JAPANESE MANAGEMENT STRUCTURES, 1920–80

JAPANESE MANAGEMENT STRUCTURES, 1920–80

Yoshitaka Suzuki

Professor of Business History
Tohoku University, Japan

St. Martin's Press   New York

First published in the United States of America in 1991

Printed in Hong Kong

ISBN 0–312–02522–X

Library of Congress Cataloging-in-Publication Data
Suzuki, Yoshitaka, 1944–
Japanese management structures, 1920–80/Yoshitaka Suzuki.
p.   cm.
Includes index.
ISBN 0–312–02522–X
1. Industrial management — Japan — History — 20th century.
I. Title.
HD70.J3S993   1991
658′.00952′0904—dc20   90–43960
                                                         CIP

Contents

List of Tables	viii
List of Figures	ix
Preface	x
Abbreviations	xiii

1 Management Resources and the Structures of Modern Firms   **1**

1.1 Modern Business Enterprise and Managerial Hierarchies	1
1.2 Some Implications of Chandler's Hypotheses	3
1.3 Management Resources and the Types of Hierarchies	7
1.4 Aspects of Japanese Management Structures	9

2 The Formation of Managerial Hierarchies, 1920–40   **13**

2.1 Management Structures and Large-scale Industrial Companies in Pre-war Japan	13
2.2 Internalisation of Human Resources	15
2.3 Management Strategies and Generating the Flow of Goods inside Firms	22
2.4 Decentralised Structures	33
2.5 Summary	36

3 Holding Companies and Corporate Control, 1920–40   **44**

3.1 External Institutions of Pre-war Large-scale Firms	44
3.2 The Development of Holding Companies	46
3.3 Corporate Control and Strategic Decision Making	51
3.4 Segmented Allocation of Management Resources	58
3.5 Change and Continuity during the War	66
3.6 Summary	71

4 Hierarchies and Federations in the Post-war Era   **75**

4.1 Introduction   75
4.2 Post-war Business Groups and Big Business: New
    Evidence   76
4.3 The Six Largest Business Groups and Large-scale
    Firms: Interpretation of Evidence   81
4.4 Giant Firms and their Affiliated Large-scale Industrials   83
4.5 Summary   86

**5 The Development of Large-scale Manufacturing Firms,
1950–80**   **88**

5.1 Large-scale Firms and their Products   88
5.2 Entry and Exit   90
5.3 Their Positions and Sizes   92
5.4 Direction of Development (I): Mergers and Horizontal
    Combinations   94
5.5 Direction of Development (II): Vertical Integration   95
5.6 Direction of Development (III): Diversification   98
5.7 Strategy and Structure of Japanese Firms   100
5.8 Summary   103

**6 The Traditionally Established Companies in Fabricated
Basic Materials**   **105**

6.1 Introduction   105
6.2 Textile Companies   108
6.3 The Paper, Printing and Materials Companies   124
6.4 Steel Companies   137
6.5 Nonferrous Metals Companies   156
6.6 Summary   167

7 New Industries in the Traditional Companies   **176**

7.1 Introduction   176
7.2 Chemical and Pharmaceutical Companies   177
7.3 Electrical and Electronic Companies   197
7.4 Heavy Engineering Companies   216
7.5 Summary   235

8 New Companies in the Post-war Mass Market **243**

8.1 Introduction 243
8.2 Food and Drink Companies 245
8.3 Oil Companies 265
8.4 Automobile Companies 277
8.5 Miscellaneous Companies in Consumer Durable Goods 302
8.6 Summary 317

9 Management Resources and their Development **324**

9.1 The Development of Management Structures in
   Japanese Industrial Companies 324
9.2 The Direction of the Development of Modern Firms:
   Types and Stages 328

Appendix: The Largest 100 Industrials of 1935 331

Index 337

List of Tables

2.1 Industry breakdown of firms with more than 1000
   employees   16
2.2 Industry breakdown of the largest 100 industrial
   companies (by sales and assets)   23
3.1 Ownership concentration and the stockholders of
   large-scale industrial enterprises   47
3.2 Changing ownership characteristics, 1920–35, of the
   largest 100 industrial companies in 1935   50
3.3 Number of transitions among the categories of executives,
   1920–35   54
3.4 Ratios of external debts of the largest 118 firms of 1935 60
5.1 Industry distribution of the largest 100 manufacturing
   firms   89
5.2 Entries and exits of the largest manufacturing firms   91
5.3 The largest 100 firms by industry (sales)   93
5.4 Mergers and divestments of the largest manufacturing
   firms   94
5.5 Diversification by product groups   100
5.6 Management structures of the largest 100 manufacturing
   firms   101
7.1 Diversification by three-digit industry classification   236
7.2 Diversification by four-digit industry classification   236
8.1 Low diversifiers by four-digit classification   244
8.2 Low diversifiers by three-digit classification   244
8.3 Management structures of Japanese automobile
   companies   300

List of Figures

1.1 Functionally departmentalised structure 3
1.2 Management resources and the organisational forms 10
1.3 Functional/line and production-unit forms 11
5.1 Diversification of Japanese manufacturing firms 99

Preface

Like many other books, the present one resulted from the interaction of a number of factors. Its original form as a research paper was hastily shaped after the author was invited to visit Sheffield, England, on an exchange fellowship between the British Academy and JSPS (Japan Society for the Promotion of Science). I was rather worried that this sort of fellowship might entail such a research paper, and, in the event, the anxiety became reality, and the paper was exposed to the debates of several seminars which waited it there. However, this topic was a means and not an end for my visit to Britain, and its initial role would have ended along with the termination of my stay in Sheffield, trailing the echo of an itinerant performer but for the fact that it became the basis of a publication in the first volume of the *Strategic Management Journal*. It happened to be discovered by Malcolm Falkus, who recommended me to write it into a book.

There was another, rather different motive for this work. For a business historian of the present day, it seems worth examining the explanations on the emergence of the modern business enterprise presented by Alfred D. Chandler, Jr., whose insights still dominate the field. Such works can be done in various ways depending on the individual, and I thought it necessary to tackle his ideas according to my own way. The result is the present book which has overstepped its original frame as a journal article, and, all in all I spent the larger part of my late thirties on this work.

Like many books, this book has sprung also from motives. Business firms are more than mighty institutions in present day Japan. They have a prodigious influence on the occupational life of the individuals concerned, and the whole aspects of their daily life and thought. Why can the firm have such tremendous strength? Is it the characteristic nature of the Japanese firm?

Various attempts have been made to emancipate description of the characteristics of Japanese firms from being purely esoteric, and to explain them by explorable and comparable hypotheses. For instance, *The Economics of the Japanese Firm* edited by Masahiko

Aoki, is one of such efforts made on the part of economists. Many propositions which had previously been put forward without exploration were examined by testable theories, by which methodologically a more rigid comparison with other industrialised economies was made possible. Similar attempts can be made by historians. The question of why the Japanese firm has such a profound influence is not confined to the present book for me, and naturally cannot fully be answered by it. However this work investigates that theme by inheriting and developing the ideas of modern firms from the works of Chandler who argued that it allocates resources through managerial hierarchies. In examining the structure of managerial hierarchies, however, the present work does not relate it so much to the strategy of the firm as to the kind and the nature of the management resources whose transactions the firm internalises. There are reasons why the author emphasises the latter aspects.

The propositions on management structures presented by Chandler have undoubtedly some general validity which can explain certain cause and effect relationships if directly applied to other places or eras. However, they were originally deduced from the historical experiences in the United States, and such an application may possibly result in an American-centred comparison or in measuring the distance from the United States. It may be that some more important aspects for modern firms in different economies are hidden when they do not appear in the United States. For instance, the internalised allocation of human resources or the formation of an internal capital market rather than the internalised coordination of the flow of goods through vertical integration might have been a more characteristic feature in the emergence and development of modern firms elsewhere, and consequently the types of managerial hierarchies which coordinated these resources might have taken different structures. This may be the question of to what degree the original propositions should be modified, a question which the author thinks vital, and which requires a return to the basic level of the nature of management resources. And the author thinks that if there is a particular coherence in Japanese firms, this may be related to the particular resources whose transactions they internalised. Except on this most fundamental point, the present book tries to use the same terms as used in the works of Chandler.

This book deals with many sample companies of each period chosen by a certain set procedure. This procedure limited the available materials to those published, or at best printed. The author has tried to supplement them by questioning the people inside the companies about the accuracy of the material which has appeared in trade or economic journals for these thirty years. Many of the materials were examined in the libraries of the National Diet, the Japan Business History Institute, the Federation of Economic Organizations, Oriental Economist, Hitotsubashi University, the Institute of Business Research at Hitotsubashi University, and some of the archives of the individual companies. Above all the library of Tohoku University, particularly the archives of former Sendai Higher Technical School, is a mine of information about pre-war industrial activities, to which the author owes much.

These materials were discovered and catalogued in exemplary fashion by Etsuko Matsumoto (now Mrs Ishizawa). Many of my colleagues commented on earlier drafts of this work or its parts which appeared in several academic journals. Professors Tsunehiko Yui and Hidemasa Morikawa made comments and criticisms which resulted in several parts being rewritten. Professors Leslie Hannah and Derek F. Channon improved the poor expression of my original papers which later developed into some of the chapters of this work, and helped in other ways. Professors Alfred D. Chandler, Shin-ichi Yonekawa, Hideki Yoshihara, and Malcolm Falkus encouraged me at the various stages of this work, while Etsuo Abe and Seiichiro Yonekura offered criticisms. Professor Falkus also read my early drafts through, and improved my expressions. The editors of *Business History* and the *Strategic Management Journal* kindly permitted me to reprint passages from articles originally published in their journals.

I have had much support from my colleagues at Tohoku University. Our office staff was helpful in improving my English, typing the manuscript, photocopying the drafts, and in many other ways. Taketoshi Nagashima arranged the materials for me. The author should like to express his thanks to all for their help.

Tohoku University   YOSHITAKA SUZUKI

Abbreviations

Ck   Chuo koron keiei mondai (Chuo koron Managemental Supplement)
Ec   Ekonomisuto (Economist)
Kh   Keizai hyoron (Economic Review)
Kik   Kindai keiei (*Management Today*)
Kj   Keiei jitsumu (Management Practices)
Kk   Kagaku keizai (Chemical Economy)
Ks   Keieisha (The Manager)
Ma   Manejimento (*The Management*)
Mg   Manejimento gaido (Management Guide)
Nks   Nihon keizai shinbun (Japan Economic Newspaper)
Nss   Nikkei sangyo shinbun (Nikkei Industry Newspaper)
Pr   Purejidento (*President*)
Sk   Soshiki kagaku (*Organizational Science*)
Tg   Toyo keizai tokei geppo (*Oriental Economist Monthly Statistics*)
Tk   Toyo keizai shinpo, Shukan toyo keizai (*Oriental Economist*)
Za   Zaikai (Business World)

1 Management Resources and the Structures of the Modern Firms

1.1 MODERN BUSINESS ENTERPRISE AND THE MANAGERIAL HIERARCHIES

The modern business enterprise is equipped with a highly developed managerial hierarchy. It allocates resources by making use of the line of authority which is operated through this hierarchy. While resources can be allocated and economic activities coordinated through other sorts of institutional arrangements such as the market mechanism, it may be asserted that the business enterprise or the firm with managerial hierarchies appears when the markets or other kinds of institutional arrangements do not effectively fulfil the function of the allocation of resources.

In advance of the allocation of resources by a business enterprise, the transactions of the resources such as labour, goods, and capital must be internalised in the business enterprise. Thus a highly developed modern firms seems to be an amalgam of such resources. These internalised resources are called 'management resources' in this book. This work starts by regarding the business enterprise as the internalised management resources which are allocated by the authority operated through the managerial hierarchies. These hierarchies are structured by certain criteria and become existing management structures which are familiar to us by the names such as the 'functionally departmentalised' or the 'multidivisional' structures.

Whereas the modern business enterprise more or less internalises the transactions of resources before their allocation, this is not always the peculiar aspect of the 'modern' business enterprise. Many firms in the past employed work forces for a long period of time and by doing so internalised the transaction of human resources. Further, there were big businesses in sixteenth-century England[1] or in nineteenth-

1

century Germany[2] which internalised the flow of goods by integrating various processes of production from extraction through smelting or refining to their final processing and sometimes to sales activities. In some cases, they were even engaged in financial activities. Whether it is modern or not, business enterprise with managerial hierarchies tends to be formed when the markets for a certain kind of skills, supplies, or products are underdeveloped, incomplete, or non-existent, which fixes the transaction costs to high levels. Thus the business enterprise with internalised transactions of resources and authority is not itself a historical stage in the development of the modern firms, just as the market is not.

Again it is not necessarily the case that there appears a marked tendency towards the formation of a firm when the market mechanism cannot effectively fulfil the function of resource allocation. Other kinds of institutional arrangements such as the domestic system, the subcontracting system, various sorts of financial or transactional affiliations, cartels, and other forms of federations can be regarded as substitutes for the market transactions or the firm. They are somewhere in the midway points between the firm and the market.

In spite of these limitations, the position of the business enterprise in economic activity became predominant and the managerial hierarchies more complex for at least the last one hundred years in Japan, as in most other industrialised nations. Although it may eventually be partly or wholly replaced by the markets or by other sorts of institutional arrangements, the firm with managerial hierarchies has taken deep root in modern industrial economies. These hierarchies are composed of vertically and horizontally specialised components parts. There may be various forms the hierarchies may take, and the typical, or 'ideal' form is what is called the functionally departmentalised structure with three levels of management (see Figure 1.1).[3] This form can be regarded as the archetypal bureaucratic organisation since the tasks are specialised by function, which is the most rational criterion of the division of labour.[4] The three levels of management, although familiar, should be defined here since there are various interpretations. At the lowest level, the managers are responsible for the operation of the units like factories; the middle management is responsible for each of the functional departments like sales or production, and coordinates the flow of goods and supervises the operating units by means of administrative decisions; at the highest level, managers are responsible for the future invest-

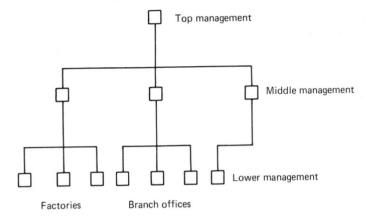

Top management

Middle management

Lower management

Factories   Branch offices

FIGURE 1.1 Functionally departmentalised structure

ment decisions and company-wide coordination. In practice, of course, such definitions are inexact, for there exist many deviations among individual firms even when they adopt this form of hierarchy.

However, divergences do not always stem from the archetypal structure. This organisational form is, as will be examined in the following sections, built up on the combination of particular sorts of management resources, and there may be other combinations which have affinities to other forms of organisational structures. Not only the divergences by industry groups which largely derive from the differences in the nature of products, but national divergences which arise more from the efficiencies of the resource markets, are discernible.

The purpose of this work is to examine analytically and empirically the characteristics of the management structures of major Japanese industrial companies since the First World War when they first appeared in various industrial branches. The author attempts to apply the same framework used to explain the characteristics of the firms of other industrialised nations, which requires some modification of such existing frameworks.

1.2 SOME IMPLICATIONS OF CHANDLER'S HYPOTHESES

In his extensive works, Chandler has examined and analysed not only the development of managerial hierarchies but that of the modern business enterprise itself.[5] His analysis is comprehensive, getting a series of important changes within its range. There is also a consistency in his works, and this enables us to get to the point of his argument. The point is the emergence of the multifunction firm, from which all the subsequent changes in the United States stem, and which distinguishes the early American big business from others.

A multifunction firm is defined as one which is engaged not only in production but also in purchasing or extracting raw materials, and sales or marketing. Such firms resulted from vertical integration, in other words, the internalisation of the transaction in goods. Among the various sorts of resources which were allocated by markets, it was the 'goods' whose transactions were internalised by the modern United States business enterprise. Firms were built upon the internalised flow of goods. Functionally departmentalised structure was formed to coordinate the internalised flow of goods, and professional managerial classes appeared as the result of the developed functional structures. As the new tasks of coordination and control were assigned to the department managers at the middle management level, the internalisation of the flow of goods can be regarded as the momentum of the formation of the middle management as well as of the modern business enterprise. How about other resources and other levels of the management hierarchies?

Prior to the emergence of big business, many American firms solved their problems at the shop floor level by means of 'scientific management' or 'systematic management'. The traditional forms of the transactions in labour such as subcontracting system were replaced by the 'visible hand' which controlled the operation of works. However, this change did not directly lead to the formation of the modern business enterprise in the United States, nor did this lead to the internalisation of the allocation of human resources. An 'internal labour market', which is accompanied by training within the firm, enterprise specific skill, inside promotion, and long-term employment, appeared long after the emergence of the modern enterprise in the United States.

One may argue that the appearance of the multidivisional structure (M-form) is decisive in the American business history. This organisational form is often explained as an attempt to create an internal capital market. This is also explained in terms of the separation of top management from operating tasks. Still it was designed by the product-market criteria just below the top management, and this divisional level is firmly based on the flow of goods. Divisions were developed to solve the problems arising from the internal flow of goods.

However, the implication of Chandler's work does not stop at the middle management level. Though American firms were largely built on the internalisation of the flow of goods, his analysis was not limited to this aspect. In Chandler's discussion of the establishment of the top management through the 'managerial revolution', he implied that the function of the allocation of financial resources was transferred from the capital market to the 'visible hand' of the inside managers of the firm. Chandler's discussion of the separation of ownership and control is not novel in itself. What is novel is the suggestion that the top management evolved in a managerial enterprise, and their decisions became independent of the stock holders or the stock market. Of course the rise of the managerial enterprise is not necessarily the only form of the internalisation of the allocation of financial resources within the firm, nor is it limited to the allocation of financial resources. For instance, the major part of the financial resources is supplied inside the firm so far as it remains a family business, often without recourse to the capital market. Furthermore, the allocation of cash flow is often operated by the firm's managers without the intermediation of the market. On the other hand, the top management is also responsible for the allocation of other resources such as labour or capital, and sometimes for the coordination of the flow of goods inside the firm. Therefore, it may be said that the investment decision by the managerial enterprise is a peculiar combination of one type of the allocation of financial resources inside the firm and one of the functions of the top management.

Thus what distinguishes the United States managerial hierarchies examined by Chandler is the importance of the coordination of the flow of goods at the middle management level. This resulted in the formation of the functionally departmentalised or the multidivisional structures. To what extent does this characteristic have theoretically and historically universal validity?

The institutional economics assumes that a firm is formed when the transaction costs of the allocation of resources by organisation are lower than those formed by the markets. However, there are varieties in the kinds of such resources. Coase explained the emergence of a firm by a particular nature of labour, or human resources. Azariadis and Doeringer and Piore discussed the conditions of the internalisation of the labour transaction. Arrow and Williamson explained the choice of market versus internal allocation in terms of goods. Jensen and Meckling, on the other hand, discussed the case of financial resources. Theoretically a firm appears when the allocation of one of these resources is internalised. A firm need not internalise the allocation of all the kinds of resources. The transaction in goods, which is characteristically observed in the American firms, is one of the kind of such resources by which the firm replaces the role of the market. Of course, that the internal allocation of other resources is discussed in America, indicates that the internalisation of human or financial resources are observed there.

In comparison with the American big business, European firms were formed by the internalisation of the allocation of financial resources while they more or less depended on the market transaction in goods and human resources. The emerging Japanese large-scale firms in the pre-war era possibly began by the internalisation of the allocation of human resources.

Why and under what conditions was the modern business enterprise in the United States built on the internalised flow of goods? What was the case in other countries? These are difficult points to demonstrate. We can only assume that a certain kind of resource was scarce or the traditional institutional arrangement was not enough in the allocation of that resource in face of the new market or technological circumstances. For the newly appearing consumer final goods which were supplied by mass production methods and directed to the growing urban markets, the existing market channel consisting of middlemen proved to be inefficient in delivering goods. The suppliers of these products such as packed meat or sewing machinery had to integrate forward into wholesales. These factors like new consumer final goods, the application of mass production, and the growing urban markets were characteristic of the United States of this period. So far as these products are concerned, we might expect the same strategy would be repeated in other places under the same conditions. However, for other industry groups like fabricated basic materials, or other consumer or producer goods, the superiority of the coordination of the flow of goods by managerial hierarchies to that by market was proved only *ex post*. Those which applied the strategies of vertical integration survived and those who did not went down.

1.3 MANAGEMENT RESOURCES AND THE TYPES OF HIERARCHIES

Chandler's studies suggest that the modern business enterprise in the United States was built upon the internalised flow of goods. However, outside the United States the internalisation of transactions in other resources may be more pressing. For example, large-scale firms may be built mainly on the internal allocation of human or financial resources. While a functionally departmentalised structure may best suit the coordinating of the flow of goods, other types of hierarchies may be more appropriate to solve problems arising from the internalisation of other resources.

In the development of big businesses in Europe we find that multiunit firms often emerged through mergers or acquisitions, but these operating units were organised on the 'holding companies', which held shares in these operating units.[6] This organisational form consists of two basic levels of management: a small head office which owns stock, and the operating subsidiaries. They were initially financial devices, and remained so except where head offices initiated reorganising product lines, and taking other measures of rationalisation of the operating subsidiaries. A group of firms organised within a holding company structure may even become a multifunction firm, or may diversify product lines if the acquisitions take place in different sectors or the industry. Although a holding company structure is inefficient in dealing with the problems of middle and lower management levels, it may be in a more flexible position in buying or selling companies than other types of organisational structures, and in that sense it is certainly efficient in allocating financial resources. A firm organised as a holding company structure can swiftly shift from one industry to another, or gain profits from the sale of stock. Such strategies may be effective in a market where industries are losing their international competitive power one after another and cannot cope with the internalisation of labour or the flow of goods.

A firm builds primarily upon the internalisation of transactions in financial resources; the adoption of the holding company structure is a reasonable solution for its central strategic objective. Empirical studies of the British, Belgian, and German companies in post-war decades indicate many transitions from the holding company to the multidivisional structure.[7] However, this does not imply that the holding company structure is backward or inferior to the multidivisional structure. Rather, this is more relevant to the nature of resources these companies intended to develop. Holding companies are not necessarily destined to be reorganised into the functionally departmentalised or the multidivisional structures. On the contrary, there may be transitions the other way round.

Such a hypothesis leaves a point to be explained: why do some companies tend to internalise the flow of goods in one country, and the transactions of financial resources in another? These are complicated questions, and their answers can only be judged *ex post*. For the allocation of particular resources, business enterprise is efficient, but for that of others different institutional arrangements are more suitable. The dominant industries or products of a certain period require a particular kind of scarce resource.

If the business enterprise is primarily built on the internal transactions in human resources, what type of management structure is most suitable for their allocation or control? This is another difficult question, since, unlike financial resources or the flow of goods, human resources are dealt with by various levels of hierarchies. Thus, which of the levels of hierarchies becomes the pivot is not certain. However, for a modern business enterprise it is initially the operating units which employ a large number of the work force, and it is the task of the lower management which controls these human resources.

If the business enterprise develops primarily on the internalised human resources leaving the allocation of other kinds of resources to its outside institutional arrangements, the position of the operating units will become strong. As the important functions of the top management such as the allocation of financial resources or of the middle management such as the coordination of the flow of goods are lacking, these management levels are relatively small. The typical example which corresponds to such requirements would be the simple 'line structure'. Here the managers of each operating unit are directly responsible to the highest level managers, while there is no coordination among the tasks, products or markets of each operating unit.

Seemingly this line structure is similar to the holding company in its outlook, because both have a simple head office and strong operating units. However, unlike the latter the head office of the line structure does not hold the stock in their operating units. The major differences between the two can be found in legal or financial forms. The managerial control in the line structure lies in the appointment of the managers of the operating units, or, more generally, making the highest level managers hold the post of factory managers at the same time. The managerial hierarchies of this form basically consist of one level. This form can be adopted in multiunit firms, or even in multifunction firms, as will be examined later. Their operating units are engaged initially in production, though some firms add procurement or sales activities by setting up their own trading offices.

Thus the three basic forms of managerial hierarchies, the line, the functionally departmentalised, and the holding company structures are organised according to the kind of the main management resources whose transactions and coordinations are internalised in these firms. In practice, however, the modern business enterprise usually internalises the transactions of one or two other resources in addition to its main management resources. The multidivisional structure is a device to differentiate the tasks of investment decisions from those of the control or coordination of daily activities as both become more complicated. Still it is firmly based on the coordination of the flow of goods. In Europe the holding company structure has often been reorganised into the multidivisional form in order to improve the coordination of their operating units. Likewise, companies which are based on the simple line structure may be required to undertake other kinds of activities such as the coordination of the flow of goods or financial control, even if their primary tasks are the control of personnel. Two directions of divergence are possible. One is to add backward or forward activities either by developing purchasing or sales functions, or more vigorously by vertical integration. Another is to choose financial control by making the operating units those of a self-supporting system. The former can be termed as the 'functional/line structure', and the latter as the 'production unit structure' (see Figure 1.2).

1.4 ASPECTS OF JAPANESE MANAGEMENT STRUCTURES

A glance at the organisational charts of multiunit large-scale Japanese industrial firms as of 1950 or 1940 frequently shows the 'functional/line structure' or the 'production unit structure' forms, in addition to ordinary functionally departmentalised structures. The functional/line structure is, as illustrated in Figure 1.3, organised by a head office which is equipped with a trading (sales and/or procurement) department in addition to a 'general affairs department' (Somu-bu), and several operating units which are directly and separately responsible to the highest level managers of the company. This

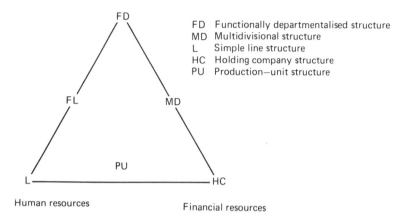

Flow of goods

FD   Functionally departmentalised structure
MD   Multidivisional structure
L   Simple line structure
HC   Holding company structure
PU   Production–unit structure

Human resources

Financial resources

FIGURE 1.2 Management resources and the organisational forms

form indicates a certain degree of differentiation of managerial tasks by functions just below the highest level managers, although control over production is not operated similarly.

The production unit structure is, on the contrary, organised by a small head office, and a few large-scale production units each responsible for placing and accepting orders, and often being the unit of self-supporting system of production. The production unit form shows some similarity with the modern multidivisional structure by product or geography, but differs in that the coordination of units is not made by the head office. (See Figure 1.3.)

Enormous changes have taken place since 1950. The American methods of modern management were extensively introduced in Japan firstly at the level of production units, and to higher levels shortly afterwards. The number of the staff with technological knowledge and administrative quality grew larger, which expanded the hierarchies by increasing the number of employees nor engaged directly in production. The management structures of many firms were reorganised into functionally departmentalised or multidivisional structures. However, the important status of production units among Japanese industrial companies still remains. The production units of Japanese companies had developed before sales or financial activities were integrated, or the flow of goods or financial resources

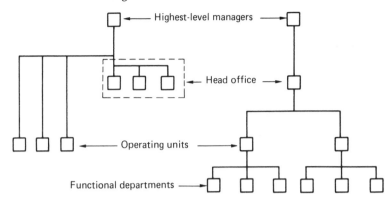

FIGURE 1.3 Functional/line and production-unit forms

were internalised. In this study we will examine how these elements originated and how they have changed.

That the production units are placed high in a company implies the relative weakness of other functions of the industrial firms. Other functions such as sales, purchasing, or financing may be partly internalised, but are not necessarily operated through the markets. The transactions of goods and financial resources inside the business groups are pointed out among Japanese industrial companies. Japanese manufacturing companies formed groups of companies for the purchase of raw materials and components, or for distribution of their products. Manufacturing companies are most prominent here, but we also find wholesale merchants or trading companies as well. As to financial groups, holding companies as well as banks or wholesale merchants play important roles, but sometimes manufacturing companies affiliate with other large-scale industrial companies financially. In any event, these varied forms of federation play a significant role in the allocation of resources. Such types of transaction are often formed on an equal basis. If such groups are formed around large manufacturing firms, the profit of reduced transaction costs falls into the hands of the manufacturers. In other cases, it is necessary to examine to what degree manufacturing companies depend on such outside federations. This work intends to examine in what sense large-scale industrial firms are responsible for the allocation of resources, and in what sense they are not. The following analysis will be based on a large number of sample companies in order to make generalisations as sound as possible.

NOTES

1. J. U. Nef, *Industry and Government in France and England, 1540–1640*, Ithaca, 1967.
2. W. O. Henderson, *The Rise of German Industrial Power, 1834–1914*, London, 1975.
3. A. D. Chandler, Jr., *The Visible Hand: the Managerial Revolution in American Business*, Cambridge, Mass., 1977, p. 2.
4. M. Weber, *Economy and Society*, ed. G. Roth and C. Wittichi, vol. 3, New York, 1968, pp. 956–8.
5. A. D. Chandler, Jr., *Strategy and Structure: Chapters in the History of the Industrial Enterprise*, Cambridge, Mass, 1962; *do.*, *Visible Hand*.
6. D. H. Channon, *The Strategy and Structure of British Enterprise*, London, 1973; H. Daems, *The Holding Company and Corporate Control*, Leiden, 1978.
7. G. P. Dyas and H. T. Thanheiser, *The Emerging European Enterprise: Strategy and Structure in French and German Industry*, London, 1976.

2 The Formation of Managerial Hierarchies, 1920–40

2.1 MANAGEMENT STRUCTURES AND LARGE-SCALE INDUSTRIAL COMPANIES IN PRE-WAR JAPAN

Managerial hierarchies are, as in big business in the West, essential characteristics of modern Japanese enterprises. This chapter deals with the organisational structures of Japanese large-scale companies throughout their formative period.

The development of such managerial hierarchies has generally been explained as the results of the internalisation and vertical integration of business functions such as sales or purchasing into manufacturing firms.[1] In the UK and USA, these varying functions were originally carried out by independent, single-unit and single-function firms. This process best fits an economy where business functions are carried on by market transactions between independent middlemen and manufacturers in advance of the emergence of the managerial hierarchies. Such a developed market in which resources are allocated by a price mechanism, however, is actually observed in some particular countries. In a less developed or less specialised economy, traditional merchants generally undertook various economic roles simultaneously at the time when the multiunit large-scale industrials emerged. Managerial hierarchies appeared and developed even in a circumstance where they had no such developed market. Of course, either of the market or other sorts of institutional arrangements outside the firm will be replaced by the internalised transactions if their costs are higher than those of the latter. In both cases managerial hierarchies tend to develop, although the process would vary in each case. The first question is why and how managerial hierarchies appeared in a country where a market mechanism had not developed well.

13

The management hierarchies may originate for reasons other than the internalised flow of goods. Of particular importance here have been internal transactions of labour and their coordination by firms. In Japan the spectacular increase in the number of industrial workers from around 1905 coincided with the emergence of the multiunit enterprises. In 1905 there were 113 manufacturing enterprises with more than 500 employees, of which 24 were multiunit firms. Of them 47 were non-governmental manufacturing enterprises with more than 1000 employees, of which 18 were multiunit firms. By 1920, industrial enterprises with more than 1000 employees amounted to 123, and the number of the multiunit firms among them had increased to 100.[2] This was the result not only of mergers among firms within existing industry branches, but also of the remarkable number of new entries and the internal growth of firms in the new industries. The difficulties for these emerging enterprises were found in recruiting workers with necessary skills which were unavailable both inside and outside the firms. This is a common problem faced by the entrepreneurs in the early phase of industrialisation. However, the nature of the skills, which was required by the new industries of the present century was far more complicated than that of the early phase. Recruitment of skilled workers was a more difficult task for Japanese large-scale firms than for those of other countries. What type of organisational structures did appear if Japanese firms had to solve such labour problems? This is the second question.

The third question relates to the general study of management structure in Japan. Research on institutional arrangements for coordinating business activities among pre-war Japanese enterprises has been concentrated on those of the *Zaibatsu* and cartels.[3] This chapter, by contrast, is an attempt to investigate the organisational structure of individual companies. For this purpose, the largest 100 manufacturing companies measured by sales, assets and the number of employees, are examined, and the evolution of the varied types of management structures are followed over the period 1920–40. The *Zaibatsu*, consisting of the headquarters and operating companies, has often been examined as a unified enterprise. Not a small number of operating companies were, in fact, affiliated with the *Zaibatsu* or cartels, but removing the umbrella of the *Zaibatsu* clarifies developments in the hierarchical structure at various levels of management. There are reasons to justify such an attempt. First, the *Zaibatsu* affiliated companies were responsible for the coordination at the middle and lower management level though not at the top management level. Second, unless at least the top management functions were carried out by the *Zaibatsu* head office, the group cannot be regarded as a unity, but this is a matter of debate. Third, individual firms might have developed their own schemes for resource allocation and managerial coordination when these functions of the *Zaibatsu* were underdeveloped. And fourth, it was these hierarchical structures that appeared later when the *Zaibatsu* were dissolved after the Second World War. Whether the top management and the strategic roles in other functions were carried out by the *Zaibatsu* or individual companies is examined in Chapter 3.

2.2 INTERNALISATION OF HUMAN RESOURCES

Generally speaking large-scale Japanese companies had to pay more attention to human resources than did their western counterparts. The spectacular expansion and changes of manufacturing firms after around 1905 required a large workforce with various types of skills. The existing labour market could not meet these demands either in quantity or quality. Table 2.1 shows the industry distribution of the largest employers in 1905 and 1920, which suggests the types of workers these firms needed most.[4]

In 1905, the largest employing firms centred on textiles, minerals, and heavy engineering. Thirty-nine of the 47 largest firms with more than 1000 employees were classified into one of these three industries, and most of the remaining part to miscellaneous industries such as brushes, matches and leather goods. In addition there were government factories mostly in heavy engineering branches, which employed more than six times as many as its related industries in private sector. On the other hand there were no firms with more than 1000 workforce in industries such as food processing, paper, chemicals (match making excepted), ceramics, oil, and electric equipment.

Two new types of workers were demanded by these industries. One was unskilled workers, particularly for cotton spinning enterprises. The other was skilled workers like mechanical engineers required in heavy engineering and shipbuilding, particularly for government enterprises. In addition there were requirements for such traditional workers as miners, and rural or urban miscellaneous unskilled labourers.

By the end of the First World War, the number of large employers in textiles had increased to 57, and that of heavy engineering to 18. In

TABLE 2.1 Industry breakdown of firms with more than 1000 employees

	1905			1920		
	firms	*employees*	*industry total*	*firms*	*employees*	*industry total*
Food	0	—	29 888	6	11 352	111 000
Textiles	29	66 389	265 689	57	273 788	754 000
Paper	0	—	5 239	4	12 146	28 000
Chemicals	2	2 576		9	24 021	
Rubber	0	—	58 000	2	2 575	72 000
Oil	0	—		2	6 143	
Glass and ceramics	0	—	13 559	4	11 046	64 000
Iron and steel	1	1 495		7	20 612	
Nonferrous metals	5	28 252	49 818	9	171 382*	155 000
Electrical equipment	0	—		4	12 936	
Heavy engineering	5	15 186	34 333	18	107 669	184 000
Miscellaneous	5	9 018	69 689	1	1 560	136 000
Total	47	125 601	526 215	123	655 230	1 611 990
Government factories	12	110 436		10	139 000	

* Includes coal mining

textiles total factory employment increased three times during the fifteen years after 1905, and the demand from large firms rose more than this. In heavy and electrical engineering, the number of workers in large-scale firms grew eight times. In contrast to stagnant traditional branches like mining or urban miscellaneous industries, large firms emerged in new industries such as food processing, paper, chemicals, rubber, oil, glass and ceramics, iron and steel, and electric equipment. Apart from electrical equipment, most of the new industries, including food (mostly sugar refining), were processing industries. The number of processing firms came to share a quarter of all the largest industrials, although the number of their employees did not increase proportionately. This evidence indicates that demand for labour from textiles and heavy engineering was rapidly expanding, but now a third type was added due to the entries of these processing industries. There were many kinds of semi-skilled jobs in these processing industries, each requiring one to three years' on-the-job training. However, these jobs are different from the semi-skilled jobs in the capital intensive modern processing industries which require the typical enterprise specific skills. Their work was accompanied by bad smell and dust, and in that sense it cannot clearly be distinguished form the urban miscellaneous industries such as match making.

Large-scale employers by the First World War needed one of these three types of workers, and none could easily be recruited from the labour markets. The process of the organisation of unskilled workers in textiles and skilled workers in engineering has already been documented,[5] and it is enough to outline what is directly related to their internalisation.

From the beginning of the present century to the First World War, the potential supply of unskilled workers was high. Such a surplus, though, was unevenly concentrated in rural areas which could not directly supply deficiencies in the areas where spinning mills existed. A special form of recruiting scheme developed utilising travelling subcontractors. But such a scheme had obvious limitations for recruiting even unskilled factory operatives, not to speak of skilled ring spinners. The scheme was expensive, and in order to reduce the recruitment costs, companies chose to entice trained workers of the neighbouring factories. They also tried to prevent labour turnover by enforcing deposits from wages, building boarding houses, and by letting the recruiting agents oversee their workers. However, during booms the labour turnover attained 200 per cent a year even in the most advanced large factories.

After around 1910, large-scale companies began to make further effort to retain their workers. Companies began to realise the importance of skills and other aspects of the quality of workers, and measures were taken to improve their technical skills and prevent their turnover. Favourable treatment on long standing employees such as pensions or other means of welfare appeared in larger companies. Some companies formed a network with some particular rural areas for a continuous supply of labour, and exclusively recruited there. Nevertheless, labour turnover remained as high as 75 per cent even in 1921. Under the pressure of shortages, labour market did not function favourably for the firms. Internalised transactions of labour could not easily replace its market transactions.

For the second type of worker, consisting of mechanical engineers or the 'blacksquad', shortage not merely continued from the beginning of industrialisation but were aggravated towards the First World War. These skilled workers were first formed in government arsenals, and later recruited by private shipbuilding and engineering companies. Their skill had a wide range of applicability to various products as well as various firms. At the beginning, a lateral labour market was formed. Some of them moved from factory to factory in order to acquire additional skills necessary to become independent as master artisans or workshop owners, and others were attracted by higher wages. From the late 1890s and particularly from the mid 1900s, the supply of this type of worker always fell short of the demand during booms, and their turnover became frequent. A government arsenal introduced a scheme of three-year fixed term employment to prevent such frequent moves, and offered premium bonuses for those who filled the fixed term. However, larger sums were often offered by other factories which needed such skilled workers. For the rising private shipyards, however, the recruitment from arsenals did not fully supply the necessary number of workers, and they also faced the recruitment from newly entering firms. The *Mitsubishi Shipyard* experienced 100 per cent labour turnover at the beginning of the present century. Under these circumstances, private firms started to evolve various levels for training within the firm, beginning from apprenticeship, to sending employees to local schools, and finally to establishing training schools within the firm. Then they tried to retain such workers within the firm by means of welfare schemes. But the tramping artisans could not easily be excluded so far as they had their own skills, while the wage system according to the length of service was not established.

During trade depressions, labour turnover declined, though many workers lost jobs by unemployment. During booms, the cycle was reversed. In the First World War years, labour turnover became very large, and measures to lower the rise proved inefficient. New companies needed skilled workers, and recruited them from other firms. Incentives for long term employment were not effective because their benefits include newcomers, and further sums were often offered by new companies.

During the post-First World War slump, the demand for labour fell immediately, and demand remained stagnant until the mid 1930s. Large-scale firms now began to discharge their employees, while labour turnover declined to less than 10 per cent throughout the 1920s. During the 1920s major companies developed their internal labour markets. They began to take on clever young boys who had just finished higher elementary schools, train them on the job as well as in training schools inside the factories, and employ them permanently. Among the largest 100 manufacturing companies by sales or assets of 1935, 16 firms, almost all of them concentrated in heavy and electric engineering and metal processing, were equipped with such training schools. The wage system changed from that based on skill to that based on length of service. These life time employees were a minority of workers, and many other workers were employed on short-term contracts so that they could be easily discharged. Nevertheless, these permanent employees were regarded as the nucleus of the workforce by the firms. Paradoxically, companies succeeded in internalising the labour market when they became able to recruit labour by market transactions. Partly, this internalisation was necessitated by the enterprise specific skills in large-scale firms where the division of labour proceeded and technology developed. Companies took the initiative of retaining highly skilled workers within their own factories even during depression.

For the third type of worker characteristically found in the newly developing processing industries, we have little available evidence.[6] In chemical branches the length of the period required to become an expert operative was shorter than in iron and steel. Unlike mechanical engineering skills, however, such specialist skills in processing had little application elsewhere. In many cases a very specific skill was required because expertise depended much on individual equipment rather than on general skill or knowledge. In enterprises such as fertilisers, glass, and dye-stuffs, 'semi-skilled' workers were needed, and companies soon learned that high rates of turnover led to inefficiency. Glass firms preferred young school leavers who could be employed longer. In other branches such as paper or cement, companies treated long-standing employees favourably by the 1920s. In *Onoda Cement* the average length of service was 12 years in the 1930s. Yearly turnover became less than 5 per cent in all the chemical branches. Similar schemes for long term employment as observed in engineering industries evolved here. The wage system was built upon length of service and promotion. However, lifetime employment had not been established firmly in Japanese firms in the 1920s. Even the nucleus of the workforce were often dismissed, while high rate of labour turnover resumed after the economic recovery in the mid 1930s.

We cannot easily explain the management structures of large-scale firms in this period entirely in terms of the internalised transactions of labour, because many firms developed beyond this. However, in these cases, the control and coordination of labour was important. We can reproduce the organisational charts of 93 firms from among large-scale firms with more than 1000 employees in 1920.[7] Forty-four are classified to the 'line structure', 27 to the functional/line and seven to the production unit forms. Only 15 had a functionally departmentalised structure. The line structure was widely developed among firms in the rising process industries and newly founded spinning firms, while established spinning companies used functionally departmentalised or functional/line forms, and heavy engineering firms used functional/line or the production unit forms. Mineral companies had few line structured forms.

However, these facts are not enough to draw conclusions about organisational forms. Firstly we may notice aspects which were more or less common to various forms. Both in the line structure or functional/line form, the workers in the operating units were placed below dual lines of command. One was concerned with production, and the other with personnel management, and both were operated through factory managers. Large textile firms promoted the standardisation of work in the 1920s, while some heavy engineering companies introduced cost management much earlier. These pioneering attempts were important, and influenced on shop floor organisation. More important still, however, was personnel management, which included appointment, allocation and promotion, as well as the control of the general life of employees. Hierarchical ranks and grades developed along this line, though various ranks and grades in the hierarchical structure were not related directly to the specified tasks or control.

As companies internalised the allocation of labour, control was centralised. While production processes were left in the hands of foremen, or in some cases entrusted to salaried engineers, allocation and appointment were centralised in personnel departments of factories, which were supervised by the personnel department of the head office. The role of factory managers became important in such an organisation. Factory managers were not only responsible for production management in their operating units, but also for personnel management there.

Above the level of the operating units, management tasks were only partly specialised by functional area, because each operating unit was directly responsible to the highest level managers. Such an organisation includes those companies which were run by simple line management or with little formal organisation. If we go back to the 1920s such a simple line management is widely found in all industries except heavy engineering and minerals, and a quarter of the firms in our sample were in this category. By 1940 this form was less common, though it was still typical among medium-sized cotton spinning companies, such as *Nagasaki Boshoku* (Nagasaki Spinning & Weaving),[8] *Izumo Seishoku* (Izumo Weaving) and *Temman Orimono* (Temman Textile Manufacturing). A manual published in the early 1930s, entitled *The Accounting and Management of Cotton Spinning*,[9] recommended this system based on the then prevalent practices. The head office of this sort of company was normally situated in one of their local factories. By the 1930s, these companies became large enough to have their trading offices in Osaka, the centre of the cotton trade. The Japanese cotton industry had established a well developed market organisation, and the major part of commercial activities were carried out by commercial houses, wholesale merchants, and agents. Still, it was convenient for cotton manufacturing companies to have their own offices in Osaka. The yarn wholesale merchants, who exclusively dealt with the products of cotton spinning companies, were located in large market centres, and the spinning companies sent their sales employees to the yarn wholesalers to make forward contracts.[10] Another important task of the spinners' Osaka offices was in purchasing raw cotton. The cost of raw cotton was a high proportion of the costs of yarn production. Spinning companies made forward contracts with cotton merchants, and their Osaka offices made a constant effort to secure a stock of cheap cotton whose price was often fluctuating. In addition to purchasing and sales, the function of the head office was gradually transferred from local head offices to the Osaka office. More than half of the directors including the presidents were stationed at the Osaka business offices with some of their service staff such as accountants.[11] Managers of the factories reported to the Osaka offices, which made the local head offices nominal ones, though some of the latter were still equipped with the 'general affairs' section. *Nagasaki Boshoku*, for example, increased the number of its operating units from two to six between 1920 and 1940, its major source of development being the acquisition of weaving companies. This example of the vertical integration was more widely repeated among firms with similar organisational structures. *Nagasaki Boshoku*, despite increasing the number of operating units, scarcely changed its organisational structure. Local factory managers reported directly to the Manager[12] in 1940 as they did in 1920.[13]

In these firms the most fundamental management tasks such as sales or production were not formalised as functions but were left to the local operating units among which there was little coordination or specialisation. Until the early 1940s when these companies were amalgamated into larger concerns, there were no drastic changes which required organisational reforms were encountered.

2.3 MANAGEMENT STRATEGIES AND GENERATING THE FLOW OF GOODS INSIDE FIRMS

After the First World War, the number of employees of the largest companies saw scarcely any increase until the mid 1930s. The number of firms with more than 1000 or 2000 workers, was approximately the same in 1920 and in 1935. However, a new aspect of managerial problems became gradually noticeable, which was caused by the following changes. The number of the operating units of the largest manufacturing firms of 1935 were twice as many as those in 1920. The number of multifunction firms among the largest firms increased by 50 per cent. A multifunction firm is termed as one which has, in addition to production units, one or more operating units either for wholesales or procurement which were coordinated by a central department.[14] This evidence indicates that many of the additional operating units of this period were used for wholesale or purchasing activities, and this must have added a new problem of coordinating the flow of goods within the firm.

Table 2.2 shows the industrial distribution of the largest 100 manufacturing companies either by sales or assets in 1920 and 1935.[15] When we look at the largest firms in both periods, we find that most of them were companies which supplied fabricated basic materials. Thus about 90 firms in 1935 mostly supplied these semi-finished goods. Twenty were engaged in the production of producer final goods. Less than 10 firms, chiefly food processing firms, supplied consumer final goods.

Another point is that in spite of the striking similarities between the industrial distributions of the sample firms in of both years, there were many entries and exits during this period. Nearly half the companies in 1920 had vanished by 1935. Nearly half the largest companies in 1935 were either non-existent in 1920 or were newly established. No other period of 15 years throughout Japan's history showed such tremendous changes among the largest companies.

Meanwhile the simple line structure was becoming less common among the largest manufacturing firms. By 1940 only eight of 108 largest firms in our sample whose organisational structures are known

TABLE 2.2 Industry breakdown of the largest 100 industrial companies
(by sales or assets)

| | 1920 | | | 1935 | | |
	sales	assets	total	sales	assets	total
Food	15	15	19	14	13	15
Textiles	31	28	37	32	30	38
Paper	5	5	5	2	3	3
Chemicals	7	9	11	14	17	18
Oil	2	2	2	2	1	2
Glass and ceramics	4	3	4	3	5	5
Iron and steel	6	8	9	8	7	8
Nonferrous metals	9	9	11	10	8	10
Electrical equipment	4	5	6	6	5	6
Heavy engineering	9	9	11	6	8	9
Miscellaneous	1	3	3	3	2	3
Total	93	96	118	100	100	118

were based on this form. By contrast, companies organising themselves along functional lines grew in number. There were various
different degrees in their evolution. In the most simple form, the
head office had a trading department, while each of the production
units was directly controlled by the highest managers of the firm. In
the most developed form, the typically functionally departmentalised
structure came. In the midway point between these two were observed companies whose head offices evolved a production or a
manufacturing department as well as a trading department, but each
production unit was not controlled by the production department but
directly by the highest managers. The functional principle was gradually spreading among the major companies, though it could not
completely penetrate them.

Although there were these variations, the functional form spread
among the firms in the fabricated basic materials, particularly among
large established firms in food (sugar and flour), textiles (cotton
spinning), paper, cement, and nonferrous metal. We now examine
the directions of the development of these firms, their managerial
problems, and their organisational structures.

Whether the products are consumer goods or producer goods, the
ratios of raw materials in production costs were high in these kinds of
fabricated basic materials, and the prices of raw materials were liable
to change. These firms learned it was important to secure stable and

low-cost supply of raw materials. Textile concerns, notably cotton spinning firms, made full use of a highly developed market mechanism, which consisted of specialised trading companies. Many firms in other industrial branches integrated backwards to the stages of raw materials either by themselves or through subsidiaries, particularly when their supply was available at home or in Japanese overseas territories. Thus most of the firms in branches other than textiles chose the second way, as found in sugar refining, paper, chemicals, oils, cement, iron and steel, and nonferrous metals. More precisely, however, not all of the firms in these industries were included in this category, because in sugar, oils, and nonferrous metals, it was the suppliers of raw materials that integrated production processes. Some steel and nonferrous metals firms, on the other hand, confined themselves to a single or downward processes of metal fabricating.

Companies in fabricated basic materials integrated less to downward processing or marketing, but more or less made use of wholesale merchants. Still, in the case of new products or new entries for which the established distribution channels were of no use, manufacturing firms had to pay attention to distribution of their own products. In the early years of their development cement companies, and some artificial fertilisers or chemical fibres companies, had to develop distribution networks in this way. Moreover, companies in cotton spinning, paper, and sugar manufacturing became independent of their distributing agents, and became gradually influential on the downward stages such as processing or distributing.

There were, however, often factors which determined the direction of the organisational development of these firms. Acquisitions of factories and mergers amounted to a high level among the firms in fabricated basic materials. The numbers of mergers or acquired companies between 1920 and 1940 for each sample firm in 1935 amounted to 2.0 in sugar refining, 3.8 in cotton spinning, 3.5 in cement, and 4.8 in nonferrous metals even though they were less than the previous two decades.[16] Whether to consolidate the management practices between the existing and the newly acquired operating units, or to leave the latter as they used to be, was a matter of choice. The choice depends on the size, the particular management resources, and the numbers of the acquired operating units. If consolidation is chosen, some kind of organisational devices were necessary.

The actual managerial hierarchies of each company in these industrial branches arose from the varied combination of vertical and horizontal integrations. Sugar manufacturing companies had depended on overseas activities, particularly in Taiwan, where they integrated various processes such as planting, transportation, raw sugar manufacturing and storage. During the First World War such companies acquired some refining factories near large cities in Japan. Sugar firms which had head offices and refining factories in Japan went the other way and acquired manufacturing interests in Taiwan. Though their growth rate measured by sales was low, partly due to such vertical integration strategies, and their number within the largest 100 companies decreased between 1920 and 1935, they still held the most important position among food industries. By 1920, sugar manufacturing companies had become multi-unit firms, consisting of at least five factories. Originating as a domestic refining enterprise, *Dai-Nippon Sugar Manufacturing* [*Dainippon Seito*] set up raw-sugar manufacturing factories in Taiwan and then acquired refining factories in the homeland by the end of the First World War. In the inter-war years they acquired or assumed control of raw-sugar factories and agricultural interests overseas. The number of production units increased from 5 in 1920, to 10 in 1930, and 17 in 1940. The size of the individual production units was small, each employing two to three hundred, and high technical skills were not required. The head office in Tokyo had a production manager and its Tokyo branch office had a sales and a purchasing manager, but its vertically integrated activities could not be coordinated easily by such a formal structure: some directors were charged with the management of the domestic factories, and under the powerful leadership of the president Fujiyama, other directors were appointed overseas branch managers who were responsible for varied activities there. Overseas branch offices were not only charged with the control of the local factories but were equipped with a full set of functions. The agricultural interests of the company, which were dispersed in various part of Taiwan, were controlled by its local factories. Though the position of the production manager of the head office was strengthened throughout the 1930s, its overseas branch offices maintained their relative independence.

Important changes in this period were observed on the commercial side of the business. *Dai-Nippon Sugar Manufacturing* set up a commerce department, which played an important role in the procurement of raw materials in its early phase. The initiative of sugar merchants dominated sales, and the intensification of sales activities depended on the increase of the number of such special agents. These agents dealt with the products of the firm's domestic factories which were allocated by their own sales territories. Even before the decline of merchant houses, however, *Dai-Nippon Sugar Manufacturing* was engaged in direct sales in Tokyo and Osaka, and they extended this system to their factory in Kyushu during the inter-war years. In addition, the trading function of the head office became more important as the export of products and import of raw materials increased. These were controlled by the head office. Another important function of the commercial department was found in the formation of a cartel. Six sugar refining companies, including *Dai-Nippon Sugar Manufacturing*, formed an association of suppliers, and the commercial department of *Dai-Nippon Sugar Manufacturing*, together with a sugar merchant, a trading company and *Meiji Shoten* (House of Meiji) were made their licenced sugar brokers, who organised the network of market channels from the wholesalers to the retailers and confectionery companies.[17] In the cases of other sugar manufacturing companies, such as *Taiwan Seito*, *Meiji Sugar Manufacturing*, and *Ensuiko Sugar Refining*, branch offices were founded in Tokyo, each of which was equipped with a sales department. The characteristic of the functional structure thus appeared with the development of the division of labour between the head offices in Taiwan and the branch offices in Tokyo and with the increase of their independence of sales agents. Such a gradual move from the line structure to the functional one, though incomplete, was noticeable in the 1930s.[18]

A similar process is observed in the cases of the large-scale textile companies such as *Kishiwada Spinning & Weaving Mills* [*Kishiwada Boseki*], *Kureha Spinning* [*Kureha Boseki*], *Kinka Boseki* (Kinka Spinning), *Tokyo Muslin Boshoku* (Tokyo Muslin Spinning & Weaving), and *Toyo Muslin*. For instance, *Kureha Spinning* was initially organised on the basis of a relatively simple form of structure whose head office was composed of ten or so salaried employees. In 1939 it acquired *Toyama Boseki*, its parent company, and the head office was formed with commercial, secretarial, and technical staff sections. The number of factories began to increase, reaching 14 in 1939 when three further companies were acquired. These 14 factories were divided into four regional groups: each of these groups constituted a department in the head office, whose manager acted as the superintendent of the regional group. The head office had, in addition, trading, technical and other departments.[19] The relative independence of the production units in a functional structure was observed also in *Kishiwada Spinning & Weaving*. Factories – not managers – gained premium bonuses or penalties according to whether they attained their monthly norm of production. This control system was abolished by the end of the 1930s when the head office was reorganised to one consisting of various sections such as sales, technology, and weaving, in addition to six factory-superintendent sections.[20] In the remaining three textile companies mentioned above, the factory managers were directly responsible to the highest level managers in spite of the formation of a production department in the head office.[21] This was mainly because of the nature of their business. In the 1920s worsted companies began to diversify into cotton manufacturing, while cotton spinning companies embarked on weaving. A lot of small-scale companies were acquired, which was the main cause of the increase in capital of these companies. The newly acquired factories had their own management practices. Commercial aspects were first unified, but the unification of production was not easy. Troubles regarding organisation or personnel at the time of mergers were avoided by forming less strict organisational structures. This was seen on the occasion of the formation of *Daiwa Spinning* by the amalgamation of *Kinka Boseki* with three other spinning companies. In the head office of the new company, sales, spinning and chemical departments were established, in addition to administrative department, but four branch offices which were derived from the previous firms still represented and coordinated the groups of factories. The main difference between the management structure of sugar and large-textile companies and that of mineral and metal companies, therefore, resulted from the difference in the relative independence of their production units, though a centrifugal tendency is more or less observed in all these industrial companies.

The largest textile companies such as *Toyo Cotton Mill* [*Toyo Boseki*], *Nisshin Spinning* [*Nisshin Boseki*], *Dai Nippon Spinning & Weaving* [Dainippon Boseki], *Fujigas Spinning* [*Fuji Gas Boseki*], *The Nippon Weaving* [*Nippon Keori*] and *Katakura Industry* [*Katakura Seishi Boseki*] went a step further and typically developed a functionally departmentalised structure by establishing a centrally controlled production department. Some had already established such an organisation by 1920, though major organisational reforms were observed in the inter-war years. The largest of them had more than 20 factories with 20 000 employees in 1920. These companies had already integrated vertically to weaving by the First World War. After the war weaving branches were expanded to supply the growing export market, and this was followed by investment in overseas interests. Towards the end of the 1920s, the production of cotton textiles was rationalised, while financial resources were directed to other textile products, including rayon, staple fibres, silk and wool. This diversification was achieved by mergers of existing companies or the foundation of new enterprises. The rationalisation movement, which mainly implied the reorganisation of production on the workshop level, also raised the problem of the unification of management on the higher level. *Nisshin Spinning* and *Toyo Cotton Mill* were the pioneers of modern centralised management. *Nisshin Spinning* formalised a management system in 1909, unifying the different managerial practices of its production units. A functional structure consisting of clerical and technical departments was formed. Though differentiation in the head office organisation had proceeded further by 1940, the company adapted itself to the increase of the number of factories, of vertical integration, and of overseas investment with fundamentally the same management structure.[22] The organisation of *Toyo Cotton Mill* also developed by the tightening of the factory management. Cost accounting and standard motion study were introduced into more than 30 factories of the company just after the war. When *Osaka Godo Boseki*, another large company, was acquired in 1931, the organisation of the former's units was brought in to line with *Toyo Cotton Mill*, and the factory managers were replaced.[23]

Other largest textile companies underwent a series of organisational changes during the period under examination. *Dai Nippon Spinning & Weaving* started in this period with a relatively simple functional/line structure. During the slump in the late 1920s the 'Meeting of Superintendents', consisting of the factory-managers and the section-managers in the head office, promoted the rationalisation and standardisation of production. By 1940, the head office had a large production department, which in turn had sections in particular product lines.[24] *Fujigas Spinning* changed its organisational structure in 1930 during the slump. The company had been administered by a loose functional/line structure. Although the production department had already been set up, the system of control was not clearly defined. The authority and responsibility for planning, trading, and production were now made definite, and these, in turn, were further sub-divided into particular sections.[25] The organisational history of *The Nippon Weaving* can be characterised as that of trial and error. Again it started from the production side: in order to unify the management practices of the factories whose number increased either by acquisition or by internal growth it introduced 'functional foremanship' in the early 1920s. However, it failed to coordinate its various production processes. A second attempt to improve production was made in the late 1920s, when the functional and departmentalised structure was laid.[26]

So far as sales functions were concerned, these companies gradually moved from heavy dependence on the established organisation of the yarn market. The first of the changes took place with the development of the overseas market. Except in the case of silk companies which advanced into direct exporting, this new channel became mainly dealt with by the trading companies. Secondly, the expansion of their weaving branches resulted in internalising the transactions of yarn within firms.[27] Thirdly, despite the above-mentioned two factors which restrained the development of the sales function of manufacturing companies, the largest textile companies intensified their sales activities in the domestic market. The number of their sales offices increased during the period, and they began to deliver goods other than to the Osaka market. By the mid-1930s most of their products became directly delivered to local weaving companies. Here, yarn transactions were made between the large spinning companies and local weaving shops, and the role of the city yarn merchants was reduced to those of remittance or pricing.[28]

The last group of companies that developed along functional lines during the inter-war years were found among chemical, pharmaceutical, and the remaining part of the food industries. Most of the heavy chemical companies specialised in either fertilisers or soda, and undertook little diversification. Even the oldest companies such as *Dainippon Jinzo Hiryo* (Dainippon Artificial Fertilisers), were no exceptions. For a long time, artificial fertilisers remained difficult to market. Firms had to develop their own marketing. In place of the traditional middlemen, *Dainippon Jinzo Hiryo* appointed local special agents, with whom the company's salesmen fixed upon the price and amount of transactions. Thus local sales offices were set up and their number increased up to seven by 1940. These offices, together with the factories, constituted the sub-units immediately below the highest level managers. The development of *Dainippon Jinzo Hiryo* was, to a considerable extent, based on mergers and acquisitions of other factories. At the time of the mergers in 1923, the operating sub-units were grouped into the functional departments. Its production department seemed to work as service staff, because the factory managers were directly responsible to the general manager.[29] In other chemical companies which developed similar types of organisational structure, marketing played an important role in the formation of the functional structure. *Dainippon Celluloid*, for instance, embarked on joint-sales activities with processing companies in the early 1930s, and affiliated local sales agents. *Showa Hiryo* developed direct sales to the Cooperative Union of Farmers in the late 1920s. In spite of the strong position of the production units in high technology industries, marketing often required a new sales function.[30]

Fine chemical companies, engaged in pharmaceuticals or dyestuffs, developed a more refined organisational structure. Pharmaceutical companies, such as *Shionogi*, *Sankyo*, and *Takeda*, originated as either wholesalers or retailers of pharmaceutical products, and made inroads into manufacturing by buying up or acquiring pharmacies. These manufacturing concerns were controlled by their production departments, which were often in charge of research and development at the same time. Their head offices retained characteristics of Japanese traditional merchants. Employees were recruited through shop apprenticeship. However, in the early 1920s, trading departments were set up and employees with higher education were recruited. The commercial side continued to hold a predominant place in these companies, which imported or dealt with pharmaceutical products produced by other pharmacies, selling through the sales network of local wholesalers. By 1930 the share of their own manufactured products increased, and further expansion during the Second World War gave a more independent position to the factories.[31] The remaining samples in food processing, such as confectioneries and brewing, though they were not the companies in fabricated basic materials, developed a functionally departmentalised structure.

These examples show that two forms of the functional structure were found among large-scale industrial companies in the inter-war years. The first was found in sugar, heavy chemical and large-scale textile companies. Not only a sales department but a technical or production department was formed in the head office. However, the production department could not directly control the production units. The production department was advisory staff to top management to whom each production unit reported. In many cases, factory managers were often members of the highest level managers. The second form was nearer to the structure described by Chandler as 'functionally departmentalised', in which each of the management tasks was divided into a series of specialised functions, and carried out under the direct control of a specialist manager. The second form was prominent among the largest textile firms, fine chemicals, and some of the food companies.

In metals and minerals, by contrast, the central coordination of the flow of goods was less developed than other branches of fabricated basic materials. By 1914, some companies had developed a head office consisting of accounting, sales, and secretarial functions, while production was performed by relatively few, large-scale production units.[32] The metal companies in this group developed rapidly throughout the period, and their growth mostly depended on forward or backward integration, either by themselves or by their affiliated companies. *Fujita Kogyo* (Fujita Mining) continued to acquire domestic mines, and *Tokyo Rope* [*Tokyo Seiko*] integrated backward by setting up *Kokura Seikojo* (Kokura Steel Works). Furthermore many companies integrated forward and diversified through adding metal processing stages. In *Fujita Kogyo*'s case the location of its production units was determined either by the location of resources or of the firms acquired. As a result, the company had geographically dispersed operating units, each of which integrated all the stages from the extraction of raw material to those of smelting and transportation. Sometimes, particularly in its early phase, sales activities were carried out by these local production units. These units were made the units of self-dependence. However, by the 1920s, functions which could not be covered by these production units became apparent. One was export. The main product of the company was copper. Like some other companies which had no metal processing branches inside the firms or among the subsidiaries, *Fujita Kogyo* had to make overseas markets their major outlet. *Fujita Kogyo* formed a trading department in its head office after the separation from its parent company in 1917. Initially export was undertaken by its parent company, it was moved to *Fujita Kogyo* when the parent company was acquired by *Fujita Kogyo* in the 1930s. Another factor which made the commercial activity of the head office increasingly important in the early 1930s was the formation of cartels among copper smelting companies. This was caused by the import of cheap American copper, and *Fujita Kogyo* took the initiative here. There were 377 salaried employees and 5464 wage workers, and the number of operating units in 1937 was 10. The organisational structure of this firm, however, remained relatively simple given its size.[33] More or less similar trends are observable in metal companies such as *Kokusan Kogyo* (Kokusan Industries), *Sumitomo Besshi Kozan* (Sumitomo Besshi Mining), *Furukawa Electric* [*Furukawa Denko*] and *Tokyo Rope*.[34]

Organisational changes directly resulting from mergers were found in some metal companies. Here there was decentralisation, with the development of a functional/line structure. Such a process is illustrated by the management structure of *Sumitomo Shindo Kokan* (Sumitomo Copper Rolling and Steel Tube) and by that of its direct descendant, *Sumitomo Metal Industries*.[35] During the period between 1922 and 1932, such an organisational form was observed for the first time in the history of this company. In 1916 a formal organisation was established in this works for the first time, though the works was not an independent firm but a copper rolling works belonging to *Sumitomo Corporation*. Activities came to be administered through dual lines of command, one through the traditional manager system, and the other through a functionally departmentalised structure. Just below the head of the works, a manager, and eventually several sub-managers and a chief engineer were appointed, and further below them functional units were formed. No structural reorganisation had taken place when a second factory was acquired in 1919. The new factory became a semi-independent field unit with a full set of functions. In 1922, the accounting, purchasing and sales functions of both factories were consolidated, though their production activities were operated separately. Steel tubes were produced in both of these factories, while copper rolling was concentrated in the First Factory. The reallocation of product lines between these two factories was soon started, and in 1926, following the firm's incorporation, this was achieved. However, the line of command was not reorganised despite the reallocation of product lines. Part of the steel tube branches continued to belong to the First Production Department even after their operations were transferred from the First Factory to the Second Factory. Such a confusing organisation was reformed in 1932. The 'manager system' was abolished, and by this means, the dual structure, which had often made the lines of authority ambiguous, was reformed into a functional one, consisting of accounting, sales, and two production departments. Furthermore, each of the production departments was made responsible for one of the product lines such as copper rolling and steel tubes. However, this functionally departmentalised structure did not last long. The 1930s saw tremendous development of the company increasing sales twenty-fold within a decade. The merger with *Sumitomo Steel* in 1935, which was one of the major sources for this rapid growth, took place in order to coordinate the kind of products which overlapped within the same *Sumitomo*. Both companies had open-hearths, and supplied similar products to a certain extent. The turnover of the steel branch of *Sumitomo Shindo Kokan* amounted to 5 million yen in 1930, which was approximately the same as the total sales of *Sumitomo Steel Works*. This merger, however, again brought about a production-centred organisation after three years of administration based on a functional structure. The sales departments were left in the head office, while the manager of each production unit was directly responsible to the top management, and this practice was strengthened under the war-time system from 1938. A similar organisational change following mergers can be pointed out in *Nippon Kokan* (Nippon Steel Tube) and in *Kokusan Kogyo*.[36]

Thus by 1930 70 of the largest firms in our sample had evolved either a crude or refined form of functional structure. The crude forms were found in mineral companies, while the modern functionally departmentalised structures were observed in the largest textile firms, fine chemicals, and a few of the consumer final goods companies. Other firms developed structures somewhere between the two. The differences have stemmed from either the strength or the weakness of the positions of the production units. When companies integrated forward, and when the position of the operating units were not so strong, a central control and the centralised coordination of the flow of goods originated.

2.4 DECENTRALISED STRUCTURES

Not all industrial corporations developed their management structure in a functional and centralising direction. Decentralised structures – on geographical or product lines, or in holding company style – were widely observed as early as the functional structures and in almost all branches of industries. These variations of the decentralised forms can be grouped into the third type of the management structures. Most of the decentralised structures started by having been based on the production units, which developed as the core of other functions such as procurement of parts, placing and accepting orders, and shipment. Of course, as in the case of European firms, but to a lesser degree, multi-firms mergers often produced such a decentralised structure.

Multiunit engineering companies, such as *Mitsubishi Heavy Industries* [*Mitsubishi Jukogyo*], *Tokyo Shibaura Electric* [*Tokyo Shibaura Denki*], *Nippon Sharyo* (Nippon Rolling Stock), and *Kawasaki Dockyard* (Kawasaki Zosenjo), developed autonomous production units. *Mitsubishi Heavy Industries*, which was incorporated in 1917 under the name of *Mitsubishi Zosen* (Mitsubishi Shipbuilding), was composed of two major shipyards, employing approximately 3000 in 1918. The organisational structure of its Nagasaki Shipyard started from a functional/line one, consisting of marine engineering, shipbuilding, and general affairs departments. Purchasing and sales were initially placed in the general affairs department. In 1930, the subcontracting department was added, and in 1932 trading function was formalised as a separate department. Kobe Shipyard had a similar, but separate, hierarchical organisation: both production and trading (purchasing and acception of orders) were carried out autonomously under the control of shipyard manager. The head office of *Mitsubishi Zosen* consisted of two relatively small sections concerning with trading, and the exchange of technological information between the main production units. In 1920 the number of administrative and technical employees of the head office who were paid monthly was 80, while those at the Nagasaki and Kobe shipyards was 1534 and 853 respectively. Though the ratio of the head office staff to such black-coated workers of the whole company rose slightly from 2.8 per cent to 4.2 per cent between 1920 and 1926, the head office organisation remained simple until the mid-1930s. The merger with *Mitsubishi Kokuki* (Mitsubishi Aircraft) resulted in the reorganisation of the head office: five commercial departments specialised by market or by products were set up at the head office, each in charge of the clerical work such as accepting and placing orders. However, the production units still had their own trading departments, and this central coordination scheme was counter-balanced by the rapidly expanding production units.[37] Few coordination or reallocation of product lines and market between its main production units was realised.

Similar organisational structures can be found among other firms formed by mergers. The problems of reallocation of product lines and marketing channels were often spontaneously solved, because the products or markets of the constituent firms differed from each other. The merger in 1937 between *The Shibaura Engineering Works* [*Shibaura Seisakujo*] and *Tokyo Electric* [*Tokyo Denki*], both among the top 100 firms in 1935, is an example. In 1920, both companies were functionally organised. *Tokyo Electric* maintained this structure, but the production units of *Shibaura Engineering* were separated from the control of the production department when a second factory was set up. At the time of merger, these two firms became 'Branches' immediately below the highest level managers, and both maintained their previous organisational forms without major changes except that the tasks of financing and purchasing materials were centralised. *Shibaura Engineering*, though it had added some household electrical equipment to its original product lines, was essentially a heavy electric and engineering firm, while *Tokyo Electric* produced electric light bulbs and communications equipment. The new enterprise was controlled by this style of holding company throughout the 1940s, and the separate systems of administration persisted.[38] Geographical division developed naturally in other heavy engineering firms, such as *Nippon Sharyo*, and in cement and ice-manufacturing firms. *Nippon Sharyo* had been operated as a series of separate factories until 1924, when two territorial sub-units were made self-supporting units, and given responsibility for both production and sales in their area. This was a single product firm, and coordination among the regional units became an important managerial task. A manager was appointed to each of these territorial branches not only to administer the semi-independent unit but to coordinate their relations with each other.[39]

Multidivisional structures decentralised by product division were also found in the 1930s. *Asahi Glass* increased its sales of soda in the 1920s, which had previously been used only as the raw material for glass manufacturing. Soda production for outside markets prompted the adoption of a self-supporting system to each of the product lines. This accounting system was completed in 1927 in order to exploit the ability of each factory to the full. However, the formal organisational chart of the company indicates a functional structure in spite of these measures: manufacturing and trading departments were placed below the managing directors, though these departments were subdivided into product lines. When *Mitsubishi Chemical Industries* was formed *Asahi Glass* was organised into two divisions in the organisational chart.[40]

In contrast to the internal growth of *Asahi Glass*, *Kanegafuchi Spinning* [*Kanegafuchi Boseki*] and *Godo Yushi* (Amalgamated Oils & Fats) became diversified either by mergers or acquisitions of factories. *Kanegafuchi Spinning* expanded its silk interests in the 1920s, then invested in chemical fibres, woollens, and linen in the 1930s. The organisational structure of its early phase is unknown, but in the mid 1920s the company was composed of 26 factories and two business offices. By 1940, the head office was divided into four product divisions, each of which was headed by a 'Superintendent of Production and Trading'. *Godo Yushi* was engaged in the production of soap and its raw materials after 1930, on the basis of a functional/

line structure. From 1937, the company acquired many local oil companies and rapidly diversified into paint, textiles, fishing, and other unrelated areas. Six product divisions were charged with production and sales functions. The new industry branches of the company was added by acquisitions, but the acquired factories were grouped by product, and the groups were made responsible to the top management.[41] In these cases, the profit responsibility of each product line was established, and the divisions were sometimes responsible for a full line of functions. However, the delegation of authority, or the separation of the top management from the operating tasks was quite incomplete.

In these various forms of decentralised structure, each sub-unit below the highest level managers had a full set of business functions consisting at least of production and sales. However, most of them were divided into sub-units not by product but by geographical basis. Each of the local operating units or the forerunner companies became self-sufficient 'divisions'. Reallocation of product lines and market among these 'divisions' rarely took place. These crude decentralised forms were found among the firms of producer final goods or some kind of fabricated basic materials which had their own local market. For the sea food, flour, cement and ship repairing firms, transportation costs amounted high when they tried to sell their products beyond a certain geographical areas. The number of their head office staff was too small to perform the staff functions in operating matters. Particularly in the cases of companies in electric or heavy engineering, the technical skills which constituted their major managerial resources belonged to the production units. However, the third type should not be simply regarded as the transitional forms from the simple line management to a refined modern multidivisional structure because this type remained for a long time. Although many organisational changes took place, particularly due to mergers, these companies would not adopt the modern form of the multidivisional structure. Rather this form was established under the war-structure from the late 1930s.

2.5 SUMMARY

Large-scale companies grew in Japan in the inter-war years as they first internalised the transaction of labour, and then added the control of purchasing or sales. By then these large-scale firms were found in all industries, though most of them supplied fabricated basic materials and a few producer final goods. Along with this, there was a transformation of the internal structure of these companies. Many of the companies we have examined evolved their hierarchical organisation to more elaborate forms, along with the parallel developments of the *Zaibatsu* and cartels.

The first feature which appeared in the management structures in Japan was a lean middle management at the department level. This was widely found among almost all organisational forms. In such hierarchies the manager in charge of each of the operating units was directly responsible to the board of directors or the general managers, and sometimes the highest level executives were appointed to manage the operating units.

The second, related characteristic of Japanese enterprise was the leading position of the production units in the company. This was not limited to high technology industries such as electrical goods and engineering, but was widely found even among industries which required financial resources or marketing techniques. In many cases, the production department of the head office worked as advisory staff to the senior managers, and the senior managers were at the same time in charge of the operating units.

A characteristic form of a hierarchical organisation which was more or less common to all the various types of the management structures was formed. Japanese industrial firms developed an organisation dividing the whole company into two parts, the head office and the production units. In this two-fold organisation, the head office was composed of some of the functional departments such as trading and accounting in addition to the highest managers and their administrative and service staff. The head office was a general term for these various sorts of managerial tasks, while the production units were a separate part of these firms. The decentralised forms of management structure, whether reorganised geographically or by product or not, developed around the production units.

The slow development of sales and marketing also influenced the form of Japanese organisational structure. This partly resulted from the industrial characteristics of the firms we have studied. Although more than half of them were engaged in the production of consumer goods, the products were not necessarily finished goods but fabricated basic materials. In addition, large-scale industrial enterprises were formed in a traditional Japanese market organisation which was dominated by wholesale merchants. This traditional organisation could not fulfil the functions that were achieved, in the West, by a highly developed network of marketing middlemen. Manufacturing companies in Japan had to equip themselves with sales or purchasing functions from the beginning. However, the development of these functions in manufacturing companies was limited, and the remaining part was carried out by trading companies. Apparently manufacturing companies could acquire raw materials and technical skills, or deliver goods at lower cost, by using the trading companies rather than by the internalised hierarchy. Furthermore, the traditional distribution channel was too firmly established to be replaced by the manufacturing companies. A centralised and functionally departmentalised structure was observed in companies which had any benefit in developing their own sales activities. Such cases were found among giant textile companies strong enough to cope with the merchant houses, fine chemical companies which had been derived from wholesalers, or some food companies which had to create new markets. These companies had many production units, but their position was not so strong. This made the coordination through managerial hierarchies both easier and necessary. Though the companies which fell into this category grew in number during the inter-war period, they were more or less subject to the influence of the general characteristics mentioned above.

In this chapter the investigation has been mainly directed to organisational schemes to coordinate various functions in individual large-scale corporations. Top management functions such as resource allocation or strategic decision making has been kept out of the discussion, and the author has deliberately avoided the term 'top management'. Whether the top management functions were really carried out by the highest level managers of individual companies, or in the hands of the *Zaibatsu* head office, or other sorts of external agents, and in what degree or in what sense the individual companies were independent businesses, still remains to be discussed in the next chapter.

NOTES

1. Alfred D. Chandler, Jr., *The Visible Hand*, Cambridge, Mass., 1977; *do*, 'The United States: Seedbed of Managerial Capitalism', ed. A. D. Chandler, Jr. and H. Daems, *Managerial Hierarchies*, Cambridge, Mass. and London, 1980.

2. *Factory Statistics* for the years 1905, 1920.
3. There are a few exceptional works. T. Yui, 'The Development of Organization of Top Management in Japan', *Meiji Business Review*, vol. XXIV, nos. 3–4, 1977.
   A word is necessary for the important role of the trading companies inside and outside the *Zaibatsu*. They were responsible for the procurement of raw materials and the sales of the products of the manufacturing companies, often maintaining exclusive transactions with the latter. This, however, does not necessarily mean that the manufacturing firms did not develop as multi-function firms, nor all the trading activities were carried out by such external institutions.
4. *Factory Statistics* for the years 1905, 1920.
5. H. Hazama, *Nihon romu kanri shi kenkyu* (A Study in the History of Labour Management in Japan), Tokyo, 1964; T. Hyodo, *Nihon ni okeru roshi kankei no tenkai* (Development of Labour Relations in Japan), Tokyo, 1971; M. Sumiya, *Nihon no rodo mondai* (Labour Problems in Japan), Tokyo, 1967.
6. *Shakai seisaku jiho* (Social Policy Review), vols 45–6; 59–62; 127–9; Chuo shokugyo shokaisho, *Shokugyobetsu rodo jijo: kagaku kogyo* (Labour by trade, chemicals), 1932.
7. In addition to the company histories of these firms, the following materials were consulted: *Nippon kogyo yokan*; *Kogyo nenkan*; *Boshoku yoran*; *Nippon kogyo taikan*.
8. When the registered English name of the sample company is known, like *The Nippon Weaving*, this is used and its Japanese pronunciation is quoted as [*Nippon Keori*]. In other cases the Japanese name of the company is used and its meaning is shown, like *Temman Orimono* (Temman Textile Manufacturing).
9. G. Okura, *Bosekigyo no kaikei to sono keiei*, Tokyo, 1933, pp. 7–39.
10. K. Inoue, 'On the Yarn Market', *Keieigaku ronshu* (Annals of Japan Society for the Study of Business Administration), vol. 7, 1933, pp. 229–48.
11. *Kaisha shokuin roku* (Personal Directory of Business Enterprises), Tokyo, 1940.
12. 'Manager' used to be a title given to the highest rank employee in a partnership. This title, however, was still observed in many joint-stock companies, and was given to the person who held the post just below the board. In a manager system the command that came from the board or president was given to the operating units through the manager.
13. Kurashiki Cotton Spinning, *Kaiko 65nen* (65 Years in Retrospect), Osaka, 1953, p. 678; *Boshoku yoran* (The textile Year Book), Osaka, 1919; *Teikoku ginko kaisha yoroku* (Directory of Japanese Banks and Companies), Tokyo, 1931; *Kaisha shokuin roku*, 1940.
14. *Nippon kogyo yokan*, 1922, 1936; *Kogyo nenkan*, 1930; *Nippon kogyo taikan*, 1925, 1931.
15. Toyo keizai shinpo sha, *Kabushiki kaisha nenkan*, 1936; Nomura shoten, *Kabushiki nenkan*; *Annual Returns* of each company.
16. Toyo keizai shinpo sha, *Kabushiki kaisha nenkan*, 1936, 1941.
17. *Nitto saiken 25nen shi* (The 25 Year History of Dai-Nippon Sugar

Manufacturing), Tokyo, 1934, p. 62; *Nitto 65nen shi* (The 65 Year History of Dai-Nippon Sugar Manufacturing), Tokyo, 1960, pp. 44–51.

18. *Meiji Seito 30nen shi* (The 30 Year History of Meiji Sugar Manufacturing), Tokyo, 1936; Y. Hasegawa, *Shaki shasoku shu* (Collected Regulations of Companies), Tokyo, 1941, pp. 433–9. In *Meiji Sugar*, both head office and Tokyo office had technical and sales departments, and several factories. The technical departments, however, did not directly control the factories.

19. *Kureha Boseki 30nen* (30 Years of Kureha Spinning), Osaka, 1960, pp. 56–81.

20. *Kishiwada Boseki 50nen shi* (The 50 Year History of Kishiwada Spinning), Osaka, 1942: *Nichibo 75nen shi* (The 75 Year History of Nippon Spinning), Osaka, 1966, pp. 273–80.

21. *Daiwa Boseki 30nen shi* (The 30 Year History of Daiwa Spinning), Osaka, 1971, pp. 226–36; *Nippon kogyo yokan*, 1936; *Kaisha shokuin-roku*, 1940.

22. *Nisshin Boseki 60nen shi* (The 60 Year History of Nisshin Spinning), Tokyo, 1969, pp. 171–4, 237–9, 255–66, 334–41, 363–9.

23. *Toyo Boseki 70nen shi* (The 70 Year History of Toyo Cotton Mill), Osaka, 1953, pp. 179–86.

24. *Nichibo 75nen shi*, pp. 160, 201–02, 314: *Kaisha shokuin roku*, 1940.

25. *Fuji Boseki 50nen ki* (50 Years of Fuji Spinning), Tokyo, 1947, pp. 146ff; Hasegawa, *op. cit.*, pp. 394–401.

26. *Nippon Keori 30nen shi* (The 30 Year History of The Nippon Weaving), Kobe, 1931, pp. 140–48. In 1925, a production department was set up in place of the 'management department' which controlled its factories. At the same time, a trading department was newly established instead of purchase and sales departments. Finally, staff functions such as personnel, research, secretary were separated from the operating lines and placed under the direct control of the top management.

27. The relative importance of yarn and cloth of these firms in their total sales can be calculated from *Menshi boseki jijo sankosho*.

28. Inoue, *loc. cit.* In *Nisshin Spinning* trading manager Murata played an important role in developing the market for their products. See, *60nen shi*, p. 368. In *The Nippon Weaving*, transition from dependence on wholesalers to its own sales offices was observed.

29. *Dainippon Jinzo Hiryo 50nen shi* (The 50 Year History of Dainippon Artificial Fertilisers), Tokyo, 1936, pp. 117–22, 188–96: *Nissan Kagaku Kogyo 80nen shi* (The 80 Year History of Nissan Chemical Industries), Tokyo, 1969, pp. 76–7. *Denki Kagaku* (Electro Chemicals), by contrast, developed through internal growth, and a similar type of organisation appeared in 1923. This system persisted until 1959, when the production department of the head office was finally charged with the control of its factories. *60nen shi* (The 60 Year History of Denki Kagaku), Tokyo, 1977, pp. 118–20.

30. *Daicel Kagaku Kogyo 60nen shi* (The 60 Year History of Daicel Chemical Industries), Sakai, 1981, pp. 13–42; *Showa Denko 50nen shi* (The 50 Year History of Showa Denko), Tokyo, 1977, pp. 31–3.

31. *Shionogi 100nen* (100 Years of Shionogi), Osaka, pp. 129–229; *Sankyo*

60nen shi (The 60 Year History of Sankyo), Tokyo, 1960, pp. 63–134: *Takeda 180nen shi* (The 180 Year History of Takeda), Osaka, 1960, pp. 63–134. A similar process and result is observed in food companies, such as *Meiji Seika* (Meiji Confectionery), *Dai Nippon Brewery*, *Kirin Brewery*, and *Noda Shoyu* (Noda Soy-Sauce). These companies developed either by expanding the market for new products or providing traditional products for the wider market, and by these reasons, marketing played an important role in the formation of the functional structure of these firms. For a dyestuffs company which developed a functionally departmentalised structure, see *Nissen 20nen shi* (The 20 Year History of Nippon Stuff Manufacturing), 1936. The technical department of the company was in charge of its factories at first, but gradually expanded their range of control and finally centralised the tasks of planning and labour management.

32. H. Matsumura, *Kozan no keiei* (Management of Mines), Tokyo, 1941, pp. 634–40.

33. The Dowa Mining, *70nen no kaiko* (70 Years in Retrospective), Tokyo, 1955, pp. 89, 94, 140–41.

34. The production units of *Kokusan Kogyo* were made units of profit responsibility. This company had set up an export department before its sales activities were taken over by *Mitsubishi Corporation*. As the commercial activity of the head office became increasingly important in the early 1930s, the head office of *Sumitomo Besshi Kozan*, which had been attached to the main production unit, was removed to Osaka with its trading department. *Furukawa Electric*, a copper rolling and cable company, was established in 1920: it inherited a sales department of *Furukawa Shoji*, a trading company, though the greater part of its sales operation was still carried out by the latter. Its sales function was strengthened when the latter was absorbed into the head office of the former.

Market orientation was clearly observed among the companies of secondary metal processing. Again, *Furukawa Electric* divided its sales department into two sub-units by products, and set up several business offices throughout the country. *Tokyo Rope* centralised its sales activities during the First World War. The company had to seek its markets among the Japanese Navy, shipping companies, and local fishermen's bosses. These activities were removed from *Okura Gumi* to its own business offices and special agents. Like *Furukawa Electric*, its head office had two sub-units for sales activities to meet with the product diversification. See, *Tobata Imono Kabushiki Gaisha yoran* (An Outline of Tobata Imono), Tokyo, 1935, pp. 18–33; *Hitachi Kinzoku shi* (History of Hitachi Metals), Tokyo, 1980; *Sumitomo no rekishi to jigyo* (The History and Present Status of Sumitomo), 1955; Furukawa Kogyo, *Sogyo 100nen shi* (The 100 Year History of Furukawa Mining), Tokyo, 1976, pp. 327–33; *Tokyo Seiko 70nen shi* (The 70 Year History of Tokyo Rope), Tokyo, 1957, pp. 67–68.

35. *Sumitomo Kinzoku Kogyo 60nen shoshi* (The 60 Year Brief History of Sumitomo Metal Industries), Osaka, 1957, pp. 24–72; 116–27; *Sumitomo Keikinzoku Kogyo nenpyo* (Chronology of Sumitomo Light Metals), Tokyo, 1974, pp. 18–77.

36. When started the head office of *Tobata Imono*, the direct forerunner of *Kokusan Kogyo*, had one sales, one technical, and two production managers. By 1930 the company became large enough to have four factories including the two which were acquired by mergers. The technical and the production functions were gradually moved to these production units, the managers of which were still responsible for the head of the factory department. By 1935, when the production units further increased owing to the mergers in the early 1930s, the factory department was abolished and these production units, each with technical and production departments, were made directly controlled by the president. *Nippon Kokan* began by criticising the management of *Yawata Iron Works* for irrational factory layout and poor sales performance. However, the production manager and the chief engineer played a critical role in its early history despite the creation of a functional structure. During the slump after the First World War the firm diversified into shipbuilding interests. At the recovery of trade in the 1930s, this company further embarked on the production of pig iron, and integrated backward the supply of raw materials such as iron ore and coal. As a result, the head office was reformed into one consisting of the trading and raw materials departments, while each of the large-scale operating units, which became independent of the head office department, belonged directly to the highest top. See, *Nippon Kokan 30nen shi* (The 30 Year History of Nippon Kokan), Tokyo, 1942, pp. 22–3, 364–7.

37. *Mitsubishi shashi* (The Diary of Mitsubishi Corporation), 1920–40; *Mitsubishi Nagasaki Zosenjo shi* (History of Mitsubishi Nagasaki Shipyard), vol. II, Nagasaki, 1951, pp. 50–56; *Kobe Zosenjo 50nen shi* (The 50 Year History of Kobe Shipyard), Kobe, 1957, pp. 56–64.

38. *Tokyo Denki 50nen shi* (The 50 Year History of Tokyo Electric), Tokyo, 1940, pp. 266–7; *Shibaura Seisakujo 65nen shi* (The 65 Year History of The Shibaura Engineering), Tokyo, 1940, pp. 134–48; *Tokyo Shibaura Denki 85nen shi* (The 85 Year History of Tokyo Shibaura Electric), Tokyo, 1963, pp. 105, 188–95.

39. *Bakushin: Nippon Sharyo 80nen no ayumi* (The 80 Year History of Nippon Rolling Stock), Nagoya, 1977, pp. 75–80, 103–04. Similar examples were found in cement and ice-manufacturing industries. The cement companies acquired many local factories in the inter-war period. From the initial phase of incorporation, *Asano Cement* was run through its two branch offices, each of which had responsibility for production, accounting and sales. With the acquisition of minor cement companies and diversification into industrial explosives in the 1920s, a functional structure was adopted, with head office technological and trading departments, the branch office system being abolished. A dual structure, with the head office on the one hand, and factories with sales functions on the other, temporarily appeared. The 'branch office system', however, was re-adopted in 1930. *Onoda Cement* was managed by a similar decentralised structure throughout most of this period, but in 1938 the head office strengthened its control over the production units. The top management was appointed to the newly founded departments of the central office, though the local production units continued to have their own sales and

production function. *Asano Cement enkaku shi* (History of Asano Cement), Tokyo, 1940, pp. 621–7; *Onoda Cement 100nen shi* (The 100 Year History of Onoda Cement), Tokyo, 1981, pp. 322–4.
40. Asahi Glass, *Shashi* (History of Asahi Glass), Tokyo, 1967, pp. 145–6, 518–37.
41. *Nippon Yushi 30nen shi* (The 30 Year History of Nippon Oils and Fats), Tokyo, 1967, pp. 177–86; *Kaisha shokuin roku*, 1940.

3 Holding Companies and Corporate Control, 1920–40

3.1 EXTERNAL INSTITUTIONS OF PRE-WAR LARGE-SCALE FIRMS

The previous chapter examined the development of the management structures of large-scale Japanese manufacturing firms. Though hierarchical structures from top to lower management were investigated, our discussion focused on the middle and lower management. The main functions of these two hierarchical levels were in coordinating the flow of goods and allocating and controlling labour. However, the top management functions of large-scale firms were not fully examined, and the financial resources of these companies were not investigated, either. Furthermore, these companies did not always make use of the market mechanism even when they did not internalise the transactions of resources. Thus the following questions still remain to be discussed. Generally, can the individual companies be regarded as independent firms which are themselves responsible for resource allocation? If their strategic decisions were made by other firms, they should not be regarded as independent firms, and analysing their management structures separately makes no sense. Was it the individual large-scale companies, the *Zaibatsu* or other sorts of institutions external to the individual firm that were responsible for top management functions? Did the *Zaibatsu* intensify their control over large-scale industrials in the inter-war years? So far as the top management functions are concerned, it is impossible to discuss the individual firms separately without examining their relationships with the *Zaibatsu* or other owners.

Middle management functions also require more investigation. Although most of the large-scale firms were multifunction firms, they may have depended on external institutions such as trading companies

44

or cartels for purchasing or sales. Were the functional departments nominal, and were the sales or purchasing activities actually undertaken by the external institutions? There may have been internal transactions among the member firms of the *Zaibatsu* even if the *Zaibatsu* was not responsible for the strategic decisions of its member firms.

Some of these points have been mentioned in existing studies. We have a large number of studies on the pre-war *Zaibatsu*. Recently, research on their control system has been started.[1] However, these studies start by regarding a *Zaibatsu* with many subsidiaries as a unified enterprise, and treat the companies belonging to the *Zaibatsu* as its divisions or branches, though they at the same time often emphasise the decentralising trends of the *Zaibatsu*. Many works, particularly in comparison with the post-war business groups, take it for granted that the head office of the pre-war *Zaibatsu* controlled overwhelmingly, if not owned, their member companies.[2] There are also some empirical works on the emergence of 'salaried managers' and the development of top management organisation in individual companies.[3] Although these are quite important studies, it is necessary to make clear whether the top management functions were actually carried out by these 'salaried' or highest level managers of the individual firms. There are some studies which have examined the separation of ownership and control in large-scale firms by analysing the dispersion of share holding.[4] However, they did not deal with the control or decision making in the pre-war large-scale firms, but directly applied the hypothesis of the separation of ownership and control. However, a company which is personally owned or controlled differs greatly from one owned by another institution such as a holding or parent company. Studies of pre-war Japanese firms either concentrate their analysis on the *Zaibatsu* as a unity, or on the individual firms by ignoring the managerial functions of the *Zaibatsu*. These two approaches have not intermixed.

The present chapter examines large-scale companies of pre-war Japan, in their relation to external institutions such as the *Zaibatsu* and trading companies. This problem is divided into two parts. First, which of the two institutions, individual firms and the *Zaibatsu*, were in charge of the top management functions? Second, was segmented coordination of the flow of goods, or allocation of financial and labour observed within the *Zaibatsu*? Did large-scale firms depend on the trading companies or other intermediate merchants for purchasing and sales, or on particular banks for financial transactions, in spite of the formation of functional departments within their firms?

Ordinary means of corporate control such as shareholding, inter-locking directorships, loans, and mutual transactions of goods which are often used to measure inter-corporate relationships are examined here. All of these four forms are related to the allocation of resources within a group, and the first two are particularly related to the top management functions. In addition, the employees of individual companies were appointed altogether by the parent companies and then allocated to individual firms, or they were moved from parent companies to other companies in the same groups. In this chapter we attempt to throw light on these aspects and ask whether and to what degree the individual firms internalised the top management functions, and also whether they were actually multifunction firms or not.

3.2 THE DEVELOPMENT OF HOLDING COMPANIES

First, the relationship between large-scale manufacturing firms and the *Zaibatsu* headquarters is examined. The largest 100 manufacturing companies either by sales or assets in 1920 and 1935 have been taken as samples. There were 118 such firms in 1920, and again 118 in 1935. Most of the *Zaibatsu* originated as diversified family firms, then separated their activities like mining, manufacturing, banking, and sometimes trading interests into individual firms, while at the same time developing holding companies which held shares in these oper-ating firms. During the period in discussion, they were composed of their headquarters (holding companies) and a large number of oper-ating companies.

A survey indicates that, in 1936, 101 companies were affiliated with *Mitsui Zaibatsu*, 73 with *Mitsubishi Zaibatsu*, 34 with *Sumitomo Zaibatsu*, and 44 with *Yasuda Zaibatsu*. 109 of them were manufac-turing firms, and their paid-up capital amounted to 1530 million yen, which were approximately 24 per cent of the total capital of all industrial companies.[5] If the other nine *Zaibatsu*, such as *Asano*, *Furukawa*, *Nissan*, were taken into account, the number of manufac-turing firms affiliated with the *Zaibatsu* became 250, and their capital amounted to 40 per cent of the total capital of all the mining and manufacturing companies. Sixty-one of the largest 118 firms of 1935 were listed among them, and 40 of them belonged to one of the four major *Zaibatsu*.[6] These figures may suggest an important position held by the *Zaibatsu*, particularly by the major four. However, in what way were many large-scale companies affiliated with the *Zaibatsu*? Are there sufficient grounds for such figures?

The largest 100 manufacturing firms (either by sales or by assets) in 1920 and 1935 had various types of shareholders shown in Table 3.1.[7] In 1935 there were 12 companies more than 50 per cent of whose shares was held by four major *Zaibatsu*: four were owned by *Mitsui*, five by *Mitsubishi*, two by *Sumitomo*, and one by *Yasuda*. If a lower bound of 10 per cent is taken, another six companies are enlisted as belonging to these four *Zaibatsu*. *Mitsui* increases its number to seven, *Sumitomo* to four, and *Yasuda* to two. Most of these shares were held by the *Zaibatsu*'s general office, but some jointly by other member companies. 'Pyramidal ownership' by the member companies is sometimes found. When compared with the survey of 1936, which was quoted in the beginning of this section, these numbers are strikingly small. However, these must be taken as the real number of the companies on which the *Zaibatsu* could enforce their influence through ownership.

How about the largest 118 manufacturing firms in 1920? The four major *Zaibatsu* owned more than 50 per cent of the shares in eight companies, and they were the minority shareholders in five companies.

TABLE 3.1 Ownership concentration and the shareholders of large-scale firms

	1920		1935	
	50% +	10–49%	50% +	10–49%
Top Holders				
Individuals	5	17	8	7
Institutional Holders	20	30	32	37
Zaibatsu				
Mitsui	(3)	(3)	(4)	(3)
Mitsubishi	(3)	(0)	(5)	(0)
Sumitomo	(1)	(1)	(2)	(2)
Yasuda	(1)	(1)	(1)	(1)
Asano	(2)	(1)	(1)	(2)
Furukawa	(2)	(2)	(1)	(1)
Okura	(0)	(2)	(0)	(3)
Kuhara	(1)	(2)	–	–
Nissan	–	–	(3)	(1)
Nitchitsu	(0)	(1)	(2)	(0)
Mori	–	–	(0)	(2)
Operating firms	(4)	(7)	(7)	(13)
Other institutions	(3)	(10)	(6)	(9)

Six belonged to *Mitsui*, three to *Mitsubishi*, two to *Sumitomo*, and two to *Yasuda*. A slight increase in these figures between 1920 and 1935 was not so much due to the acquisition of the shares in the independent companies by the *Zaibatsu*, as to the separation and incorporation of their operating branches.

If the major *Zaibatsu* did not hold the controlling shares of the greater part of the largest firms, did the remaining many control themselves? There were 43 companies in 1920 and 34 companies in 1935 which can be characterised as having 'dispersed ownership'. In addition, there were 22 companies in 1920 and 15 companies in 1935 whose majority or minority shareholders were individuals. In these two groups the *Zaibatsu* or other external institutions had no relationships with these large-scale firms through shareholding.

In 1920 besides the 13 companies which had the four major *Zaibatsu* as their majority or minority share holders, there were 37 firms whose shares were more or less owned by other companies. In 12 cases, other companies were their majority share holders. Of 51 companies whose shares were more or less held by other companies in 1935, 20 were owned by the majority share holders. In total 66 of the largest 118 firms of 1935 had other companies as majority or minority share holders, of these 32 were owned by majority holders. These exceed other forms of ownership in number. Eight were owned by private majority holders, seven by private minority holders, and the remaining 34 by widely dispersed shareholders. In some industries such as iron and steel, nonferrous metals, electrical equipment, and heavy engineering, companies were owned by the institutional shareholders, while in textiles and chemicals by other forms of ownership as well.

Among these institutional holders of large-scale firms, were operating companies, 'nominal' holding companies, financial institutions, the rising *New Zaibatsu*, in addition to the established four or other *Zaibatsu*. They were holding companies, and the differences between them were often vague, though they can be classified roughly into two groups. First, there are the industrial or other sorts of operating companies which set up or acquired the control of other large-scale industrial firms. Many large-scale firms such as *Shanghai Seizo Kenshi* (Shanghai Spinning), *Kurashiki Kenshoku* (Kurashiki Rayon), or *Chosen Chisso Hiryo* (Chosen Nitrogenous Fertilisers) were set up by such large-scale industrial companies. In some cases, the majority shares of large-scale firms were acquired by other companies. 97.3

per cent of the shares of *Kyoritsu Muslin* was undertaken by *The Nippon Weaving [Nippon Keori].*[8] In other cases, trading companies set up or took over the shares of large-scale firms. *Iwai Shoten* (Iwai Commercial House) held 70 per cent of the shares of *Nippon Soda Kogyo*, and *C. Itoh & Co. [Itochu Shoji]* owned 19.1 per cent of the total shares of *Kureha Spinning*. Thus nearly half of 66 firms were owned directly by other operating companies, though some of these operating holding companies were themselves owned by pure holding companies or *Zaibatsu*. Many of the operating companies which held the majority or minority shares in large-scale firms continued their own operating activities, as in the cases of *Kanegafuchi Spinning [Kanegafuchi Boseki], Kurashiki Cotton Spinning [Kurashiki Boseki]*, or *The Nippon Weaving*. But a few, such as *Nippon Chisso* (Nippon Nitrogenous Fertilisers) intensified their standing as holding companies in the 1930s. The number of large-scale companies whose majority or minority shareholders were operating companies was less in 1920.

Second, there are the pure holding companies which were not directly involved in operating activities. These pure holding companies were formed by being separated from operating companies. Among them were nominal holding companies, comprised of a few partners and employees. These were incorporated in order to maintain the value of properties of the founders' families as well as to evade legally the payment of income tax. *Terada Gomei* (Terada & Co.) owned 21.2 per cent of the shares in *Kishiwada Spinning & Weaving Mills [Kishiwada Boseki]*, and *Shiobara Gomei* 27.9 per cent of *Sankyo's* shares in 1935. Such holding companies had a limited staff in their general office, making them incapable of working as the top management organisation of their subsidiaries. Each of them held shares in one or two companies. Even in such a case, however, they were capable of tightening control over the subsidiaries, or setting up new operating companies with the intention of controlling them. However, the number of large-scale firms whose shares were held by such nominal holding companies to more than 10 per cent was larger in 1920 than in 1935. Such nominal holding companies were more predominant in 1920. Many of the pure holding companies of 1920 failed to hold shares in their subsidiaries until the 1930s, though their subsidiaries remained among the largest 100 firms. Furthermore, few holding companies of 1935 extended ownership just for the purpose of increasing the security of their properties. Holding companies increased the number of their subsidiaries to control them.

The various types of ownership which appeared in the above discussion are summarised as follows:

1: More than 50 per cent of the shares in a firm are owned by a single or a joint shareholders.
2: 10 to 50 per cent of the shares in a firm are likely owned.
3: A firm with ownership dispersion.
A: A firm whose shares are personally or jointly owned by individuals, for instance, by family members.
B: A firm owned by other companies.

Table 3.2 indicates how the largest 118 manufacturing firms in 1935 changed their ownership characteristics between 1920 and 1935. Twenty-nine firms did not exist in 1920, and four were not known. Fifty-one companies remained unchanged, while 39 converted to other types of ownership. The ownership of 16 companies was dispersed because they moved from '1' to '2' or to '3', while nine went the other way round. Did the holding companies intermediate in the change between '1A' and '2' or '3'? Seven companies moved from A to B, and six from B to '3', although there were four firms which moved from dispersed ownership to ownership by holding companies ('3' → B).

To sum up the discussion on the institutional owners of the largest 118 firms, the nominal holding companies decreased, while the industrial or other sorts of operating parent companies increased between 1920 and 1935. Various intermediate forms remained. Some of the parent companies which had been engaged in operating activi-

TABLE 3.2 Changing ownership characteristics, 1920–35, of the largest 100 industrial companies in 1935

Ownership types	1A	1B	2A	2B	3	Others	
1A	4	3					7
1B	1	11		7			19
2A			5	4	3		12
2B	1	2	1	11	6		21
3		1	2	3	20		26
non-existent	6	11	1	7	3	1	29
unknown		1		1	2		4
	12	29	9	33	34	1	118

ties intensified their nature as holding companies by transferring operating activities to their subsidiaries. Others, though incorporated as pure holding companies, increased the number of subsidiaries among large-scale firms. Most of the *Zaibatsu* retained controlling functions. In all these cases, the ownership of industrial firms was moved into the holding companies, but the operating and some of the middle management functions were retained in the individual firms.

It was not the complete dispersion of stock ownership of large-scale firms, but a gradual move of their ownership to holding companies that occurred between 1920 and 1935. Although there were four major *Zaibatsu*, their positions were lower than generally supposed. What about the controlling or the top management functions? Did they belong to the operating companies or to the holding companies?

3.3 CORPORATE CONTROL AND STRATEGIC DECISION MAKING

Pre-war Commercial Law authorised the shareholders meeting to be responsible for overall decisions of the company. Still, the board of directors was formally regarded as policy making and executing institution. In practice, as full-time directors were engaged in daily management, they had easy access to the inside information of their firms. How did such full-time managers take over the positions which were formerly held by the owners? Another question is whether the highest level managers were internal or external directors. An external director is a director appointed or sent by other institutions such as the *Zaibatsu*, holding companies, or other operating companies. He is a salaried manager, but represents institutional shareholders. Let us begin with the second question by examining the careers of the senior executives of large-scale companies.

In this chapter chairmen, presidents, senior managing directors, and managing directors of the largest 118 manufacturing firms (the largest 100 manufacturing firms either by sales or by assets) in 1920 and 1935 are examined.[9] Ordinary directors are excluded, though the board of directors was a formal organisation in policy making and execution. Data on the careers of ordinary directors are incomplete. Furthermore, it is doubtful to what extent they were involved in decision making particularly when they held a number of posts as directors. For this investigation, these executives are grouped into the following three categories.

a: owner managers who held the positions of senior executives by holding shares in their firms. Directors who were listed among the top 10 shareholders in their firms are called owner managers.

b: managers sent by holding or parent companies, or those who were appointed as directors by other institutions which were listed as the large shareholders of the firms or promoted to the positions of the senior executives immediately after they left holding or parent companies.

c: salaried managers who cannot be classified into 'b', and a few ex-governmental officials.

Types 'a' and 'c' are internal directors. Though these two have been distinguished from each other in the discussion of ownership and control, both were internal directors who carried out top management function independent of outside institutions. Executives of type 'b', in contrast, are external directors. Firms with such external directors may be regarded as parts of larger units when important decisions are made by such larger units.

Two hundred and sixty-two senior directors of 116 firms in 1920 are examined. For the firms in 1935, the careers of 347 directors of 116 firms are known. Sixty-four, or a quarter of them were sent from their parent companies in 1920. In 1935, the number rose to 83, but no noticeable changes took place in the overall ratio. They were outnumbered by 'internal' salaried managers ('c'). The number of internal salaried managers was 98 in 1920, and 188 in 1935. Owner managers ('a') numbered 74 in 1920 and 75 in 1935. Internal directors whether salaried or owner managers prevailed in their numbers.

However, hierarchies existed in the top management organisation of Japanese firms.[10] Such a top management organisation was composed of several hierarchical positions from chairman or the president to auditors. Moreover, each member of the top management did not necessarily specialise in one of the functions and take part in making decisions. In such an organisation the highest ranking manager may have played far more important roles than other members. The number of highest ranking managers who were sent from parent companies was 48 among 118 firms in 1920, and 44 among 118 firms in 1935. Some companies had both a chairman and a president in 1935, and if both of them are taken together their number increases to 45 among 118 firms. The number of internal salaried managers who held the highest rank was relatively small. It was 24 in 1920 and 27 in 1935.

The remainders were owner managers. There was a large number of owner managers and their number did not decrease during these 15 years. Some of them acquired a large amount of their companies' shares after being appointed their directors. If both types of internal managers are taken together, they occupied 60 per cent of the highest positions of the largest firms in 1920 and 1935. In short, few changes took place. However, lower ranking managers who were sent from parent companies may have played important roles in decision making through informal means. This was a possibility in all the companies that were not composed completely of internal managers. The number of companies whose boards were entirely composed of internal directors was 59 in 1920 and 61 in 1935. This approximately matches the ownership characteristics, though there was an increase in the number of firms owned by holding companies. There was no increase in the number of firms which had at least one managing director sent from parent companies. There were some companies without any outside directors on their boards, although at least more than 10 per cent of their shares were owned by other firms. In 1935 *Teikoku Seito* (Teikoku Sugar Manufacturing), *Toyo Seito* (Toyo Sugar Manufacturing) and *Kuhara Mining* [*Kuhara Kogyo*] in 1920, and *Nanyo Kohatsu* (Nanyo Company), *Meisei Boshoku* (Meisei Spinning & Weaving), *Toyo Muslin*, *Kurashiki Kenshoku* (Kurashiki Silk Weaving), *Asahi Benberg Kenshi* (Asahi Benberg), *Onoda Cement*, *Toyo Seikan* (Toyo Can Manufacturing) are examples of such companies. Their holding companies were minority shareholders, and half of them were 'nominal' holding companies. Some holding companies appointed their employees as rank-and-file directors of these companies, but these directors were not necessarily involved in the top management functions.

In conclusion, the posts of executive directors of 14 companies in 1920 and 1935 were entirely occupied directors sent from holding companies ('b'). As a half of the companies were entirely staffed with 'a' and 'c' executives, the remaining one-third had at least one 'b' in addition to 'a' and/or 'c' executives. How many of these firms were fully equipped with the top management functions? At least 59 in 1920 and 61 in 1935, whose executives were entirely composed of 'a' and 'c' were independent enterprises. In addition, some of the firms whose directors represented 'nominal' holding companies have been included in this category. In these cases, a nominal holding company could not allocate resources or make decisions independent of its own subsidiary because the holding company was set up exactly for

TABLE 3.3 Number of transitions among the categories of executives,
1920–35

I	No change	30
II	a → b, b → c	17
III	a → c, a → ac, ac → c	14
IV	c → b, c → ac, b → ac	19
V	Others and unknown	2

the purpose of holding shares in a particular operating company. In 1920, for instance, *Kawasaki Dockyard* had K. Matsukata as president, who was at the same time a member of *Matsu Shokai* (Matsu & Co.) which owned 16.5 per cent of the shares of the former. *Kawasaki Dockyard* was, at that time, not a part of *Matsu Shokai*, but an independent large-scale company. At least 15 similar examples were found in 1920 and 10 in 1935. Therefore, in 44 remaining firms in 1920 and 49 firms in 1935, executives sent from holding companies were found.

Table 3.3 classifies various forms of transitions among the types of senior managers of the firms of 1935 between 1920 and 1935. No remarkable change was observed. Companies which were staffed by the employees of holding companies continued to remain in group I. Companies whose executives changed from owners to salaried managers by being intermediated by holding companies are grouped in II, but their number is small. Group III companies moved directly from owner control to salaried managers control. Group IV changes in the opposite direction. Holding companies did not play an important role in the rise of the salaried managers. Holding companies could not successfully retain control of the companies in which they held shares.

Did holding companies have direct influence on the decision-making of their subsidiaries? In some cases, subsidiaries' boards made decisions independently of their parent companies, though their directors were appointed by parent companies. In others, parent companies put senior executives on the subsidiaries' boards, but the latter made different decisions from the parent companies. In these cases holding companies were not responsible for the top management functions of their subsidiaries. Whether holding companies can take over the top management functions of their subsidiaries or not often depends on the size of the head office staff. However, this is not always the case, because in some *Zaibatsu*, personal leaders continued to manage their subsidiaries without the support of such general staff.

The only possible solution is to clarify the method chosen by each of the holding companies. Most of the *Zaibatsu* had rules for the control of subsidiaries, though their methods differed from company to company and from period to period.

Five firms in 1920 and six firms in 1935 had one or more executives who were sent from *Mitsui* or its group companies. In 1920, the Supervisory Department of *Mitsui Gomei*, which controlled their subsidiaries, was abolished. Although *Mitsui Gomei* continued centralised management of its 'Directly Affiliated Companies', only one firm – *Mitsui Mining* – among the five and six of the largest companies of 1920 and 1935 respectively belonged to the Directly Affiliated Companies, while other four firms in 1920 and five firms in 1935 were controlled in a different way. For the Directly Affiliated Companies, the practice changed in 1933. Only fundamental management policies, such as personnel or investment required approval by the *Gomei* head office.[11]

Mitsubishi Goshi sent their staff as directors of four and three of the largest firms in 1920 and 1935 respectively. The personnel, budget, operation, and finance of their 'Branch Companies' were placed under the control of the *Goshi* head office in 1918. Three firms in 1920 and one in 1935 were Branch Companies. Towards the end of the 1920s, financial control by the *Goshi* head office was abolished, and in 1931 only control over new projects and investment contracts were retained in the hands of the *Goshi* head office.[12]

The number of the companies whose executives were appointed by *Sumitomo Goshi* was three in 1920 and four in 1935. *Sumitomo Goshi* had developed a head office with more than 200 staff which enabled them to supervise centrally the personnel, finance, and the management of its 'Connecting Companies'. One firm in 1920, and three in 1935 were Connecting Companies. The control by the head office extended to investment decisions and management of the Connecting Companies. However, decentralisation began in the late 1920s. For instance, *Sumitomo Hiryo* (Sumitomo Fertiliser), the predecessor of *Sumitomo Chemical*, decided to make inroads into the production of ammonium sulphate and presented the plan to the *Goshi* in 1928. Although the board of *Goshi* hesitated to approve this project, it had to approve its execution in 1929.[13]

The head office of *Yasuda Holding Company* had a Secretarial Department which was responsible for the personnel of its subsidiaries and a Subsidiaries Department which supervised subsidiaries. *Yasuda* had more than 40 subsidiaries in 1935, but only two of them were listed among the largest 100 firms in 1920 and 1935, though they had interests in many financial and public utility branches. *Teikoku Seima* (Teikoku Linen) was grouped with the secondary related companies and *The Japan Paper Manufacturing* [*Nippon Shigyo*] with the primary related companies in 1926. The head office intensified control once, in 1921, however, decentralisation proceeded after 1929, and the head office withdrew from the management of its subsidiaries.[14] Though there was a period of centralised management, these two firms were autonomously administered for the major part of the period examined.

Asano Dozoku (Asano Family Company) was a holding company as well as an operating company. As an operating company it had branches in trading and transport, and as a holding company it had large subsidiaries like *Asano Cement* or *Asano Kokura Seikojo* (Asano Kokura Steel Works). In addition, *Asano Dozoku* held most of the shares of *Asano Zosenjo* (Asano Shipbuilding). Little is known about the control of subsidiaries. The first and second Soichiro Asano became president of these subsidiaries, and autocratic aspects of decision making were often observed in the early phase of their development, though other shareholders influenced separately the policies of each firm.[15]

Furukawa Gomei and the companies of its group held shares and appointed presidents of *Osaka Denki Bundo* (Osaka Electric Copper Smelting), *Furukawa Kogyo* (Furukawa Mining), *The Furukawa Electric* [*Furukawa Denki Kogyo*] in 1920. In 1935 *Furukawa Kogyo Gomei* (Furukawa Mining & Co.) and the group members held shares and appointed senior executives of *The Furukawa Electric* and *Fuji Electric* [*Fuji Denki*]. The Supervisory Department controlled budget, performance, and planning of direct and indirect subsidiaries in 1920. In 1935 the control of subsidiaries was intensified by the formation of the President Office.[16] At informal levels however, the management of subsidiaries was decentralised. For instance, *The Furukawa Electric* was set up on the initiative of K. Nakajima, director of *Furukawa Gomei* and later president of *The Furukawa Electric*, but was administered by S. Nakagawa, senior managing director of *The Furukawa Electric*. Even very important matters such as the formation of *Fuji Electric* were decided by *The Furukawa Electric*. However, these facts did not immediately indicate that top management functions were systematically carried out by the managers of the subsidiaries. Rather these were caused by the lack of unity in the *Gomei* headquarters.[17]

Okura Gumi held minority shares in *Akita Mokuzai* (*Akita Wood Products*) in 1920, and in *Nippon Jidosha* (Nippon Motor) in 1935. In addition it acquired minority shares in *Toyo Muslin* by the mid 1930s. However, *Okura Gumi* developed their interests in home and over-sea trade, mining, and civil engineering. Their operating units were dispersed from each other, and no efficient management system was formed. Their manufacturing interests arose from the activities of K. Okura as a leader of business circles, and not from integration or diversification.[18] Manufacturing firms remained autonomous even after becoming subsidiaries of *Okura Gumi*.

Nippon Sangyo consisted of large-scale manufacturing firms such as *Nippon Mining* [*Nippon Kogyo*], *Hitachi* [*Hitachi Seisakujo*] and *Hitachi Shipbuilding* [*Hitachi Zosen*] which *Nippon Sangyo* took over from *Kuhara Mining*, and of *Kokusan Kogyo* (Kokusan Industries), *Kyodo Gyogyo* (Kyodo Fishery) and *Nippon Shokuryo Kogyo* (Japan Food Products) which G. Ayukawa either founded or acquired. Among them, *Nippon Sangyo* maintained only a minority share in *Hitachi* and *Kokusan Kogyo*. Before long the shares in *Hitachi* became dispersed, and *Nippon Shokuryo Kogyo* was short-lived. Until 1933, *Nippon Sangyo* was a nominal holding company which held shares and sent G. Ayukawa as chairman of *Nippon Mining*, *Hitachi Shipbuilding*, and *Kokusan Kogyo*. In 1934 a central office was formed whose departments took charge of planning, super-vision and finance. Acquisition was the major source of development of the *Nissan Zaibatsu*, but centralised control by head office depart-ments was rejected by its subsidiaries. Soon *Nippon Mining*, *Hitachi*, and *Nippon Suisan* – formerly *Kyodo Gyogyo* and *Nippon Shokuryo Kogyo* – regained their autonomy, while these subsidiaries sent their senior executives to the central board of *Nissan Zaibatsu*.[19]

Nippon Chisso Hiryo (Nippon Nitrogen Fertilisers), an operating as well as a holding company, had two large-scale subsidiaries, namely, *Chosen Chisso Hiryo* and *Asahi Benberg* in 1935. These subsidiaries were either set up or separated to promote vertical integration further. Despite their legal independence, these two subsidiaries were actually part of *Nippon Chisso*. *Nippon Chisso Hiryo* appointed directors of these subsidiaries and made decisions for them. These three companies formed an accounting unit. It is dubious to count these companies as individual large-scale firms.[20]

Finally, *Mori Kogyo*, the minority share holder in *Showa Hiryo*

(Showa Fertilisers) and *Nippon Denki Kogyo* (Nippon Electro Chemicals) in 1935, had a weak central office organisation. *Showa Hiryo* and *Nippon Denki Kogyo* were personally managed by T. Mori, and each of them had other large share holders. *Mori Kogyo* had little power to control its subsidiaries.[21]

All the *Zaibatsu* that had at least one subsidiary or affiliated company among the largest 100 firms were investigated. The *Zaibatsu* headquarters played top management functions in seven firms among 22 'affiliated firms' in 1920. The number amounted to ten among 27 'affiliated firms' in 1935. These figures included the 'Directly Affiliated Companies' of *Mitsui*, 'Branch Companies' of *Mitsubishi*, 'Connecting Companies' of *Sumitomo*, and the 'Primary Related Companies' of *Yasuda*, although a certain degree of management decentralisation is observed here. In these cases strategic decisions were more or less made by the hierarchies formed outside individual companies. On the other hand, the 'nominal' holding companies were still a part of the large-scale firms and not the reverse, though they had the potential to become larger by forming a central office staff. In addition, there were subsidiaries of other operating companies among the largest firms in 1935. Their parent companies were giant manufacturing or trading companies. Managerial control by parent companies was not necessarily strong, but the coordination of the flow of goods or vertical integration between parents and subsidiaries may be more important.

In sum seven large-scale firms of seven *Zaibatsu* in 1920 and ten firms of ten *Zaibatsu* in 1935 were not individual firms. Other large-scale companies belonging to the *Zaibatsu* maintained autonomy in top management functions. Even the subsidiaries which were formerly subject to the *Zaibatsu* head office became less strictly controlled later.

3.4 SEGMENTED ALLOCATION OF MANAGEMENT RESOURCES

Though most of the large-scale manufacturing firms made their own strategic decisions, they may not have used outside markets, but may instead have depended on particular agents for their supply of labour, raw materials, financial resources, or outlets for their products. In fact, financial resources were partially supplied by various types of holding companies which held shares in manufacturing firms.

There may have been other types of transaction such as the appointment of new employees, exclusive transactions of goods, or loans. These types of transaction are worth examination since, they create an interdependence in the transactions of resources among the firms in the *Zaibatsu*. This subject can be divided into two parts. One is whether a segmented circle of resource allocation occurred among the member companies of the *Zaibatsu*. The other is whether individual companies were dependent on a particular bank or a trading company in the transactions of materials, products, or financial resources; in other words, whether the banks or trading companies inside the *Zaibatsu* acted as the intermediaries for other members.

The supply of raw materials and their processing within segmented circles are sometimes pointed out as factors in the development of some *Zaibatsu* such as *Furukawa* and *Nippon Chisso*. Were large-scale firms also involved in this type of transactions?

The first example is *Furukawa* and its 'Related Companies', which were comprised of 17 operating firms including three among the largest 118 firms in 1935. These firms ranged over mining, metal smelting, metal processing such as wire and cable, electrical equipment, communication equipment, and chemicals and rubber. The total sales of these firms for the latter half of 1937 amounted to 120 million yen, 40 million yen of which came from transactions among themselves. Of those 16 million yen, or 13 per cent were transactions of raw materials for downward branches.[22]

Another example are the Connecting Companies of *Sumitomo*. Four firms, which represented all of its main Connecting Companies in manufacturing branches, are found among the largest firms in 1935. *Sumitomo Besshi Kozan* (Sumitomo Besshi Mining) supplied two of the Connecting Companies, *Sumitomo Shindo Kokan* (Sumitomo Copper Rolling and Steel Tube) and *Sumitomo Densen Seizosho* (Sumitomo Cable Manufacturing), with two-thirds to one-half of its products. *Sumitomo Shindo Kokan* and *Densen Seizosho* purchased approximately half of their raw materials from copper suppliers outside their group. In addition, a few per cent of *Besshi Kozan*'s sales were to *Sumitomo Chemical* and its forerunner in the 1920s, but this amount was even lower than the sales derived from some fertiliser producers outside their group. Meanwhile, *Shindo Kokan* (or *Metal Industries*) and *Sumitomo Chemical* sold little to other members of their group. *Densen Seizosho* found its main markets among outside customers. In 1935 3 per cent of its orders came from the Connecting Companies, and 10 per cent from *Nippon*

TABLE 3.4 Ratios of external debts of the largest 118 firms of 1935

	1920	1935
50% +	3	8
40–49	6	10
30–39	9	16
20–29	9	20
10–19	24	15
0– 9	31	43
Unknown	7	6
Non-existent	29	–
Total	118	118

Electric, while the remaining 87 per cent was sold outside.[23]

In the other *Zaibatsu*, mutual transactions among member companies must have been less than *Furukawa* and *Sumitomo*. In the 1930s the number of operating companies which held majority or minority shares in other large-scale firms increased. The relationship between *Meiji Sugar* and *Meiji Seika* (Meiji Confectionery), and *Kobe Steel Works* and *Harima Zosenjo* (Harima Shipbuilding) are such examples, but except for a few cases such as that of *Nippon Chisso* and its affiliated companies, their mutual transactions were not remarkable.

In relation to the segmented allocation of financial resources, the ratio of external debts (debentures, loan capital, and notes payable) to the total capital of each of the largest companies are known.[24] Unlike shareholding, however, evidence which directly identifies the creditors of these external debts is still incomplete.

Table 3.4 indicates the distribution of external debts of large-scale firms. The ratios are low in comparison to those of post-war companies. External debts were less important forms of financing in the pre-war large-scale firms. In terms of the *Zaibatsu*, the closely affiliated companies of *Mitsui*, *Mitsubishi*, *Sumitomo*, and *Yasuda* (including *Asano*) indicated lower ratio of external debts than other firms. Though these *Zaibatsu* had financial institutions among their subsidiaries, their closely affiliated firms did not have to depend on credit from their parent companies and the banks within the same *Zaibatsu*. Similarly, companies which were less closely affiliated with the *Zaibatsu* showed lower ratios of external debts. Although the majority or minority shares of this second group of firms were held by the *Zaibatsu* and their executives were sent from the *Zaibatsu* head office, these firms had their own top management functions. In general, the financial positions of these two groups of companies were better on the average than those of large-scale companies. For the companies which were traditionally regarded as affiliated companies of the *Zaibatsu*, but had no relations with the *Zaibatsu* in shareholding and personnel, the ratio of debentures, loaned capital and notes payable was, in general, low. However, there are several exceptions to this third group. Some textile companies showed high ratios of debentures or loaned capital. They are regarded as having been affiliated with *Mitsui*, but there is little evidence to show that they were financed by *Mitsui*. Moreover, their dependence on loaned capital or debentures began after the mid 1920s. In the early 1920s, they did not depend so much on such external debts. Finally, there were six companies outside these three groups of companies whose debentures were exclusively undertaken by either *Mitsui*, *Mitsubishi* or by *Yasuda*.

In contrast, the affiliated firms of *Furukawa, Nippon Sangyo, Nippon Chisso, Okura* and *Mori* showed remarkably higher ratios of loaned capital and/or debentures. Their external debt ratios for 1920 are not available, since many of them did not exist then. However, they had no influential banks among the member firms, and they could not generate a segmented flow of financial resources among group members. If they wanted to form such a segmented flow of money, holding companies had to act as intermediaries in introducing outside financial resources and allocating them among subsidiaries.

There were about 50 companies in 1935 which had no relation with *Zaibatsu* groups. In 20 such firms, particularly textile companies, the ratio of their external liabilities was higher than average. Though they may have been involved in a certain segmented flow of money generated by local banks or trading companies, they were not included in the capital market inside the major *Zaibatsu*.

The next question is whether the headquarters, trading companies, or banks inside the *Zaibatsu* acted as intermediaries for other members in transactions of resources. To what extent were these carried out by various forms of federations such as the recruitment of the employees of member firms by the headquarters, exclusive distributorships, sole-sales agents, and syndicates? And to what extent were these coordinated by the market?

Some of the affiliated companies relied on the *Zaibatsu* head office for the supply or recruitment of salaried employees. *Mitsubishi Goshi* took high school-graduates as 'Regular Employees' and allocated them among its Branch Companies. A similar practice was observed in *Sumitomo*, and later in *Furukawa, Nippon Chisso*, and *Yasuda*, though *Yasuda* had no such large-scale companies. Little is known about *Asano. Nippon Sangyo* had no such practice. Therefore, this practice roughly accords with the control and decision making of the holding companies discussed in the previous section, and the number of companies whose employees were recruited through their parent companies was less than ten among the largest sample firms for each of the years 1920 and 1935.

For the supply of raw materials, little information is available. In the first half of the 1930s, nearly 20 companies, particularly those in marine produce, sugar manufacturing and refining, cement, and nonferrous metals, integrated upward into extraction and plantation. However, a portion of necessary raw materials had to be supplied by *Mitsui Trading* or *Mitsubishi Trading*. Chemical companies used long-term contracts for procurement, particularly of coal, electricity, and some mining by-products. About half of them including pharmaceuticals bought their raw materials from particular producers. They also had subsidiaries in lime ore mining and electricity generation. In electrical or heavy machinery, the kinds of materials ranged over various products of other industrial branches inside and outside these companies. It was unlikely that a single trading company became the sole supplier of their raw materials. Textile companies can not be classified into any of these groups. Senior executives and their Osaka offices played important roles in purchasing, while the number of importers of raw cotton were limited and naturally such importers had great influence over the supply of materials. *Chuo Keito Boseki* (Chuo Wool Spinning), whose raw materials were exclusively supplied by *Iwai Trading* throughout the 1920s and 1930s, is an exception. Little is known about steel companies. This evidence indicates that a particular trading company could not become the sole supplier of one or a group of industrial firms. Rather, patterns of purchasing were related more to the nature of raw materials.

Companies which used their own organisations for distribution were found in food processing, pharmaceuticals, ceramics, electrical engineering, and minerals. Except for those in minerals, these companies supplied finished and differentiated products which were directly used by a large number of final customers. The number of final goods suppliers among the pre-war large-scale firms was limited. At least 18 of the largest 118 firms of 1935 used their own hierarchies and trading offices for sales in 1920, and 23 did in 1935.

Various types of federations between the manufacturing firms and wholesalers are widely observable. In some cases, manufacturing firms assigned sole agents by area or product, and such agents were exclusively engaged in dealing with that product for particular manufacturers. This agency system reflects the underdevelopment of internal hierarchies and the weakness of the sales activities of manufacturers. However, by 1920, many manufacturing companies grew stronger than their distributors. In 1920, at least 13 of the largest 118 firms of 1935 used such merchants, and by the mid 1930s 27 firms did so, though many of them depended partially on their own distribution channels at the same time. *Meiji Sugar Manufacturing* and *Tokyo Electric* had sales subsidiaries. By the mid 1930s, five firms had such sales subsidiaries.

In other cases, intermediate merchants were stronger than large-scale manufacturing companies. Some merchants acquired exclusive distributorship in part or whole, of the products of the manufacturers. However, the number of large-scale manufacturing companies whose sales activities were exclusively carried out by a particular trading company was not large; eleven in 1920 and eight in the early 1930s. As has often been pointed out, some trading companies such as *Mitsubishi Trading* or *Mitsui Trading* held the exclusive distributorship of manufacturing companies, and other trading companies like *Iwai Trading* set up large-scale manufacturing subsidiaries.[25] However, in many cases these manufacturing subsidiaries were not listed among the largest firms, or only a part of their products or markets were dealt with by particular merchants. Even in *Sumitomo Zaibatsu* which had a more unified structure than others, the central trading department did not deal with all the products of the group companies. In 1921, *Sumitomo Goshi* (Sumitomo Corporation) had eight branch offices throughout the country. The 'Copper Sales Office' belonged to *Sumitomo Besshi Kozan* (Sumitomo Besshi Mining) in 1928, and the remaining seven branch offices dealt with from 40 to 50 per cent of the products of its Connecting Companies throughout the 1920s and 1930s. *Sumitomo Shindo Kokan* (Sumitomo Copper Rolling and Steel Tube) sold from 30 to 50 per cent, and *Sumitomo Seikojo* (Sumitomo Steel Works) sold 60 per cent of their products through *Goshi*'s trading offices. *Sumitomo Densen Seizosho* (Sumitomo Cable Manufacturing) sold more than 70 per cent of its products in the interwar years through *Goshi*'s trading offices. However in *Sumitomo Chemical* this ratio was less than 10 per cent;[26] the remaining part of its products being sold directly by the manufacturing companies.

Mitsubishi Trading made exclusive contracts for distribution with some manufacturing companies in the latter half of the 1920s. Nine of them were found among the largest 118 firms companies of 1935. However, these contracts were often limited to a particular region, a particular product line, or special activities such as export. Only *Tobata Imono*, the forerunner of *Kokusan Kogyo* (Kokusan Industries) sold all its products through *Mitsubishi Trading* since 1931. *Mitsubishi Electric* sold all its products through *Mitsubishi Trading* between 1921 and 1924, but after that this exclusive contract system was reorganised into a syndicate. *Mitsui Trading*, on the other hand, exclusively dealt with the products of *Taiwan Seito* (Taiwan Sugar Manufacturing), *Toyo Rayon*, *Dainippon Jinzo Hiryo* (Dai Nippon Artificial Fertilisers), and *Onoda Cement* during 1920s and 1930s. The products of these companies were semi-finished goods and had to be distributed more widely.

What about the subsidiaries of the operating companies? *Suzuki Shoten* (Suzuki Trading) was a trading company with its own subsidiaries among the largest firms such as *Kobe Steel Works* in 1920. *Suzuki Shoten* supplied its manufacturing subsidiary with raw materials. However, the products of *Kobe Steel* were not necessarily distributed by *Suzuki Shoten*. *Iwai Shoten* (Iwai Trading) was exceptional in that it took over the exclusive distributorships of *Chuo Keito Boseki* (Chuo Wool Spinning) and *Nippon Soda Kogyo*. Large-scale subsidiaries of manufacturing companies did not depend on their parent companies in supply and sales. In 1920, the number of such subsidiaries was small, but in 1935 their number increased to sixteen. Most of these manufacturing subsidiaries had outlets for their products. For instance, *Furukawa Electric*, whose controlling share was held by *Furukawa Coal Mining* in 1935, developed its own organisation for distribution, but *Fuji Electric* whose minority share was in turn, in the hands of *Furukawa Electric* also developed its own distribution channels. In many case these large-scale subsidiaries depended on sole sales agents. In almost all cases, large-scale subsidiaries started from the diversified branches or downward processes of their parent companies. They were separated as subsidiaries because their products and markets differed from those of their parents. Parent companies could not engage in sales activities for their subsidiaries even when the parent companies supplied their subsidiaries with raw or intermediate materials.

On the other hand, at least six firms in 1920 and eight in 1935 used middlemen for their distributors. Such a practice was found among cotton textile firms, but large-scale cotton spinning companies began to use their branch offices for distribution.

Finally, there were many firms which cannot be classified into any of these types of transactions. They manufactured to orders and directly delivered goods to the orderers. Sometimes these orders and their payments were intermediated by trading companies. Such a pattern was prominent among shipbuilding, heavy electrical, and some nonferrous metals companies. Here again, product-market characteristic rather than the affiliation with a particular business group determined the types of transactions.

For financial transactions, banks inside the *Zaibatsu* intermediated outside resources with the large-scale firms of their groups. When the *Zaibatsu* had no such financial institutions, who played this role? *Mitsui*, *Mitsubishi*, *Sumitomo*, and *Yasuda* had one or more financial institutions inside the *Zaibatsu*. However, large-scale manufacturing companies which were more or less related to these *Zaibatsu* were in good financial positions. They did not have to depend on outside financial resources at least until the mid 1930s; on the contrary, the dividend from these large-scale firms flowed through holding companies or their financial institutions to outside companies.

How about the *Zaibatsu* which had no banks inside their group? *Furukawa Kogyo Gomei*, for instance, did not advance money to its subsidiaries, though it depended heavily on external debts.[27] *Nippon Sangyo* increased loaned capital throughout the 1930s, because its own capital and premium income derived from issuing shares could no longer meet the increasing demand derived from its subsidiaries. *Nippon Sangyo* borrowed money from various banks to finance its subsidiaries. However, when the supplies from such means proved insufficient, the subsidiaries of *Nippon Sangyo* began to find financial resources by themselves.[28] *Nippon Chisso* relied on the *Mitsubishi Bank* for their financial resources until 1933. After this time the debentures of *Nippon Chisso* and its subsidiaries were undertaken by *Nippon Kogyo Bank* and *Chosen Bank*. These loans were made separately, but actually *Nippon Chisso* and its subsidiaries were not financially separated from each other.[29] Two subsidiaries of *Mori* did not raise money through their holding company, but financed themselves individually.[30]

This examination of the allocation of financial resources indicates that financial affiliations in the form of loans were less pronounced than shareholding. Furthermore the ratio of equity capital was generally high throughout the larger part of the interwar period. However, there was another type of financing which may have been related to financial affiliations. In pre-war companies, only part of the shares which were raised in the capital market were actually paid up. Afterwards, companies requested payment of the unpaid part, and the share holders often asked for bank loans secured on these companies' shares. In these cases, banks did not loan to individual companies, but through their shareholders in the form of equity capital. It is not possible to measure the extent of this type of financing in the equity capital of large-scale firms.

3.5 CHANGE AND CONTINUITY DURING THE WAR

Shareholding, the interlocking directorships, exclusive transactions, and selective financing by the *Zaibatsu* were not so extensive as to support their control on large-scale firms. Most of the large-scale manufacturing firms allocated resources and coordinated economic functions on their own initiative for the major part of the interwar years. Only a limited number of companies among the large-scale firms, particularly in minerals and metals, were controlled by the *Zaibatsu* head offices.

However, the *Zaibatsu* may have controlled non-manufacturing companies or small-scale firms, or they may have used some informal means for control. Firstly, the share of manufacturing branches in GDP stayed around 25 per cent throughout the 1920s and the early 1930s, then rapidly rose to 30 per cent in the mid-1930s, and stood at around 30 per cent throughout the greater part of the post-war years. Secondly, large-scale companies may not have been found among manufacturing firms. Taking the largest 100 companies by assets in 1970, two-thirds of them were manufacturing companies. Manufacturing firms accounted for two-fifths of the largest 100 companies by assets in 1930. These figures indicate an important fraction of non-manufacturing firms among the pre-war large-scale firms. However, a large number of these non-manufacturing firms were electricity supply and railway companies, which were not directly controlled by the *Zaibatsu*. Finally, the *Zaibatsu* may have indirectly controlled the manufacturing firms by forming strong foothold in mining, distribution and finance. This may have been partly true, but it is impossible to prove that the *Zaibatsu* indirectly controlled manufacturing firms through these mining, distribution and financial firms. Even if the influence of the *Zaibatsu* on the national economy as a whole was large, individual large-scale companies independently made decisions regarding resource allocation or the coordination of economic functions.

However, the growing influence of the *Zaibatsu* after the mid-1930s is often pointed out. The *Holding Companies Liquidation Committee* (Mochikabu kaisha seiri iinkai, or *HCLC*) reports that the share of the major *Zaibatsu* of the total paid-up capital of all joint stock companies increased between 1937 and 1944. The shares of the four major *Zaibatsu* increased from 10.4 per cent in 1937 to 24.5 per cent in 1944. They increased their shares in heavy industries from 14.6 per cent to 32.4 per cent. If the ten (in 1937, nine) *Zaibatsu* are taken, the share rose from 15.1 per cent to 35.2 per cent of the stocks of all the companies, or 24.9 per cent to 49.0 per cent in heavy industries between 1937 and 1944. Figures rose under the wartime-structure, particularly among the companies in heavy industries.

Though this evidence indicates the changing position of the *Zaibatsu* in resource allocation since the mid-1930s, they do not necessarily indicate a growing control by the *Zaibatsu* of large-scale companies. Among the largest 118 firms of 1935, 32 firms were listed by the *HCLC* documents as affiliated companies of the *Zaibatsu*. In 21 cases shareholding by the *Zaibatsu* decreased since the mid-1930s, while in six it increased. For interlocking or appointment of the senior directors of large-scale companies, few changes were found during the same period.

As a new factor in the late 1930s, external debts of large-scale firms increased. The large-scale companies in the interwar years, particularly those affiliated by the *Zaibatsu*, primarily depended on equity and other sorts of owned capital. After the mid-1930s however, the rapid development of manufacturing firms in branches of heavy industry necessitated a large amount of additional capital. The average ratio of the external debts of all companies stood at around 40 per cent until 1938, then rose to 43 per cent in 1939, 45 per cent in 1940, and finally to 55 per cent in 1943. For the largest firms of 1935, the average ratio was 17 per cent in 1935 and 27 per cent in 1940. Questions arise as to whether the capital was supplied or intermediated by the banks inside the *Zaibatsu* or not, whether the manufacturers' need for money helped to generate segmented flows of financial resources, and whether the *Zaibatsu* intensified their control on the large-scale firms by allocation of additional financial resources. The *Zaibatsu* head office could no longer supply additional financial resources in the form of loans, debentures or bills.

It has been pointed out that industrial companies began to depend on 'organ banks' inside the *Zaibatsu*, in addition to increasing their equity capital in the late 1930s. The rising new *Zaibatsu* which had no such banks fell behind in adapting themselves to rapid development due to scarcity of financial resources.[31] It has also been pointed out that 'indirect financing' had its origins in the 1930s. At the same time, it is known that the industrial companies began to depend on financial resources outside the *Zaibatsu* in the 1930s.

However, both 'organ banks' and 'indirect financing' are vague terms. The banks inside the *Zaibatsu* were not set up to supply capital for the companies inside the *Zaibatsu*. In this sense they were not organ banks. The term 'indirect finance' is even more confusing; many financial intermediaries held shares in operating companies, but insurance companies and some holding companies held portfolios in operating companies too. In these cases, indirect financing cannot easily be distinguished from direct financing. In other cases, the shareholders of operating companies often asked for bank loans to supply additional or unpaid equity capital when these companies requested payment. Therefore, these are not necessarily the best terms to explain the pattern of financing of this period.

Recently, some empirical works have appeared, in which the nature of the financial transactions between the banks and the industrial companies have been clarified: firstly, in the cases of the large-scale industrial companies such as *Mitsui Mining, Oji Paper, Kanegafuchi Spinning, Tokyo Shibaura Electric, Taiwan Sugar Manufacturing*, and *Toyo Rayon* which are regarded as having been related to *Mitsui Zaibatsu*,[32] their equity ratio continued to rise until at least 1936, and in some cases until 1939. Additional shares were not held by the *Zaibatsu* head office. The external debts of these firms began to increase after 1937, while their deposits at the *Mitsui Bank* decreased. *Oji Paper* fell into debt to *Mitsui Bank* in 1930, again between 1934 and 1936, and again from 1938 and beyond. *Kanegafuchi Spinning* fell into debts to the *Mitsui Bank* in 1935. From 1939 and after, *Tokyo Shibaura Electric* (Toshiba) and *Mitsui Mining* also borrowed from the *Mitsui Bank*. However, *Oji* and *Toshiba* borrowed from the *Mitsubishi Bank* and the *Sumitomo Bank* as well. Companies in the munitions industries such as *Toshiba*, issued debentures. In 1944 public funds were introduced into munitions companies through the *Mitsui Bank*, and the segmented allocation of financial resources was completed. However, the extent of such loans should not be exaggerated, because they still only made up 3 or 4 per cent (at most 8 per cent) of the total capital of these companies in 1940. In addition these companies had a large amount of bills payable, and a certain part of them must have been loans from banks in the form of bills. However, they cannot be distinguished from ordinary type of bills accepted by the transactions of goods.

The nature of the relationships between the banks and the member companies of *Mitsubishi Zaibatsu* is not clear. The internal capital of the member companies was used for their small-scale investments. The internal capital of the *Zaibatsu*, used for large-scale investment, became insufficient by the late 1930s, and the member companies had to seek external capital.[33] Long-term capital was raised by equity outside of the *Zaibatsu*, while short-term capital was supplied within the *Zaibatsu*. However, there are no documents which support this presumption. After 1937 the pattern of financial transactions amongst *Mitsubishi* companies began to change. The rapid development of the companies in heavy industries was financed by their greatly increasing profits, which continued until 1944, and by equity capital as well. However, these companies also used other methods; debentures were raised by *Mitsubishi Mining* and *Mitsubishi Heavy Industries*. These were offered to the public by the *Mitsubishi Bank* and *Mitsubishi Trust and Bank*. *Mitsubishi Heavy Industries* and *Mitsubishi Chemical Industries* (formerly, *Asahi Glass*) asked for loans, *Mitsubishi Mining* and *Mitsubishi Electric* depended on bills payable (which were actually loans). Financial transactions between these industrial companies and the banks inside *Mitsubishi* are not clearly observable. At least one of them borrowed from the *Sumitomo Bank*, though the amount was not large, and they also borrowed from the government banks. In 1940 the ratios of loans to total capital was 6 per cent in *Mitsubishi Heavy Industries* and 20 per cent in *Asahi Glass*. Those of bills payable were 11 to 12 per cent in *Mitsubishi Mining* and *Mitsubishi Electric*. This evidence indicates that the manufacturing companies were not necessarily lacking capital for their development, though patterns varied from company to company. They combined the increase of equity capital and the call of unpaid capital with other methods of financing.

Little information on the financial resources of the companies of the *Sumitomo Zaibatsu* is available. Although members made use of equity capital, debentures, and loans,[34] their financial transactions with the banks inside *Sumitomo* decreased by the time loans became more necessary. Until 1940, their deposits surpassed their loan debts, and after 1940 they began to depend on government banks without intermediation by the banks inside *Sumitomo*. *Sumitomo Metal Industries* (formerly, *Sumitomo Copper Smelting and Steel Tube*) and *Sumitomo Electric* (formerly, *Sumitomo Densen*) borrowed from the *Sumitomo Bank*, in addition to its debentures and loans from government banks. *Sumitomo Mining*, *Sumitomo Chemicals* and *Nippon Electric* borrowed from both the *Sumitomo Bank* and *Sumitomo Trust and Banking*. Loans amounted to 2 to 20 per cent of their total capital in 1940 and from 15 to 28 per cent in 1943. Clearly an increasing trend towards loans is visible.

The *Yasuda Zaibatsu* had two firms among the largest 100 firms, and the ratio of loans to total capital of these two firms was high. Companies which were not related to these four *Zaibatsu* lacked banks inside their groups. The external debt ratios of these companies were traditionally higher than those of the companies inside the four major *Zaibatsu*, and remained high after the mid-1930s. However, external debts in the form of loans were remarkably lower than those of the firms inside the four major *Zaibatsu*. The companies which were related to the four major *Zaibatsu* preferred bills payable and debentures.

This evidence indicates the following: 1) the rapid development of manufacturing companies, particularly in heavy industry branches after the mid 1930s required additional capital. 2) The external debts of these companies rose after around 1938. 3) Firms which were affiliated with the four major *Zaibatsu* increased their loans and bills payable, though the degree and the timing differ in each case. 4) The post-war pattern of financial transactions had not yet appeared by 1940.

Though the allocation of financial resources through banks inside the *Zaibatsu* was even after the mid-1930s not predominant among the largest firms, and most of large-scale firms were supplied with additional financial resources without the intermediation of particular banks, the members of such large-scale firms may have changed much during the decade after 1935. The banks inside the *Zaibatsu* might have financed the rising heavy industrial firms which were engaged in the production of munitions. However this is another difficult fact to prove, since there were still few changes in the membership of the largest firms until the end of the 1930s, while sales in 1944 which were influenced by various factors under the abnormal wartime-structure make no sense. It is rather more appropriate to compare the large-scale firms in 1935 with the samples from 1950 when Japanese industrial production returned to the pre-war level. A quarter of the largest 118 companies had disappeared due to mergers during the War – particularly amongst textile industries – and to the loss of overseas equipment during the 15 years since 1935. Of the largest 100 firms of 1950 either by sales or by assets, 72 were also among the largest 118 firms in 1935. Six firms came into existence by the forceful divisions of the post-war reforms. Approximately two-thirds of the firms in 1935 were still found among the largest firms in 1950. These entries and withdrawals are less significant than the changes which took place during the previous 15 years to 1935 and again less significant than those of the 15 years after 1950. Furthermore, withdrawals were prominently found among food and textiles, while there were many new entries in food, textiles (chemical fibres), paper, and chemicals. Apparently, companies which were financed by banks inside the *Zaibatsu* were short-lived, and this pattern of finance was not continued by the next generation of large-scale firms.

In sum, shareholding by the *Zaibatsu* head offices increased after the mid-1930s. However, their shares in large-scale firms decreased. It has been pointed out that the pattern of finance changed under the wartime-structure; traditionally the *Zaibatsu* used internal capital for outside financing via their banks, but under the war-structure, external financial resources were introduced into the firms inside the *Zaibatsu* through their banks. However, so far as the large-scale firms are concerned, this was not necessarily the case. The pattern differed from firm to firm, but affiliated financing by the banks inside the group was observed only in limited cases. Most of the large-scale companies supplied financial resources through debentures and bills payable in addition to equity capital, which had no relationships to particular banks.

3.6 SUMMARY

In this chapter we examined whether pre-war large-scale companies made their own decisions, allocated managerial resources, and coordinated the flow of materials and goods by means of their own hierarchies. The conclusion is as follows.

First, with regard to top management functions, approximately one-tenth of our sample companies of both 1920 and 1935 were controlled by their parent companies in the sense that a greater part of strategic decisions were made by the parent companies. In spite of their legally independent status, they cannot be regarded as individual firms. Two-thirds of the largest firms in 1920 and 1935 had only internal senior executives on their boards, while the remaining one-third had at least one senior executive assigned from parent companies.

Second, for the coordination of the flow of goods, many companies used loose federations for purchasing and sales, such as sole sales agents for particular products or regions. Syndicates also developed towards the latter half of the 1930s. The number of companies which mainly used their own hierarchies was not small, but taking into account the formal development of internal management structures with a number of functional departments and operating units, their number was not large. Exclusive distribution by trading companies inside and outside the *Zaibatsu* was rare among the largest firms.

Third, segmented allocation of financial resources such as share-holding by holding companies and loans was widely found. But the affiliated companies of *Mitsui*, *Mitsubishi*, *Sumitomo*, and *Yasuda* did not have to depend so much on debentures or loans undertaken by their parent companies. This pattern did not change significantly throughout the 1930s.

Finally, there were some companies which relied on their parent companies for the supply of higher school-graduates. The parent companies recruited salaried employees and allocated them among their subsidiaries. The number of such companies in the largest firms was not large, but such a practice strengthened the identity of the groups.

NOTES

1. Hidemasa Morikawa, *Zaibatsu no keieishiteki kenkyu* (Business History of *Zaibatsu*), 1980; Shoichi Asajima, *Senkanki Sumitomo Zaibatsu keieishi* (Business History of the *Sumitomo Zaibatsu* in Inter-war Period), 1983.
2. Yoshikazu Miyazaki, *Sengo nihon no kigyo shudan* (Business Groups of Post-war Japan), 1976; Ken'ichi Imai, *Gendai sangyo soshiki* (Modern Industrial Organisation), 1976; Kozo Yamamura, 'Zaibatsu pre-war and Zaibatsu post-war', *Journal of Asian Studies*, vol. 23, 1964; Kazuo Shibagaki, *Nihon kinyu shihon bunseki* (Analysis of Japanese Financial Capitalism), Tokyo, 1965.
3. Tsunehiko Yui, 'The Development of the Organizational Structure of Top Management in Meiji Japan', *Japanese Yearbook on Business History*, 1984.
4. Yojiro Masuchi, *Kabushiki gaisha ni okcru shoyu to shihai* (Ownership and Control in Joint Stock Companies), 1933; T. Mito, H. Masaki, and

H. Haruyama, *Dai kigyo ni okeru shoyu to shihai* (Ownership and Control in Big Business), 1973.

5. It is often difficult to distinguish mining from manufacturing.
6. K. Takahashi and J. Aoyama, *Nihon Zaibatsu ron* (On Japanese *Zaibatsu*), 1938; Holding Companies Liquidation Committee, *Nippon Zaibatsu to sono kaitai* (The Japanese *Zaibatsu* and their Dissolution), 1962; Shigeaki Yasuoka, *Nihon no Zaibatsu* (The Japanese *Zaibatsu*), 1976, pp. 55–69.
7. Tokyo Koshinjo, *Ginko kaisha yoroku* (Banks and Companies Digest), 1922; Daiamondo (ed.), *Zenkoku kabunushi yoran* (Stock Holders Digest), 1920; Osakaya (ed.), *Kabushiki nenkan* (Stock Yearbook), 1921; Toyo keizai shinpo sha (ed.), *Kabushiki gaisha nenkan* (Joint Stock Companies Yearbook), 1936.
8. Some companies had registered English names like *The Nippon Weaving*. In such cases, their English names are used and the Japanese pronunciation is quoted as [*Nippon Keori*]. In other cases, the Japanese name of the company is used, and its meaning is shown, as in *Shanghai Seizo Kenshi* (Shanghai Spinning).
9. Jinji koshinjo, *Jinji koshin roku* (Personal Directory), 1921, 1931, 1940; Tsuzoku keizai sha (ed.), *Zaikai fusu hi* (Who's who in the Business World), 1923, 1931.
10. Yui, *loc. cit.*
11. Hiroshi Matsumoto, *Mitsui Zaibatsu no kenkyu*, Tokyo, 1979, pp. 64, 239–41.
12. Yasuo Mishima (ed.), *Mitsubishi Zaibatsu*, Tokyo, 1981, pp. 94–100; Yasuzo Suzuki, *Mitsubishi Zaibatsu ni okeru shikin chotatsu to shihai* (Financing and Control in *Mitsubishi Zaibatsu*), Tokyo 1953, pp. 116–17.
13. A. Mikami, 'Sumitomo Kagaku no seiritsu to hatten', (The Rise and Development of Sumitomo Chemicals), in M. Miyamoto and Y. Sakudo (eds), *Sumitomo no keieishiteki kenkyu* (Business History of *Sumitomo*, Tokyo, 1979, pp. 346–59.
14. *Yasuda hozensha to sono kankei jigyo shi* (History of *Yasuda* Holding and its Related Enterprises), 1974, pp. 530–39, 672–85.
15. Yoichiro Kobayakawa, '*Asano Zaibatsu* no takakuka to keieisoshiki' (Strategy and Structure of *Asano Zaibatsu*), *Japan Business History Review*, vol. 16, no. 1, 1981.
16. Furukawa Mining, *Sogyo 100nen shi* (One Hundred Year History), 1976, pp. 362–3, 505.
17. Morikawa, *Zaibatsu no keieishiteki kenkyu*, pp. 147–50.
18. Seishi Nakamura, 'Taisho showa shoki no *Okura Zaibatsu*' (The *Okura Zaibatsu* in Taisho and Early Showa Japan), *Japan Business History Review*, vol. 15, no. 3, 1980.
19. Masaru Udagawa, *Shinko Zaibatsu* (The Rising New *Zaibatsu*), Tokyo, 1984, pp. 52–64.
20. Ibid., p. 120.
21. Ibid., p. 162.
22. Furukawa Mining, *op. cit.*, pp. 467–69.
23. Asajima, *op. cit.*, pp. 112–13, 151, 184–86, 242, 260–61.
24. *Kabushiki nenkan*, 1920; *Kabushiki gaisha nenkan*, 1936. Similar trends

have been pointed out regarding some of the subsidiaries of the *Zaibatsu.* (Shibagaki, *op. cit.*, p. 226).

25. Takahashi and Aoyama, *op. cit.*, pp. 116–17; Shibagaki, *op. cit.*, pp. 416–17.
26. Asajima, *op. cit.*, pp. 347–52.
27. Furukawa Mining, *op. cit.*, p. 511.
28. Udagawa, *op. cit.*, pp. 64, 68.
29. Ibid., pp. 120–21.
30. Ibid., p. 151.
31. Shibagaki, *Nihon shihonshugi no ronri* (The Logic of Japanese Capitalism), Tokyo, 1971, ch. 5.
32. M. Sakamoto, 'Manshu jihen igo no *Mitsui Zaibatsu*', *Hitotsubashi Ronso*, vol. 86, no. 1.
33. H. Patrick, 'Japanese Financial System in the Inter-war Period', in *Senkanki no nihon keizai bunseki*, ed., by T. Nakamura, Tokyo, 1981; S. Asajima, 'Senji taisei ki no *Mitsubishi Zaibatsu*', *Senshu keieigaku ronshu*, vol. 39, 1985.
34. S. Asajima, *Senkanki Sumitomo Zaibatsu keieishi* (Business History of *Sumitomo Zaibatsu* in the Inter-war Period), Tokyo, 1983.

4 Hierarchies and Federations in the Post-war Era

4.1 INTRODUCTION

This chapter presents an overview of the development of resource allocation and the coordination of economic activity among large-scale companies in post-war Japan. We will examine particularly the business groups, which have been the major form of federation for the larger part of the period. Cartels were another form of federation, but they were related to particular groups of industries such as fabricated basic materials, and, therefore, are best be dealt with in later chapters.

These business groups had been one of the major subjects of industrial economists. As the role of business groups declined, such interests of industrial economists became shrunken. With the advantage of hindsight, historians can now examine post-war business groups and compare them with the pre-war *Zaibatsu*.

The previous chapter has shown that the orthodox view of the role of the pre-war *Zaibatsu* cannot be upheld for their control over transactions and financing of large-scale companies and even their constituent firms was in fact limited. On the contrary, most large-scale industrial companies were responsible for their own strategic resource allocation and the coordination of economic functions throughout the inter-war years. Even for companies affiliated with the *Zaibatsu*, the main functions of the *Zaibatsu* head offices became nearer to those of typical holding companies whose main concern was the allocation of financial resources. Given that the pre-war *Zaibatsu* was unable to exercise extensive control over most large-scale industrial firms, we must ask how the *Zaibatsu* differed from the business groups established after the Second World War?

During the immediate post-war years, many of the largest industrial

75

concerns were joined into 'groupings', or 'Kigyo shudan'. These groupings, and their differences with the pre-war *Zaibatsu*, have been the subject of a number of studies and of contrasting interpretations.[1] We shall examine here these new groups by the largest 100 industrial companies either by sales or assets in 1970 (if we look at the largest 100 companies by sales, and the largest 100 by assets, there was a great deal of overlap, so that we have 114), and analysing their relations with the business groups. We can ask which of the two, large-scale firms or business groups, played strategic roles in resource allocation.

Among the business groups which had relationships with large-scale firms, there are two types. One was 'the Six Largest Business Groups', and the other the groupings formed around giant industrial companies.

4.2 POST-WAR BUSINESS GROUPS AND BIG BUSINESS: NEW EVIDENCE

The names of 'the Six Largest Business Groups' are well known: they are *Mitsubishi*, *Sumitomo*, *Mitsui*, *Fuyo*, *Sanwa*, and *Daiichi-Kangin* Some of them had their origins in early post-war years, while others, which were formed around the large-scale city banks, came later. However, it is difficult to confirm the exact dates of their origins, because such confirmation relates to the idea of the 'business groups'. Each of these six groups formed a meeting of the presidents of its member firms, and the admittance to attend the periodical meeting distinguishes them from the outside companies. About 180 firms attended one of these six groups in 1970, of which 113 were manufacturing companies. Among the largest 114 industrial companies in 1970, 63 firms were members of one of these six largest business groups. Ten belonged to the *Mitsui* group, 9 to *Mitsubishi*, 7 to *Sumitomo*, 11 to *Fuyo*, 13 to *Sanwa*, and 16 to *Daiichi-Kangin* group. These manufacturing firms were not always confined to just one group: *Hitachi* was a member of three groups and *Kobe Steel* a member of two. The *Mitsui*, *Mitsubishi* and *Sumitomo* groups consisted of companies which had already been large-scale industrial firms in the pre-war era. In the other three groups there were relatively few such old-established firms. The activities of members of the six groups ranged throughout industry, but were especially well represented in heavy industry. However less than half the largest firms were found in food, oil, automobiles, and household electrics. Of 38 firms in fabricated basic materials, 25 belonged to one of the groups, of 37 firms in finished producers' goods, 24 were members of the groups, while in finished consumers' goods, 14 firms out of 39 samples belonged to the groups.

Some have argued that the business groups, by promoting economic concentration, have become an 'organic entity'. Unity derives from a number of factors, from the meeting of presidents, preferential finance from the member banks, mutual shareholding, and mutual transactions within the group, that is, from ordinary means of corporate control.[2] However, we should note that these factors do not always lead to corporate control. Also, even where corporate control is effective, we should look in addition at the concentration ratios. Moreover, the purpose of such unity was not clearly explained. Finally, such arguments assume the unity of groups in advance, though they have to prove it.

Some scholars, on the contrary, have denied the existence of unified control within the groups.[3] Evidence presented by Hadley and Yoshino show looser relationships among the group members, but these authors do not explain why such groups are formed and what their roles are. Other studies regard the business groups as 'information clubs'. By forming a group of companies from various branches of industry, the costs of information necessary for the transaction of goods and financial resources are reduced below those of the market. This certainly provides a coherent hypothesis to explain business groupings,[4] but, like other interpretations, needs to be judged on the basis of concrete evidence.

Despite different views as to the nature of business groups, there is no disagreement about some of their basic characteristics. Thus preferential finance by the banks inside the group and mutual share holding among the group members is a common practice. In addition, each group has a meeting of the presidents of the member firms, which range along almost all the industry branches including banking and general trading, but has no controlling centre. When we examine in detail the 114 largest industrial companies, we should begin with such basic characteristics.

As to mutual shareholding, though relatively new in their development, *Fair Trade Commission* quoted its average ratio: 26 per cent of the issued shares of the member companies was held by other members of the same groups in 1981.[5] Each company held 1.8 per cent of the shares of other members of the same group. In 1960, the ratio ranged from 23.6 per cent for *Sumitomo* to less than 6 per cent for *Sanwa*, while in 1970 the former was 20.1 per cent while the latter had increased to 11.2 per cent.[6] These figures include all the companies that were the members of the meeting of presidents of each group, which were not necessarily among the largest manufacturing companies. If we take the 63 firms among the largest 114 manufacturing companies which belong to one of these groups, the ratio has always been lower than that quoted above. Twenty per cent of the shares of the 66 industrials of 1980 were, on the average, held by other members of the same groups including financial institutions.[7] The rates of *Mitsubishi* and *Sumitomo* were higher than this, while those of other groups showed lower than 20 per cent.

The ratio continued to increase from 1960 through to 1970, though the timing of the rapid increase differed from group to group. The increasing trend towards mutual shareholding was accelerated when *Nippon Shoken Hoyu Kumiai* (Japan Securities Holding Association) and *Nippon Kyodo Shoken* (Japan Associated Securities) sold shares in 1966 for the first time. Mutual shareholding also increased when the Japanese firms had to deal with excessive liquidity since the early 1970s. They bought shares in other members by using such internal capital. The problem is how to understand the function of such mutual shareholding. Some writers suggest that mutual or collective control may be gained through shareholding. However, this is not always the case, for mutual shareholding may lead to mutual non-intervention, or strengthen the separation of ownership and control. The fact is that there have been few cases in which such mutual shareholding directly influenced the decision making of the member companies.

Interlocking directorships within the group members are also found. In 1981, more than 70 per cent of the companies which were the members of the meeting of the presidents of the six major business groups had at least one director sent from other member companies of the same group. Two-thirds of them were sent from the banks of the same group. The average ratio of these 'outside' directors was 8.7 per cent of all the directors of these companies, nearly half of them from banks. These data were provided by the *Fair Trade Commission*.[8]

However, the data from the *Fair Trade Commission* should be assessed with care. We find that if we look at the directors sent to the largest 100 manufacturing firms from other members of the same group, the proportion actually contracted sharply in the three decades since 1950. Furthermore, there were few 'outside' directors among the senior members of directors. Few outside directors were found among the *Mitsui* and the *Daiichi-Kangin* groups, though the member firms of *Mitsubishi* and *Sumitomo* had a slightly larger number of outside directors. Yet the total number of such outside directors sent from the same groups to the largest 100 manufacturing firms was consistently about 20 throughout the two decades since 1960, or only 4 per cent of the number of directors of these firms.[9] Less than one-third of the companies which are the members of one of the six business groups had directors sent from other members. The differences shown above from the data of the *Fair Trade Commission* may be partly explained by the fact that interlocking directorships occurred less frequently among large industrial concerns. But it would certainly appear that the concentration ratios measured by the interlocking directorships were lower than have often been assumed.

Such interlocking directorships occurred in particular situations such as mergers and financial difficulties. When shares of member companies were taken by foreign companies, or when they had foreign directors, the members of the group often sent directors as if to counterbalance the constitution of the boards. Such a practice is observed even when the companies were not the joint ventures between foreign companies and the groups. This is a kind of collective defence to maintain the control by management over ownership. There are also interlocking directorships which are not accompanied by these special cases. The problem is how to understand the function of the last type of outside directors.

Preferential finance by particular banks and financial affiliations occurred at a much earlier period than mutual shareholding, the interlocking of directors, and even the formal meetings of presidents. The relative importance of external debts in the capital of the Japanese firms can be explained by the difficulties of raising equity capital against the ever increasing financial demands from manufacturing firms. Japanese firms have made use of loans and bills for raising necessary funds for their investments. The *Fair Trade Commission* found that the ratio of loans of the firms from the banks inside the six groups to their total loans was 18.1 per cent in 1981.[10]

The ratio of loans from member banks was higher in the earlier post-war period, and also higher within the *Mitsui*, *Mitsubishi*, and *Sumitomo* groups than in others. The average ratio of the largest 100 manufacturing firms (by sale or assets) within the *Mitsui* group was 28.9 per cent in 1960 and 25.6 per cent in 1980. Within the *Mitsubishi* and *Sumitomo* groups, ratios were 29.0 per cent and 28.9 per cent, and 38.5 per cent and 28.0 per cent respectively. We may notice that the external debts decreased its relative importance for raising capital during these two decades, though it was still high.[11]

There are several causes as to how and why the dependence on external debts by the major Japanese firms originated. One such cause was as early as 1945, when as an anti-depression measure money was supplied by city banks. Financial resources were originally so scarce that funds had to be supplied by the central bank and allotted equally among city banks. The city banks had to finance preferentially to particular industrial companies. Eventually, additional funds in the form of deposit came from people who could not easily have access to the equity market, and financed to industrial companies through the same channels. The cost of loan capital was approximately half of the equity capital.

We have little data concerning the volume of the transactions of goods with the groups. Though this aspect has often been emphasised, it is difficult to estimate volumes of such transactions from published data. The investigation made by the *Fair Trade Commission* indicates that in 1981 the manufacturing firms of the six major groups were dependent on the same group members for 20.4 per cent of their total sales, and on the same group members for 12.4 per cent of their total purchases.[12] These include firms outside the largest 100 manufacturing firms. The ratios were higher in the cases of the former *Zaibatsu* groups. The internal sales ratio of three former *Zaibatsu* groups amounted to 29 per cent of their total sales, while that of three other groups was 14.9 per cent. Likewise, the internal ratio of purchasing of the former *Zaibatsu* groups was 14.9 per cent, and that of the other groups 8.2 per cent. Also the manufacturing firms of these groups sold to and bought from the general trading companies of the same groups. On the average, 15.8 per cent of the total sales of the manufacturing firms of these six groups were directed to passes through the hands of the trading companies in the same groups, and 8.3 per cent of the total purchases of these firms was through the trading companies in the same groups. Here again the ratios of the transactions were significantly higher in the cases of the former *Zaibatsu* groups, and in some cases the sales ratios would amount to more than half of their total sales.

However, the reliability of the data presented by the *Fair Trade Commission* may be questioned. The transaction of goods within the group is a mutual transaction among members, and therefore, the numerators, or the total amount of sales, must always become equal to purchasing among the members. As to the denominators, their total amount of sales including those to outside members is normally, except in a very rare case, larger than that of purchasing. This means the ratio of inside purchasing must become higher than that of inside sales. The very rare case that makes the total purchasing larger than the total sales occurs only when the firms within the groups invested in expensive fixed assets all at once, and such equipment is supplied from outside their own groups. In practice it is out of the bounds of possibility. The total sales of the manufacturing firms which were the members of the six groups – two unlisted aluminium companies excepted – can be computed as 52 778 029 million yen (or £125 363 million) while their total purchase, that is the raw materials and the increase in the fixed capital, was approximately 27 487 531 million yen. The total amount of the fixed capital formation of these companies was 2 440 232 million yen, that is, less than 10 per cent of their total purchasing. Therefore, if as the *Fair Trade Commission* shows the ratio of sales inside the group was 20.4 per cent of their total sales, the ratio of purchase inside the group must become 39.2 per cent, or to continue the speculation, if the ratio of inside purchase was 12.4 per cent, that of inside sales should be 6.5 per cent.

It is impossible to estimate the sum relating to the largest 100 manufacturing firms for the past three decades. What is definite is that the ratio was higher than in the pre-war period. There is an explanation which stresses the leading position of the general trading companies within each group by mentioning the high amount of transactions between the group members and them. However, this cannot explain the high amount of direct transactions among group members. The transactions with the trading companies of the same groupings do not necessarily mean the leading positions of such trading companies.

4.3 THE SIX LARGEST BUSINESS GROUPS AND LARGE-SCALE FIRMS: INTERPRETATION OF THE EVIDENCE

The analysis in the previous sections suggests that we must re-assess explanations of formation of the meeting of the presidents, mutual shareholding, interlocking directorships, preferential finance to the group members by the banks inside the groups with the relatively high ratio of the external debts of the Japanese companies, and mutual transactions inside the groups. The critical defect of the arguments which regards a business group as a unity is two-fold. Some presuppose the unity of the group members in economic activities before they prove this unity. Others deduce the unity by the supposed means of control. However, the scale of joint activities within groups was small, and the shareholdings or interlocking directorships were also little developed.

If these relationships between the group members do not work as a means of control, it is necessary to explain why the groups were formed. Some writers argue that the groups are institutions which facilitate commodity and financial transactions among the members. In other words, mutual commodity and financial transactions are, according to these explanations, not primarily a means of control by the groups but the very purpose of the groups. Mutual shareholdings and interlocking directorships also help to facilitate mutual transactions. Financial or commodity transactions bear costs when carried out in the market. The most significant cost is information cost about the other party. Financial transactions, which are normally made between different points of time, require more information on the reliability or the ability of repayment than those of the ordinary transactions of raw materials or goods. This leads to continual transactions, or the formation of customer relationship. Mutual transactions of intermediate materials also benefit the group members. By forming a group, each company can obtain information necessary for such transactions while avoiding the outflow of its own information among its rivals. This is possible because there is one company from every industry branch in the group, each company offering information to its customers among the group members which cannot be obtained in the case of normal transactions because of fear of its rivals. However, this benefit, if there exists such a benefit at all, is received only by former *Zaibatsu* groups, such as the *Mitsubishi*, *Sumitomo*, and *Mitsui*, in which the ratios of internal transactions were high. The remaining three groups, such as the *Fuyo*, *Sanwa*, and *Daiichi-Kangin*, are not composed of one company from every branch of industry. Several companies often compete with each other in the same group. Moreover, the ratios of internal transactions are not high, their average internal purchasing ratio being 8.2 per cent. The ratios accounted for *Fuyo*, *Sanwa*, and *Daiichi-Kangin* groups in the total purchase of the Japanese manufacturing firms were 5.2, 3.7, and 5.1 per cent respectively, while those of sales were 5.8, 4.9, and

6.4 per cent. If, for instance, a company in *Daiichi-Kangin* group buys intermediate materials at random, more than 6 per cent come from the other members of the same group. The marginal advantage derived from membership was just a small percentage.

4.4 GIANT FIRMS AND THEIR AFFILIATED LARGE-SCALE INDUSTRIALS

Giant industrials such as *Toyota Motor*, *Hitachi*, and *Nippon Steel*, which were the members of the six major groupings, have formed another type of group around them. There are some firms among the largest 100 manufacturing firms which are the affiliated (subsidiary or associated) companies of these giant companies. Shareholdings and interlocking directorships from the giant parent firms to their large-scale affiliated companies are one-way rather than mutual. The relations among members of this second type of group, or at least the relations between the parents and the affiliates, may be much closer than those within the first type of business group.

The first thing is whether the largest 100 firms are the affiliated companies of other large-scale companies and cannot be regarded as independent firms that are responsible for their own resource allocation. Among the 114 largest industrial companies in 1970 (the largest 100 firms either by sales or assets), the number of firms whose more than 10 per cent of the shares were held by other firms was 22. Ten of them were true subsidiaries where majority of shares were held by other giant firms. Two were owned by *Hitachi*, one by *Matsushita*, one by *Toyota*, two by *Nissan*, and the remaining four were the subsidiaries of foreign oil firms. *Nippon Steel* had no such subsidiaries, though it had two associated firms among the largest 100 firms. The remaining 12 were associated companies where less than 50 per cent were held by other large-scale industrial companies. *Matsushita* and *Toyota* had each one large-scale associated company, but other firms such as *Toray Industries*, *Taiyo Fishery*, or *Fuji Electric* had also minority interests in large-scale firms which were sometimes larger than themselves. *Taiyo Fishery* was in its turn the associated company of *Hayashikane Sangyo*, which has never been among the largest industrial firms. Again, foreign oil companies had minority interests in Japanese oil refining or petrochemical companies. There were also five companies among the largest 100 industrial firms whose minority shares were held by quasi-holding companies –

pure holding companies are forbidden by law – or by foreign investors. *Nissei Real Estate* had a 12 per cent interest in *Dainippon Ink and Chemicals*, and *Moxley* in *Matsushita* and in *Sony*. At one extreme, there were giant parents and large-scale subsidiaries. At another extreme, there were smaller holding companies and their large-scale associated companies. And there were various intermediate forms between. Before analysing the control exercised by the parent, it would be appropriate to examine how these inter-firm relationships were formed.

There are three ways in which these 22 large firms came under the wing of other giant firms. First, there was financial, technological, or managerial assistance from the giant firms to the large-scale industrial companies which needed reconstruction or support. This type of affiliation often appeared as horizontal combinations, but occasionally emerged as the forward integration of the giant firms. *Nissan Shatai* and *Victor* were examples of the former which came under the wing of other giant firms, while *Nisshin Steel* became affiliated with the supplier of their materials. Some of the large-scale firms were subsidiaries of foreign companies, especially among oil firms. Among such oil firms, foreign parents supplied not only capital but crude oil, and sometimes took charge of the sales activities in the domestic market as well.

The second way in which giant firms became associated with other firms came about by the separation of some branches of giant firms. *Hitachi* and *Toyota Motor* separated some of their activities in the early post-war period, though *Toyota* was still a small-scale local firm when the separation took place. The product lines of these firms were very wide before the separation of some of their activities.

The third way in which subsidiaries or associated companies were formed was a joint enterprise with other large-scale firms for new fields of activities. Such joint enterprises usually remained as a single parent-subsidiary relationship, not developing into a large grouping of companies. We are none the less interested here in this form of affiliation, since our focus of interest is whether subsidiaries or associated companies found among the largest 100 firms are responsible for their own resource allocation or not. In addition to the above 22 firms, the giant industrial companies also, of course, had many smaller companies within their group.

The nature of the relations of firms inside the group is to a certain extent conditioned by the ways in which such affiliations originated. In the first way we have considered above, affiliations were formed between previously independent companies, one company buying shares in another. The major change which followed was not in the proportion of shares but in the number of directors sent from the parent company. That is, the number of directors sent from the parent company gradually decreased as the subsidiaries were reconstructed, while ownerships remained the same. Sometimes the parent reorganised the product lines of the subsidiaries by making the latter specialise in some particular product line of the former. Often, however, the subsidiaries continued to supply the same sorts of products that were manufactured by their parents. Moreover, the subsidiaries gradually acquired ability in technological or managerial development. They were able to accumulate these managerial resources in a way which could not be controlled by their parent companies.

In the second way, the proportion of shares held by the parent firms was high and did not change throughout their history. Again, the number of directors sent from the parents gradually decreased since the separation took place. These companies were set up because their product lines or activities were different from those of their parent companies, and would better be administered by separation. This separation can be explained by the scarcity of management resources of large-scale firms at a time of rapid development. If all business was included in a single enterprise, it would have been very difficult to allocate managerial resources appropriately. After separation, the subsidiaries continued to depend for the supply of materials on their parents or became engaged in processing some of their parents' products on commission. Most of the subsidiaries gradually became independent of their parents, and began to produce directly for outside markets.

Finally, in the case of joint enterprises, the post-war fast-growing companies such as oils or petrochemicals were typical examples. Such enterprises evolved partly because of the large amounts of initial or additional capital required, and partly by a need for foreign technology. Furthermore, the supply of crude oil was monopolised by the big international oil companies. New companies had either to depend on foreign companies for the supply of these resources or to maintain the least independence in face of their limited supply. There were several ways to solve this. A Japanese large-scale company set up a joint subsidiary with a foreign company. The Japanese side provided assets, while the foreign partner brought technology and capital. The Japanese company was able to avoid control by a foreign company because the ownership by the foreign partner was limited to their joint subsidiary. In this case the coordination of the flow of goods was not in the hands of the subsidiary but in its parent's. The decisions of the subsidiary was normally made jointly by the directors sent from both parents. Another type of the joint subsidiary was formed by several Japanese companies of various industries, which used the products of oil industry. In the course of time, the subsidiary became independent of the parent in the transactions of materials or products. However, the problem that which of the two, the subsidiary or the parents, was responsible for the decision making of the joint subsidiary remained. At least it can be said that the decision making of joint subsidiaries tended to be more complicated than that in the case of single ownership, such as the first, or the second types of affiliations we have considered. If none of the partners hold remarkably higher shares than others, the management of the subsidiary will resemble that of an independent firm.

4.5 SUMMARY

This chapter has dealt with the relationship between the large-scale industrial companies and their affiliated companies in post-war Japan. These large-scale firms made use of affiliated firms in the supply of raw materials and parts, processing, and distribution, in addition to utilising the market mechanism and their internal organization. However, they were often themselves members of larger groups, and sometimes were the affiliated companies of other large-scale firms. Two types of business groups which comprised these large-scale firms have been pointed out, which have played an important role in resource allocation in the post-war Japanese industries. The first type of business group was formed around the giant industrial companies, which sometimes included large-scale firms as their members. There was a parent- subsidiary relationship between the giant firms and other members, though their origins and the degree of control varied much among the different groups from each other. Large-scale subsidiaries tended to accumulate technical skills within the company and become independent of the control by their parent companies. The second type of business group was formed by the large-scale firms of varied industry branches, each of which consisted of one firm from all basic industries. Transactions in financial resources, and sometimes in goods, inside the group was characteristic.

The function of the second group can best be understood as that which reduces transaction cost by generating a flow of information inside the group. Neither of these two groups replaced individual firms in strategic decisions in resource allocation.

NOTES

1. In addition to many works written in Japanese, the following works are useful. Y. Yoshino, *Japan's Managerial System*, Cambridge, Mass., 1968; E. M. Hadley, *Antitrust in Japan*, Princeton, 1970.
2. Y. Miyazaki, *Sengo nihon no kigyo shudan* (The Business Groups of Post-war Japan), Tokyo, 1976; H. Okumura, *Shin nihon no rokudai kigyo shudan* (The Six Major Business Groups), Tokyo, 1983; Heiwa keizai keikaku kaigi, *Kigyo shudan* (Business Groups), Tokyo, 1978.
3. Yoshino, *op. cit.*; Hadley, *op. cit.*
4. H. Odagiri, 'Kigyo shudan no riron' (The Theory of Business Groups), *Quarterly Journal of Economic Theory*, vol. 26, no. 2, 1975; A. Goto, 'Kigyo shudan', *Business Review*, vol. 30, no. 3/4, 1983; *do.*, 'Business groups in a market economy', *European Economic Review*, vol. 19, no. 1, 1982; I. Nakatani, 'Kigyo shudan no keizai kino' (Economic Functions of Business Groups), *Quarterly Journal of Modern Economics*, Summer, 1984.
5. Fair Trade Commission, *Dokusen kinshiho kaisei*, (The Amendment of the Anti-trust Law), 1979, pp. 179–202; *do.*, *Keizai no henka to dokusen kinshi seisaku* (Economic Change and the Anti-trust Policy), 1984, pp. 155–81.
6. Miyazaki, *op. cit.*, pp. 29–30.
7. Figures are author's.
8. Fair Trade Commission, *Keizai no henka*, *loc. cit.*
9. Figures are author's. These were examined by the information in the *Stock Exchange Year Book* and *Keiretsu no kenkyu* (Researches on Affiliation). All the directors that were appointed to the members of the boards within four years after leaving the previous companies are counted.
10. Fair Trade Commission, *Keizai no henka*, *loc. cit.*
11. Figures are author's.
12. Fair Trade Commission, *Keizai no henka*, *loc. cit.*

5 The Development of Large-Scale Manufacturing Firms, 1950–80

5.1 LARGE-SCALE FIRMS AND THEIR PRODUCTS

In the previous chapters we have found that most large-scale Japanese firms made decisions regarding the allocation of resources in the inter-war period. These firms formed managerial hierarchies and became independent of holding companies. For most companies the internalisation of labour and of labour's technical skills was important, and these factors were reflected in their managerial hierarchies. This chapter presents an overview of the development of large-scale firms and their management structures in the post-war period.

The direction of development of post-war large-scale firms has been determined by the nature of goods which they produced, or of the markets to which these goods were supplied. Here, the most important factor is whether products were semi-finished or final goods, and whether they were consumer or producer goods. Furthermore, whether goods supplied were traditional or new, and subsequently whether their markets were traditional or new were also important factors. Finally, whether products were diversified or not also determined the types of management structures that developed.

Table 5.1 shows the industrial breakdown of the largest 100 industrials either by sales or assets at various points between 1920 and 1980.[1] Post-war large-scale firms can be classified into the following three groups.

Companies which had already been established in the pre-war era can be divided into two groups. The first consisting of companies which continued to supply in the post-war period the same products

TABLE 5.1 Industry distribution of the largest 100 manufacturing firms

	1920			1935			1950			1965			1980		
	S	A	T	S	A	T	S	A	T	S	A	T	S	A	T
Food	15	15	19	14	13	15	12	8	12	15	8	15	8	4	8
Textiles	31	28	37	32	30	38	23	22	24	12	11	13	3	6	6
Paper	5	5	5	2	3	3	8	6	8	6	4	6	5	7	7
Chemicals	7	9	11	14	17	18	13	13	14	11	17	18	16	14	18
Ceramics and rubber	4	3	4	3	5	5	5	6	6	3	6	6	2	5	5
Oil	2	2	2	2	1	2	5	6	6	10	8	10	18	16	18
Steel	6	8	9	8	7	8	11	9	11	9	10	10	6	7	7
Nonferrous metals	9	9	11	10	8	10	7	10	10	7	9	9	8	8	9
Electricals	4	5	6	6	5	6	4	5	6	10	10	11	14	13	14
Engineering	9	9	11	6	8	9	9	12	12	6	8	8	6	11	11
Automobiles	0	0	0	1	0	1	3	3	3	9	9	9	12	8	12
Others	1	3	3	3	2	3	0	0	0	2	0	2	2	1	3
Total	93	96	118	100	100	118	100	100	112	100	100	117	100	100	118

Note: S = Sales, A = Assets, T = Total.

that they did in the pre-war period. These were companies in industries which produced fabricated basic materials (semi-finished products), such as textiles, paper, glass and ceramics, steel, and nonferrous metals. In 1965 and 1980 almost all large-scale firms in these industries are also found among pre-war large-scale companies. Thus they are traditionally established companies in traditionally established industries. In some industrial branches such as food, however, pre-war firms which mainly supplied semi-finished products like sugar or flour disappeared. In textiles and nonferrous metals, most of the traditionally established firms reduced in size. The number of the first group of large-scale firms continued to decrease throughout the post-war era.

The second group of companies, most of which are also found among the pre-war large-scale firms, began to supply new kinds of products after the war. Many of them manufactured producer final goods, such as ships and electrical equipment. Chemical and a few textile companies also fall into this group. This second group of companies gradually increased their numbers among the largest 100 firms, and changed their product lines after 1950.

The third group of companies are new companies, and manufactured completely new products that were unknown in the pre-war period. These firms were found among consumer final goods industries such as household electrical equipment, automobiles, gasoline, cosmetics, watches, cameras, musical instruments, and processed food and drinks. Most of them appeared in the post-war era, and developed rapidly.

Although some companies can be simultaneously classified into two of these groups, 86 companies of the largest 118 firms in 1935 mainly manufactured semi-finished products, and only 14 produced consumer final goods. By 1965 the number of firms which produced semi-finished products decreased to 52, while those of consumer final goods increased to 45. Forty-seven firms of the largest 118 firms in 1980 primarily produced consumer final goods. Companies which supplied producer final goods such as industrial machinery, electrical equipment, and transportation machinery also grew in number. Thus, in contrast with pre-war large-scale firms, which mostly manufactured semi-finished products, post-war large-scale companies included those which supplied final goods either for producer or consumer use. Although there were entries into and exits from every group, there were considerably more exits than entries in the first group, more entries than exits in the second group, and far more entries than exits in the third group. The circumstances which these groups of companies faced differed a great deal from each other, but their strategies also determined their success or failure throughout the post-war three decades.

5.2 ENTRY AND EXIT

Table 5.2 presents the number of entries and exits of the largest 100 manufacturing firms either by sales or by assets in the post-war period, and classifies them into three product groups. All the groups have entries and exits. Until 1970, however, the number of firms decreased in the first group (fabricated basic materials), and increased in the second group (producer final goods). There were more exits than entries in the first group. In the second group, there were many exits, both in the 1950s and the 1960s, but there were more entries than exits, especially in the 1960s. In the third group (consumer final goods), there were more entries than exits.

In the 1950s exits were observed among the textiles, paper manufacturing, chemical, and food companies. Firms in chemical and food industries used to supply traditional semi-finished products such as fertilisers, and oils and fats, and were not concerned with consumer final goods. There were remarkable entries in the 1950s by food and

TABLE 5.2 Entries and exits* of the largest manufacturing firms

			1950/60	*1960/70*	*1970/80*
Product group	I	Entries	10	8	10
		Exits	16	15	11
	II	Entries	5	13	9
		Exits	7	6	4
	III	Entries	13	9	4
		Exits	5	3	5

* The total number of exits is not equal to that of entries since, firstly the number of the largest 100 companies (either by sales or assets) in 1950, 1960, 1970 and 1980 differs from each other, and secondly there were decreases due to amalgamations between large-scale companies.

automobile companies. In the 1960s, exits were observed among textile, cement, iron and steel, and chemical companies, with entries in electrical equipment, engineering, and automobiles. In addition there were some entries by companies which were newly established in the 1950s. These new companies were formed by separation of other large firms but grew large in the 1960s.

After 1970, a new trend appeared. Entries were observed among the first product groups, while exits were in the third group. Most of the new large-scale firms in the early 1970s were oil-refining companies. Until the early 1970s the oil companies were classified into the third group which supplied consumer goods, because more than half of their sales were made up by gasoline and paraffin oil. Companies which became large in the 1970s were refineries which were formed to supply materials for 'Industrial Complexes' (*kombinato* refineries). Withdrawals from the third product groups are noticeable in the food companies. Mass production goods for mass markets became less important and gave way to differentiated products. Large firms do not always have an advantage over smaller ones under such conditions. Another characteristic of the 1970s is that more than half of the new entries were companies whose shares were unlisted. Many of them were subsidiaries of other companies.

Looking at the largest 114 manufacturing firms (the largest 100 firms either by sales or assets) in 1970, 71 of them or their direct predecessors were listed among the largest 112 firms (the largest 100 firms either by sales or assets) in 1950. Eighty-six appeared amongst the largest 110 firms in 1960. Ninety-three of the largest 114 firms in 1970 still appeared among the largest 118 in 1980. There are some technical problems in the identification of some companies, because mergers and acquisitions took place during these three decades. Some companies amalgamated with others on an equal basis, and some in turn were acquired by others. To solve this difficulty, as a rule all direct forerunners are counted if the mergers took place on an equal basis.

5.3 THEIR POSITIONS AND SIZES

Various figures indicate the share of large-scale companies in the allocation of resources. The share of the largest 100 manufacturing firms in total manufacturing assets continuously declined. 56.9 per cent of the total gross assets were held by the largest 100 firms in 1950. This figure fell to 41.6 per cent in 1960, 37.6 per cent in 1970, and 33.8 per cent in 1980. Figures for tangible assets are incomplete, but declined from 40.2 per cent in 1960 to 34.2 per cent in 1970. Consolidated accounts are available only for the year 1980. The largest 100 manufacturing firms in 1980 had 2984 subsidiaries of whose equity capital more than 50 per cent was owned by these 100 firms. In total, assets amounting to 82 billion yen or 44.1 per cent of the total manufacturing assets were owned by the largest 100 firms in 1980.

The share of the largest 100 firms (unconsolidated) in the total manufacturing output changed as follows: 39 per cent in 1950, 31 per cent in 1960, again 31 per cent in 1970, and 34 per cent in 1980.[2] There has been no remarkable increase or decrease since the mid-1950s. In comparison this is quite the opposite to, or at least completely different from trends in other industrialised countries such as Britain or West Germany. In Britain the share of the largest 100 firms in manufacturing output rose from 22 per cent in 1949 to 32 per cent in 1958, and 41 per cent in 1970, while in West Germany it moved from 33.6 per cent in 1954 to 40.1 per cent in 1960 and 45.6 per cent in 1966.

The share of the largest 100 firms (by value-added) was around 22 per cent throughout the 1970s, although precise figures are not available for the period before 1970.

For the largest 100 firms by sales, a comparison with large-scale firms of other countries is possible, The size of firms in Japan ranged from £83 million (or DM 697 million) to £1503 million (or DM 12 625 million). As the range went from £64 million to £2352 million in

TABLE 5.3 The largest 100 firms by industry (sales)

	Japan	*Britain*	*Germany*
Automobiles and parts	11	4	7
Rubber	1	1	3
Oil	8	4	6
Iron and steel	9	1	11
Metals and minerals	7	5	5
Heavy engineering and aircraft	7	11	9
Light engineering	2	5	2
Building products and glass	2	5	1
Paper and printing	6	8	5
Chemicals	8	7	12
Electricals and electronics	13	8	10
Textiles	8	6	2
Food, drink, and tobacco	10	29	8
No dominant industry	8	6	19

Britain and from DM 550 million to DM 15 800 million in West Germany, the largest 100 Japanese firms were slightly larger in the bottom group and smaller in the top. Few super-giant firms have existed in the Japanese market until the end of the 1970s.

The composition of large-scale firms by industrial branches is shown in Table 5.3.[3] Several industries require comment. The number of Japanese firms was larger than that of Britain in the areas of automobiles, oil, and steel, and smaller in food and drink. The composition of Japanese firms was very similar to that of West Germany. In automobiles, the sales of five Japanese companies were relatively small – below £150 million – and the total sales of 11 Japanese companies amounted to £3930 million (or DM 33 012 million). The sales of four British automobile companies amounted to £1830 million, and that of seven German companies amounted to DM 39 970 milion. In oil, total sales of eight Japanese companies was £1932 million, which was even less than the sales of *British Petroleum*, the British second largest oil company, but was similar to the total sales of the German firms. In steel, nationalisation has turned more than ten large companies into a single state-owned enterprise in Britain, while Japan, like West Germany, had a strong steel industry by 1970. The large-scale food and drink companies were not of substantial importance in the Japanese and German markets.

5.4 DIRECTION OF DEVELOPMENT (I): MERGERS AND HORIZONTAL COMBINATIONS

Horizontal combinations were used by those firms which manufactured semi-finished products. Table 5.4 shows the number of mergers and separations in which the post-war largest 100 firms were involved. The largest 100 firms either by sales or assets in 1960, 1970 and 1980 are taken, and the number of the firms acquired or separated by these companies during each previous decade are counted. This table includes all the mergers regardless of their sizes. Of course mergers or separations did not necessarily take place among the firms in the same industrial branches. Even if all of them are counted, post-war Japanese firms did not depend so much on mergers for their development as did their European or pre-war Japanese counterparts. Instead the number of the separations of companies was as many as that of the mergers in the development of the post-war Japanese large-scale firms.

Although there is a well-known period in the post-war Japanese industrial history referred to as the 'Age of Large-scale Mergers', mergers were not an important source of development in the history of large-scale firms. The number of firms among the largest 100 firms which existed as a result of mergers was only one in the 1950s and four in the 1960s. No large-scale mergers are found in the 1970s. In other cases mergers took place between the members of the largest 100 firms and companies outside the largest 100 firms. Three of the mergers were carried out on equal terms, while two others were acquisitions. There was another case in which a company outside the largest 100 firms took over a company among the largest 100 concerns.

Until 1970, large-scale mergers were observed in industries such as

TABLE 5.4 Mergers and divestments of the largest manufacturing firms

	Samples 1950–60			Samples 1960–70			Samples 1970–80		
	(1960)	M	S	(1970)	M	S	(1980)	M	S
Semi-finished products	51	18	13	36	40	20	40	20	48
Producer final-goods	25	16	18	37	20	22	36	16	29
Consumer final-goods	34	7	18	39	4	9	40	7	5

Note: *M* = mergers, *S* = separations.

textiles, paper, iron and steel, cement, and engineering and ship-buildings. Mergers among engineering and shipbuilding firms took place between firms whose products differed slightly from each other, while mergers of companies in consumer final goods took place between their sales subsidiaries. The number of mergers was not large in consumer final goods companies. Therefore, horizontal combinations were observed only among companies which supplied semi-finished products. And among the post-war mergers, horizontal combination were most popular. In general mergers did not contribute much to diversification or vertical integration throughout the three decades since 1950.

Most of the firms which manufactured semi-finished products experienced mergers, and this strategy was limited to firms in this group. However, these mergers took place in different phases of their development. In textiles and steel, mergers were used to eliminate redundant investment among firms in the same industrial branches. In others, like paper or steel in their early phase, mergers were used to acquire particular kinds of technical skills. In cement, one company used mergers to expand its market share. Some of the industrial branches in basic materials had finished their development by the time of mergers, while others were still developing rapidly in the 1960s. However, in all of these cases the number of firms which made mergers their major source of development is not large. Mergers were used for defensive purposes in the first group of firms. Only those which took part in large-scale mergers have maintained their positions as the largest firms, and those which did not, withdrew from the largest 100 firms.

5.5 DIRECTION OF DEVELOPMENT (II): VERTICAL INTEGRATION

Forward integration intended to coordinate the flow of goods inside the firm was promoted by post-war Japanese large-scale firms. Such vertical integration was the major source of development for firms in the third product group (consumer final goods).

It is not easy to estimate the degree of integration in each of the largest 100 firms. However, it is possible to show the integration of wholesale or other distribution channels in manufacturing firms. In 1960 of total manufacturing output, 6.2 per cent was sold by the trading offices of manufacturing firms. Manufacturing firms integrated forward, and used their operating units for wholesale activities. In other cases, they more or less depended on intermediate merchants. The ratios of wholesales by manufacturing firms rose to 10.4 per cent in 1970, and 14.4 per cent in 1980.[4] These figures indicate a gradual move towards forward integration by manufacturing firms. This trend is particularly remarkable in such products as cosmetics, chemicals, machinery, and metals. The figures may be higher in the largest 100 firms than in other firms. However, the classification of these statistics differs from that of our product groups, and it is not clear in which product groups the ratio was higher than others.

However, forward integration of manufacturing firms should actually be higher than the ratios estimated above. These figures were quoted from the *Commercial Statistics* (*Shogyo tokei*) which investigated the operating units being engaged in sales activities. The trading offices of manufacturing firms were included in this statistics. However, as the head offices of these (whose trading departments were often engaged in sales activities) were excluded from the commercial statistics, and included instead with the industrial statistics. The extent of integration of wholesale activities by manufacturing firms should be higher than the above figures if the wholesale activities by trading departments of the head offices is counted.

More spectacular than the forward integration through internalisation of sales functions was the affiliation of the distributors with manufacturing firms. By doing so manufacturing firms were able to reduce transaction costs and get high-quality information without a serious investment of financial or human resources. Two types of affiliating distributors were found: one at wholesale stage, and the other at the retail stage.

The Basic Survey of Commercial Activity and Structure (*Shogyo jittai kihon chosa*) of 1967 and 1979 investigated the number of wholesale units of various sizes affiliated with manufacturing firms. By combining the data in the *Commercial Statistics*, it is possible to estimate the amount of sales that passed through outlets affiliated with the manufacturing firms. In many cases manufacturing firms affiliated wholesale companies, but the direction was often the other way round. Nineteen per cent of the total output of manufacturing firms passed through their affiliated wholesale merchants in 1967. The ratio was 20 per cent in 1979, while 7 per cent of the output was produced by wholesalers' affiliated manufacturers. Affiliation includes various sorts of leadership and control on the part of manufacturing firms through shareholding, interlocking directorships, and technical and financial supports. The statistical data show a high ratio of affiliation in automobiles, oils, and cosmetics. In these industrial branches, not only wholesale merchants but retailers were often affiliated by manufacturers. In this system, manufacturers did not have to invest fully in distribution organisation, and were able to enjoy a higher quality of information than could be obtained from the market.

In total, more than 30 to 40 per cent of all manufacturing products passed through distribution channels which were either integrated to or affiliated with manufacturing firms. This means nearly half of all transactions were carried out outside of the classical market mechanisms. If products supplied to the domestic market are counted, this ratio would be even higher than these figures.

The importance of backward integration, by contrast, reduced throughout the post-war era. Backward integration was once a very important strategy for the pre-war firms, particularly in semi-finished products. Large-scale firms in silk, paper, chemical, cement, and steel and nonferrous metal industries had material branches of their own or in their subsidiaries. Cotton spinning, and woollen and worsted companies purchased their raw materials from all over the world, making full use of merchants. In textiles, however, the competitive advantages derived from low cost purchasing were reduced by the appearance of new kind of materials such as chemical or synthetic fibres. In other branches, it became utterly impossible to supply raw materials from domestic sources in either sufficient quantity or reasonable cost. Although overseas investment aimed at the development and import of raw materials is occasionally observed, companies tended simply to buy the cheapest available materials from all over the world.

Backward integration by companies in final goods ceased to be significant, as they became able to purchase parts from outside suppliers. Shipbuilding, electrical equipment, and later, automobile companies became less dependent on internal supplies of parts than they had been previously. However, these parts were not automatically supplied by the outside market; the suppliers were raised and supported technologically by large-scale companies in final goods, and the products of these suppliers were often purchased exclusively by a particular large-scale firm.

Thus, forward integration was most characteristically observed among large-scale companies in consumer final goods, while the separation of upward branches proceeded in firms in semi-finished products. Companies in semi-finished products intensified their interests in downward processes, while those in producer final goods no longer supplied some of their parts or components internally. Textile companies began to organise textile processing, and iron and steel companies secondary and tertiary processing. In electrical and heavy engineering, the development of specialised component suppliers, no longer the subcontractors of large firms, began to appear during the same period.

5.6 DIRECTION OF DEVELOPMENT (III): DIVERSIFICATION

The diversification of Japanese large-scale firms is shown in Figure 5.1, in which the largest 100 firms in 1970 either by sales or assets – and their direct forerunners – are classified according to a well-known definition.[5] Their product lines are grouped by the three-digit Industry Classification. Diversification is most remarkable among the firms in the second group, but completely negligible in the third group.

Single product   Firms whose growth is at least 95 per cent dependent on the expansion of one main product lines (according to three-digit Industry Classification).
Dominant product   Firms which diversify into other product lines to the extent of up to 30 per cent of total sales.
Fully diversified   Firms which diversify to more than 30 per cent of total sales. If diversification occurs by entrance into related markets, either by using a related technology, or by combining the processes which have vertical relationships, it can be called 'Related diversification'. If the firm diversifies into other businesses with which it has no market, technological or vertical relationship, it will be referred to as 'Unrelated diversification' or 'No-dominant industries'.

There may be other ways of measuring diversification, such as grouping products by the four-digit Industry Classification, or by the two- or three-digit Standard Commodity Classification. If the four-digit Industry Classification is applied, many firms become fully diversified from the beginning. If the Commodity Classification is used, the outcome becomes somewhat different from Figure 5.1. In

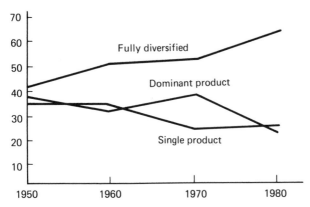

F<small>IGURE</small> 5.1 Diversification of Japanese manufacturing firms

some industry branches, particularly in semi-finished products such as textiles, steel, and nonferrous metals, firms become less diversified if the two-digit Commodity Classification is applied.

Figure 5.1 indicates a gradual move towards diversification of large-scale firms in Japan. The number of single product firms decreased continuously during these three decades. However, companies which fully diversified increased rapidly in the early phase, and remained unchanged throughout the 1960s and the 1970s. When compared with the European firms, Japanese large-scale firms diversified early in the post-war era, but did not depend so much on diversification later. When the four-digit Industry Classification or the three-digit Commodity Classification is used, diversification of Japanese firms in the early phase is more remarkable. Japanese firms diversified within a narrow range from the beginning. This is related to the strategy of large-scale companies in a narrow and small domestic market. As their markets expanded, they did not have to depend on diversification for their growth.

Table 5.5 shows the difference in diversification by product groups. Company diversifies in order to make full use of its managerial resources, by applying related technology, making use of the common market, by providing semi-products or processed goods, or by investing surplus financial resources in other fields. Companies that diversified in the post-war period were remarkable in the second group, like those in heavy engineering, electrical engineering and chemicals. They were 'technological diversifiers', and their diversification is extremely high compared with other product groups.

TABLE 5.5 Diversification by product groups

	Number of Firms	1950			1960			1970			1980		
		S	D	F	S	D	F	S	D	F	S	D	F
Group I	38	9	13	17	10	12	18	2	19	17	3	14	21
II	37	1	17	19	3	9	26	2	6	29	2	5	30
III	39	24	8	4	21	11	7	20	12	7	20	10	9
Total	114	34	38	40	34	32	51	24	37	53	25	29	60

Note: S = single product, D = dominant product, F = fully diversified.

Companies in semi-finished products have not diversified remarkably. Most of them increased sales of semi-products such as pulp in paper manufacturing companies, or secondary products in steel or nonferrous metals companies. This was diversification derived from process integration. In addition, companies in semi-finished products sought new products because their traditional markets had reached maturity. Neither of these measures was strong enough to change the make-up of their product lines, or their degree of diversification. Companies in consumer final goods have not diversified at all. The product lines of Japanese firms in this group have been very narrow, though there have been some variations from industry to industry. Japanese oil companies have always been completely single product firms, automobile and beverage companies gradually promoted product differentiation, and home electrical companies diversified within a limited range. Some made use of the related market of their main products, but they lacked technical skills which could be applied to other fields of activity. Furthermore, their development was too rapid to accumulate surplus managerial resources within the firm for application to diversification.

5.7 STRATEGY AND STRUCTURE OF JAPANESE FIRMS

The three types of strategy observed in large-scale firms were composed by their organisational structures. Companies which mainly produced fabricated basic materials faced problems in the coordination of the flow of materials and goods inside the company. These firms are found among the pre-war large-scale companies, but were quickly reduced in number among the post-war large-scale firms. The functional/ line, or sometimes, the functionally departmentalised structure developed in these firms. By contrast, companies which supplied producer final goods developed in the post-war era, and this development was realised through product diversification. Some of them used crude forms of decentralised structures as their organisational system. The third group of companies, which appeared in the post-war period, developed through forward integration by building up their own market organisation. From the beginning they were forced to form their own management structures in order to promote their activities.

Table 5.6 shows the organisational structures of the largest 100 firms in 1970 (either by sales or assets) in 1950, 1960, 1970 and 1980. Like American or European large-scale firms, the most remarkable organisational change in the post-war Japanese firms was found in the widespread adoption of the multidivisional structure. Twenty-nine of the largest 100 firms in 1970 (or their direct forerunners) had adopted this form by 1960, and 55 had by 1970. There are various intermediate forms between the multidivisional structure and other structures, and it is often difficult to classify existing firms into one of them. Many firms partially introduced the divisional system, though their main activities were operated through the functional structure. These firms are classified into (F/D). Companies whose management tasks at the level immediately below top management are specialised by functions such as sales and manufacturing are classified into (F). In addition, companies termed functional/line form are also classified into (F). In the multidivisional structure, management tasks are specialised at the level immediately below top management by product-market or geographical criteria, and each division which at least has manufacturing and sales functions is made a profit-centre. However, in classifying existing firms in the multidivisional structure, all of these requirements are not necessary.

TABLE 5.6 Management structures of the largest 100 manufacturing firms

	Number of Firms	1950 F	F/D	M	O	1960 F	F/D	M	O	1970 F	F/D	M	O	1980 F	F/D	M	O
Group I	38	34	0	2	3	28	3	8	1	13	10	15	0	8	12	18	0
II	37	26	0	6	5	19	3	16	1	5	1	30	1	3	2	31	1
III	39	29	0	1	6	28	4	5	2	22	5	10	2	24	5	8	2
Total	114	89	0	9	14	75	9	29	4	40	16	55	3	35	19	57	3

Note: F = functional structure, M = multidivisional structure, F/D = partly divisionalised, O = other decentralised forms like holding companies and production-unit structures.

There were many transitions from the functional structure to the multidivisional structure. There were some cases in which the 'production-unit structure' – a pre-war decentralised form – changed into a modern multidivisional structure. However, there were few examples of holding companies which were reorganised into the multidivisional structure. There are few holding companies or few multi-firm mergers in post-war Japan. Japanese large-scale firms had many subsidiaries but few of them have been reorganised into the divisions of their parents, nor have the parents been reorganised into holding companies. These changes first took place in the late 1950s and ended by 1970. Like in European firms, American practices had an influence on the introduction of the multidivisional structure in Japanese firms. One point of divergence from European firms, however, was that many of the European firms employed American management consultants individually in planning organisational reforms,[6] while the Japanese firms did not. Therefore, the divisionalisation of Japanese firms was incomplete, and left some historical legacies. Some Japanese firms even introduced the multidivisional structure independently of the practices in America.

The divisionalisation of the Japanese companies was prominent in the group of firms which supplied producer final goods. These firms diversified into related products by utilising of core technology. As they were the most diversified firms, managerial tasks became more complicated than in firms of other groups. The multidivisional structure was more efficient than traditional decentralised structures such as the 'production-unit structure' if the reorganisation of product lines among factories was desired.

By contrast companies which supplied consumer final goods were based on the functional structure. Firms in beverages, oils, and automobiles either applied the functional structure, or employed sales subsidiaries by specialising themselves into manufacturing activities. The multidivisional structure spread among household electrical companies. The multidivisional structure by geography was found among dairy and sea food companies. However, these divisional structures in consumer final goods were unstable, and many of them returned to the functional structure.

Companies in fabricated basic materials were located at the midway point between the second and the third groups. These firms attempted to diversify into new products through integration of upward and downward processes. They developed into downward stages by strengthening processing branches as soon as the rapid growth was over. However, differences in technology and markets between the new and the old branches placed a barrier in the way of their diversification, and this became the background of their incomplete divisionalisation.

5.8 SUMMARY

This chapter examined the role of large-scale firms in resource allocation in post-war Japan. The position of these large-scale firms in the Japanese economy did not change much throughout the three decades after 1950, though there were frequent entries and withdrawals in the constituent companies. The way of resource allocation and the coordination of the flow of goods by large-scale firms changed rapidly. These changes were deeply related to the direction of development of the firms, of which three noticeable types were observed.

The first group of companies were traditionally established firms in semi-finished products, such as textiles, paper, cement and ceramics, steel, and nonferrous metals. The number of firms in this group among the largest firms was quickly reduced. However, it was this group of companies that first adopted mass production methods in the early post-war era, which caused deficiencies in the traditional system of supplying raw materials. Although they sought raw materials at home and abroad, and further integrated forward into processing, both integration and diversification were restricted. Eventually horizontal combination by merger became the major source of development for these firms. Organisational development in response to such strategic changes is found in the partial adoption of the divisional system, while main product lines were operated through the functional structure.

The second group of companies was also traditionally established firms, but they diversified after the war and swiftly changed their product lines. They were found in industries which supplied producer final goods, such as heavy engineering and shipbuilding, and electrical engineering. In addition, chemical firms were included in this group. Most of them diversified by making use of their core technical skills, equipment, and human resources. They adopted the multidivisional structure in order to coordinate their diversified activities.

The third group of firms are found among industries such as foods, oils, automobiles, household electricals, and other consumer goods. The emergence of large-scale firms in these industries is the product of the post-war era in Japan. These firms expanded rapidly together with the development of the mass market. They did not diversify but grew along with their main product lines, and developed distribution channels. These large-scale firms made use of affiliated firms in purchasing, processing, and distribution, in addition to utilising the market mechanism and their internal organisation. They either integrated wholesale activities or affiliated local wholesalers and sometimes retailers as well. These activities were coordinated through the functional structure.

NOTES

1. Nomura Shoten, *Kabushiki nenkan*, 1921; Toyo Keizai Shinposha, *Kabushiki kaisha nenkan*, 1936; Nihon Keizai Shinbunsha, *Kaisha nenkan*, 1952, 1967, 1982. For unlisted companies various sources were used.
2. Figures are author's. *Gendai nihon no sangyo shuchu* (Industrial Concentration in Japan) quotes a different figure for the year 1980: the share of the largest 100 manufacturing firms in the total *sales* was 27.3 per cent. As the samples were almost the same, the major difference came from the gap between the *shipment* and the *sales*.
3. D. F. Channon, *The Strategy and Structure of British Enterprise*, London, 1973, pp. 52–63; G. P. Dyas and H. T. Thanheiser, *The Emerging European Enterprise*, London, 1976, pp. 141–51.
4. *Commercial Statistics for the Years 1960, 1970, and 1980.*
5. Channon, *op. cit.*, pp. 12–13.
6. Ibid., pp. 239, 242.

6 The Traditionally Established Companies in Fabricated Basic Materials

6.1 INTRODUCTION

The first group of companies consists of traditionally established firms which supplied fabricated basic materials in the pre-war era and continued to supply the same sort of products in the post-war period. The industrial branches of these firms ranged over textiles, paper and pulp, iron and steel, non-ferrous metals and metal fabricating, and ceramics and other materials. Companies in these industry groups are widely found among the largest pre-war firms, but have gradually declined after the war.

It is not appropriate to look upon the strategy of the firms in these semi-finished products as protective under the changing circumstances. Textiles, paper manufacturing, steel, cement, and non-ferrous metals companies recovered quickly from the war damages and technological delays during the war, and had reconstructed themselves by 1950. There were few changes in the ranks of the largest firms between 1935 and of 1950. They began by reorganising their workshops by the mass production method and foreign technologies in the early 1950s. The size of the plants and the scale of their equipment expanded enormously; in steel, huge plants of previously unimagined size appeared. The quality of products, particularly in chemical fibres, paper manufacturing, and non-ferrous metals also improved significantly. They took the lead over other industries in various innovations. Major changes in the production process are the characteristic of this group of firms.

Firms in semi-finished materials were also pioneers among Japanese firms in international activities. Paper manufacturing and non-ferrous metals firms attempted to secure their supplies of raw materials by investing overseas, and applied their skills to searching for and handling them. Other firms such as those in textiles also went abroad in the early post-war era, labour intensive processes gradually being transferred to Asian countries. Thus it was that the companies in fabricated basic materials became the pioneers in overseas production and investment.

They have shown similarities in their strategies and structures. The competitive power of these firms lay in their cheap and stable supplies of raw materials which constituted a great part of production costs. For the pre-war large-scale firms, there were two ways of attaining this. One solution was to make full use of the market mechanism, adopted by the cotton spinning companies. The vertical integration of raw materials and manufacturing, prominent in paper manufacturing, non-ferrous metals, cement, and, particularly sugar manufacturing companies was the other. After the war, however, both methods began to change. For the cotton spinning firms cheap supplies of raw cotton no longer meant competitive power in the face of cheaper cotton substitutes such as chemical or synthetic fibres. Companies in other industrial branches attempted to continue vertical integration, but the growth of their productive capacity easily exceeded the domestic supply of raw materials. Again two basic patterns of adjustment appeared. One was to import the cheapest raw materials from all over the world, as was done by iron and steel companies. The other was to invest in oversea mines and forests, as observed in non-ferrous metals and paper manufacturing firms, and later, in iron and steel companies. These were the first and basic differences from their pre-war strategies.

Secondly, post-war companies integrated downward to processing or upward to producing intermediate materials. Textile and paper manufacturing companies intensified their interests in processing which had previously been the territory of traditional wholesale merchants, and then advanced into the supply of materials such as solvent naphtha for synthetic fibres or pulp for paper manufacturing. Similarly, steel companies entered into iron smelting, and non-ferrous metal companies tried to secure supplies of ores both at home and overseas. Eventually these firms reorganised secondary processing firms into their subsidiaries, or made inroads into metal processing by themselves. Cement, glass and rubber companies followed a similar line of development. There are reasons for this commonality. Firstly, trading or wholesale companies which had originally used to organise small-scale manufacturers had withdrawn from the secondary processing branches. Secondly, it became necessary for the firms in these industries to shift their activities from low value-added to high value-added products. Thirdly, they had to coordinate the flow of goods in accordance with the rapid increase in their manufacturing products.

Companies in semi-finished products such as the above, were neither fully diversified like firms in producer final goods (Group II), nor were they single product firms like those in consumer final goods (Group III). If the four-digit Industry Classification is applied, some of them still remain in the 'dominant product' category, and even if the two-digit classification is applied, the result does not change much. On the other hand, if they are classified by the Standard Commodity Classification, they become less diversified. This is exactly because their diversification resulted from vertical integration, namely, diversification through semi- or processed products in addition to their main product lines.

In mergers and cartels, those companies in semi-finished products stood out clearly from those in the other two industrial groups. Companies in semi-finished goods merged in order to reinforce their weak branches or to expand their scales. However, most of the mergers were essentially horizontal, and defensive; they narrowly maintained their positions as the largest firms through mergers. Otherwise many of them would have fallen from 'largest-firms status', in the post-war period. Apart from illegal cartels which are forbidden by the Anti-monopoly Law, counter-recession cartels are often observed in these industries.

Firms in these industries had to solve various problems arising in their management structures from mergers, while at the same time, they had to coordinate the flow of raw materials efficiently.

Traditionally, most of the companies in this group operated through a 'functional/line' structure. Their production units were directly controlled by the highest managers, while other activities were managed through the functional departments of the head office. Except for cement and cotton textiles, which had a large number of factories, the number of their plants was often small but the size of those themselves was large. Each production unit stood high in the companies' organisation, leading to a functional/line structure. These companies gradually introduced a divisional system into a part of their activities, and these new divisions were often put in charge of their downward processes.

Another common characteristic of the management structures of these firms is found in the frequent changes in their basic structures during the three decades since 1950. Many companies which had once introduced the multidivisional structure returned to the previous functional forms. These changes were particularly notable in textiles and steel. They introduced the divisional system not as a result of diversification but as a prerequisite to it. However diversification was not so effective as they had intended. In the following sections, their diversification through forward or backward integration is examined, and the organisational problems along with their solutions will be made clear.

6.2 TEXTILE COMPANIES

Japan had been the world's largest textile producer in the pre-war era both of cotton and chemical fibres, and textile firms had always accounted for more than one-third of the 100 largest companies, and among them were included the giant firms. Even in 1970 eight textile companies are still found to be amongst the 100 largest firms. Some were the descendants of the giant cotton spinning companies of the pre-war period, but others were synthetic fibre companies derived from pre-war chemical fibre firms. However, there were no giant textiles firms in post-war Japan of the likes of *Courtaulds*, whose sales (£627 million in 1970) amounted to more than the total sales of the five largest textile firms in Britain. The sales of the Japanese firms amounted to £250 million in 1970. Recovery and the boom of the early post-war period were eventually followed by a long 'structural' slump in the early 1960s, which brought restraints on production capacity.

Cotton spinning firms had already extended their activities into chemical fibres, and integrated downward into textile processing. Thus by 1950 they had become diversified, though each of them still had their own strong fields, such as cotton spinning (*Toyobo*), vinylon (*Kuraray*), and nylon (*Toray*). Furthermore, downward processes such as spinning and weaving were gradually separated from the main bodies and transferred to subsidiaries or subcontracting factories. At various levels, between these large-scale textile firms and the retailers of finished goods, intermediate merchants still played an important role in coordinating the flow of products from processors to retailers. As a response to the decline of their international competitiveness, textile companies invested in overseas subsidiaries.

Despite some similarities in strategy, the development of their organisation differed. Chemical fibre companies had traditionally maintained a few large production units, and their rapid growth depended much on these production units. By contrast, cotton spinning companies had many factories that were controlled by their head offices, which took the initiative in diversifying into chemical and synthetic fibres. Mergers happened in cotton spinning companies during the post-war period. These factories worked together to form the organisational structure of the textiles companies.

Toyobo[1] was a manufacturer of natural and rayon fibres in 1950, whose product lines ranged over cotton, woollen, and silk yarn and cloth, staple fibres, and rayon. Natural fibres amounted to more than 80 per cent of its total output during the 1950s, but synthetic fibres grew rapidly in proportion during the early 1960s. Synthetic fibres accounted for one half of total sales by the mid-1960s, and for more than 60 per cent by the late 1960s. The company had to deal with several organisational problems throughout these two decades. Diversified textile branches whose production and supply of materials differed from each other had to be coordinated. The company had to deal with scheduling the effective flow of products as its main products shifted from natural textiles to synthetic fibres. Organisational problems accompanying a large-scale merger also had to be solved.

Toyobo adopted a multidivisional structure in 1948 in preparation for the impending dissolution of the firm under the Deconcentration Act, but maintained this organisational form well after the crisis was past. Four divisions, namely, cotton production, cotton trading, woollen, and chemical fibres, were founded, the latter two being divisions with sales, production, and purchasing functions. This structure was reinforced in 1951, being equipped with a board of directors as the top management, together with a general staff and controller. The board coordinated the various divisions and promoted company-wide rationalisation. Managerial problems caused by product diversification were solved by this structure. To ensure the effective scheduling of flows, from the purchase of raw materials, to production to distribution was another problem. The Commercial Department of each product lines was made responsible for purchasing and sales functions, while the Engineering Department supervised production. Both departments reported to the managing director who was in charge of the product lines. However, in 1963 the firm abolished the multidivisional structure in its main textile branches, and until 1974 when it was readopted into the whole company, divisions were found only in minor industrial branches of the company.

In the first half of the 1950s, forward integration into cotton products occurred, and this absorbed the surplus workers of these existing branches. As the extension of the equipment of existing branches was restrained, financial resources were allocated to the development of synthetic fibres, though they had to solve technological problems before the project could be started. During the decade after 1955, synthetic fibres took the place of cotton goods and in order to meet this change in products, the firm strengthened its planning function. The Investigating Section, which had been responsible for planning, came under the control of the management committee so that the management committee was able to grasp the company-wide plans. A self-supporting system for each product line was also introduced. Each unit was made a full-division with production and sales functions, and controlled by one of the members of the management committee. All these measures were taken in the 1950s.

Toyobo abandoned the multidivisional structure at the time when many Japanese companies were introducing it. The multidivisional structure of *Toyobo* contributed to the arousal of concerns amongst its employees about profit, but also prevented cooperation among product lines. The company, planning to develop synthetic fibres became aware of the necessity of combining new products with the lines of existing textile branches. Though the multidivisional structure was partly maintained in Toyobo's minor product branches, the profit responsibility of each product line still being continued, main lines were reorganised into a functional structure. As to the background of this organisational reform, a new company strategy is observed. T. Taniguchi, the president (later the chairman) of *Toyobo*, proposed that the cotton spinning company should grow into a supplier of final consumer goods rather than remain either a speculator in purchasing or a low cost producer. Synthetic fibre companies integrated forward earlier than the cotton spinning companies, and *Toyobo* followed the similar lines of development.

After around 1960 investment in synthetic fibres, particularly in polyethylene projects, increased. *Toyobo* rationalised the production of cotton textile branches starting in the mid-1960s; from 1965 to 1973, 526 billion yen was spent in the rationalisation of cotton branches, and 714 billion yen in that of synthetic fibres.[2] In 1966 *Toyobo* amalgamated with *Kurehabo*, which was a large cotton spinning company with a strong interest in nylon production. Though *Kurehabo* was a large firm, one of the largest 100 firms in 1965, the organisation of the new company was structured after that of *Toyobo*. Fourteen of 16 directors of *Kurehabo* retired at the time of the merger, and duplicated posts were reduced by sending managers to subsidiaries. This merger was intended to increase mixed fabrics and promote specialisation of factories. Various attempts were also made to strengthen marketing, such as vertical integration into final goods, and affiliation of subsidiaries. Sales functions were also reorganised as the final products were made of various mixed materials. In the 1970s, the firm reduced textiles, diversified into non-textile branches, and adopted various methods of increasing high-value-added products. These changes were also carried out in more than 80 subsidiaries, and *Toyobo* specialised in supplying materials for these companies. *Toyobo* also undertook planning and sales activities for these subsidiaries in finished products, and in 1974, the multidivisional structure again took over from the functional structure. Each divisional headquarters controlled several divisions, subsidiaries, and sales functions, and was made responsible for its own profit. Investment decisions were also made by the division headquarters, which to extent took over the functions of the general office.

Kanebo[3] was similar to *Toyobo* both in size and product lines in the 1950s. *Kanebo*, like *Toyobo*, had to solve organisational problems arising from the purchase of traditional textile materials, diversification, and to a lesser degree, mergers. As a response to the problems caused by diversification, the company had once adopted the multidivisional structure in the pre-war period. However, *Kanebo* introduced a functional structure in the early post-war period. The units below the top management were sub-divided into departments in charge of each of the functions of a particular product line, like the Cotton Sales Department or the Cotton Spinning Department. This system was reorganised, by product, into a normal multidivisional structure in 1958, and the multidivisional system lasted until the late 1970s when the sales function of divisions were separated to form new companies.

After the textile boom caused by the Korean War and the rationalisation of equipment in 1952, the company intended to develop rayon staple branches throughout the 1950s. However, severe competition with chemical fibres companies, making inroads into new synthetic fibres, had distressing results for *Kanebo*, and the multidivisional structure was introduced as a reconstruction measure. Each division was engaged in the purchasing of raw materials for, as well as cost control, sales, and production planning of its own product lines. Rationalisation, including the reduction of unprofitable products followed this organisational reform. The crisis was miraculously overcome and President Muto put forward the Greater Kanebo Plan. The plan advocated starting nylon production, and diversification into non-textile branches to make up for the risk arising from *Kanebo*'s late entry into nylon production. Cosmetics, chemicals, and food firms were acquired and reorganised into several subsidiaries. Investment in these subsidiaries increased by eight times in the first half of the 1960s.[4] Financial resources were allocated in downward processes such as weaving or sewing, and further down in sales organisations. *Kanebo* exceeded *Toyobo* in these respects. It promptly developed access to final consumers through integration of processing and of sales. Unlike the synthetic fibre companies which backed processing firms indirectly, *Kanebo* organised retailers directly into the *Kanebo Circle*, through which *Kanebo*'s products were distributed to consumers. In cosmetics, these measures were particularly thorough; in place of traditional wholesale merchants, *Kanebo* formed a distribution channel of sales subsidiaries and retail chains, into which a large amount of financial resources were invested. The organisational problems arising from mergers, diversification, and vertical integration were solved without much difficulty, because, the planning and controlling departments centrally controlled the whole company.

Various changes took place within *Kanebo*'s multidivisional structure since its introduction. During the 1960s, some divisional headquarters' full lines of functions were set up in response to the company's aggressive expansion. Five important product lines were chosen and unprofitable ones were again eliminated . In textile branches, financial resources were allocated among domestic and overseas subsidiaries. 135 billion yen, or more than 30 per cent of its total investment during five years from 1968,[5] was spent on these interests. More important was the shift from textiles to non-textiles. This change yielded good results because the textile depression in the mid-1970s extended not only to traditional branches but to synthetic fibres as well, while much of *Kanebo*'s profit by this time came from food and cosmetics.

A drastic separation taking place in the late 1970s again modified the multidivisional structure. Natural textile branches were separated and reorganised into new companies, though this reorganisation of natural textiles was incomplete. Food branches were also separated. In synthetic fibres, sales functions were separated and a sales company was set up. The explanation for this was that the responsibilities of sales and production had become vague, although profit could be measured by adopting the multidivisional structure. Under the new structure, cosmetics, chemicals, and industrial materials remained as full divisions. Textile branches were reorganised into divisions mainly consisting of planning and control, while their field units were operated either by subsidiary companies or by functional departments. Owing to the separation of various interests, sales decreased by 40 per cent in the latter half of the 1970s.

Unitika[6] was formed in 1969 by the merger of *Nichibo* and *Nippon Rayon*. *Nippon Rayon*, which produced rayon and silk, was set up in the pre-war era as a subsidiary of *Nichibo* (Dai-nippon Boseki). *Nichibo* was engaged in the production of various lines of natural textiles. *Nippon Rayon* began nylon production in the early post-war period, and after establishing itself as a synthetic fibre company, its growth rate rose quickly. The sales of *Nippon Rayon* were less than one-tenth of those of *Nichibo* in 1950, but had caught up by the early 1960s.

Nichibo (Dai-nippon Boseki) had been administered by a functional structure quite similar to that of *Kanebo*. Production promotion immediately after the war was soon met by production restraint due to government policy after 1956, and the company closed its six factories by 1962. Since then, the firm restrained diversification, compared to those natural textile companies which had already enlarged their non-textile or synthetic fibre branches. On the other hand, *Nichibo* tried to develop processing and sewing branches, which were increasingly handed over to the subsidiaries or subcontracting firms but with the final products being distributed by *Nichibo*'s sales organisation and bearing *Nichibo*'s brand name. The organisational reform in the early 1960s reinforced the functions of general staff. Reorganisation also tightened control over subcontracting companies in the downward processes of textile goods. For such purposes a Subcontracting Department was set up. The new organisation also intensified marketing by subdividing its department by market.

Nippon Rayon began its post-war development by reconstructing production equipment for rayon and staple fibres, then by going into synthetic fibres such as nylon and polyester. These activities were carried out by a divisional structure, but in 1950 the divisional system was reformed into a functional system. By the mid 1960s, the organisational structure of this firm became quite similar to that of *Nichibo*, a sub-divided functional form, but *Nippon Rayon* gradually adopted the divisional system in its subordinate products such as ester and plastic.

By the time of the merger, the sales of both companies had become approximately the same, but *Nippon Rayon* was in a better financial position than *Nichibo*. Both companies had concentrated their financial resources on synthetic fibres, though in different sorts of products and in differing amounts of investment. *Nichibo* had invested 95 billion yen in vinylon while *Nippon Rayon* had invested 268 billion yen in nylon during the decade after 1955.[7] The rapid expansion of *Nippon Rayon* was prominent even among the growing chemical fibre firms. The merger was expected to bring about the integration of the whole processes from the production of raw materials for synthetic fibres to the manufacturing of finished textile products. The expansion of oversea production, the reinforcement of research and development, and the development of compound textiles which were only possible by combining the products of both companies, were also expected.

In fact, their production, sales, and resource allocation were not readily rationalised by this merger. At the time of the merger, *Nichibo* was composed of 20 departments, and *Nippon Rayon* of 40; *Unitika* started with 50 departments. In 1970, a large-scale organisational reform which was intended to diminish redundancies was planned, but postponed due to a disagreement with one of its trade unions. This reform ended in the resignation of the chairman and the president of the new company. The organisational structure just after the merger was a mixture of functional and divisional forms, and was not easily transformed into a division headquarters structure. Finally the company reduced the number of departments, enlarged staff functions, and established profit responsibility. The new company tried to remove duplicated functions and to prevent the extreme specification of tasks. In 1972, the multidivisional structure was introduced, and nine divisions, each with production and sales, were formed.

After the merger, *Unichika* had to confront a severe depression. Its international competitive power, particularly in spinning, declined. The firm closed down its natural fibre plants and attempted to diversify into non-textile branches. By 1980 plans had been made to enlarge non-textile interests to 30 per cent of the total sales, which at the time actually amounted to 24 per cent in spite of the decrease of sales of textile branches. Organisational reform again took place in 1973; eleven divisions were reorganised into six division head-quarters, the number of textile divisions was reduced, and financial resources were gradually transferred to plastic or film branches, though much was still spent in synthetic fibres.[8]

Among the five concerns that started as chemical fibre companies, *Teijin*[9] fell behind others in entering synthetic fibres. In the early post-war period, *Teijin* integrated downward into rayon spinning staple fibres, weaving, and distribution through a subsidiary trading company. With this background, the organising power of trading companies, which had played an important part in the distribution of textile goods, diminished, and the manufacturing companies had to handle sales activities. The major trading companies were reorganised into smaller firms under the Anti-Concentration Law, and their financial position, through which they had attained superiority over manufacturers upward and downward, declined. Chemical fibre manufacturers such as *Teijin* advanced forward in order to fill the gap which had used to be the field of activity of trading companies. *Teijin* set up a weaving subsidiary, reconstructed a processing and dyeing firm, and formed a sales company. Thus, in comparison to their pre-war activities which were heavily inclined towards production function, their post-war activities included the coordination of the flow of goods inside the firm. Its early functional structure was still incomplete; the head office was not equipped with a production department, and production was carried out independently by each factory. Then S. Oya was called back to the post of the president, and he set out to reconstruct the firm. First he formed a management committee, and separated the tasks of the managing directors from daily operations, and this management committee was used as an advisory committee for decision making by the president. A production department was set up, and in 1957 and 1958 the sales department was sub-divided into departments by product lines; this action was taken after similar sub-division in the production function. The functions of line and staff were made clear in the late 1950s. In spite of these inclinations toward the divisional system, a multidivisional structure was not introduced. The company was planning to expand its synthetic fibres branches, and financial resources were concentrated on polyester and nylon.[10] With the coincident changes in technology and market demand, synthetic fibres rapidly overtook rayon and other chemical fibres.

The second series of organisational reforms was started in 1960, again at the initiative of president Oya. A very strong top management was set up; he abolished the management committee and the traditional 'referral system'. The top management organisation was divided up into two parts. One was the controlling department, or the 'General Headquarters', consisting of the president and the senior managing directors. This Headquarters took charge of strategic planning, development and personnel. The other, or the 'Operating Headquarters', was composed of the departments of sales, production, development and management. Directors were appointed to the managers of the Operating Headquarters, and they were authorised to perform all operational activities. This system was called paradoxically 'multidivisional structure by function'. However, the system made the responsibility of each functional manager clear, bringing about swift decision making and execution, specialised the top management, and facilitated internal communication and an improvement of morale. A need for general coordination between departments, however, still remained.

A strategic change took place in the mid-1960s; the company retreated from rayon, and integrated backward into synthetic fibres materials. Heavy investment in 'Tetron' (polyester) continued towards the end of the 1960s. Throughout the period of increasing overseas investment, exports, including those of plant and equipment also increased. In the domestic market, sales of finished products, manufactured by subcontract companies, increased until 1970, but these were replaced by raw materials for synthetic fibres by 1970.[11] Finally diversification into non-textile branches, such as petroleum oil, was attempted. All these were prompted by a structural slump in the polyester industry. The company reorganised its functional headquarters structure into a normal functional structure in 1968. The main point of this reform was to separate the vice-presidents from the tasks of the headquarters and to make them specialise in top management. The staff departments were also separated from the lines, and made into new sub-units according to product lines, in an attempt to unify sales and production staffs. In 1969 management reorganisation in the operating levels followed. A divisional structure was introduced, although not necessarily a complete divisional system. However, in textile branches the new unit was equipped with production and sales functions. The results of these strategic changes became clear after 1974; non-textile branches had proved to be unsuccessful and chemical products derived from textile production had continued to increase. The integration upward to intermediate materials caused a crucial new problem because the kind of materials began to change from DMT to PTA. The multidivisional structure did not last long, and by 1980, with the reinforcement of the sales functions, a functional structure had been revived.

Toray Industries[12] manufactured chemical fibres which were classified as chemical industry, while yarn and cloth accounted for less than 30 per cent of its output. The company swiftly changed its products from rayon to synthetic fibres, and their success in nylon, though several years were spent before its realisation, enabled them to enter into polyester, plastic, and other synthetic fibres in the late 1950s. Investment in nylon plants superseded that in others during the ten years after 1955. The new product lines and rapid technological changes created an enormous amount of daily work for the top management. Until the early post-war years, the company was structured with a simple line organisation, while sales were carried out by *Mitsui Bussan*. In the late 1940s, the company formed its own sales organisation, and developed it in the early 1950s. With this background, their products became increasingly diversified to nylon and rayon fabrics, and their activities included the weaving process of these products. Toray became much more interested in the downward processes than they had been previously. Organisational reform started with the formation of the Staff Department. In 1955, the production function was departmentalised and the research and development became independent of the production unit. A managing director assumed each function, and the company modified the tradition of its decentralised management with extensive power over production units; directors were made to engage in general management, and the top management function gradually became clarified towards the end of the 1950s. By 1960, the company had formed a general staff, such as the 'Executive Department' for controlling, and the 'Inquiry Department' for corporate planning. These were separated from the six operating departments, and more authority was invested in these two departments. Management decentralisation, accompanied by swift decision making was not realised easily, because the planning function was concentrated in the Executive Department, and coordination among operating departments was carried out by the top management.

After the slump of the mid-1960s, the firm experienced rapid growth for the second time, led by exports. Backward integration into materials was planned in order to economise the cost of production as well as in order to enter chemical industries. Overseas investments increased with exports, though the proportion of investment to export differed by country. The restriction of imports by Asian countries began in the 1960s, which forced the company to set up local subsidiaries to produce secondary textile products. These were accompanied by the export of industrial plants and technologies. Capital expenditure in synthetic fibres continued throughout the 1960s, but investment in non-textile branches amounted to nearly half of that in textiles.[13] The share of each product did not change proportionately. The sales of chemical products expanded only gradually, and in textiles, finished products, mostly manufactured by subcontracting companies, increased. Cloth and other finished goods came to represent one-third of its textile products in 1965, but in 1973 it amounted to nearly half of the latter. As in the cases of other textile firms, the materials supplied by *Toray* were processed by subcontracting companies, and branded and sold through Toray's sales channels.

Such development resulted in organisational reform in the mid-1960s. The firm sub-divided its sales department into departments by product lines, each in charge of subcontracting companies in textile processing. Soon this system evolved into a multidivisional structure. The whole company was grouped into three division headquarters to diversify and promote oversea business.

The purpose of the divisionalisation of 1970 was the tightening of the profit control. However, there was a technical problem in achieving profit control because it was difficult to divide the production units into corresponding division headquarters with profit responsibility. The chemical division headquarters extended to upward processes, while textile and plastic divisions extended to the downward stages of the same continuous process. In 1971, the two downward division headquarters were divided into several divisions, and were made profit centres. Each division was composed of a sales and a controlling department, while production was carried out by the production units which were directly controlled by the production department. The division manager was authorised to decide the amount and the cost of products of his own division. The controlling department of each division was charged with profit responsibility for both production and sales.

After the oil crisis, strategy was changed; overseas investment and production increased drastically[14] and the rate of export both in textile products and in plants and technologies slackened. The production of synthetic fibres, particularly of yarn and cloth, decreased, and the company decided to concentrate its managerial resources on some special products. These changes were readily reflected in the organisational structure; the multidivisional structure caused overlapping of similar functions, particularly of staff, and gave rise to sectionalism among divisions, and charged top management to do the tasks of division managers at the same time. The company adopted the functional structure in 1976, but with the recovery of its financial performance, the divisional system was revived. The new system was a mixture of the divisional and the functional structure: sales activities were operated through divisions while production was controlled and coordinated by production headquarters.

Mitsubishi Rayon[15] started as a subsidiary of *Shinko Wool Textile*, and was merged into *Japan Chemical Industries* (later *Mitsubishi Chemical Industries*) in 1937. *Shinko Rayon* was merged with *Japan Chemical Industries*, and became the Textile Division Headquarters of *Mitsubishi Chemical Industries* in 1947. However, not only production and sales functions but financing was also delegated to the textile division headquarters. In 1950, this headquarters was separated from the main body, and began to break into the downward process of the rayon staple industry. The new firm integrated spinning and weaving processes in the early 1950s. Its organisational structure evolved from a simple line system consisting of a sales department and four factories, into a functionally departmentalised one in the early 1960s, and in the late 1960s a resin division was added. It was in 1976 that the whole company was divisionalised.

Under the line system of the 1950s, the head office had a sales department, while production was carried out by four factories. These four factories, directly responsible to the top management, were profit centres until 1954, when a centralised accounting system was introduced. Managing directors were appointed to the factory managers. The organisational reform of the early 1960s was a typically modern one. A functionally departmentalised system consisting of the sales and the production headquarters was set up, and the managing directors were separated from the operating tasks and made specialised in general management. Thus top and middle management were formally established.

The strategy of this company was more or less similar to that of other chemical fibres companies. Until the mid-1950s the share of yarn and cloth in its total output increased, and in the following decade, an entry into synthetic fibres was attempted, while the rayon branch was gradually reduced. This required new kinds of materials and new outlets. *Mitsubishi Rayon* set up subsidiaries for the procurement of intermediate materials for synthetic fibres. All *Mitsubishi Rayon*'s technologies and licenses relating to synthetic fibres were supplied by foreign companies, and foreign companies wanted to have shares in the Japanese projects. This was the main reason why subsidiaries were utilised. In the case of polypropylene, however, a subsidiary was not set up, but *Mitsubishi Petrochemicals* supplied intermediate materials. Downward processes were also important, because these were new products, and local weaving factories hesitated to use these fibres. *Mitsubishi Rayon* gave them technical guidance and financial support, and formed outlets for its products. Though synthetic fibres became the main product, amounting to 70 per cent of total sales, the rationalisation of rayon equipment required a fairly large amount of financial resources.[16] Since the mid-1960s, capital expenditure in synthetic fibres was gradually shifted to resin.[17] The organisational structure during this period was relatively simple. Three headquarters, i.e. textile production, textile marketing and resin constituted the units below top management. On the organisational chart, factories came under the control of the production headquarters. However, senior directors were often appointed as factory managers.

After the mid-1970s, the company rapidly discarded its existing interests. Spinning processes which, compared to chemical processes, required more intensive labour were separated. Engineering interests were also separated. Twenty-seven per cent of employees were transferred to new firms. In 1976, the rayon staple interests were closed down, and 1200 employees, or 19 per cent of all workers were laid off. As a result, the company come to specialise in the upward processes of textile production, and little increase in sales is observed after 1975. Organisational reform followed in 1976; a multidivisional structure consisting of textile, resin, and subsidiary divisions was set up. An international division and the new business division were soon added. These reflected increasing investment in subsidiaries and overseas interests.

Kuraray[18] was set up as a subsidiary of *Kurashiki Spinning* in the mid-1920s, but in 1935, it was already listed among the largest 100 firms. After the war, the company entered the production of synthetic fibres, making use of their own technology. The products of the firm consisted mainly of intermediate materials for textile goods until the early 1950s, then by 1955 gradually shifted to those of downward stages such as yarn and cloth. *Kuraray*'s management structure saw frequent changes. Originally the company was administered by a functionally departmentalised structure, but its functional departments were gradually sub-divided into functional departments by products during the early 1950s. In 1962 a multidivisional structure was introduced, which in turn gave way to the functional structure in 1968. It was again divisionalised in 1971, and again gave way to the functional structure in 1976.

Kuraray's product lines also changed frequently. Vinyl had taken the place of rayon and rayon staple by the mid-1960s. However, in spite of its stability in price, vinyl production proved to be unprofitable, and in the early 1960s the company had had to consider entry into other synthetic fibres by introducing foreign technologies. *Kurashiki Rayon* had moved away from vinyl by the mid-1960s, though capital expenditure was still concentrated on vinyl branches.[19] The production of raw materials increased, and that of cloth remained the same, while yarn decreased, though both cloth and yarn were produced by subcontracting companies and supplied to the market by *Kuraray*. A merger with *Kurashiki Spinning* was proposed in the mid-1950s, but was not realised. Although *Kuraray* made use of small-scale mergers, its main strategy in expanding downward processes of chemical or synthetic fibres.

In spite of the frequent changes in its management structure, the production units remained powerful in the early phase of development. In 1962, some divisions were set up as staff and sales divisions, and the production units remained independent of the divisions. In 1971, synthetic rubber and intermediate material divisions were made profit centres. Their main textile products were severely hit by the slump of textile industries, and marketing and the concentration of managerial resources on particular fields became more important. The multidivisional structure was often characterised by a lack of close relationships among divisions, and was also particularly inefficient in the development of areas which extended over several divisions or of new markets. Thus the company changed again into a functional structure, and simplified its organisation in the mid-1970s. The existing divisions were consolidated, and some general functional headquarters were formed. The controlling and the planning departments undertook coordination among the functional headquarters, and also took control of the allocation of resources.

Asahi Chemical Industry,[20] which originated in electrochemistry and had diversified into various lines of chemical products by making use of ammonium, was fundamentally a chemical company in 1950. By 1980, the firm was fully diversified. In the early post-war era, the company supplied materials for rayon and industrial chemicals. By 1980, successfully pursuing a unique idea of its first president S. Noguchi, they fully utilised self supplied materials and by-products such as ammonium gas, caustic soda, chlorine gas, and hydrochloric acid. Diversification derived from vertically integrated processes of materials through intermediate materials to fabricated basic materials or final products. Their product lines ranged over rayon, gunpowder, synthetic fibres, condiments, synthetic resins, building materials, and various other chemical products. Such diversification was made possible by domestic technologies, making each branch large enough to attain minimum optimal scale. Except for a few textile products, *Asahi* became the largest producer or at least attained a market share necessary to enable them to compete with other firms in each industry branch. Traditionally the company was administered by a management organisation, in which the main units below the top management were composed of factories, while the head office took charge of sales. The multidivisional structure has been adopted since 1959, though there have been modifications in it.

The company's strategy in the 1950s formed the background of the transition to the divisional form. By 1955 the company had tried to integrate downward into textile products, and in the recession of 1957 it began to change the gas source of ammonium from electro chemicals to petrochemicals. New materials and by-products were made possible by this change, although their share of new products were still low. However, the idea of the first president was developed over the following two decades. A long-range management plan, which was first drafted in the late 1950s, also promoted the rationalisation of existing branches such as chemical fibres. The introduction of the management plan in place of budget control led the way to the divisionalisation of the whole company. Five divisions, each with sales and production functions, were set up. They were grouped into two parts; the textile group had a headquarters in Nobeoka (Kyushu), while the non-textile group was based in Tokyo. The branch office at Nobeoka supplied services to the production units of both groups there. The production units of the non-textile group were supplied with services and controlled by the Tokyo office.

However, the profit centres were placed at the divisions, and each division was made responsible for drafting its own long-range plans. In spite of this delegation of authority, the division managers were appointed from the members of the management committee. At the head office, the management committee was supported by general staff such as the budgetary or the technology committees, but some general staffs assisted with the planning of each division.

After 1965, the company began various chemical products, expanding rapidly and catching up with *Toray Industries*. Investment was made in synthetic fibres, building materials, and chemical products, while export and oversea investment stayed at a low level.[21] Eventually textile branches fell to 50 per cent of the sales of the firm. Petrochemical projects were promoted jointly by the *Asahi* group.

The multidivisional structure, which had been adopted since 1959, raised new problems towards the end of the 1960s. Various textile products which were supplied by the firm competed on the same market. The adjustment among divisions took time and delayed the decision making of the top management. The company tightened administrative and coordinating departments, and then adopted the division headquarters structure in 1970. Company-wide projects were planned and promoted by the Development Headquarters. Three division headquarters were made profit centres. Textile division headquarters consisted of several divisions and sales departments. Activities common to the divisions, such as export or the distribution through the same market channels, were made into common subunits. Thus throughout the 1970s, priority was moved from production to marketing. In contrast to such decentralisation in operating levels, planning and control were centralised in the division headquarters.

The management structure of the textile companies alternated between several basic types of organisation. Such changes were caused by vertical integration, dis-integration, and product diversification. Most of them once or twice adopted the multidivisional structure after the war. The divisions were originally organised as product divisions, each requiring different technology. However, the products of different divisions were supplied to the same market and were mutually substitutable. The companies' strategy also influenced the reverse change from multidivisional to functional structure. The share of one product in their total sales rose overwhelmingly and the balance among divisions could not be sustained, and where diversification was attempted through effective utilisation of semi- or by-products, it was not successful either. Furthermore, these firms moved upward into supplying raw materials for synthetic fibres and other chemical products, and separated downward processes from the main bodies. Such a strategy made it difficult to divide these processes into product divisions because different finished products used the same raw materials. As downward processes were separated from large-scale textile companies, upward processes became their main activities. Finally, an increasing necessity for marketing required the unification and centralisation of sales functions. This increasing market-orientedness resulted in the introduction of the division headquarters structure in which a small number of the division headquarters controlled the production divisions and a sales department.

The differences between those companies which originated in cotton spinning and those which developed from chemical fibres also became clear. The cotton spinning firms had established functionally departmentalised structures with centralised top management, and had become diversified by the war. Functional departments were formed in each of the main product lines, and such organisations were easily reformed into multidivisional structures by product. The purchasing of raw materials eventually reduced in importance as various new materials appeared. Cotton spinning firms used mergers to maintain their competitiveness. The chemical fibre companies, by contrast, were alike in having relatively small numbers of large production units. They did not use mergers for expansion, management was centralised and the top management was separated from daily operations in the early post-war period. They also intensified control over downward processes, which had traditionally been coordinated by trading companies.

6.3 THE PAPER, PRINTING AND MATERIALS COMPANIES

Paper and materials industries had seven concerns among the largest 100 firms in 1970. Four were paper manufacturers, and there was one each in cement, tyres, and glass. In addition there were two printing firms. Unlike their European counterparts, paper manufacturing and printing have not been vertically integrated with each other. It is doubtful whether all of these products qualify as fabricated basic materials. According to the Standard Commodity Classification, tyres are classified as final goods, and printing is unclassifiable in any products. Thus their treatment here is strictly for convenience.

Paper manufacturing was a traditionally established industry often based in large-scale firms. The supply of raw materials and, in the pre-war era, of electricity and water were the main determinants of the success of these firms. For these reasons, they were integrated backwards in the pre- and early post-war eras. After that they attempted to secure supplies through their overseas interests. As the supply of raw materials from the market became much easier, diversification making use of by- or intermediate products was begun. The narrowest range of diversification in the paper industry was in adding paperboard to ordinary printing papers. The second stage was in pulp and container production through backward and forward processes, and the third in timber or finished paper products. In 1970, more than 70 per cent of the sales of two of the paper manufacturing companies remained in the first range, while the other two went beyond the second stage. Mostly, they have partially or wholly adopted the divisional structure when they added new products to their original lines.

From the dissolution of the former *Oji Paper* into *Tomakomai* (present *Oji*), *Jujo*, and *Honshu*, until the mid 1950s, paper companies competed in rationalisation of production and in the introduction of new technologies. The boom for them came earlier than for other industries and so did the long slump. An inter-firm agreement for the reduction of production was attempted, and this was followed by a governmental recommendation for the reduction of operation in the late 1950s. In the early 1960s, major firms attempted jointly to restrain their investment, and in the mid-1960s a cartel for the restraint of equipment was formed. Finally in 1968, these three companies reached an agreement on a merger, although this finished in vain.

The former *Oji Paper*[22] used to have 33 production units in and outside Japan in 1945. The present *Oji* started as a single unit firm in 1949, and soon set up a second factory in central Japan (Kasugai). A powerful head office was set up, control of factories intensified, and the division of labour between the head office and factories clarified. Under the new system, sales functions were transferred to each factory, while the head office specialised in its own functions. Finally in the late 1960s, the trading headquarters of the head office undertook the coordination of production and sales. For its supply of raw materials, the forerunner of the present *Oji* relied upon the state forest in *Sakhalin* for a stable supply of wood. After the war, the company had to switch to domestic conifer wood, which was supplied by small-scale private forestries. But their supply was vulnerable to market fluctuation. *Oji* thus planned to acquire half of its raw materials from its own forests. Research was made regarding the improvement of wood, and efforts were made to rationalise cutting and transportation.

The first series of management reorganisations took place in the mid-1950s. *Oji Paper* introduced the American type of management practices, such as the management committee and controllership. A production department was set up in the head office, and the head office was equipped with a full-line of functions. Instead of increasing the number of production units, the new company tried to attain an economy of scale of factories, whose location was no longer limited by easy access to raw material and electricity or water power. Self-supply of raw materials could not suffice in satisfying demand, although the company developed its forestry branch, switched its materials from conifer wood to fast-growing broadleaf trees, and made full use of scrap wood. Their level of self-supply was approximately 10 per cent in 1960 in contrast to 50 per cent in the original plan.

The second large-scale organisational reform, which took place in the early 1960s, was initiated by the impending liberalisation of foreign trade. The firm pursued specialisation into a few product lines of paper products up until the mid-1960s. They increased the functions of the head office for the second time, and formed a planning headquarters. The production and sales functions were moved into each of the factories. Each factory became a division though there was mutual overlapping of products. Purchasing was done centrally. Wood Headquarters took charge of overseas development and of long-term contract purchasing. Instead of using intermediate merchants such as local paper and pulp companies and trading companies, the Wood Headquarters of the company directly imported chipped wood. Special ships were used between berths overseas and their berths at Tomakomai and Nagoya. Formation of a cartel was considered in order to avoid excessive competition with other paper manufacturing companies. Even a merger of the three offshoots of the former *Oji Paper* was discussed; but it only resulted in a loose association of companies with an exchange of shares. The coordination of production equipment and joint ventures overseas were promoted through this association. Parallel to such measures in the paper branch, *Oji* tried to diversify into non-paper markets by investing in them more than one-third of its financial resources between 1965 and 1973.[23] Diversification had proved unprofitable by the mid-1970s, and the firm gave priority to the production of high-value-added paper, which was accomplished by the acquisition of *Kitanihon Paper*. Operations had to be reduced several times, but *Oji* tried to make a profit nevertheless. In the head office, a trading headquarters to which production and sales functions were moved was set up.

Honshu Paper[24] took over seven factories which used to belong to the former *Oji Paper*. These factories were situated in the central part of Japan, and they were able to acquire more than half of their conifer wood supplies from their own forests. However, the company nevertheless soon faced difficulties in getting supplies of raw materials. In the early 1950s, the slump in the paper manufacturing industry hit *Honshu Paper* more seriously than other paper companies, and costly materials became an outstanding and urgent problem for the reconstruction of the company. Attempts were made to utilise broadleaf trees, which were cheaper and in part supplied by the company's own forests. Then the firm made inroads into paper-board production for industrial use, by making use of these broadleaf trees. Factories were modernised, a new method of quality control was introduced, and the production units were enlarged. However, the paper-board market proved to be unstable. Management reform started with a complete change of top management. In 1956 a new president and a managing director were sent from *Oji*. Planning and controlling functions were fortified and a self-supporting system was set up in the production units. The new management then centralised sales activities, which had been more or less subordinate to the production units. Such innovation resulted in the adoption of a functional structure consisting of five headquarters, each of which was managed by a member of the top management.

Towards the end of the 1960s there was a diversion of investment from paper-board production to the secondary processing of paper products, paper containers and wood.[25] Such shifts to downward products were made partly in order to reduce the quantities of raw materials, whose supplies were becoming increasingly costly. The multidivisional structure followed diversification. New divisions were full-divisions not only with sales but also with production units, and these were responsible for profits. Heavy investment in equipment, however, brought difficulties at the time of the oil-crisis by putting an end to the drastic increase of demand for paper containers. The strategy adopted during the slump was to develop those subsidiaries which were in charge of the downward stages of paper products. This had not brought good results by the end of the 1970s.

Honshu Paper was the only concern in the paper industry that introduced the multidivisional structure throughout the company. This firm was more diversified than the rest, and such diversification continued throughout the 1970s. Division headquarters were laid in established product lines, while in others, divisions were made administrative units. However, the firm began to centralise its management towards the end of the 1970s. The number of divisions and division headquarters was reduced, and vice-presidents and senior managing directors were appointed as their heads.

Jujo Paper[26] also took over seven factories located throughout Japan, which had belonged to the pre-war *Oji Paper*. The rationalisation of equipment and backward integration into pulp production was attempted. With new production technologies, managerial techniques were introduced from foreign companies. Soon after the board of directors was established, a management committee was formed to perform the function of general management. The firm then set up functional departments, though production units were still directly controlled by the president who was assisted by the production staff department. The firm adopted a long-range plan in the early 1960s, and intended to invest heavily in machinery and to achieve a drastic increase in production. These early innovations in managerial practices, quite similar to those of other paper companies, were promoted extensively. However, the actual increase in production and sales was much less than had been expected. Production reached 554 thousand tons in 1964 against the long term plan of 650 thousand tons. In terms of sales as well as in financial performance, the company had caught up with *Oji Paper*. From its formation to the early 1960s, difficulties in raw material supplies arose, and these were aggravated by the firm's expansion strategy. New sources of materials were sought one after another, and since the beginning of the 1960s, mass-production was being reexamined because of the expense of raw materials.

From the mid-1960s onward, strategy was modified into one which intended the production of high value-added paper products. It was planned that sales from the non-paper branch would reach 30 per cent of the firm's total sales. Along with diversification, the firm stepped up rationalisation of production in order to increase its international competitive power. Inefficient mills were closed down. A pulp manufacturing company, *Tohoku Pulp*, was acquired in the northern part of Japan. These measures resulted in an increase in sales and a decrease in profit, and influenced the form of the company's management structure.

Until *Tohoku Pulp* was completely consolidated into *Jujo Paper*, the new company had two sales departments, each controlling its own branch offices. In 1970, a functional headquarters structure was introduced. In addition to the engineering, sales, wood, and planning headquarters, a few divisions with sales and production functions were formed in downward processes. The managers of the production units still reported directly to the top management. However, in the 1970s, the divisions in lessor branches were abolished, probably due to the difficulties in managing production processes by product-market criteria.

Daishowa Paper Manufacturing[27] was unique in that it did not develop any modern management structures. Originating as a functional/line form, the structure of the company came to resemble that of a single function firm when it separated its trading activities in 1967.

Daishowa Paper was a family-controlled firm, having started its post-war development on a far smaller scale than the three offshoots of *Oji Paper*. By 1960, the firm had grown as large as those same three companies as the result of its aggressive policies in the early 1950s. This strategy was continued until the mid-1960s, by which time the company had become the largest paper manufacturer in Japan. Such expansion, despite the slump in the paper industry, was achieved by innovations in securing raw materials. The firm made use of broadleaf trees, and of foreign chipped wood which was carried by ships which were exclusively for company use, and finally of imported cheap raw wood. All these measures contributed remarkably to the reduction of the product costs. In comparison with other paper manufacturing companies. *Daishowa* had a wide range of product lines because the management preferred to avoid the risk of specialising in a few lines. However, their products were still limited within the areas of printing paper and paperboard. Organisationally, top management positions were filled mainly by the Saito family, who owned 10 per cent of the shares in 1955 and 3 per cent in 1970. Below the top management, a functional structure was formed from the beginning, though each of the production units and branch offices reported directly to the top.

Other companies and the government often expressed objections to the expansion strategy of *Daishowa* Paper. In most cases, *Daishowa Paper* insisted on free competition. In the latter half of the 1960s, the firm invested overseas for the supply of raw materials and also in subsidiaries for downward activities and diversification.[28] These new strategies resulted in the organisational reform of 1967. Particularly sales activities, which were operated through complicated traditional distribution system, needed transformation. Though the company separated its trading functions and set up a sales subsidiary, the top management of *Daishowa Paper* held important posts in this subsidiary. After its separation, the head office became very simple, consisting only of the staff, while operating activities were controlled by factories and the sales subsidiary.

The purchasing of raw materials was the most important and difficult task faced by the post-war paper manufacturing companies. It did not, however, influence directly their organisational structures, but rather indirectly, through pressure to shift their main lines to high-value-added or downward products.

Two printing companies have long been administered by the geographically based multidivisional structure. Their strategies and sizes were similar to each other. Despite remarkable innovation in printing technology through the initiatives of their central offices, these companies have maintained decentralised structures. Neither of them diversified nor integrated vertically.

Toppan Printing[29] started its post-war reconstruction on the self-supporting production unit system. During the first half of the 1950s, *Toppan Printing* introduced foreign technologies in printing processes and ink manufacturing to fill the technological delay caused by the war. The company first applied synthetic resin ink produced by one of its subsidiaries which had been set up with the technological support of *Interchemical*. Financial resources were concentrated on printing machines,[30] while diversification into the production of office machinery, films, and synthetic resins was carried out by their subsidiaries. These varied activities were coordinated by the head office, which consisted of a full line of functions such as technical, trading, and planning departments and also of factories. By 1955, however, each production unit, which had its own tradition, acquired all functions except financing and staff functions. This system resembled the 'production-unit structure', which was widely observed among engineering firms. Even when the company had several factories in the same localities, each of them was made a self-supporting unit, between which there was little coordination. In 1964 this system was reformed into a geographically-based multidivisional structure. However, as each division was based on one of the local factories, there emerged more than two regional divisions in the same localities without any territory of their own. Coordination between neighbouring divisions was not attempted.

After the mid-1960s, the shortage of labour became a serious problem. *Toppan Printing* tried to solve it, first with a subcontracting system, then they began to employ many local printing firms for labour intensive processes. Soon half of the total output of the company was being undertaken by subcontractors. The company then went into production oversea, and finally, embarked on manufacturing high value-added products. The number of subsidiaries and investment in them increased remarkably between 1965 and 1973.[31] The long-range plan of 1970, however, gave priority to investment in speciality processing and paper-container branches. These investment policies brought about a complicated structure made up of geographical and product divisions by 1970. An overseas division and four divisions by products were added to the traditional geographical divisions in the 1970s.

Dai Nippon Printing,[32] which was smaller than *Toppan Printing* in 1950, extended its activities towards speciality printing branches and the affiliation of local printing firms. By 1964, the number of subsidiaries had increased to 42, making the company slightly larger than *Toppan Printing*. *Dai Nippon Printing*'s organisational structure also became similar to that of *Toppan*. In 1950, it had a functional structure. By 1955 the trading function was moved to each factory, and by 1964, the structure was further reformed into multidivision by geography.

These strategies observed prior to 1964 continued well after the late 1960s. Production was rationalised by utilising a subcontracting system. In 1970, sales from subcontracting plants accounted for 40 per cent of the company's total sales. Development in speciality printing, such as micro-electronics, was a new field of activities. Regional divisions were divided into regional trading headquarters and regional divisions, and the new regional divisions were composed of production departments and factories. This probably checked the centrifugal trend in the production units. This dual structure was reformed into a normal multidivisional structure by geography in the latter half of the 1970s. Some product divisions, those in charge of the new fields of activities such as containers or micro-electronics, were added to the geographical divisions.

The remaining three materials companies developed differently from each other, though their diversification was constrained. In the early post-war period, one of them produced intermediate materials, while the other two utilised their distribution channels for diversification. However, the market for the main products of the latter two companies grew rapidly along with the development of consumer durable industries such as television or automobiles. In the 1970s they began to diversify into finished products.

Among them, the strategy and structure of *Onoda Cement*[33] was similar to that of paper manufacturing companies though there was several years' time lag. The management structure of this company started with the production-unit form, but was soon reformed into a functional one in the 1950s, and partly divisionalised in the 1970s. In the inter-war years, the firm had developed by merger and invested overseas where two-thirds of its assets was located. However, its post-war recovery was rapid, and the growth continued well after the boom of the Korean War. Traditionally, their production units were situated near lime mines throughout the country. Though each production unit had its own sales department, products were handled by *Mitsui & Co. (Mitsui Bussan)* through sole-sales agent contract and distributed by the latter's affiliated local wholesalers. As the sole-sales contract was stopped after the war, *Onoda* had to organise new distribution channels. Special agents were chosen from among the local wholesalers who had used to belong to *Mitsui & Co.* For activities in upward processes, the company redeveloped old lime mines and bought up new ones near their factories. Lime was the only natural resource whose domestic supply was possible at a cheap cost. However, it became necessary to rationalise the transportation of goods and coordinate the regional flow of goods. Central control was established in the early 1950s. Before that time, *Onoda*'s head office was situated in one of the main factories, but eventually moved to Tokyo. The sales function was centralised in the head office.

The depression in the cement industry came in the mid-1960s, and hit the company severely. *Onoda Cement* had to reduce the number of its employees, simplify its head office, and strengthen its management committee. Decision making, which was being carried out through the referral system, was improved. After the recession, the firm integrated forward into supplying raw concrete, and diversified into non-cement areas such as building materials and mineral products. Sales of raw concrete increased, representing 34 per cent of the firm's total output in 1966 and 59 per cent in 1973. Though *Onoda Cement* lagged behind other companies in developing raw concrete branches, the emergence of such products was marked enough to change the functions of local agents, who thereon undertook downward activities such as wholesale, transportation, and providing customers with credit. *Onoda* had to set up local raw concrete firms undertaking risks and financial burdens. These risks and burdens enlarged parallel with the growing size of each transaction. In integrating downward processes, *Onoda* set up separate firms partly for financial reasons, and partly because local firms were much more familiar with local environments. *Onoda* sent management to these local raw concrete companies. Divisionalisation took several steps; as the sales of non-cement branches increased, the company separated its mining branch from the production department, and sub-divided its sales department into two units to deal with these new products. Then the self-supporting system was set up in non-cement interests, which, in the early 1970s, became two divisions with production and sales functions.

It may not be appropriate to deal with a tyre manufacturer here since its products are classified as producer final goods, or even as consumer final goods if not as fabricated basic materials. Nevertheless, the nature of its products as well as the firm's strategy had much in common with some of the chemical companies discussed in the next chapter.

The strategy of *Bridgestone Tire*[34] has been influenced by Isibashi, the firm's founder. It's post-war development started with the replacement of outdated equipment. Technological innovation brought about the creation of tyres of rayon cord and new technologies were introduced from *Goodyear*. Aggressive investment during the slump in the early 1950s pushed the company to the top of the tyre companies. Structurally a functionally departmentalised form, in which main functions were assigned to two senior managing directors, was adopted in 1951. However, this structure soon gave way to a simple line structure again, making its production units directly controlled by the president. The position of the production function was important throughout the early phase of the development of this company.

Technological innovation – the introduction of synthetic rubber and nylon cord – produced a disparate development in the company.

For its materials, the company joined a synthetic rubber company, and also set up a liquefied gas company. The firm also joined with a textile company which supplied tyre code. Thus *Bridgestone* attempted to gain control over various sorts of materials which were specified and could not easily be supplied by the outside market. These measures were necessary when *Bridgestone* was competing with other tyre companies to take the lead in supplying new products. The production of tyres expanded with the development of the sales network and exports. Besides transport and automobile companies, new markets began to develop widely among the final consumers. *Bridgestone* affiliated local sales agents as their wholesalers and also added garages as new outlets for the sales of replacement tyres. Diversification into rubber products for industrial or home use was also attempted. Traditionally the firm had had interests in the bicycle industry, and added motorcycles as new products. *Bridgestone* entered car production through shareholding in two automobile companies, which were eventually amalgamated by the leadership of Ishibashi. These activities were initiated by the founder of *Bridgestone*. Such backward and forward integration brought about product diversification and a high rate of growth in the late 1950s. Among the aggressive policies adopted by the company, however, mass-production of automobile tyres is what led it to success. Organisational reforms went ahead of the change in owner-management and the public offering of its shares in 1961. Rapid expansion under one owner-manager gave rise to various organisational problems such as sectionalism among sub-units, the weakness of control and command, the inefficiency of reporting system, the increasing routine work-load of the managing directors, and the lack of profit responsibility of the product lines. The management committee was set up at the end of the 1950s, and the delegation of authority to the managing directors was attempted in 1962. Gradually the firm built up a formal management structure.

Although diversification continued after the mid-1960s, capital expenditure was actually concentrated on tyre production,[35] and the share of tyres in its total sales increased from 70 per cent in the first half of the 1960s to more than 80 per cent in the 1970s. To strengthen the top management, and to distinguish strategic decision making from operational responsibilities, a senior management committee consisting of vice-presidents was formed. These two types of activities were formerly carried out by the managing directors who were at the same time departmental managers. On operating levels, a divisional structure by products was introduced in 1970. However, the Tyre Division was so large that organisational problems to the functional structure arose in that division. The coordination of production and sales in the Tyre Division was made by the president and not by the division manager.

The oil crisis of 1973 drastically changed the state of the tyre industry. The market shrank while the price of rubber material rose. The tyre industry had few technological or market relationships with other industries, which limited its diversification either to the fields of the same materials or to unrelated areas. A measure that was taken was overseas investment, which served to further expand its tyre interests. Organisational structure was reformed into a functional one in the late 1970s.

Asahi Glass[36] took over two of the divisions of the former *Mitsubishi Chemical Industries* when the latter was dissolved after the war. These divisions, namely the Glass and the Soda Divisions, were sub-divided into functional departments by products, each of which came below the highest managers. This functional structure by products was further reorganised into a normal functional structure in 1957, but again subdivided into products departments, which was eventually changed into the divisional structure in 1964. The supply of raw materials, such as silicic sand, soda ash, and after the company began to self-supply soda ash, salt, has long been the main problem of the company. The supply of silicic sand of good quality was geographically limited, while salt was expensive. After the war, the company tried to find stable sources of supply of these two materials, and naturally diversified their sources. In 1950, the company had a large soda branch, which later became the centre of organic chemicals and refractories. The diversification of *Asahi Glass* is characterised by utilization and combination of the semi- or by-products of glass manufacturing. These by-products consistently amounted to 40 per cent of their total sales, and more recently have increased up to 50 per cent.

The glass market began to develop from the late 1950s, particularly in automobiles, furniture and television tubes in addition to the traditional building materials. In both of these branches, *Asahi Glass* introduced technologies from *A W G* and other foreign companies to compensate for the technological delay during the war. Towards the early 1960s, the company became aware of the necessity of strengthening its soda branch, since the liberalisation of glass imports was approaching, and this would cause competition in the glass branch.

Financial resources were spent in soda branch,[37] which resulted in the formation of a divisional structure, and eventually management decentralisation. A management committee was formed in 1957, when the functional structure was adopted. However, once the top management was established, managing directors were released from the tasks of the departmental managers. Divisionalisation was also initiated by the need to change production oriented organisation into a market oriented one.

The glass market which had expanded by the mid-1960s was stable, but its growth rate declined towards the end of the 1960s. The chemical branch grew more rapidly. *Asahi Glass* diverted its main interest from soda to petro-chemicals, and investment in new areas it had started in from the early 1970s.[38] The high output of the chemical branches in the 1970s, however, was not accompanied by profit. Profit came from speciality glass for automobiles and televisions, and financial resources were again directed to the glass branch. The Glass Headquarters became a large division, and was divided into a number of product divisions. Their number continued to increase until the early 1980s. The managing directors, who became heads of headquarters, were again released from operating responsibilities and made to specialise in top management.

A decentralised management was common among the firms in paper manufacturing, printing, and materials, particularly in the early post-war era. A greater part of them centralised their management control, accompanied by the transfer of coordinating functions from factories to the head office. Paper and materials firms showed this in their strategy and structures. The rapid development of paper manufacturing companies ended in the early post-war era, while glass and tyre companies only began to develop in the 1960s. The supply of raw materials, and eventually the coordination of the flow of raw materials to the semi-finished products, was the main strategic and structural problem. Later, these companies intensified downstream branches and began to diversify into processing their semi-products. Divisionalisation did not seem to be a general trend of the organisational development in this group of companies, though some of them partially adopted the divisional structure. In 1960 all were administered through varied functional structures. In 1970 two were based on a multidivisional structure, and two others had partially accepted the divisional form. During ten years prior to 1980, five of them changed their structures, but the number of distribution in each form remained the same. Three went along with divisionalisation and two discarded it. The reason for the instability in the divisional structure of this group of companies can be explained from their difficulty in expanding into new fields of activities; their technical skills or markets are unapplicable to other products. Diversification through upward integration, such as that into wood from paper manufacturing or soda from glass, proved to be unprofitable and diversification into downward products was made by their subsidiaries which were equipped with managerial resources for particular purposes. Even of the firms, which were divisionalised in the 1970s, many return to the functional form.

The two printing companies have evolved a multidivisional structure by geography, in which central control was weak and inter-divisional coordination was underdeveloped. Certainly such a structure was sufficient due to the easy access to local markets and by cheap transportation costs. However, divisions were formed around local factories, and even within the same localities, the formation of the divisional structure in printing companies required a spontaneous process, and the strength of the production units continued long after its formation. Such spontaneous growth was possible throughout the larger part of the three decades since 1950. Probably these factors placed restrictions on the diversification of these companies through upward integration, which required a central reallocation of financial resources. These companies were characterised by their extensive use of subcontracting companies. Here again, instead of well organised internal hierarchies, a much looser organisation is used for the coordination of the flow of goods. Recently these companies added some product divisions for new fields of activities, though printing still holds dominant share in their total sales.

6.4 STEEL COMPANIES

The rapid development of the post-war Japanese steel industry is often quoted as symbolizing the rapid growth of the post-war Japanese economy. In 1950, Japan produced 5 million tons of crude steel, and production went up to 92 million tons by 1970. Such rapid increases in production ceased as the rapid growth of the Japanese economy came to an end: in 1980, in spite of the growth in exports during the 1970s, production of crude steel remained at 96 million tons. Such growth of steel production was attained by three series of rationalisations, the introduction of foreign technologies, intensive investment, the purchasing of low cost materials, extremely most efficient coordination of the flow of production process. Among the nine concerns of 1970, there were five major integrated steel companies. Their development was started by the setting up of large-scale furnaces and integrating the whole processes of steel making. The market share of these five companies accounted for approximately 80 per cent of the total crude steel production in Japan in 1970; a figure as high as that of 1950. The development of the scale economy of production is well documented: in 1950 17 of these companies' production units produced less than 4 million tons of crude steel, but in 1970 21 of these companies' production units produced 73 million tons. The other four firms were producers of special or alloy steels.

The industrial structure of steel also symbolized the post-war Japanese economy. Excessive competition and government intervention were typical here. The dissolution of *Nippon Steel*, which broke the division of labour between it, the pig iron supplier, and other steel manufacturers, was one of the causes of such competition. The Ministry of Trade and Industry controlled the rationalisation plans and investment policies, first in order to promptly attain the reconstruction of the Japanese economy, then to equip the steel companies with international competitive power. The Public Sales System, according to which all the steel companies simultaneously announced their production quantities and prices two months in advance, has often been seen as a kind of cartel.

Other aspects of the business environment, however, had a much stronger effect on the management structure of the steel companies. Forward integration into raw materials and their transportation were very important as was the case in other semi-finished product industries. To secure low costs and stable supplies of iron ores, steel companies often invested in overseas mines, though such investment was not remarkable until 1970. More commonly, steel companies endeavoured to buy the cheapest iron ores from all over the world, rather than being limited to always importing them from particular regions. After 1970 iron ores which were developed by the Japanese agencies began to increase their share in total ore imports. This ratio was around 24 per cent in the early 1970s, but had doubled by the mid-1970s. Overseas mines were developed by the joint activities between several steel companies and trading companies rather than the direct investment by individual steel companies. Throughout the first two decades, efforts were made in the location and lay-out of large-scale integrated steel mills. Large-scale special-purpose ships for ore transport were built, though they were gradually replaced by multi-purpose ships. Steel mills were sited at the sea-side to economise transportation costs, and the continuing processes of steel making were laid out as efficiently as possible to secure a fluent flow of materials and economize the fuel costs. Similar systems were found among secondary steel processing. These downward processes were the territory of small processing companies, which had been affiliated with one of the major five companies. These processing companies were gathered in industrial parks near large cities for convenience of transportation and easy access to the market. Marketing agents often coordinated these continuing stages. In the sales of primary steel products, for instance, the major steel companies nominated wholesale merchants for them. Some of these wholesalers were general trading companies, and others were specialised trading companies affiliated with a particular steel company. These wholesalers often employed special agents who acted as middlemen between them and the customers. Some of the functions of marketing and of collecting bills were carried out by these wholesalers. In many cases only large-scale orders from automobile companies were dealt with directly by the steel companies. The sales of *Kawasaki Steel*, for instance, was approximately 900 000 million yen in 1975. The sales of the sole-sales trading companies affiliated with *Kawasaki Steel* were slightly more than the above figure, and the sales of the secondary processing companies affiliated with *Kawasaki Steel* were approximately three-quarters of that of the *Kawasaki Steel*. The same goods were counted three or four times as they passed the various stages from ore handling to the finished products. In this section, the internal hierarchies of the steel companies are examined, and special reference will be made to the influence of their strategy on the coordination of the flow of goods.

Kawasaki Steel,[39] having its origin in the steel making department of *Kawasaki Shipbuilding*, was separated as an open-hearth steel firm immediately after the war. Backward integration of iron-smelting and the expansion of scale were its major lines of development, and the firm maintained a functional structure as the basic form of its organisation until it was partly divisionalised in the 1970s.

During the period of reconstruction and reorganisation of business enterprises after the Second World War, Y. Nishiyama, one of the directors of *Kawasaki Heavy Industries*, proposed that the disparities in profit and production process between steel and shipbuilding were too large to be managed by a single enterprise. Destined to become the president of *Kawasaki Steel*, he further insisted that the responsibility of each branch should be clarified. The vertical integration of steel and shipbuilding was thus abandoned. When the first rationalisation scheme of the steel industry was put into action in 1951, *Kawasaki Steel* planned to construct its own blast furnaces and supply pig iron by themselves. The firm aimed at the expansion of steel and rolling facilities at the same time. Nishiyama preferred the American style of mass-production of steel by integrated steel mills instead of the traditional European one. The new blast furnace in Chiba, which had met with wide opposition before its completion, soon became the model for Japanese steel companies, and particularly for other open-hearth furnace companies because of its giant scale and the integration of its steel making processes. The second rationalisation, beginning in 1956, required large-scale investment in rolling processes, but in fact heavy expenditure was made in blast furnaces as well.[40] The scale of the third rationalisation was not so large when compared with those of other steel companies, but its early aggressive strategy contributed to its high growth rate and high profitability in the 1960s.

A strong top management was necessary for the rapid growth of the firm. Their large-scale plants in Chiba autonomously formed a second head office in Tokyo for geographical reasons. However, to unify lines of command, this quasi-regional structure was reorganised into a normal functional structure in 1959. Then followed the formation of the top management organisation in place of president Nishiyama's strong leadership. The meeting of senior managing directors, the executive committee, was delegated with executive authorities in important matters and supported by the planning department. Four vice-presidents were appointed to supplement the deficiencies of the previous one-man management. Rapid growth also required a change in the company's downward strategy and organisation. Having originated in the shipbuilding industry, *Kawasaki Steel*'s early main products were steel plates. A steel trading subsidiary was set up to sell products on a mass-marketing scale, and in the late 1950s several companies in the secondary processing of steel were affiliated with *Kawasaki Steel*. Within the company, older production units were made to specialise in high-grade product lines. Purchasing also changed substantially. Traditionally it was an open-hearth company, and raw materials were supplied either in the form of pig iron or slug. *Kawasaki Steel*'s new integrated mills required a large amount of iron ores, and as the necessity increased imports of ores from Asian and

South American countries, using special purpose ships were begun. These ships were constructed in conjunction with other steel companies and shipping companies.

Expansion continued after the mid-1960s. A second large production unit was built during the 1960s in expectation of the increasing demand for steel products. Fixed capital investment between 1965 and 1973 amounted to 9144 billion yen,[41] and the company's sales increased five times. Exports played an important part in this rapid growth. This expansion has long fixed its organisational structure in the following form: just below the top management there were several production units and a relatively simple head office consisting of financing, sales, procurement, and technology functions. The position of the production units became rather more important as they grew larger. The sales function became more important in face of severe competition brought about by the merger between *Yawata Steel* and *Fuji Steel*. The sales department was divided into the line and the staff, and the former was further reorganised into Domestic and Overseas headquarters. Under each Headquarters, departments were formed according to product lines, and department managers took charge of profit responsibility. Important changes were also observed in purchasing. Procurement of ores and other materials was made separately by each factory. In 1966 these functions were consolidated in the head office, and control was centralised. Local necessities were now centrally coordinated and purchase prices came to be centrally negotiated. Another rationalisation was also made in purchasing. Until the mid-1960s, the company had employed special purpose ships for ore transportation, which meant that the ships were actually fully loaded for half of a voyage. Thus, to lower transportation costs, they began to use these ships for other purposes on the unloaded portion of voyage. The senior managing directors meeting was dissolved, and the management committee was founded, and it was this through which the firm attempted both coordination extending to several departments, and monitoring. After the oil-crisis the company started to strengthen engineering interests in the face of the severe environment of the steel industry. They also changed purchasing policies from one of buying the cheapest possible materials from all over the world to one of developing overseas mines in areas such as Australia, Canada, Brazil and the USSR, and importing the products of these jointly with other steel companies.

Sumitomo Metal Industries[42] developed along the lines of expansion and specialisation through vertical integration. Steel pipes, forging products, rolling stock, and nonferrous metals were the company's main products in 1950. The integration of blast iron-smelting furnaces took place through the acquisition of an independent iron smelting firm; up to that point *Sumitomo Metal* had used scrap iron as its raw materials. The chief motive of this acquisition was to secure a supply of cheap materials, and to reduce the cost of steel products to international price levels. Relatively cheap American slugs could no longer be relied upon due to rises in transportation costs. Mergers as opposed to building new indigenous blast furnaces were chosen as the first step in getting low cost which quality pig iron. Such measures were believed to be a more reasonable way of acquiring new technical skills, and they enabled *Sumitomo Metal* to concentrate their own managerial resources on rolling processes.

A thorough rationalisation plan aimed at increasing the company's competitive power started in 1956, the main target of this was to the setting up of a large-scale and vertically integrated steel plant. According to the rationalisation plan of 1956, 60 per cent of capital expenditure was to be used for this newly integrated steel plant, while less than 10 per cent was allocated to nonferrous metal branches. Consequently, the company specialised in steel manufacturing. The production of steel tubes and ordnance had been the core between the steel and the nonferrous metals branches of the firm, and this type of diversification had once given stability in performance when the size of the business was small. However, these two industrial branches lost their common technology and market, and these differences became larger in the post-war period.

The organisational structure of the company in the early post-war era was a mixed form of the functional and the divisional systems. In the mid-1950s, aircraft and magnet branches were divisionalised, and the rolling stock branch was made a division in the late 1950s. Then came the separation of these non-steel branches and by 1963 these divisions as well as nonferrous metal interests were handed over to the newly formed companies.

The evolution of the top management organisation was gradual; the board of directors, which had been set up in 1950, was to wait fifteen years before having its own written rules order. The duties of the management committee, set up in 1955, were also made clear by the same rules, although there was still some ambiguity concerning the authority of decision making. Some important matters were discussed by the board, while others were dealt with by the management committee. For long-range planning, a controlling department, in charge of controlling and budgeting, was set up in 1957. In spite of these centralising measures, each production unit retained its autonomy power. These production units were made profit centres, though they were not divisions by products. Such autonomous and centrifugal tendencies of the production units were coordinated by 'the Meeting of the Factory Managers', which, in a sense, laid importance on the position of the production units.

An aggressive policy hidden behind moderate ideas, which always characterised the performance of the firms of the *Sumitomo Group*, was revealed in the recession of the mid-1960s, when governmental guidance in adjusting the quantity of steel production started to show results. *Sumitomo Metal* did not agree to this guideline and took action to build a new steel plant. The company decided to construct huge-scale furnaces and mills to achieve rationalisation and the cost reduction. Financial resources were concentrated on the scrap-and-build of blast furnaces.[43] The output of forging and rolling stock branches decreased. Sales increased six times in the eight years after 1965, and this drastic expansion necessitated the reinforcement of the top management again. A committee of the highest level managers, consisting of the president, the vice-president and the senior-managing director, was set up. After 1975 demands for steel pipes for oil extraction ceased, and the sales of *Sumitomo Metal* which were highly dependent upon exports, began to stagnate. However, the forging and rolling stock branches revived, and the company introduced the divisional structure into some of its activities.

Like *Kawasaki Steel* and *Sumitomo Metal Industries*, *Kobe Steel*[44] had been a steel manufacturer in the pre-war period, and had been based on open-hearth furnaces. Unlike the former two, *Kobe Steel* began to diversify after it integrated iron making process, and eventually adopted a multidivisional structure. Despite similarities observed in the early 1950s, the management strategies of *Kobe Steel* and the organisational problems which *Kobe Steel* had to deal with during the three ensuing decades differed much from those of the other two companies. The multidivisional system had been used until the late 1970s, when the company introduced the functional structure into the main part of its activities.

Kobe Steel separated its electrical appliance, nonferrous metals and wire branches during its post-war reconstruction, and diversified modestly in steel and engineering. In the early 1950s, both steel and engineering products amounted to one-third of the firm's total sales respectively. At that time *Kobe Steel* depended on *Fuji Iron & Steel* for its supply of pig iron. To secure thus supply *Kobe Steel* first joined the management of an iron smelting company, then built their own blast furnaces in the late 1950s. In spite of such large investment in iron and steel branches,[45] diversification was maintained.

The firm had reorganised its production unit structure into a functional one by 1950, and management tasks at the level immediately below the top were specialised by function for each of the product lines, though the production units still belonged directly to the top and not to these production departments. The decentralising trends inherent in such a structure were well evident and were counter-balanced by the formation of a planning department in the head office. Then the company adopted the multidivisional structure in 1955. Having been engaged in manufacturing of a wide range of products, each product line had its own functional departments. In addition, there were subsidiaries and production units. Such complex business caused disorder in the line of command; each factory could specialise in a particular product line, but its products were often the materials of other factories of the same firm. The allocation of production units among each division was a difficult task but was solved by the introduction of the transfer price system. Each of the four divisions took charge of production and sales, and was made a profit centre. The board of directors decided the fundamental policy of the company, while the management committee, though informal, discussed its execution. After the introduction of the multidivisional structure, however, it was gradually noticed that the delegation of authority to the division level was incomplete. Division managers were members of the top management at the same time, and the general staff, in charge of the planning of strategy, organisation and budget, were at the same time division staff.

After 1965, when other steel companies concentrated their financial resources on steel interests, *Kobe Steel* continued to allocate its resources equally among steel, engineering, and nonferrous metals.[46] The company was belated in enlarging its steel capacity, and as a result, the growth rate of its sales fell behind those of others. In steel, the company mainly produced traditional wire rods, but was weak in the growing market of steel pipes or plates. At the end of the 1960s, the company began to develop its steel interest on a full scale. First, *Amagasaki Seitetsu*, an integrated steel company, was acquired to strengthen the plates and bars branches. Then at great expense a large-scale steel plant was founded in Kakogawa.

The autonomous growth of each division and the strategic development of steel interest sometimes conflicted and the divergence of engineering products went beyond the organic relationship among divisions. Heavy investment in the steel branch was, once started, carried out at the cost of other branches, and made the expansion of other branches fall behind other companies, and this pushed the company to incessant investment. Furthermore, one of the advantages of a diversified enterprise, i.e. one branch being able to support others in times of a slump, was no longer functioning because fluctuation had begun to occur simultaneously. Organisational responses to this new situation were as follows; when *Amagasaki Seitetsu* was acquired, it was organised as the Second Steel Division. Then product lines of *Amagasaki* and *Kobe*'s were consolidated in the early 1970s. In the mid-1970s the structure was reformed to strengthen the organic relationship among product lines. One of the reasons behind this reform came from outside of the company; the market for systematised products requiring various sorts of technologies had emerged. The multidivisional structure was dissolved, and the steel division was divided into the production and sales headquarters. However, the engineering branches remained as divisions connecting themselves organically with steel production.

Nippon Kokan[47] had integrated vertically by 1950, having at first been engaged in iron-smelting, shipbuilding, and heavy engineering. The company organised a joint purchasing committee with two other integrated steel companies in 1952 to secure supplies of iron ores, and then developed overseas mines in India, Brazil, and Australia. However until the early 1970s, the company imported its materials from every possible part of the world, and tried to buy ores on long term contracts. The company moved into a multidivisional form in 1970, after which there were also several periods of fundamental changes during the 1970s.

The organisational structure which coordinated the continuing processes evolved from a typical functional/line one. Below the board, each of the production units, the trading and the financing departments of the head office were formed. The head office gradually grew large through being equipped with the management committee and a planning department. Thus the centrifugal tendency of each production unit was checked. The steel and the shipbuilding branches developed alternately. The rationalisation of the steel branch started in the early 1950s, *Nippon Kokan* reconstructed rolling equipments, which costed 183 billion yen, or two-thirds of the total investment of the first half of the 1950s.[48] During the steel industry slump between 1956 and 1958, the shipbuilding branch grew large. Then diversification into building materials and other engineering products, and the expansion and integration of steel production all took place simultaneously. From the early 1960s, diversification into secondary steel products was carried out by subsidiaries. However, the steel branch began to require huge amounts of capital both in absolute terms and in comparison to other branches. Thus, during the Third Rationalisation of the early 1960s, whose main purpose was to improve the financial position of steel companies, *Nippon Kokan* had to concentrate its financial resources on its steel interests. Diversification into secondary steel products, which cost a great deal, had to be carried out by subsidiaries. As a result, 98 per cent of expenditure was directed to the steel interests between 1960 and 1965,[49] though the share of heavy engineering products in total sales did not decline. The organisational reforms between 1955 and 1964 proceeded along with the reinforcement of the steel interest. When the Mitzue Steel Works was built in the late 1950s, the top management was strengthened. The managing directors were charged with the line functions, while control, coordination and monitoring of factories were centralised in the controlling department. The self-supporting system of the shipbuilding department was maintained, and this made the shipbuilding department a kind of division because it autonomously carried out planning, sales, and production functions. Even the operation of the production units was transferred to the shipbuilding headquarters. When a second steel works was built, the planning and inquiry department was formed, and production, cost, and budgetary management were centralised in the Management Department of the general office.

In the process of recovery from the slump of the mid-1960s, the company developed its steel interest on the one hand, and began to build a large-scale shipyard on the other. The latter expanded substantially, and its production capacity, if its affiliated company is included, became the third largest of Japanese shipbuilding companies. The heavy engineering branch was expected to become the third main branch of the company; shipbuilding depended heavily on overseas markets while demand for heavy engineering products came from the domestic market. In 1970 these three branches were reorganised into headquarters; all were made divisions with production and sales controlled by their own headquarters, and with profit responsibility. The general office took charge of planning and control, and the production units and branch sales offices belonged directly to the general office. The steel branch was soon divided into two functional headquarters. The top management organisation was composed of two committees, one which discussed important matters of the whole company, and the other which made decisions and coordinated the headquarters. In 1973 the multidivisional structure was introduced for the second time, and the three divisions which had once been made headquarters in 1970, were charged with management, planning and control. The steel division was equipped with its own production units, though other divisions lacked them. Meanwhile the share of shipbuilding declined in the 1970s, and finally in 1979 the shipbuilding and the heavy engineering divisions were consolidated. This reorganisation was carried out not only to meet the decreasing demand for shipbuilding but to meet the changing *nature* of demand. With this reorganisation, the new division came directly to control its production units.

Nippon Steel[50] was formed in 1969 by the merger between two large-scale integrated steel companies, both of which had themselves come into existence as a result of the dissolution of the former *Nippon Steel* in 1950. Both of the forerunners of the present *Nippon Steel* were administered through a functional/line structure, and after the merger the new company partially adopted a divisional form.

One of its partners, *Yawata Iron & Steel* had been the largest steel company in Japan, though it was a single unit firm for the first five years following dissolution. Throughout the 1940s, this works was much behind in modernising its equipment, and had to start with the introduction of foreign technologies and the reconstruction of idle furnaces. The replacement of rolling and drawing facilities soon led the company to both improve the lay-out of factories and construct new iron works. The high production cost of *Yawata Iron & Steel*, however, was not only due to its superannuated equipment, but, as was gradually noticed, to the type of management. Although this *Yawata* had only one iron works, it was in turn divided up into various factories and departments, and each of these such branches constituted a semi-independent managerial unit. Centralisation and the adoption of a functionally departmentalised structure in the early 1950s created the basic framework of its new organisation. The Controlling Bureau, in charge of planning and adjustment of every kind of problem, was formed in the works in 1952. In the head office the management committee was established and its members were separated from departmental tasks. Thus the organisational structure was composed of the head office in charge of financing, sales and the staff function, and of one iron works consisting of the Controlling Bureau and various factories. The controlling function became much stronger, because an auditing section was formed in the head office and the financing department was divided into financing and budgeting departments.

Between 1955 and 1964, *Yawata* planned a series of expansion projects including a new large-scale integrated ironworks. Nearly 4000 billion yen (400 million pounds) was invested in fixed equipment,[51] and such expansion elevated the company to the world's fourth largest steel producing firm. Strong production units had to be balanced by strong top management in order to meet increasing competition among steel companies. A senior management committee was formed in addition to the existing management committee, and the former was charged with making decisions on the company's basic policies, while the latter was engaged in the execution of such policies.

Fuji Iron & Steel was another partner in the formation of *Nippon Steel*. This company succeeded four production units of the former *Nippon Steel*, and acquired a large production capacity of pig iron. Capital expenditure was directed to rolling facilities in the first half of the 1950s. The firm began to affiliate secondary steel products companies during the same period. Its production units were distantly located in various parts of the country. The head office had the trading and the technology functions, while each production unit belonged directly to the top management. The first thing *Fuji Iron & Steel* had to do was to unify the accounting methods of the production units, which had all been different from each other, and to introduce a profit responsibility system to each ironworks. Measures to redress the balance of the various ironmaking processes were continuously taken in the latter half of the 1950s, and the weakest process, that of rolling, became the most important area of investment.[52] In production quantity, the company did not show a remarkable expansion.

From the beginning of the 1960s, the company turned to an expansion strategy of acquiring of a large subsidiary and further investment in the rolling process. The top management of *Fuji Iron & Steel* gradually developed from the early 1960s. The planning committee, consisting of the president, vice-president, managing directors and the president of *Tokai Seitetsu*, which was a joint venture with the local interests, was formed to deal with important matters. The management committee was formed by the managing directors in Tokyo. In 1962 the number of vice-presidents was increased to six.

Half of these were managers of production units. They were all made the representatives of the company, who, by their own judgement, dealt with raw materials, engaged in negotiations with local councils, and hired workers.

The merger of these two companies has often been justified as follows: steel companies had to increase their international competitive power, intensify their research and development, and avoid the danger of duplicate investment. These two companies had their origins in the same forerunner, i.e. *Nippon Steel*, and resembled each other in terms of scale and product lines. Interlocking directorships began in 1963. The new company had to complete consolidation of the management structures of prior companies, and cope with the new situation in the steel industry where over-supply was becoming serious. The new company had to reconsider changing its expansion scheme and reducing costs. A well-organised system of sales, production and administration was planned, with the intention of rationalising the allocation of product lines and of transport among regions. However, each production unit was very large and geographically separated from the head office. It was these iron works that constituted the basic units of administration. To solve these problems, the new firm intensified the highest level management by concentrating decision making in the president and vice-presidents. This structure restrained new investment, the greater part of which was allocated to engineering branches.[53]

Nisshin Steel[54] was formed by the merger of two iron processing companies. One of the forerunners, *Nippon Teppan* (Japan Iron Plate), produced rolled and galvanised steel sheets. In the latter half of the 1950s, it planned to embark on the production of stainless steel, which was at that time quite new to the Japanese market. Raw materials were supplied by *Yawata Iron & Steel*. *Nichia Seiko* (*Nichia Steel*), the other partner of the merger, was an open-hearth and rolling company, whose materials were again supplied by *Yawata Steel*. *Nichia Seiko* started as a zinc sheet processor, but to secure a stable supply of steel sheet it moved backwards into steel making processes and gradually discarded tertiary processing branches. After the war, the company suffered from insufficient supplies of pig iron the same as other open-hearth or rolling mills such as *Nippon Teppan*. The relationship between these two companies and *Yawata Steel* became close in the 1950s. To ensure a stable supply of materials, primary and secondary processing companies affiliated themselves with one of the six big companies. Under the pressure of slump in the late 1950s, a complementary relationship between these two subsidiaries of *Yawata Steel* was sought to avoid duplicate investment. The organisational, personnel, and equipment problems accompanied by the merger were solved by the intervention of *Yawata*.

The management structure of *Nippon Teppan* was an incomplete functional one, consisting of three factories, plus sales and finance departments. *Nichia Seiko*'s was an incomplete functional structure, consisting of several factories, sales and financial departments. The head office of *Nichia Seiko* was placed in its oldest factory, while the sales department formed a branch office. The leading position of the production units, characteristic since the late 1920s and accelerated by the introduction of the quasi-divisional system of 1942, was reduced by the formation of the planning department in 1960, the year following the merger. The head office took over production planning, and also began to coordinate technology and sales.

The strategy of *Nisshin Seiko* changed several times since its formation in 1959. The period just after the merger saw a rapid increase in demand, and the new company concentrated on the integrated production of stainless steel. To cope with giant steel companies with blast furnaces, the company modified its long-range plan and made inroads into constructing its own blast furnace. As soon as the new plant was built however, the company had to change their policy into one of forward integration, so that they did not have to compete with such giant steel companies. During the slump of the Japanese economy in the mid-1960s, the company enjoyed high profit levels, and surplus financial resources were directed to the extension of blast furnaces and the conversion of open-hearth furnaces into converters. Investment in rolling facilities amounted to a substantial figure when compared with that of the giant steel companies,[55] while expenditure on blast furnaces was minimal.

When the company was faced with the slump of the late 1960s, its expansion strategy had to be re-examined. The members of the top management were replaced. A new president was sent from *Yawata Steel* and the vice-president from *Sanwa Bank*. The new policy placed its emphasis on special steel for the third time. Organisation followed this strategic change. At the top management level, a management committee with planning and controlling staff was introduced. The functional/line structure was reformed into the functional headquarters system, in which each functional headquarters was made a profit centre. The production units came under the control of the production headquarters, and were reallocated with a particular line of products instead of various kinds of products. The research and development function which had previously belonged to each production unit was centralised to form a research and development headquarters. These functional headquarters were delegated with some of those managerial functions which had formerly belonged to the president. This structure however, soon reverted to the former one, in which the heads of each production unit directly reported to the top management.

Daido Steel[56] evolved as a special steel company after several periods of mergers and reorganisation of its works. After the war, the present *Daido* succeeded eight factories of the former *Daido Steel*, though the new company had to dispose of their steel plate branches. The factories *Daido* inherited were small and located separately from each other. Acquisitions were made between 1955 and 1964, and these were followed by the rationalisation of redundancies and the reallocation of product lines among factories. Investment was concentrated on the development of special steel products. The organisational structure evolved from a simple functional/line one, as was typical among metal companies, then moved into a multidivisional structure in 1960, and once again returned to the functional form in 1967, and was again partly divisionalised by 1970.

The demand for special steel came from the increasing production of automobiles. *Daido* had gone through several series of mergers by the mid-1960s and had rationalised its own equipment together with that of the acquired firms. The firm set about specialising each of its production unit into particular product lines. (for example, Tsukiji Works was made to specialise in forging and Takakura Works in machinery and instruments.) On the other hand, the company built a new steel works adjoining *Tokai Seitetsu*, which had blast furnaces. The scrap iron which they used for the production of ordinary steel proved to be insufficient for that of special steel, so that they had to look to an integrated steel company for material supplies.

Organisational reform followed this reallocation of product lines. Product divisions were formed by being centred around the production units. The main purpose of divisionalisation was to introduce a self-supporting system into each product line. Management centralisation was an important source of expansion in *Daido*. Demand for special steel frequently fluctuated along with fluctuations in the automobile industry, and in the mid-1960s came a severe market recession. To reduce production costs and improve productivity, rationalisation on the shop floor level was taken, but in the long run a shift to high-grade products became central policy. Diversification into fabricated steel products was restrained and financial resources were concentrated on special steel branches.[57]

The organisational structure saw frequent changes in the latter half of the 1960s. In 1967, the multidivisional structure was abolished, and four sales departments divided by products; the sales control department and the production units stood in a line below the top management. However, non-steel branches were gradually reorganised into divisions again, and by 1969 three divisions had been formed. A functionally based structure took charge of the steel products branch, which were beginning to hold a dominant place in the company. A production control department was formed to supply staff services to individual steel works which were in turn directly administered by the top management. A mixture of divisional and functional principles is observed here, and this structure did not change much in spite of the merger in 1976. The problems of the over-supply of special steel products was solved by the merger of three companies affiliated with *Nippon Steel*, and *Daido Steel* became the nucleus of this merger. The production department was finally established as the line and three factories were consolidated into one. Since the merger the new firm modified its strategy which had previously depended heavily on special steel, and concentration and rationalisation in forging interests became effective towards the end of the 1970s.

The Japan Steel Works[58] was set up as a joint venture among *Vickers*, *Armstrong* and *Hokkaido Colliery & Steamship*, and had been engaged in armament production in the pre-war years. Its management structure from a production unit form in 1950 to a functional one in the early 1950s. The functional structure remained for a long period of time until the late 1970s, when the multidivisional structure was introduced.

In the early post-war period, the company carried out a mass dismissal of its employees in order to switch from armaments and heavy engineering to steel products. Each of their production units had fully-fledged functions and were each made into profit centres. In the early 1950s the firm centralised its management by forming a management committee and the planning office, and by introducing the controller system. In spite of these measures, the production units were still made profit centres, and they maintained their leading position throughout the company. The firm's slow development, depending as it did on steel and forging products, was improved by a new policy in the early 1960s, the major purpose of which was to develop the firm's engineering interests. The *Mitsui* group supported this strategic change, and it was followed by increasing investment in the downward branches of the firm.[59] By then the firm had set about rearranging its product lines among production units. Together with the introduction of long-range planning in the first half of the 1960s, the head office gradually established a place for itself in the industry.

The late 1960s brought with them a rapid growth in the company's sales. High-value-added machinery and construction materials contributed to this growth. Financial resources were concentrated in one of the production units[60] where the firm attempted forward integration into steel construction products. There was no fundamental change in the company's organisational structure until the late 1970s. The four production units took the lead of the whole company and continued to remain as profit centres. The sales function, which had been divided into departments by product lines, was consolidated and reorganised into a headquarters, and the research and development function was made to constitute a separate headquarters, and purchasing was also centralised. Unlike the ordinary steel companies which integrated blast furnaces, acquiring raw materials was not difficult for *Japan Steel Works* as they were supplied in the form of slug, and gradually from overseas. However, as the firm's products shifted from forgings to engineering, the supply of parts and components became more important. A central purchasing committee was formed, and suppliers were organised into groups to maintain mutual effective collaboration. As a background to this management centralisation, marketing became obviously important in the course of the slump.

The growth of the company in the first half of the 1970s depended on the expansion of overseas markets, and when exports declined growth thus began to slow down. In 1977, autonomous production units were revised for rapid adjustment to the changing market. A production headquarters was set up to administer these production units, and the management committee, from which production managers were excluded, was built up to discuss the allocation of managerial resources. The new production headquarters became a profit centre and a Plant Division was set up. Divisional structure was further extended to the whole company in 1980. Though the company gradually moved forwards the multidivisional structure, divisional profit responsibility had not been established yet. Four division headquarters were set up and they assumed production and sales functions together with profit responsibility, while the control headquarters was made to monitor the performance of these divisions.

Hitachi Metals[61] has its origin in an iron-casting company which was acquired by *Hitachi* in 1937. In 1956 *Hitachi Metals* was separated from *Hitachi*. Product lines consisted in special steel and secondary steel products, and the firm concentrated primarily on steel fabrication branches. The management structure was composed of several departments by products which were mainly engaged in sales, as well as several factories and branch offices. The chairman of *Hitachi* also assumed the chairmanship of *Hitachi Metals*, though there was no interlocking directorship between these two companies. Unlike other special steel companies, *Hitachi Metals* was not severely hit by the recession of 1965 and the slump of the early 1970s. The company retreated from mass-produced goods relatively early, and promoted diversification into highly processed products, as well as specialisation into high-grade products in special steel. Eventually it gained a substantial market share in products such as joint, malleable castings, and rolls. After 1965 each production unit was made to specialise in one or two of these product lines. Based on specialisation of operating units in sales and production, *Hitachi Metals* introduced the multidivisional structure in 1972. The main purpose of this organisational reform was explained as being to unify the activities of factories and the sales function of each product line, and to clarify the profit responsibility for each product. Division managers were appointed from among the vice-presidents and managing directors. Below the division managers came production units and the sales department (in other words, the direct line form remained after the introduction of the multidivisional structure). Increases in the number of product lines was not so prominent in the 1970s. Financial resources were not concentrated on one of these branches but were distributed among production units.[62] Each division worked at expanding itself. Exports increased enormously starting at the end of the 1960s to the mid-1970s, but were gradually replaced by overseas production. These activities were operated through the Overseas Headquarters. The position of the production units was high within the divisions. Each division did not have a production department but did have a planning department and one or more factories. The division managers, who were at the same time managing or senior managing directors of the head office, were often factory managers.

The organisational structures of the steel companies developed along similar lines throughout the period 1950–80. Their organisation started from either a function/line or production-unit forms, and retained these elements after these production units became large. They had a relatively small number of large production units to which a huge amount of financial and human resources were allocated. Naturally the control on these production units was beyond the power of the managers of the production department.

Diversification has been constrained until recently. Japanese steel companies competed to build huge integrated steel mills, in which almost all available fixed capital was invested. Some companies which diversified into other metals or metal fabricating separated these activities and specialised in steel production. Others tried to maintain diversification but the share of the steel production in their total output continued to increase. Even the special steel companies pursued the scale merit. The main organisational problems were in the efficient layout of the continuous production processes, and the coordination of the flow of goods and these were mostly solved on the factory level.

The timing of divisionalisation differed between companies, though most of the concerns partially adopted accepted the divisional structure by the end of the 1970s. *Kobe Steel* and *Daito Steel* adopted the multidivisional structure in the early post-war period, while *Nippon Steel Works* and *Hitachi Metals* adopted it in the 1970s. Initially the full multidivisional structure was introduced, though reorganised into a partially divisional system. Other companies began to develop engineering branches and since this required a different type of works from those of the steel mills, divisional form was introduced into these engineering interests in the 1970s. In the earlier period, much attention was paid to upward processes such as iron smelting and the integration of the whole processes of steel making. The supply of raw materials was important, and supplies were sought in various parts of the world, mostly on long term contract bases. Later the above mentioned integrated companies intensified their control over the supply of raw materials by investing in and developing ore mines abroad. Recently, large-scale integrated steel companies have embarked on downward branches, while special steel companies have inclined towards product differentiation and place much importance on high-graded products. The gradual decline of the steel industry hit special steel firms first, and the number of concerns listed as the largest firms decreased in the 1970s. The management structure changed more frequently along with this back-down. Whether successful or not, these were the backgrounds of the divisionalisation of Japan's steel companies. So far, their recent diversification has been limited to civil engineering. Indigenous diversification into secondary processing or metal fabricating is not widely observed because these are still carried out by their affiliated companies.

6.5 NONFERROUS METALS COMPANIES

Of eight companies which were classified in nonferrous metal industries, five were primarily engaged in mining and smelting. The products of these five companies were determined by the ore which they got either from their own mines or by buying up other mines. They were more or less diversified from the beginning into various kinds of nonferrous or precious metals. Their activities were limited to the upward stages of metal industries in 1950. As the mining companies were the main branches of the pre-war *Zaibatsu*, each of these mining companies was divided into several new companies in the early post-war period. Technological delay during the War necessitated that they introduce foreign technologies for smelting, or collecting by-products such as sulfuric acid or zinc. Immediately after these innovations the recovery of trade followed in 1951, and caused deficiencies in domestic ores. Two different strategies for maintaining stable supplies of ore developed at this point. One involved the continuation of pre-prospecting and domestic mine development and the other involved investment in foreign mines and supporting overseas mining companies technologically. Since the early 1960s, Japanese nonferrous metals companies began to embark on the downward stages of metal industries.

The second factor which influenced the organisational structure of mining and smelting companies was that they were multi-unit firms from the beginning of the period covered here. In the 1950s, each company consisted of two to 20 mining works, several smelting works, one or more refining and processing factories, and two or more business offices. The number of mines decreased starting in the 1960s, while the number of factories tended to increase. Having a large number of operating units which extended vertically over a wide range of processes raised a problem of coordination of flow of materials among these various branches. However, their development towards downward processes posed another problem, particularly of adapting themselves to diverged market needs.

The sales function of these firms make up the third factor which influenced their structures. Originally one of the firms sold directly to metal processing companies in its same grouping; another one was engaged in sales activities using its own sales network; the others utilised general trading companies in the same groupings. In spite of these varieties, they were multi-function firms from the beginning. All of them, however, came to use general trading companies in the 1950s, partly for financial reasons.

The remaining three concerns were metal fabricating firms from the beginning. The market for metal fabricating companies saw an enormous expansion in the early post-war years and they were able to develop within their primary product lines: wires and cables. Diversification was constrained at first. Since the mid-1960s, the share of new products was gradually increased and by 1980 two of them had become fully diversified by making use of their technology in handling materials.

Mitsui Mining and Smelting[63] had a strong interest in zinc, the production of which amounted to approximately half of the firm's total sales in the early 1950s. The firm first made great efforts in mechanising its mining branch, though substantial capital had to be invested in the modernisation of smelting equipment. The company had a large zinc mine, which supplied a greater part of its ores for smelting zinc and lead, although scrap zinc and lead were used from the early post-war period. By the mid 1960s the output of copper, processed metals and chemical products had increased. The copper ores were purchased from outside the company. Interests in processed metals were developed by acquisition. The basic form of the vertically integrated enterprise, consisting of mining, smelting and metal processing, was established by the early 1960s. These new policies necessitated an alteration in its management structure. The company used to be administered by a functional/line structure. In the early 1960s, its head office was reorganised into one consisting of trading, mining and smelting departments with two independent divisions by products. However, each of the mining and smelting works was directly controlled by the top management. The downward branches which were acquired by the merger of 1962 were organised into divisions. These works and divisions were made profit centres, and were given a highly independent status.

From the mid-1960s, capital was invested in mining, metal processing, and overseas subsidiaries, in addition to smelting.[64] This resulted in the increase of the output of zinc on the one hand, and of processed metals on the other. The output of ores from *Mitsui*'s own mines continued to increase, though the amount of ores bought from outside increased more rapidly and accounted for approximately a quarter of the company's ore consumption by the early 1970s. In comparison with other mining companies, which eventually withdrew from mining interests, *Mitsui Mining and Smelting* continued to depend on its own mines, and the world largest zinc company in the early 1970s. The company's profits, however, were dependent upon the international price of zinc, which fluctuated greatly. To ensure stable profits, the firm adopted a new strategy which strengthened the activities of the downward branches. In the long run, the company shifted its main field of activities to metal processing, while gradually dissolving a tight integration between mining and smelting activities. Then the firm reorganised its structure into one consisting of accounting, trading and technological headquarters, mining and smelting works, and four divisions in charge of metal processing.

Mitsubishi Metal Mining[65] came into being as the result of the dissolution of the former *Mitsubishi Mining*, and started business with metal mining, smelting, and metal processing branches with its 10 mines, 2 smelting works, and 4 factories. The high profits of the early 1950s were reinvested in *Mitsubishi Metal*'s power station and mines at home and abroad. Product lines were made up of most types of nonferrous metals though copper accounted for a majority of total sales. From the latter half of the 1950s, while continuing with prospecting and the development of mines, the company closed down its exhausted mines. Financial resources were equally allocated to the mining, smelting, and processing branches.[66] The metal processing branch which had originally consisted mainly of copper wire and other copper products, added alloy tools and industrial machinery to its product lines, and gradually increased its share in the total sales of the company. The management structure of the company started from an incomplete functional one consisting of both the head office with the sales and the production staff departments, and mines, smelting works and factories. The mining and the smelting departments were placed in the head office later, and their departmental managers were appointed from among the directors, though operating field-units reported directly and belonged to the top management.

As nonferrous metal materials began to lose their market, *Mitsubishi Metal* planned to strengthen its downward branches of metal processing. Inefficient domestic mines were closed down and between 1955 and 1964 investment was shifted from smelting to processing.[67] Through this new strategy the share of alloy tools and machinery in the total sales of *Mitsubishi Metal* increased rapidly towards the 1970s. This also influenced the form of the organisational structure. The metal processing branch was gradually separated from the existing organisation, and finally a Metal Processing Head-quarters was set up, consisting of several department by product lines with technology and sales functions, and sales offices. This was followed by the formation of the Development Headquarters in charge of atomic energy, and of the Mining Headquarters consisting of management, mining and overseas departments. The structure below the top management in the early 1970s was composed of the functional departments of metal smelting, finance, purchase and personnel, while the upward and downward processes lost their long-standing integration with the smelting process and formed semi-divisional units. Mines were further separated in the 1970s, and organisational reform continued; in the mid-1970s four divisions were set up: two in the metal processing headquarters and two that were independent. In 1976 the headquarters were abolished and five divisions were newly introduced. The smelting branch was finally divisionalised, with new production staff and sales function. Though incomplete, this divisional structure lasted one and a half years, and was further reorganised into five functional headquarters. The new management structure was again functional in the smelting branch, and was divisional in the upward and downward branches, though the latter sometimes lacked production or sales functions. Such rapid organisational reform in the 1970s suggests the difficulties in con-trolling the vertically integrated branches which were always under pressure of change. Furthermore, it became necessary to build up a strong top management in the 1970s. The managing directors, who had long been the heads of mines or of operating sub-units, were separated from the lines so as to be able to work as full-time general managers, and the planning or development departments were set up in the head office.

Sumitomo Metal Mining[68] separated its coal mining branch and started its post-war development with the reconstruction of its *Besshi Mines*, and the new acquisition of copper mines. These mines had been devastated by excessive exploitation during the war, and it was only after the mid-1950s that the company could change its main supply of raw materials from scrap copper to its own copper ores. For their own reconstruction, mining and smelting branches were made self-supporting profit centres. Like *Mitsui Mining & Smelting* and

Mitsubishi Metal, the organisational structure of *Sumitomo Metal Mining* evolved from a functional/line form, and later several divisions in charge of the downward levels of metal processing were added to its original form.

Differences in the management practices among the acquired mines had to be consolidated first. The firm set about centralising management on the works level. In spite of the development of home mines in the latter half of the 1950s and active investment in prospecting and mining, these fields appeared to be unprofitable. Gradually the supply of copper ores from its *Sumitomo* mines took the place of scrap copper. However, the supply of their own ores was still insufficient and was first replaced by imported ores in the nickel branch, and then by the mid 1960s in the copper branch as well. Existing domestic mines were closed down and excess assets were sold. These measures became necessary with the liberalisation of trade and consequent competitive threat. The cost of imported nickel was less than half the ores from *Sumitomo*'s own mines. In copper refining too, domestic production costs exceeded those of other countries. Organisational changes followed them. The general staff was formalised, and the production staffs such as the mining or the smelting departments were set up in the head office. Long-range plans were introduced in 1960 to reconsider existing operations. New operations such as building materials or electronic metals branches were divisionalised. The tasks of the management committee, which had been vague since its formation, were clarified so that it could act as the top management. All these changes had taken place by the mid 1960s. As the divisionalisation of new branches was slightly earlier than that of the former two companies, so was the start of the company's reconstruction in the 1960s. The development of metal processing branches through its own divisions or its subsidiaries was planned, but financial resources were, in practice, expanded to the mining and smelting branches in the first half of the 1960s, and the sales of new branches did not increase rapidly.[69]

After the mid-1960s the company had to reform itself drastically. The rise of the 'Resource Nationalism' gave rise to a restricted supply of raw materials while competition became severe in the smelting industry. To secure supplies of raw materials, the company began to invest in mines in Canada, Australia, Chile, and several other countries. Smelting capacity was also enlarged so as to be able to cope with foreign competition. Naturally, the company strived to make high value-added products. All its home mines, including *Besshi*

Mines, were closed down, and upward branches were reduced. Financial resources were put into metal processing and other new fields since 1974[70] and management planned to increase the sales of the new branches up to 40 per cent of the total sales, and this resulted in an actual increase to 30 per cent. The management structure was reorganised, too. In 1975, headquarters in charge of functions or product lines were set up. Related businesses were brought together, and made the unit of profit responsibility. Authority was further delegated to the headquarters either from the head office or from the operating units. In the general office, a planning and controlling headquarters was set up for the long-range planning and control. On the general management level, centralisation was promoted. Managing directors also held positions by which they could directly control the operating managers. Thus lines of authority and responsibility were made clear.

Nippon Mining[71] started as a mining company, having branched out into copper smelting and oil industries in the pre-war era. Unlike other mineral companies, it has adopted the full multidivisional structure since 1960. Their post-war reconstruction programme invested management resources in copper interests, but it was the refining and processing branches such as oil or alloyed metals that remarkably increased the company's profit. Its early management structure resembled that of other nonferrous metal companies except in its oil branches. The head office was divided into mining, smelting, trading and oil sales departments while its numerous production units belonged directly to the highest managers. The president's staff, referred to as the 'Consulting Room', engaged in the strategic planning, and the management advisory committee, consisting of the departmental managers, made proposals to the board.

The introduction of the multidivisional structure had its background in the strategic changes of the late 1950s. Following rationalisation and the separation of mining works, the firm developed its nonferrous metal smelting and processing as well as oil refining activities. In both of these branches, they preferred development of works on the coast for east transportaion of foreign raw materials to continued dependence on traditional refining works adjacent to mines. The multidivisional structure consisted of four division headquarters, namely those of mining, metals, oil, and metal processing. These division headquarters had their own trading and production management departments, and were made profit centres. At the same time the top management organisation was improved and staff services were unified in the Long-range Planning Committee. Through these measures, systematic business policies as opposed to the autonomous development of each of the industries became possible.

However, such a vertical-divisional structure brings about disintegration among the various levels from mining to metal processing, and allows each division to develop in its own way. It was planned to strengthen the mining interest by investing in overseas mines and in metal processing interest as well. In practice financial resources were at first allocated to four divisions, and then concentrated on oil and smelting branches.[72] The system of the divisional structure was reformed and the middle management organisation was simplified. The group work of the general office, based on the sections, was broken apart and distributed to each member. The number of managers was decreased and the lines of communication and command were shortened. The company maintained the balance among its diversified product lines throughout the 1960s, but the position of oil came to outrival the others in the 1970s and the supplementary relationship between oil and nonferrous metals came to an end. Organisationally, management decentralisation was promoted: the division headquarters were allocated production units of their own, and were further divided into several divisions in the 1970s.

The Dowa Mining[73] had established itself in the pre-war years as *Fujita Mining*, and had originally been engaged in the supply of electrolytic copper and pyrite ores. After the war, family ownership was terminated, it became a public company. The management structure has basically been a functional/line one, with mining works at the nucleus.

The company devoted much effort to the development of home mines, which cost 5000 million yen (5 million pounds) from 1955–64.[74] This proved successful and brought about an increase in copper production as well as diversification within nonferrous metals. The market for nonferrous metals developed with the increase of investment in other industries, and eventually demands for new kinds of nonferrous metals increased. Although other companies had begun to depend on overseas ores by the end of the 1950s, *Dowa Mining* continued to make use of their own ores by developing smelting technology which enabled them to utilise low quality ores. Mining works were at the centre of its organisation, while the head office was composed of a trading section. The function of the head office gradually became increasingly important in the latter half of the 1950s. In the head office, planning and labour management departments were set up, and these functions were assumed by managing directors. The mining works, which were equipped with smelting works, were directly controlled by the highest manager. The function of the head office had become that of the general staff by 1960, since the greater part of its sales activities were transferred to a separate company in 1957.

Prospecting and the development of home mines continued well after the mid-1960s, resulting in restraint of investment in the smelting branch; the investment in smelting equipment was mainly for rationalisation and not to increase of production. In mining, however, the production of pyrite ores became unprofitable and some inefficient mines were closed down. Nevertheless dependence on the company's domestic mines for copper and zinc ores continued into the 1970s. Although the company joined one or two coastal smelting works, the initiatives for such large-scale joint works came from other nonferrous metal companies. Twenty per cent of copper ores came from *Dowa*'s domestic mines. This brought high profit but a slow rate of growth. Another aspect of *The Dowa Mining*'s strategy is to be found in its high proportion of primary smelting and refining, while other companies had turned to secondary smelting, refining, and metal processing and fabricating in the 1970s. *Dowa*'s downward company branches were thus weak.

Organisational change proceeded slowly. The staff function, which had been mostly attached to the mining works, was differentiated from the operating production function and the former was gradually taken over by the head office. By 1970, the structure of the head office had become similar to those of other nonferrous metal companies, and in the 1970s a metal processing branch was added.

The Furukawa Electric[75] had already been fully diversified by 1950, and started out in the production of rolled copper, light metals and electric wire, demand for the latter coming largely from the electrical industry and *Nippon Telegraph and Telephone Corporation*, who purchased the dominant part of the company's products. *Furukawa Electric* became independent of its holding company, *Furukawa Mining & Co.*, in the early post-war period. The management structure established in the pre-war era with the trading departments and production units just below the highest managers was maintained until the late 1950s, at which point divisionalisation was begun. The firm completed its multidivisional structure in 1960 under the new president Uematsu.

Organisational reform started in 1956; the general staff was concentrated in the Inquiry Office to support the management committee. Until that time, both the management committee and the board of directors deliberated important matters. But with this reform some managing directors were appointed as managers of the trading departments, such as of electric wire or metals, and these were subsequently charged with control over production of these same products. By 1958 these trading departments were loosely combined into sales divisions, and developed into normal divisions in 1960. The sub-units which were supervised by each division were sales and technological departments and factories. These divisions were made responsible for their own profit.

In 1971 the copper drawing branch was separated and set up as a manufacturing subsidiary, whose products were, like those of the light metals branch which had been separated since 1959, distributed by *The Furukawa Electric*. *The Furukawa Electric* specialised in wire and cable, while diversification was promoted by these subsidiaries. The organisational structure of the company came to consist of wire and cable divisions, each with a full set of functions, and of sales divisions in light metals and copper drawing.

However as the number of divisions in the cable branch increased and the products specified, the company found it difficult to adapt itself to the changing market. In 1972 the sales functions of the cable branch were separated from the divisions, and reorganised into new sub-units in line with market channels such as electricity or railway companies. The division managers were still ultimately responsible for sales and profit, and were supported by the planning and controlling staff of each division. The authority of the managers supervising such irregular divisions, however, was weaker than that of those in other divisions, and was not necessarily adequate for profit responsibility. In the sales departments, on the other hand, the command of the divisions often came to restrict the activities. An early experiment in the matrix structure did not last long. Furthermore, investment in cable fell behind *Sumitomo Electric Industries* (which had also strengthened its metal interests) because *The Furukawa Electric* had to put a great deal of effort into the rationalisation of equipment.[76] In 1976, the production divisions in cable branches were completely dissolved, and replaced by production and trading headquarters. Both of the functional headquarters were made profit centres. Other branches such as electric equipment, copper drawing, or light metals were administered by the divisional form, though in the last two cases, divisions were not equipped with production functions. Finally, a subdivided divisional structure was adopted in 1980 instead of the two functional headquarters of the cable branches.

Sumitomo Electric Industries[77] had developed a modern form of the functional structure previous to the Second World War, but reorganised it into a factory-centred one during and after the war. Divisionalisation started in the mid-1950s and had extended to the whole company by 1960, but the organisation of the company eventually changed into a division headquarters structure in which several divisions were coordinated by corresponding division headquarters.

Immediately after the war, many organisational problems were noted in the management of *Sumitomo Electric*'s production units. To these problems of distribution channels were added, after the dissolution of *Sumitomo General Office*, which had handled some aspects of the trading function for *Sumitomo Electric Industries*. As the firm diversified into non-cable products, its trading department was sub-divided into two departments by products. A Technology Department with a production section had been formed in its head office by 1955, though this department did not directly control individual production units. A centralised coordination of technology became important when the company introduced foreign technologies; first getting into a technical partnership with *ISE*, and then in the late 1950s developing their own technologies.

In the latter half of the 1950s, wire and cable branches were expanded to meet increasing demand from the public sector. However, when the first long-range plan was drafted in 1960, it was recognised that the development potential in the domestic wire and cable market was limited, and that the company should seek diversification and overseas markets. The wire and cable branches formed the nucleus of the Wire Division Headquarters, which was composed of several divisions and a sales department. Such a form could respond both to the trends in production technologies which tended to specify and in market demands which tended to be systematised.

In the two plans which covered 1965 and 1973 a policy objective was set for investment in alloys, fabricated wire products, and other metal products. Such decisions were made as a response to the decrease in the share of cables in the total sales. Meanwhile, cable fittings and construction work interest increased. A construction work department was added to the Cable Division Headquarters. The organisational structure of the company was made more complicated by the autonomous growth of the Tokyo Department, which had several trading departments as well as a construction work department. When the oil-crisis hit the firm, it suspended the execution of its long-range plan and investment. In 1975 a new management plan was drafted, in which export, overseas investment, and diversification were emphasised. There were few changes observed in the organisational structure: there were large division headquarters, each with trading departments and divisions, and ordinary independent divisions with production and sales functions.

Hitachi Cable[78] was formed in 1956 as a copper drawing and cable firm which separated from *Hitachi*, though the company shared its chairman with *Hitachi*. Its organisational structure just below the top management was composed of trading departments by products and a factory. Though it was a single unit firm when formed, the company introduced the multidivisional structure consisting of only two divisions in 1963. New divisions were 'sales divisions' without production units, though the specialisation of product lines by production units was completed. Each division was made responsible for sales of the factories' products. The firm invested its financial resources in copper drawing, and then in the cable branches.[79]

After the mid 1960s, the firm began to integrate forward; the sales-division structure was reformed into a mixture of division headquarters system in the main product lines, and independent divisions in copper rolling and rubber. The divisions in turn controlled factories. *Hitachi Cable*'s sales were not insignificant when compared with those of other cable companies. However, its limited diversification revealed itself in the formation of a relatively simple organisational structure. In the 1970s the company developed export markets and overseas investment, as well as high-qualified cable processing. For these reasons the firm grew much slower than the other cable companies.

In summary, it was shown that nonferrous metal industries had large-scale companies both in smelting and secondary processing. For smelting companies in the steel and nonferrous metal industries, the supply of raw materials, particularly of ores, was very important. However, the strategies of these industries differed a great deal from each other. Iron and steel giant companies emerged, and they gradually equipped themselves with international competitive power, which they enjoyed till the end of the 1970s. In nonferrous metals, though the initial growth of the domestic market was remarkable, companies gradually lost their established positions. By the mid 1960s, the production costs of Japanese copper and nickel smelting companies had become twice as much as their foreign counterparts. From the beginning, iron and steel companies were dependent on foreign ores, but in nonferrous metals companies shifted gradually from home mines to overseas ores. Some tried to set up coastal smelting works for economies of scale and transportation costs, but this was not sufficient to revive their declining positions and they thus embarked upon developing downward processing branches.

The evolution of management structures in metal companies was gradual, and the companies examined here showed quite similar trends of development. They started from incomplete functional structures, in which each of the mining and smelting works was the centre of the company, then moved towards management centralisation. Divisionalisation began in the 1960s. A greater part of these companies gradually adopted the divisional system in their metal fabricating branches, though a few were delayed in their structural and strategic adaptation. Towards the end of the 1960s, the management structure of these companies became a mixture of the functional and divisional systems, that is functional in their upward branches and divisional in their downward and overseas branches. Such organisational reforms were brought about by the downward integration of metal processing branches.

In metal fabricating branches, all the large-scale firms started as wire and cable companies and extended their product lines to other metal products. The supply of raw materials was not necessarily an incisive problem for them. Metal fabricating companies introduced the multidivisional structure by the mid-1960s. All of them had started as cable and wire companies and they introduced new forms of management structure in order to justify into other metals and materials. However, due to the imbalance between their main and subordinate branches, the main branches were often reorganised into division headquarters while others were left as single divisions.

6.6 SUMMARY

Of largest 100 firms in 1970 there were 34 which were engaged mainly in the production of semi-finished materials. Most of these were traditional large-scale companies which are also found among the largest companies of earlier periods. Most of them supplied the same sorts of products as had done in the pre-war era, although there were many changes in both their quality and their markets.

The number of large-scale firms decreased in the four industry branches examined in this chapter. Many of them disappeared altogether as the results of mergers among large-scale companies. Even those which were ranked among the largest firms dropped their status in spite of mergers. There were some exceptions to such a generalisation, particularly among the largest iron and steel firms, nonferrous metals firms processing, as well as glass, rubber, and synthetic fibre firms. They adapted themselves to new markets which appeared with the expansion of consumer or producer final goods. However, not all of the firms were equally successful. For the companies in natural and man-made fibres, paper, cement, steel processing, special steel, nonferrous metal smelting, the development of the markets came to the peak much earlier.

For those which were traditional large-scale firms, the control of raw materials used to be the major sources of efficient management coordination. Except for textile firms, they tended to integrate backwards to raw materials branches. Textile firms made use of the market for purchasing, but the importance of raw materials to them was in no way less than it was to firms in other industries. In textiles, new materials appeared, and in other industries internal company supplies became exhausted, or too costly. Such companies became dependent on overseas supplies, and this was often accompanied by overseas investment to assure a stable supply.

For the growing iron and steel companies too, the significance of the supply of raw materials changed. For those with newly integrated iron smelting processes, the supply of ores became important, and for those which had been integrated steel mills, rapid expansion also required new supply sources. The flow from raw material to primary steel products was generally solved efficiently by this group of companies. For other companies, however, the integration downward to processing or diversification became their major strategies.

In the earlier periods, companies can be divided into two groups according to their management structures. Companies in light industries consisted of a large number of relatively small factories as well as trading offices. They had developed a functionally departmentalised structure above these operating units. The three decades since 1950 saw little increase in the number of factories, though there were increases in the number of trading offices. Even if they acquired factories by mergers, many were run down. Companies in heavy industries, by contrast, consisted of a small number of large production units. Their head offices and trading departments were relatively small in size. The main line of authorities ran from the highest level managers directly to the factory managers. The head office organisation and the trading departments along with their operating units expanded significantly during these three decades. Corporate staff departments were added, and the special staffs, such as production or technology were organised in the head office. However, the managers of the production units still enjoyed a high position and most of them reported directly to the top management and not to departmental managers.

Among 34 companies which supplied semi-finished products, seven partially adopted the divisional structure, while ten adopted the divisional structure through the company in 1970. In 1980 their numbers were ten and seventeen respectively. The full divisional structure was preferred to partial divisions. The motives or the period of adoption differed from each other. The full divisional structure was adopted relatively early. In the 1950s, eight companies had adopted it. Conversely both the partial divisions and the mixed form were more modern phenomena. Companies that introduced the full divisional structure, such as those in steel or metals did so because they were diversified. Those which introduced the divisional structure only partially had relatively large scale equipment producing a single sort of materials, and these companies began to advance into downward processes or to diversify their product lines. There was a great deal of difference between the traditional products and the new ones in terms of scale, technical skills and markets. This was necessary because the traditional products were faced with severe competition and excessive production capacity.

NOTES

1. *The Seventy Year History of Toyobo*, 1953; Kunio Kawasaki, 'Toyobo', in *Kindaiteki* keiei *soshiki no jitsurei*, *op. cit.*, pp. 119–46; Susumu Takamiya (ed.), 'Toyobo', *Kaisha soshiki* (Company Organisation), 1959, pp. 323–50; 'The Amalgamation of Toyobo and Kureha spinning', *Anarisuto* (Analyst), Jan. 1966, pp. 45–7; 'Toyobo', *Tk*, 4.2.1961, pp. 68–9; see also ibid., 27.3.1971, pp. 106 09; 15.10.1977, pp. 84–9; 29.7.1978, pp. 92–5; *Nks*, 27.5.1959, 27.6.1963, 27.1.1964, 23.4.1966, 25.4.1970, 27.11.1974, 14.12.1976, 24.12.1976, 22.8.1978. (For abbreviations see list at beginning of book.)
2. Calculated from *Reports to the Minister of Finance*, 1965–73.
3. Ken-ichi Koshiba, '"Greater Kanebo" and Rationalisation', *Kh*, Jan.

1959, pp. 112–21; Yasuo Kadose, 'Kanegafuchi Spinning', *Kigyoho kenkyu*, July 1963, pp. 26–31; Kazuo Noda, 'Integrated Enterprise Covering Food, Clothing and Shelter', *Ck*, vol. 3, no. 4, 1966, pp. 351–7; 'Kanegafuchi Spinning', *Tk*, 28.1.1961, p. 82; see also ibid., 4.2.1961, p. 70; 6.6.1970, pp. 78–9; 'Kanebo'. *Tk*, 8.11.1975, pp. 90–95; see also ibid., 5.11.1977, pp. 90–95; 'Kanebo', *Tg*, Jan. 1977, p. 5; 'Kanegafuchi Spinning', *Ec*, 25.6.1968, pp. 52–5; *Nks*, 21.11.1957, 6.7.1958, 7.9.1958, 16.9.1958, 19.9.1958, 12.1.1965, 25.10.1967, 24.5.1968, 3.6.1972, 14.12.1976, 24.12.1976.

4. *Reports to the Minister of Finance*, 1960–64.
5. See also ibid., 1968–73.
6. Nihon kagakusen-i kyokai (Japan Chemical Fibre Association) (ed.), *Nihon kagakusen-i sangyoshi* (The History of Chemical Fibre Industry in Japan), 1974, pp. 894–1091; 'Dai Nippon Spinning & Weaving Mill', *Tk*, 4.2.1961, p. 71; 'Nippon Rayon', *Tk*, 3.3.1962, pp. 62–4; 'Unitika', *Tk*, 7.2.1976, pp. 112 17; see also ibid., 24.4.1976, pp. 98–9; 'Unitika', *Tg*, Jan. 1977, p. 6; 'Nichibo and Nippon Rayon', *Ec*, 8.4.1969, pp. 68–71; *Nks*, 24.2.1964, 22.2.1965, 20.3.1969, 23.9.1969, 2.4.1970, 23.5.1970, 1.8.1972, 6.4.1973, 18.6.1973, 23.5.1975, 14.12.1976, 24.12.1976.
7. *Reports to the Minister of Finance*, 1955–64.
8. See also ibid., 1974–80.
9. 'Teijin', *Tk*, 20.5.1961, pp. 86–7; see also ibid., 5.6.1971, pp. 94–7; 4.9.1976, pp. 82–6; 'Teijin', *Ck*, vol. 7, no. 3, pp. 128–30; 'Teijin', *Kk*, Nov. 1976, pp. 26–8; 'Teijin', *Ec*, 17.4.1979, pp. 20–22; *Nks*, 8.2.1956, 31.8.1960, 17.6.1963, 18.6.1963, 14.10.1963, 4.11.1963, 11.11.1963, 18.11.1963, 22.4.1968, 28.6.1969, 31.1.1977.
10. *Reports to the Minister of Finance*, 1955–64.
11. See also ibid., 1965–73.
12. *The Thirty-Five Year History of Toyo Rayon*, 1962; *The Fifty Year History of Toray Industries*, 1977; Susumu Takamiya (ed.), 'Toyo Rayon', *Kaisha* soshiki, *op. cit.*, 1959, pp. 143–76; Japan Productivity Center (ed.), 'Toyo Rayon', *Choki keiei keikaku*, *op. cit.*, 1961, pp. 92–100; Hiroyuki Baba, 'Organisation and Operation of Strategic Management', in *Kigyo senryaku to keiei soshiki* (Enterprise Strategy and Management Organisation), ed. Japan Productivity Center, 1973, pp. 280–96; Hidetane Ijima, 'Organisational Development of Matrix Function', in *Senryaku taisei to katsuryoku soshiki no shintenkai* (New Development in the System for Strategy and the Structure for Excellence), ed. Kigyo kenkyu kai, 1979, pp. 86–95; Keizai Doyukai (Japan Committee for Economic Development) (ed.), Growth Strategy Based on its Own Technology', *1980 nendai no kigyo keiei* (Business Enterprise in the 1980s), 1980, pp. 161–73; Koichi Ida, 'Organisation and Administrative Structure of Overseas Business Activity', in *Sozo ni chosen suru soshiki kakushin*, *op. cit.*, pp. 223–9; Hiroshi Kurahashi, 'Modernisation of Management Organisation and the Ideal Way of Middle Management', *Kj*, Dec. 1964, pp. 13–16; Yasuo Okamoto, *et al.*, 'Toyo Rayon', *Ck*, vol. 2, no. 1, 1963, pp. 347–72; Yasuo Okamoto, 'Toyo Rayon and its Flexible Organisation', *Ck*, vol. 3, no. 4, 1964, pp. 248–54; 'Toyo

Rayon', *Ec*, 19.9.1961, pp. 64–7; Kazuo Noda, 'Toyo Rayon', *Ec*, 13.8.1963, pp. 72–6; 'Toray Industries', *Kik*, Mar. 1972, pp. 12–13; 'Toray Industries', *Tk*, 19.7.1975, pp. 86–93; 'Toray Industries', *Kk*, Nov. 1976, pp. 28–31; *Nks*, 25.3.1959, 23.12.1960, 18.2.1963, 6.1.1965, 17.8.1965, 2.6.1970.

13. *Reports to the Minister of Finance*, 1960–69.
14. *Reports to the Minister of Finance*, 1974–80.
15. 'Mitsubishi Rayon', *Tk*, 2.8.1975, pp. 91–2; see also ibid., 15.10.1977, pp. 84–9; *Nks*, 24.9.1975, 21.1.1976.
16. *Reports to the Minister of Finance*, 1955–64.
17. See also ibid., 1965–73.
18. *Nks*, 8.3.1956, 29.4.1964, 2.11.1964, 1.6.1976, 7.6.1976.
19. *Reports to the Minister of Finance*, 1960–69.
20. Japan Productivity Center (ed.), 'Asahi Chemical Industry', *Choki keiei keikaku, op. cit.*, pp. 80–90; Ikuo Kamei, 'Problems of Management Organisation under the Low Growth Economy', in *Kozo henkakuka no soshiki tenkai* (Organisational Development under the Structural Change), ed. Kigyo kenkyu kai, 1975, pp. 16–28; *do.*, 'Decision Making System and its Function in a Diversified Enterprise', in *Senryaku taisei to katsuryoku soshiki no shintenkai, op. cit.*, pp. 121–8; Yukio Sawanabe, 'Asahi Chemical Industry', in *Saishin choki keiei keikaku no jitsurei* (New Cases in the Long-Range Management Planning), ed. Toyohiro Kono, 1978, pp. 122–46; *do.*, 'Strategic Reorganisation of Middle- and Long-Range Management Planning', *Kj*, Jun. 1978, pp. 22–5; 'Asahi Chemical Industry', *Tk*, 12.9.1959, pp. 28–39; see also ibid., 28.12.1974, pp. 124–5; 11.10.1975, pp. 88–93; 13.9.1980, pp. 86–9; 'Asahi Chemical Industry', *Tg*, Jan. 1977, p. 7; 'Asahi Chemical Industry', *Kk*, Nov. 1976, pp. 23–5; see also ibid., Jan. 1980, pp. 38–9, *Nks*, 15.1.1958, 8.6.1959, 7.9.1964, 29.9.1978, 30.10.1980.
21. *Reports to the Minister of Finance*, 1965–73.
22. *The History of Oji Paper*, 1982; Japan Productivity Center (ed.), 'Oji Paper', *Choki keiei keikaku, op. cit.*, pp. 102–3; Norio Saito, 'Oji's Policies towards the Economic Fluctuations since 1955', *Ibaragi Daigaku Seikei gakkai Zasshi* (The Journal of Political Science and Economics), no. 37 1977, pp. 13–27; 'Oji Paper', *Tk*, 29.9.1962, pp. 58–9; see also ibid., 15.3.1969, pp. 82–6; 28.2.1970, pp. 74–7; 24.7.1971, pp. 84–7; 12.2.1972, pp. 76–9; 5.7.1975, pp. 80–83; 9.7.1977, pp. 97–8; 21.10.1978, pp. 88–92; 31.5.1980, pp. 112–15; 'Oji Paper', *Ec*, 27.1.1976, pp. 94–95; *Nks*, 17.8.1964.
23. *Reports to the Minister of Finance*, 1965–73.
24. *The History of Honshu Paper*, 1966; 'Honshu Paper', *Kj*, Jan. 1956, pp. 19–20, 28–9; 'Honshu Paper', *Tk*, 10.9.1977, pp. 95–7; see also ibid., 3.3.1979, pp. 82–5; 'Honshu Paper', *Tg*, Jan. 1977, p. 11; *Nks*, 2.5.1956, 28.1.1957, 7.6.1962, 17.2.1972.
25. *Reports to the Minister of Finance*, 1965–73.
26. *The History of Jujo Paper*, 1974; Toyoaki Ono, 'Jujo Paper', in *Kindaiteki keiei soshiki no jitsurei, op. cit.*, pp. 39–67; *do.*, *Nihon kigyo no soshiki senryaku* (Organisational Strategy of Japanese Enterprises),

1979, pp. 279–305; 'Jujo Paper', *Tk*, 13.3.1965, pp. 116–19; see also ibid., 7.12.1968, pp. 82–7; 'Jujo Paper', *Ec*, 5.9.1961, pp. 64–6; *Nks*, 20.10.1967, 17.3.1968, 10.2.1970, 2.3.1973.

27. Kazuo Noda (ed.), *Sengo keieishi* (Postwar Business History), 1965, pp. 611–17; Toshio Kikuchi, 'The Champion for Free Competition', *Kik*, Nov. 1965, pp. 33–9; 'Daishowa Paper Manufacturing', *Tk*, 6.8.1966, pp. 96–9; see also ibid., 11.1.1969, pp. 90–93; *Nks*, 28.6.1965.

28. *Reports to the Minister of Finance*, 1965–73.

29. *The Sixty Year of Toppan Printing*, 1961; *TOPPAN: The History of Toppan Printing*, 1985; 'Toppan Printing', *Tk*, 3.11.1973, pp. 100–01, *Ns*, 13.9.1961.

30. *Reports to the Minister of Finance*, 1955–64.

31. Ibid., 1965–73.

32. 'Dai Nippon Printing' *Tk*, 10.4.1971; *Nks*, 18.8.1960, 7.4.1961, 8.2.1965, 26.3.1963.

33. *The Seventy Year of Onoda Cement*, 1952; *The One Hundred Year History of Onoda Cement*, 1981; Akitoshi Takamune, 'The Present State and Rationalisation of Cement Industry', *Shakaito*, (The Socialist Party), May 1966, pp. 99–117; 'Onoda Cement', *Ks*, June 1965, pp. 47–9; Akira Mizusaki *et al.*, 'The Management Organisation in Cement Enterprises', *Soshiki kagaku* (Organisational Science), vol. 2, no. 1, 1968, pp. 52–68; *Nks*, 2.3.1964.

34. *The Fifty Year History of Bridgestone Tire*, 1982; Tsunetada Kawate, 'Long-Range Management Planning and Operation of General Staff System', in *Kozo henkakuka no soshiki tenkai*, *op. cit.*, pp. 87–96; *do.*, 'Bridgestone Tire', in *Saishin Choki keiei keikaku no Jitsurei* (New Cases in the Long-Range Management Planning), ed. Toyohiro Kono, 1978, pp. 229–43; Eiji Watanabe, 'Bridgestone Tire', *Ma*, June 1978, pp. 41–8; Jun Mori, 'Timing of Diversification', *Ck*, vol. 3, no. 4, 1964, pp. 260–67; 'Bridgestone Tire', *Tk*, 31.7.1965, pp. 78–9; see also ibid., 29.11.1975, pp. 84–9; 9.7.1977, pp. 82–7; *Nks*, 26.2.1960, 22.9.1960, 12.8.1963, 23.12.1970.

35. *Reports to the Minister of Finance*, 1965–73.

36. *The History of Asahi Glass*, 1967; Susumu Takamiya (ed.), 'Asahi Glass', *Kaisha shoshiki*, *op. cit.*, pp. 100–16; 'Asahi Glass', *Tk*, 16.7.1977, pp. 82–6; 'Asahi Glass', *Tg*, Jan. 1977, p. 16; *Nks*, 1.4.1964.

37. *Reports to the Minister of Finance*, 1960–69.

38. *Reports to the Minister of Finance*, 1970–73.

39. *The Twenty-Five Year History of Kawasaki Steel*, 1976; Sei-ichiro Yonekura, 'The Innovative Behavior of Kawasaki Steel in Post-War Japanese Industry', *Hitotsubashi Ronso* (Hitotsubashi Review), vol. 90, no. 3, 1983, pp. 69–92; Hiroshi Kuroda, 'A Study of the New Management Planning', *Kj*, June 1978, pp. 26–9; 'Kawasaki Steel', *Tk*, 30.4.1977, pp. 76–81; 'Kawasaki Steel', *Tg*, July 1980, p. 7; 'Kawasaki Steel', *Ec*, 23.12.1975, pp. 90–91; *Nks*, 5.7.1958, 7.10.1963, 30.1.1969, 1.9.1973.

40. *Reports to the Minister of Finance*, 1955–60.

41. Ibid., 1965–73.

42. *The Sixty Year History of Sumitomo Metal Industries*, 1957; *Recent Ten*

Year History of Sumitomo Metal Industries 1957–67, 1967; *Recent Ten Year History of Sumitomo Metal Industries* 1967–77, 1977; 'Witness to the Post-war Industrial History' 47,48, *Ec*, 23.11.1976, pp. 78–85, 30.11.1976, pp. 78–85; 30.9.1975, pp. 94–5; 'Sumitomo Metal Industries', *Tk*, 26.2.1972, pp. 92–6; see also ibid., 2.11.1974, pp. 75–9; 16.8.1975, pp. 110–15; *Nks*, 6.1.1953, 2.12.1963.
43. *Reports to the Minister of Finance*, 1965–73.
44. *The Fifty Year History of Kobe Steel*, 1954; *The Seventy Year History of Kobe Steel*, 1974; *The Eighty Year History of Kobe Steel*, 1986; Susumu Takamiya (ed.), 'Kobe Steel', *Kaisha soshiki* (Company Organisation), 1959, pp. 221–35; 'The Multidivisional Structure of Kobe Steel', *Mg*, Feb. 1964, pp. 16–19; 'Kobe Steel', *Tk*, 8.7.1961, pp. 76–9; see also ibid., 30.10.1965, pp. 86–9; 24.11.1970, pp. 107–11; 7.6.1965, pp. 78–83; 13.12.1975, pp. 92–7; 18.2.1978, pp. 90–95; *Nks*, 19.11.1953, 8.1.1955, 15.2.1956, 23.3.1956, 3.5.1956, 24.2.1964, 30.11.1964, 23.4.1975, 21.9.1976.
45. *Reports to the Minister of Finance*, 1955–64.
46. Ibid., 1965–73.
47. *The Forty Year History of Nippon Kokan*, 1952; *The Fifty Year History of Nippon Kokan*, 1962; *The Sixty Year History of Nippon Kokan*, 1972; *The Seventy Year History of Nippon Kokan*, 1982; Japan Productivity Center (ed.), 'Nippon Kokan', *Choki* keiei *keikaku* (Long-Range Management Planning), 1961, pp. 306–9; Yoshihiro Maekawa, 'Mechanisation of Management Procedures in Nippon Kokan', *Tekko kai* (The Steel Industries), June 1964, pp. 14–20; Gen Oyama, 'Organisational Reformation of Nippon Kokan', *Sk*, vol. 12, no. 1, 1978, pp. 28–39; 'Nippon Kokan', *Tk*, 14.10.1978, pp. 82–4; *Nks*, 5.6.1959, 2.11.1960, 1.7.1963, 23.12.1969, 17.12.1971, 24.4.1978, 7.4.1979.
48. *Reports to the Minister of Finance*, 1950–55.
49. Ibid., 1960–65.
50. *Hono-o to tomoni – The History of Yawata Iron & Steel*, 1981; *Hono-o to tomoni – The History of Fuji Iron & Steel*, 1981; *Hono-o to tomoni – The History of Nippon Steel*, 1981; Michimoto Arita, 'Yawata Iron & Steel', in *Kindaiteki keiei soshiki no jitsurei* (Cases of Modern Management Organisation), ed. Susumu Takamiya, 1953, pp. 245–58; Japan Productivity Center (ed.), 'Yawata Iron & Steel', *Choki keiei keikaku, op. cit.*, pp. 282–7; 'Yawata Iron & Steel', *Ec*, 27.3.1962, pp. 64–7; 'Yawata Iron & Steel', *Tk*, 20.1.1962, pp. 98–101; 'Yawata Iron & Steel', *Kh*, Jan. 1964, pp. 106–15; *Nks*, 5.5.1956, 9.5.1956, 2.4.1959, 12.9.1960, 30.7.1962, 28.1.1963, 2.12.1963, 20.10.1964, 10.1.1965; Tetsuo Hayashi *et al.* 'Fuji Iron & Steel – Hirohata Factory', *Kh*, Aug. 1959, pp. 90–98; *Nks*, 1.7.1960, 20.9.1960, 30.7.1962, 17.8.1963; Keizai Doyukai (Japan Committee for Economic Development) (ed.), 'Improving Performance by Management Reorganisation and Rationalisation', *1980 nendai no kigyo keiei* (Business Enterprise in the 1980s), 1980, pp. 105–15; Toshihiro Okuyama, 'Organisational Reform to Strengthen Engineering Business', in *Sozo ni chosen suru soshiki kakushin* (Organisational Innovation Aiming at Creativeness), ed. Kigyo Kenkyu Kai, 1981, pp. 210–22; Masayasu Araki, 'Apprehensions of Employees and Trade

Japanese Management Structures

Unions towards the Big Merger', *Ck*, vol. 7, no. 3, 1968, pp. 136–49; Kinya Ninomiya, 'Why did Nippon Steel recover?', *Ck*, vol. 18, no. 2, 1979, pp. 226–39; Seinosuke Suzuki *et al.* 'Nippon Steel – takes the leadership in "Cooperative" Oligopoly', *Kh*, Oct. 1970, pp. 209–21; Shuji Ohashi, 'Growing Oligopolistic Trends of the Steel Industry', *Ec*, 7.5.1968, pp. 14–20; see also ibid., 3.8.1971, pp. 76–81; 8.4.1975, pp. 10–21, pp. 22–5, pp. 26–9; 'Nippon Steel', *Tk*, 18.7.1970, pp. 50–55; 2.8.1975, pp. 88–90; *Nks*, 18.5.1963, 12.3.1970, 13.11.1970, 10.6.1977, 5.6.1979.

51. *Reports to the Minister of Finance* (Yawata Iron & Steel), 1955–64.
52. *Reports to the Minister of Finance* (Fuji Iron & Steel), 1955–60.
53. *Reports to the Minister of Finance*, 1974–80.
54. *The History of Nippon Teppan, 1956*; *The Fifty Year History of Nichia Seiko*, 1960; *Nisshin Steel: Ten Years since its Formation*, 1969; Takao Naganuma, 'Policies for Controlling Affiliated Companies: in Case of Nisshin Steel', *Kj*, Aug. 1978, pp. 10–13; *Nks*, 9.1.1953, 14.11.1954, 14.6.1958, 1.4.1959, 9.4.1969, 21.6.1980.
55. *Reports to the Minister of Finance*, 1965–6.
56. *The Fifty Year History of Daido Steel*, 1967; 'Daido Steel', *Tk*, 2.12.1961, pp. 60–61; *Nks*, 29.1.1957, 1.8.1963, 1.9.1967, 27.4.1976.
57. *Reports to the Minister of Finance*, 1965–73.
58. *Documents on the History of The Japan Steel Works: Supplement*, 1978; Naokatsu Sudo, 'The Japan Steel Works', in *Kindaiteki keiei soshiki no jitsurei*, *op. cit.*, pp. 379–93; Etsuhiro Goda, 'Knowledge Intensification and Organisational Efficiency', in *Kozo henkakuka no soshiki tenkai* (Organisational Development under the Structural Change), ed. Kigyo Kenkyu Kai, 1975, pp. 43–9; Masanori Ueki, 'Organisation Reform of The Japan Steel Works', *Keiei shiryo geppo* (Monthly Report on Business Records), 1980, no. 674, pp. 26–33; 'The Japan Steel Works', *Tk*, 30.9.1978, pp. 96–9; *Nks*, 9.12.1961, 18.4.1973, 23.5.1977.
59. *Reports to the Minister of Finance*, 1955–64.
60. Ibid., 1965–73.
61. *The History of Hitachi Metals*, 1980; 'Hitachi Metals', *Tk*, 9.1.1971, pp. 129–30; see also ibid., 20.11.1976, pp. 146–7; *Nks*, 11.3.1972.
62. *Reports to the Minister of Finance*, 1974–80.
63. 'Mitsui Mining and Smelting', *Tk*, 29.10.1977, pp. 106–110; see also ibid., 5.5.1979, pp. 124–7; 'Mitsui Mining and Smelting', *Tg*, Jan. 1977, p. 10; *Nks*, 23.3.1964.
64. *Reports to the Minister of Finance*, 1965–73.
65. Toichi Noda, 'Mitsubishi Metal Mining', in *Kindaiteki keiei soshiki no jitsurei*, op. cit., pp. 270–75; 'Mitsubishi Metal Mining', *Tk*, 23.8.1975, pp. 82–7; see also ibid., 1.7.1978, pp. 98–9; *Nks*, 14.1.1954, 1.3.1965.
66. *Reports to the Minister of Finance*, 1955–64.
67. Ibid., 1965–73.
68. *The Twenty Year History of Sumitomo Metal Mining*, 1970; Keizai Doyukai (ed.), 'Adaptation to Business Environment by the Leadership of the Top Management', *1980 nendai no kigyo keiei*, *op. cit.*, pp. 131–46; Yasuo Hashida, 'Strategic Management by the Leadership of the Top Management and Policy Setting', in *Senryaku keiei keikaku sakutei*

no jissai (The Practice of Strategic Planning), ed. Kigyo Kenkyu Kai, 1982, pp. 203–14; *Nks*, 12.1.1980.

69. *Reports to the Minister of Finance*, 1960–64.
70. Ibid., 1974–80.
71. *The Fifty Year History of Nippon Mining*, 1957; *The Fifty Year History of Nippon Mining: A Supplementary Volume, 1967*; Toshiaki Yoshizumi, 'Nippon Mining', in *Kindaiteki keiei soshiki no jitsurei, op. cit.*, pp. 287–300; Takamiya *et al.* (ed.), 'The Abolishment of Sections in Nippon Mining', in *Nihonteki keiei to dotai soshiki* (The Japanese Management System and the Organisational Dynamics), 1968, pp. 139–55; 'Nippon Mining', *Ks*, Nov. 1967, pp. 42–5; 'Nippon Mining', *Tk*, 7.1.1961, pp. 162–3; see also ibid., 5.6.1971, p. 93; 1.11.1975, pp. 90–95; 'Nippon Mining', *Ck*, vol. 7, no. 3, 1968, pp. 126–8; *Nks*, 28.7.1960, 29.7.1960, 2.9.1963, 27.4.1980.
72. *Reports to the Minister of Finance*, 1960–73.
73. *The Seventy Year History of The Dowa Mining*, 1955; *The Ninety Year History of The Dowa Mining*, 1974; *The One Hundred Year History of The Dowa Mining*, 2 vols, 1985; 'The Dowa Mining', *Tk*, 19.11.1966, pp. 92–6; see also *ibid.*, 19.4.1980, pp. 94–6; *Nks*, 26.3.1957, 10.9.1957.
74. *Reports to the Minister of Finance*, 1955–64.
75. Tatsui Suzuki, 'The Furukawa Electric', in *Kindaiteki keiei soshiki no jitsurei, op. cit.*, pp. 369–73; Shinji Kirimura, 'Management Strategy and General Staff', in *Kozo henkakuka no soshiki tenkai, op. cit.*, pp. 69–86; 'The Furukawa Electric', *Tk*, 30.10.1976, pp. 108–11; *Nks*, 22.4.1957, 15.3.1965, 29.9.1971, 29.3.1976, 2.4.1980.
76. *Reports to the Minister of Finance*, 1965–73.
77. *The History of Sumitomo Electric Industries*, 1961; *The History of Sumitomo Electric Industries*, 1979; Takeya Motoyoshi, 'Monitoring of Research and Development Project', in *Kenkyu kaihatsu hyoka jissen shiryoshu* (Practical Materials for Monitoring Research and Development), ed. Kigyo kenkyu kai, 1982, pp. 201–3; Hideaki Sasaki, 'Re-examination of Long-Range Vision and Middle & Long-Range Planning', in *Senryaku keieikeikaku sakutei no jissai* (The Practice of Strategic Planning), ed. Kigyo kenkyu kai, 1982, pp. 167–78; Shigeru Tsutsumi, 'Control of Affiliated Companies in Transition', *Kj*, Aug. 1978, pp. 14–17; 'Sumitomo Electric Industries', *Tk*, 24.12.1977, pp. 142–4; *Nks*, 7.1.1959, 19.7.1960, 5.10.1964, 20.3.1967, 17.7.1968, 26.9.1978.
78. *The History of Hitachi Cable*, vol. 1, 1980; *Nks*, 26.7.1979.
79. *Reports to the Minister of Finance*, 1960–64.

7 New Industries in the Traditional Companies

7.1 INTRODUCTION

Companies in chemicals, electrical equipment, and heavy engineering developed along similar lines in their organisational structures. Most of them manufactured producer final goods, except for some companies that specialised in cosmetics, films, or household electrical equipment. This chapter deals with the development of management structures in 27 firms which mainly supplied producer final goods.

Most of these 27 concerns had already been established as large-scale companies in the pre-war era. There were entries into and withdrawals from the largest 100 firms during the post-war three decades, and consequently these industrial branches increased their numbers among the largest concerns. In the pre-war era, most of these 27 firms manufactured a single product like fertilisers, electrical motors, and ships. They not only changed their product lines dramatically in the post-war period, but diversified substantially.

These groups of companies show some similarities with each other in the introduction of the multidivisional structure. Of the 53 companies among the largest 100 firms which were administered by the multidivisional structure in 1970, 25 belonged to these three industrial branches; that is to say, 25 of the 27 firms adopted the multidivisional structure, and this number was still 25 in 1980. Another important characteristic of the organisational structure in these industrial branches, however, was found in the stability of the multidivisional system after adoption. Unlike firms in other industries, the divisional structure was maintained for a long period of time, and was not replaced by the functional form again. Though the nature of these companies' products changed rapidly, the initiative for diversification came not only from the top management but from operating levels as well. The first problem one encounters in investigating the organisational change in these firms is the question of how the operating units or the divisions promoted diversification.

These branches of industries applied core technologies either introduced from overseas or developed independently to diversification. Firms grew more or less in the manufacture of new products, and this was brought about either through the introduction of new technologies or the application of existing technical skills to new products. Such characteristics pushed these firms to diversification. In the case of the firms in semi-finished products, diversification originated either in downward integration to processing or in mergers or acquisitions. Here, diversification began in the application of the companies' technical skills, and such technical skills had to be accumulated in order to be applied to related areas of activities, because these industrial branches did not automatically confirm upon their members, core technical skills necessary for diversification. This is the second point of interest in this chapter.

Whatever the process that brought it about, diversification led to the introduction of the multidivisional structure. Divisionalisation was not a phenomenon observed only in American firms. The experiences in European companies,[1] and our preliminary research on Japanese firms[2] indicates a similar co-relationship. In this chapter, the process of the adoption of the multidivisional structure by individual firms, its background and the characteristics of Japanese multidivisional structure are examined in more detail. In the pre-war period and during the war as well, companies in producer final goods were administered by a decentralised structure, in which each production unit had a wide scope of authority. This is called the 'production-unit system'. The divisionalisation of these firms is characterised as a centralisation process rather than one of decentralisation. The third problem this chapter will deal with is therefore, how such a decentralising force influenced the modern multidivisional structure and how it was reorganised.

7.2 CHEMICAL AND PHARMACEUTICAL COMPANIES

Eleven concerns were classified as being in chemical industries in 1970. Of them nine firms are examined here, and the remaining two which supplied consumer final goods are discussed in the next chapter. Chemical companies had already established a leading position for themselves in the inter-war period. In 1935, 14 such firms were found among the largest 100 companies by sales, and 17 were among the largest 100 by assets. Most of the largest firms of 1970 had also existed in 1935, though only three of them could be found among the largest 100 at that time. Six chemical companies were engaged in full lines of chemical products in 1970, while the other three supplied either chemical intermediaries or final products.

The general chemical companies mostly started by producing fertilisers or coal products around 1950. These firms developed by diversification, first within fertilisers or into urea. With the change of sources of ammonium gas from coal or the electrolysis of water to oil, various petrochemical products or their intermediaries came into existence. This enabled them to supply new products with wider markets, such as polyethylene, synthetic fibres and resins, and to thus put an end to their close relationship with nonferrous metals or mechanical engineering.

The development of the general chemical companies was also accompanied by rapid growth in the size of production units. The size of firms, however, stayed relatively small throughout the post-war period. Unlike in Britain or Germany, no giants are found among Japanese chemical companies. The concentration ratio was traditionally low (except in film products), and competition was high. The government may have partially contributed to such a high competition rate, and came to be deeply concerned with the policies of individual companies. For the production of fertilisers, the rationalisation of equipment and business organisation was promoted by the government. In petrochemicals, three series of petrochemical projects were initiated by the government, according to which the plans of the individual companies were deliberated or coordinated by the government, investment in chemical plants being similarly regulated.

Three other companies specialised in a particular area of chemical products such as urea, ink, or pharmaceuticals. The difference between these three and some of the firms discussed in the previous chapter (cement, rubber, and glass) may in part be nominal, derived only from their Industry Classification. However, they also differed from each other in their strategy and structures.

Mitsui Toatsu Chemicals[3] was formed in 1968 by a merger of two large chemical companies within the *Mitsui* group. One of the forerunners, *Toyo Koatsu*, had been a small fertiliser firm when it was acquired by *Mitsui Mining* in the inter-war period. Between 1950 and 1955, the major product of *Toyo Koatsu* was still fertilisers, particularly ammonium sulphate. Then, in the second half of the 1950s, utilising its technology, the firm entered into the production of urea. Diversification into other chemical products was still limited during this period, but by 1960 the ratio of fertilisers in the total sales of the company had fallen to less than 70 per cent. Organisational reforms were carried out all at once in 1959, when the firm adopted the multidivisional structure to deal with the problems caused by diversification. Three divisions, fertilisers, industrial chemicals, and resins, were made profit centres and were made responsible for the development, production and sales of each of their product lines. Divisional management was assumed by a managing director, who was delegated with the authority necessary for the operation of his own division. *Toyo Koatsu* also established a top management organisation. The management committee was reorganised into a body that deliberated on major policies and plans, and a general staff department responsible for long-range planning was formed. Research and development departments were consolidated into a single unit. The necessity for diversification was made acute by the unbalance of supply and demand, price control, and 'the deficit export' of fertilisers. The differences in production processes, technologies, product markets, sales method, and research and development among the three divisions, were large. So that enough attention be paid to new products, risks should be dispersed. The sectionalism arising from the functional structure deteriorated the general performance of the company. Finally, due to the increase of coordinating tasks of the top management, they came to be pressed with daily work and were therefore deprived of swiftness in making important decision.

Advances into petrochemicals by *Toyo Koatsu* were curbed. Instead, a joint scheme was planned by chemical companies of the *Mitsui* group. It was necessary that any plan by the group members to move into a new area of business be carried out by the member company whose technology was most suitable and by the factory whose equipment was most competent for that particular business. Diversification, or 'de-fertilisation', was thus belated. The ratio of fertilisers was highest among the large-scale chemical companies during the 1960s. Large scale investment into fertilisers continued until the end of the 1960s,[4] while the firm also attempted an advance into petrochemicals through a joint venture with other members of the *Mitsui* group.

Meanwhile, the performance of *Mitsui Chemicals*, which originated in coal chemistry and produced industrial chemicals, resins, and dyestuffs, worsened. Y. Ishige, the chairman of *Toyo Koatsu* took over the presidency of *Mitsui Chemicals*. There was little overlapping of product lines between the two companies, but in order to promote a joint petrochemical project vigorously, they amalgamated. Due to the nature of this merger, an economy of scale in the new enterprise could not be expected, but the number of product lines increased. Among them, the management planned an expansion of industrial chemicals and resin, which was soon realised.

The structural reorganisation which followed this merger was not necessarily delayed. *Mitsui Chemicals* had originally been based on an incomplete divisional structure. The resin and industrial chemical branches of each company constituted separate divisions within the new company (i.e. there were two resins and two industrial chemicals divisions). Eight divisions were allocated internal capital and made profit centres. Each division was put in charge of production, sales, and research and development, but they were not responsible for purchase, personnel, and finance. The existence of a duality of divisions in similar products, and the new problems that accompanied the specification of product lines were solved by the adoption of the division headquarters structure in 1970. Five division headquarters, four by product and one by geography, were set up to coordinate and cooperate divisions when they had production technology, customers, and sales channels in common. Special staff were concentrated on the division headquarters to reduce overhead costs, and the interchange of personnel was promoted.

The classical divisional structure was challenged when pollution became a problem and the safety of chemical plants came to be widely questioned. The most suitable allocation and utilisation of factories was required from the standpoint of the total company. This necessitated the centralisation of authority and the intensification of the general staff. Factories were separated from divisions and placed directly under the production control department of the head office. Factories were made profit centres instead of divisions, which were grouped together and reorganised into headquarters in charge of production management and sales. For example, the chemical product division and the industrial chemical division were reorganised into chemical product headquarters. Thus together with solving the factory allocation problem, the firm attempted to strengthen market orientation and forward processes. However, this reorganisation was not decisive, and some minor divisions were not reformed into headquarters. This system could not, however, monitor the performance of factories well. The firm eliminated such irregularities by the end of the 1970s, when independent divisions were organised into headquarters, and the production control department was abolished, making the headquarters more responsible for their own activities.

Showa Denko,[5] which came into existence through the merger of two electro-chemical companies in the pre-war era, was predominantly engaged in the production of fertilisers in 1950. In addition, the company produced aluminium and electrodes through the utilisation of cheap electricity. The organisational structure of the firm changed from a divisional to a functional one in 1952, and was divisionalised again in 1967. The divisional form was reinforced in the 1970s.

Just after the Second World War, the divisional structure, under which each 'division headquarters' was made a self-supporting unit responsible for its own product lines, was introduced in order to rebuild the firm. However, this measure was taken casually and lacked a definite foundation, and was unable to solve the problems arising from the existing complex managerial situation. Management recognised this situation and began research on the organisational reform. In 1952, the company introduced a functional structure, which at that time, was viewed as the most modern form of management organisation. Authority was made clear by forming a written rule – the first such attempt among Japanese companies. Although this company had been diversified by that time and well appreciated the merit of multidivisional structure, the management preferred a centralised functional structure. Managing directors were appointed, but the management committee was not fully established. The internal control system was still insufficient. Organisational reform which started on the shop floor, gradually came to necessitate the reorganisation of the whole company.

The firm planned a drastic two directional expansion in the second half of the 1950s. One direction was into petrochemicals, and the other into aluminium interests. For petrochemicals, the plan was at first motivated by the change of sources of gases used for the production of ammonium sulphate. It was intended that the production costs of fertilisers would be reduced by changing the raw materials used. However, the company had not accumulated the necessary technical skills when it formed these plans to make inroads into new areas. All the technology had to be introduced from foreign companies. From 1959 the production of organic chemical products, instead of fertilisers, became *Showa Denko*'s main endeavour. This plan was implemented by a subsidiary which had the technological support of *Philips Petroleum*. At the same time, interests were being developed around electro chemicals by integrating the whole process necessary for the processing of aluminium, including electrical generation. Until the mid-1960s, capital was invested mainly in equipment for aluminium production.[6] This reflected the proportion of each product line in the company's total output and the company was quickly discarding its role as a fertiliser firm in the second half of the 1950s.

Organisational reform at the higher level of hierarchy started in 1956. Neither the position and function of the board of directors, nor the authority of the president had been clear and to solve this problem, a planning committee, composed of the managing directors, was formed as the advisory staff for decision making. By 1961 the planning committee had established its position in the firm as the final deliberating and decision making authority.

After 1965 the firm came to promote petrochemical projects on a more extensive scale, and this was realised by the construction of an industrial complex in conjunction with four other companies. The allocation of factories became a severe problem, slightly earlier than in the case of other chemical companies, because of mercury poisoning and the high cost of electricity. So far as the latter is concerned, *Showa Denko* planned to set up production units overseas by forming companies like *New Zealand Aluminium Smelters Ltd*. Fertilisers continued to decrease in importance and aluminium was not able to recover its place in spite of these measures. Instead, the company diversified into a wider range of products during the decade following 1965. Industrial chemicals, resins, gases, ferro-alloys, and chemical products were also developed.

The introduction of the multidivisional structure had been examined since the mid-1960s. The necessity of organisational reform was recognised in the following light. Firstly, the products of electro-chemicals required a strategy different from that of petrochemicals. Secondly, business policy had to become market oriented, and the integration of each function was more necessary than it once had been. Thirdly, the responsibility of each unit should be made clearer. An organisation reformed in this way would be able to respond quickly to drastic changes. The posts of division managers were largely assumed by the managing directors. Furthermore affiliated companies were grouped together and placed under the divisions. The recession of the early 1970s came after this organisational reform, and it hit nonferrous metals and petrochemicals severely. Aluminium interests were separated, while forward integration in petrochemicals was attempted. Financial resources were moved to foreign countries.[7] Meanwhile, the multidivisional structure was strengthened by the adoption of the internal capital system. In contrast to *Mitsui Toatsu* whose divisional system was weakened in the face of severe market circumstances, *Showa Denko* met them by moving in the opposite direction.

Sumitomo Chemical[8] was already considerably diversified by 1950, although sales of fertilisers amounted to nearly half of its total output. The main product lines of the company changed from fertilisers and dyestuffs to aluminium and resins in the 1960s, and finally to industrial chemicals in the 1970s. Its organisation changed in parallel with changes of its products. In 1950 the company was based on an incomplete functional structure consisting of the sales departments in the head and Tokyo-branch offices, and of production departments in the factories. Divisionalisation started in the early 1960s, and the geographical system was reformed into a product-market one, in which the trading departments were divided into sub-units according to products. Towards the end of the 1960s, the divisional structure extended to the whole company, though it was still a 'staff-divisional' system, although between 1973 and 1975, divisions were equipped with their own production units.

In the early 1950s, *Sumitomo Chemical* laid emphasis on the development of production capacity. In order to compete with cheap European fertilisers in the South-east Asian market, equipment had to be modernised in order to reduce the cost of ammonium gases. Then the usefulness of petroleum was gradually noticed, not only in ammonium gases, but also for the production of polyethylene. A series of technologies were introduced from foreign companies, although *Sumitomo Chemical* also began research of its own. In aluminium and dyestuffs, the company developed new products by applying its own technologies. Thus, the company diversified into new products with both borrowed technology and technology of their own. These activities were coordinated through a very crude form of a functional structure. In the aluminium branch, there was a division of labour between two companies of the Sumitomo group: *Sumitomo Chemical* was in charge of refining, and *Sumitomo Metal Industries* undertook rolling.

The divisional structure was first introduced in 1961 in the pharmaceutical branch and then in the aluminium branch in 1964. Both

divisions were equipped with production, sales, and research functions. Until that time, company departmental managers were located
in various parts of the country, and this frequently caused a lag in
decision making and serious problems also occurred in the coordination of functions. Both fine chemicals and aluminium were particular in the production process and in marketing. The market for fine
chemicals was particularly competitive and required swift decision-
making. However, these divisions were not formed as 'full' divisions
entrusted with profit responsibility. These partial organisational reforms were taken in response to the management policy of strengthening the aluminium and fine chemical branches. Investment was,
however, built up mainly in aluminium and resins, but not in fine
chemicals. The advantages of the divisional structure were thus
appreciated, but the remaining parts of the company were not readily
divisionalised. Instead, they adopted a headquarters system within
the sales function in 1963. The sales department was divided into six
headquarters, each in charge of the sales of a particular sort of
products. This, in turn, integrated the function of sales which had
been geographically divided between the Osaka head office and the
Tokyo branch office. By these means they aimed not only at the
self-sufficiency of each kind of product, but also at securing swift
decision-making capabilities and clear responsibility. At the same
time, the Marketing Development Department was set up to reinforce the staff function, while purchasing activities were integrated
into one headquarters under the head office. Further reorganisations
were made, intending centralisation of management. Such centralisation was further promoted in 1969–70, when the divisional system
was extended to the whole company. In agricultural chemicals,
industrial chemicals, and resins, the development of new products
was desperately needed, and each sales headquarters acquired research and technology and became a division. Newly formed divisions lacked production functions. The profit responsibility of each
factory played an important role in maintaining the leading position
of the production units, although in formal, investment and production, planning was carried out by the head office.[9]

Just after these organisational reforms, *Sumitomo Chemical* had to
face a number of severe business environments, and a shake-up of
the top management took place. A vicious spiral of petrochemical
plant expansion and falling prices had to be solved, and this pushed
the company one step further into fine chemicals. In actual fact, the
company successfully increased the proportion of fine chemicals in

the total sales of the company without heavy capital investment. The aluminium division was, like in other chemical companies, reorganised into a separate company. Divisions spread over the whole company in the first half of the 1970s, and undertook control of factories. Such reorganisation appeared to bring about an organic integration of production and sales, but this did not last long; factories were separated from divisions again, and were put under the direct control of the head office. The attempted co-operation between production and sales was unsuccessful. In the chemical industry, production processes were intricately combined, making one product the raw materials for others. When a division was to control production, a whole factory had to belong to a particular division. However, the products of a factory ranged over a variety of types that were dealt with by several divisions. Factories did not return to their former production units with profit responsibility. Under severe circumstances, it was necessary that the production function be controlled with the interests of the whole company in mind, and should thus not be left as a factory level problem.

Mitsubishi Chemical Industries[10] had its origins in a coal chemistry firm, and was engaged in the production of coke and fertilisers in 1950. The company had experienced the adoption of a divisional structure when the former *Mitsubishi Chemical Industries* was formed by the merger of three companies in 1944. Its management structure was turned into a functional structure in the following year, divisionalised again in 1947, and finally, due to the separation of fibre and glass concerns in 1950, the structure of the firm changed into an incomplete functional one. In 1950 the head office had sales and technological departments, while the production departments were located in the factories. The divisional structure was adopted in 1964, though the factories and other operating units were not included in divisions. Such a 'staff divisional' system was reinforced by the organisational reform of 1969.

Coke played an important role in the post-war reconstruction of the company. *Mitsubishi Mining* supplied raw materials and undertook products for *Mitsubishi Chemical Industries*, which specialised in the production of coke. Fertilisers were produced as by-products of coke-making through the application of coke gas to ammonium production. The firm stepped up into petrochemicals jointly with *Shell* and the other companies of the *Mitsubishi* group, and set up *Mitsubishi Petrochemical*. However, after 1960 *Mitsubishi Chemical* embarked on petrochemicals by itself, and at the same time advanced into aluminium smelting which though a late-comer, was the growing industrial branch. These two industries required vast amounts of financial resources exceeding the total investment of the previous decade. The company was able to introduce the latest aluminium smelting technology, and built a factory at Naoetsu where they had easy access to cheap electricity. Raw materials were supplied by *Alcoa* in the form of alumina. Having appreciated fully its potential use, the company became aware of the necessity of entering petrochemicals independently, although it had joined with *Mitsubishi Petrochemicals* and sent many staff to the latter. Coordination had to be made between *Mitsubishi Chemical Industries* and *Mitsubishi Petrochemical*, and the project of the former was set out along lines that would avoid duplication with the latter. Here again, main technologies were introduced from foreign countries, though the company tried to develop its own as well.

In the beginning of the 1960s, strategic targets were set in preparation for the coming liberalisation of foreign trade. The whole company attempted to reduce the costs of, and increase the amount of production. Among petrochemical products, raw materials for synthetic textiles showed a remarkable growth. This field was chosen in consideration of the products made by *Mitsubishi Petrochemical*. Based as it was on product diversification, *Mitsubishi Chemical* introduced the divisional structure in 1964. Prior to this move, the divisional system was introduced into its dyestuffs branch in 1959, which at that time was facing difficulties. In the dyestuffs division, sales and technology were effectively integrated under the division manager. The divisional structure of 1964 resembled this form because newly founded divisions were equipped with sales and technology functions, and were mainly engaged in sales planning, production planning, and marketing. These were the 'staff divisions'. Local branch offices were put under the direct control of the head office, as were the factories. As in the case of other chemical companies, factories could not be divided up for technological reasons. Along with the reinforcement of the special staff of each division, the general staff departments were established.

Large investment in aluminium and petrochemicals made *Mitsubishi Chemical Industries* the largest chemical company in Japan.[11] However, its scale was still small when compared with that of its Western counterparts. The company's strategy of expansion continued after 1965, and included the introduction of foreign capital. This long-term plan was re-examined towards the end of the 1970s when chemical companies began to recognise the strain of vigorous growth. Eventually the company moved into fine chemicals and environmental control systems. Internal organisation was made more flexible at the same time. Sub-units in a division, such as the sales or the development departments, were abolished, and departmental managers were each made responsible for a particular project. These strategic and structural changes were not readily reflected on the changing share of each product in the total sales of the company. After the oil-crisis, however, this policy was promoted more earnestly. Aluminium smelting was separated as an independent company because of its high production costs. New divisions were set up to deal with precision machinery, pharmaceuticals, and food. Investment in new interests showed slight increase.[12] The sales grew, and of them, petrochemical products still showed noticeable growth.

Ube Industries[13] was formed during the Second World War from a merger of four local companies which themselves were originally derived from a single company, and situated in Ube. As a result, *Ube Industries* appeared as a diversified firm with interests ranging over coal, fertilisers, cement, and machinery. Soon the new company set up a central purchasing department as well as a sales department.

The coal mining branch was first to be reconstructed after the war, and the construction of ammonium equipment followed, which naturally led the firm to diversify into nylon material. Although this company was heavily committed to coal mining, source of gases were quickly changed to those of petroleum by 1960, and several years later a petrochemical project was started. The company tried to reduce the production costs of ammonium by making use of their own coal and technology. However, these were too expensive, and they thus decided to introduce new technologies from various American companies.

In 1962 the multidivisional structure, in which the divisions succeeded their forebear companies was introduced. In practice, however, the process of transition was more complicated than this. In anticipation of the dissolution of the company, the firm had been divided into four sub-units with a full set of functions by 1950. In 1950 the firm strengthened the function of the head office so as to be able to promote its smooth reconstruction. In the same year an Accounting Headquarters was set up in the head office in order to coordinate the flow of money and materials more efficiently. The operating functions were reorganised into 'Coal' and 'Manufacturing' headquarters, both of which became divisions. The trading function, which had previously been independently subject to each factory or mining works, was centralised into each of these headquarters. The reinforcement of the head office continued. In 1952 the controlling department was formed in the Accounting Headquarters to carry out internal control, and the financing department was separated. In this type of unrelated diversifier, the top management often found difficulties in making correct judgements as to the condition of their own company. In 1955, four management sub-committees were formed to draft strategies for each of the companies' main industrial branches.

The introduction of the multidivisional structure followed these preceding measures. Towards the early 1960s the company's activities became highly complex, and the relationships among these activities began to change through the introduction of petrochemicals. The management became aware of the necessity to clarify the profit responsibility of each industry branch. Different salary systems among divisions, for instance, were not a result of different practices among the four forerunner companies, but of the principle of the profit responsibility of each division. Here management control was looser than in the ordinary divisional structure, but the strong leadership of the president Nakayasu checked this centrifugal tendency. This tendency, however, vanished partially as the company changed its product lines, retreating particularly from coal mining and diversifying into petrochemicals and chemical plants. Capital investment into petrochemicals was high during the decade after 1964.[14] From the beginning of the 1970s, however, investment into cement increased,[15] directly reflecting the increase of the share of cement and raw concrete in the total sales of the company.

Dainippon Ink and Chemicals[16] was a general chemical company, having its own petrochemical plants as the basis for various chemical products such as dyestuffs, intermediaries, resins, building materials, and printing machinery. In 1950, however, the product lines had come to consist primarily of printing ink, dyestuffs, and pigments. The firm was smoothly reconstructed as a result of the publishing boom immediately after the war, and rapid development changed the firm from a family concern to a public company. The company's capital investment preceded that of others. The first five year plan made the improvement of the quality of ink and the modernisation of equipment as policy objectives. This is first observed in the change of raw materials for ink from the traditional linseed oil to synthetic resins. This was enabled by a technological tie-up with *RCI* of the United States. This change of raw materials gave the company an opportunity to diversify. In 1955 the share of resins reached 40 per cent of the total output of the company.

In 1950, when other companies were engaged entirely in the introduction of new technologies and management techniques at the shop floor level, the *Dainippon Ink and Chemicals'* management became aware of importance of higher level management, and adopted the multidivisional structure. K. Kawamura, the newly appointed senior managing director appreciated, as a result of his career in a trading company, the necessity of establishing the profit responsibility of each sub-unit. Each division was made a profit centre with sales, production and technology functions, and controlled by a senior managing director. Division managers were delegated with the authority over acceptance of orders, production, purchasing and pricing all of which were necessary to attain the sales and profit objectives of each division. As a further measure for management decentralisation, local branch offices were charged with sales profit responsibility and factories were charged with production profit responsibility. Thus a territorial responsibility system was established, and in order to control such a decentralised organisation, a long-range management plan had to be completed. Each division made short-term profit plans and reported to the head office. The formation of many profit centres required a well-established internal transfer-price system. In the chemical industry, in which the raw materials of a division very frequently depended on the products of other divisions, such a procedure becomes troublesome, and many other general chemical companies chose a different type of divisional structure in order to avoid such difficulties.

The production of resins was undertaken by a subsidiary, a joint venture of *RCI*, while *Dainippon Ink and Chemicals* either distributed this subsidiary's products or processed part of them. Diversification since the latter half of the 1950s went in two directions: one was forward integration into finished resin products, and the other into market related products such as printing machinery. In order to prepare for the coming liberalisation of trade, the size of the company needed to be enlarged. For this purpose investment in chemicals and resins, and the acquisition of a production subsidiary were carried out. By the mid-1960s, the company's heavy dependence on ink and resins had been reduced.

After 1960 *Dainippon Ink and Chemicals* went into petrochemicals for the self-supply of raw materials. During the decade after 1965 the expansion strategy of the company resulted in a 5-fold growth in its sales, though the share of each product in the total output did not change remarkably. Organisational structure changed little either, but expanded due to the increase of product lines. In 1968 a division manager system was introduced. The division managerial posts, which had formerly been held concurrently by managing directors, were made independent. Even after the oil-crisis the share of each product in total sales changed little. The multidivisional structure which was adopted in 1950 was still unchanged 30 years later. Sales and production functions as well as technology belonged to each division, while the head office was responsible for financial management. Internal capital was allocated to each division, and interest was imposed by the head office upon such capital. Some of the staff functions, such as the pre-estimation of demand and raw material prices, were assumed by the divisions. Divisions were also made responsible for the management of the factories. This type of divisional structure was considered as the motive power of the company in the end of the 1970s. However, reorganisation into a more market-oriented system came to be discussed. Such an improved structure would be able to deal with large scale orders which were concerned with several divisions. The top management function, especially initiative in the allocation of managerial resources, as well as the general staff, were strengthened amidst the severe business environment after 1974.

Mitsubishi Petrochemical[17] was set up in 1956 as a joint petrochemical project of the *Mitsubishi* group and *Shell*. Its main product lines were in basic organic chemicals and intermediaries such as ethylene and propylene. The ratios of these products to the total output of the firm changed little throughout the following 25 years. Its president as well as its technological and administrative staff were sent from *Mitsubishi Chemical Industries*. The top management was composed of four directors, and decisions were made by the management advisory committee which consisted of departmental managers.

The products of the company were classified as fabricated basic materials. But the company was distinguished from companies in semi-finished products not only by its rapid growth but by the breadth of its products. Until 1975, *Mitsubishi Petrochemical*'s strategy was one of the expansion of each product line. The divisional structure was adopted in 1966. As in the case of other petrochemical companies, its divisions were composed of sales and staff, separated from production functions.

Sekisui Chemical[18] was formed as an offshoot of *Nippon Chisso*, one of the large-scale chemical companies of the pre-war era, and after the Second World War it commenced plastic processing. Soon vinylon pipes and processed plastic products became its main products. The rate of its growth in the 1950s was extraordinarily high, making the company into an exception; a giant among thousands of small-scale plastic processing firms. Factories were primarily controlled by the sales manager, but in 1951 the functional structure was adopted and the board of directors was formed. Following this move to the functional structure, the firm adopted the divisional structure in 1958, which was reorganised as the 'operating-units' structure in 1965. However, shortly after the decentralisation of 1965, the multidivisional structure was revived in 1966. The multidivisional structure was maintained until 1975, when the functional structure took its place.

As new kinds of resins such as polyethylene began to appear towards the end of the 1950s, competition among plastic companies became acute. *Sekisui Chemical* was able to adapt itself to this new situation by innovating new technologies. A five year plan, beginning in 1960, aimed at a 33 per cent annual growth, with proposed shares of construction materials at 49 per cent, processed products at 15 per cent, and synthetic products at 37 per cent of their total sales. To attain these objectives, some organisational reforms were made. A central research institute was founded. For the housing market, a subsidiary was set up. To compete with thousands of small-scale manufacturers in such an industry dealing with bulky products, local *Sekisuis* were set up to attain economic transportation costs, and seven such companies appeared in sequence. And finally, the multidivisional structure was adopted in 1958, prior to which, the financial position of the company had worsened. Profit responsibility had to be established by allocating the production and sales function to each unit. The head office needed to be simplified and to be specialised into a staff function, and for that purpose surplus head office employees were moved to operating divisions. The integration of production and sales under one division was justified as follows: as *Sekisui Chemical* was concerned with newly appearing products for a mass market, a close relationship between supply and demand was required. This reorganisation into the multidivisional structure proved to be effective. A top management organisation was established by forming a management committee, although its members also assumed division managerial posts, meaning that the separation of the top management and the operating units was incomplete.

Towards the end of the first five-year plan, the company was intending to integrate backwards to secure raw materials for themselves. However, these aggressive and expansionist policies came to an end when the company encountered the severe recession of 1965. Expansion was financed by loans, whose interest became a burden when expansion terminated.

The new president, invited from *Asahi Chemical Industry* recognised that most of the company's products had outlived themselves, and were rapidly losing out to new products, and that therefore the development of new products, rather than integration into raw materials or mere continuation of an expansionist policy was the first task that should be faced. The new management noticed potential opportunities in the production of unit-housing as a new area of activities. The company had been engaged in the production of pipes for building materials, and then expanded into various housing parts and plumbing fixtures. The production of unit-housing was a forward integration through the extension of the company's own products. During the slump and reconstruction period, the multidivisional structure was abolished. The defects of the divisional structure, namely, the acceleration of unnecessary competition among divisions, the overstressing of short-term performance, the prevention of the reallocation of technological skills or personnel among divisions, and the duplication of responsibilities between divisions and subsidiaries, were also noted. However, the reforms were curious in this respect, because factories and local branches were made profit centres, and management decentralisation was thus further promoted. The head office staff was reinforced in order to be able to plan long term strategy.

In the course of reconstruction, the divisional structure was revived. Seven divisions were made profit centres again, and authority was delegated to the division managers, who were non-executive directors. However this time, factories and local branches did not belong to the divisions. Instead these operating units were put under the direct control of the president, while the divisions became responsible for planning and directing production and sales. Since the re-introduction of the multidivisional structure, excessive decentralisation was avoided, and for the same purpose divisions were grouped into three division headquarters. The sales channel rather than the technological core was used as the criterion of reorganisation. This criterion became more pronounced in 1969, because the multidivisional structure by product was reformed into the multidivisional structure by market. The divisions were charged with developing new products and marketing, while daily sales activities were carried out by the sales offices. However, this was not the final large-scale reorganisation. In 1971, in order to simplify the management structure, the division headquarters were abolished, and four divisions were put immediately below the president. Furthermore, local branches were placed under the control of the divisions, and the division managers were made responsible for production and sales again, in addition to the development of new products. In 1973 the division headquarters system was adopted for the second time. An international division headquarters, which was to control production subsidiaries in Europe was also added this time.

The oil-crisis hit the housing-unit interests of the company. However, existing plastic branches were more severely hit. *Sekisui Chemical* reexamined its diversification and as a result management resources were allocated to housing-unit interests. The multidivisional structure was abolished in 1975. A sales and a production headquarters were founded to control the production and sales departments which had formerly belonged to the divisions respectively. All sales activities were operated through the sales headquarters. The managers of the nine major trading offices, who came under the control of the headquarters manager, were made responsible for the sales and profits of their own branches. In the same manner, eight factories were made responsible for their own production costs. In both headquarters several staff departments were set up. In the sales headquarters, for instance, six planning departments by market were set up in addition to the general sales staff department. By the end of the 1970s, however, this functional headquarters system with some degree of decentralisation had given way to the multidivisional structure.

Takeda Chemical Industries[19] was engaged primarily in pharmaceuticals in 1950, but by 1970 had diversified into various chemical products. The market-oriented nature of its products prompted the firm to establish a functionally departmentalised structure in its early phase. As the company diversified into new product lines, it introduced an accounting system by products in 1957, which prepared the way for the introduction of the multidivisional structure in 1960. First of all the problems such as strikes and surplus workers were solved. For production, synthesising and fermenting processes were modernised and distribution channels were built up for sales, and this brought about the employment of 2000 well-organised special agents.

The functions of the top management were made clear with written regulations, which served to gradually lower family influence. A planning department was established, and the first five-year plan, beginning in 1950, was proposed. These strategic and structural changes in the first half of the 1950s resulted in a relative increase in production of pharmaceuticals, which came to represent more than 90 per cent of total sales in 1955.

Throughout the following two series of long term plans, investment was made in the final process of pharmaceuticals.[20] In spite of excesses in equipment and increasing competition in the pharmaceutical industry, diversification was nevertheless limited. Only modest diversification into condiments, medical machinery and foods, coupled with gradual moves toward the divisional system, was seen in the latter half of the 1950s. In the sales department, the controlling function was separated from the operating function, and the controlling department was established. Next to be introduced was a separate calculating system for each product line to monitor the contribution of each product to the company as a whole. This was done at the same time as a measure for determining from the situation of the non-pharmaceutical branches, whether or not it was worthwhile to embark full-scale on new fields. The answer was found in promoting diversification, and for that purpose the divisional structure was adopted in 1960. The largest division was food, which began with vitamin-enriched rice in the early post-war period. *Takeda Chemicals* gained control over an outlet consisting of rice wholesalers and retailers, and also supplied soft drinks and condiments through these channels. These products were developed with the company's own technology. Diversification into chemical products, including agricultural chemicals, was carried out with foreign technologies.

Takeda Chemical's divisionalisation took an irregular form. Foods and chemicals constituted divisions of their own, each with production and sales functions, while the pharmaceutical branch was divided into two divisions, one in charge of production and the other of sales. The main reason behind such irregularity was that the pharmaceutical interests of this company were, compared to other branches, too large to be assumed by one division manager. Furthermore the pharmaceuticals sales division dealt not only with the products of the production division, but also with those of the affiliated companies and of foreign companies, to an extent of more than 40 per cent of the *Takeda*'s sales. These divisions were not necessarily made profit centres in the strict sense of the term. In the two pharmaceutical divisions, performance was jointly monitored. The posts of the division managers were concurrently assumed by managing directors, who were at the same time, concerned with company-wide policy making. The main reason for this was that the division managers were responsible for the external relationships with the government and other companies, and this necessitated that they have a higher status in the company as a whole. It is of interest that each of these divisions was situated in a different place, each most suitable for access to markets or information.

For sources of profit, the company had been dependent on vitamin compounds until the mid-1960s. When this reached its peak, full-scale diversification was attempted. Foods, chemicals, and toileteries were again chosen as areas for diversification. Investment in chemical branches rose to high levels between 1965 and 1973.[21] Products other than pharmaceuticals had increased to more than 40 per cent of total sales by 1973, although these new products did not quickly improve the company's overall performance. After 1965 marketing policy was also changed. *Takeda* devoted great efforts to medicines for hospital use as opposed to those for popular use that were sold at chemists. The two pharmaceutical product divisions were integrated into a full division with production and sales in 1972. Although investment declined after 1974, research and development funding continued at a high ratio, attaining 5 per cent of the total sales. These changing strategies had been proved to be successful by the end of the 1970s.

As was observed in Chapter 2, many chemical concerns had already appeared among the largest firms of the pre-war era. They were either fertiliser companies which utilised electricity or fine chemical companies which supplied pharmaceuticals or dyestuffs. Most of them, however, disappeared from the ranks of the largest firms of the post-war period. The largest post-war firms, though already in existence in the pre-war era, were engaged in electro- or coal-chemistry. After the mid-1950s they began to diversify through the application of petrochemical technologies, but they were unable to use their own technologies which they had developed in the pre-war era. The introduction of petrochemicals was initiated by necessity of reducing the cost of ammonium gases, which was required for the cheap supply of fertilisers. However, it did not stop at this since petrochemicals had wider applications in the production at lower cost of various chemicals such as polyethylene, resins, synthetic rubber, synthetic fibres, detergents, and fine chemicals. Some of these products had been unknown and others had been supplied by different companies. As new technologies were introduced from foreign chemical companies, there came to be little market relationship with former products.

The six general chemical companies had adopted the divisional structure by 1970. However, prior to the introduction of the modern multidivisional structure, four of them had undergone management decentralisation by adopting the 'production-unit system' during the post-war period of reconstruction. The sub-units in this old decentralised structure were referred to as either divisions or headquarters. This structure was introduced either to control subsidiaries created by acquisition, or to promote the self-supporting production unit system. Only one company has maintained its original system, while the others had moved to the functional structure by the mid-1950s. Centrifugal tendencies were not eliminated, however, partly because of the traditional strength of the production units and partly because of the technological nature of the chemical processes. These had influence on the multidivisional structure of the chemical companies. A full-fledged division with at least sales and manufacturing function did not become dominant. Many divisions were, instead, 'staffdivisions' with no operating department, or at best they were 'sales divisions' in which factories formed independent sub-units. Reorganisation into the normal divisional structure was attempted from time to time, and by 1980, three of the firms had adopted the full divisional structure and the remaining three the 'sales divisions'. In general chemicals, one product acts as the raw material for other products, and internal transfer becomes very complicated if the self-sufficient divisional structure is adopted. In addition, it is very difficult to divide a series of chemical processes into several product divisions. And finally, as it became more and more difficult for a chemical plant to maintain a good relationship with the inhabitants the production function had to be dealt with in the light of the overall survey of the situation by the company in question.

The remaining three companies in chemicals and pharmaceuticals, which were engaged either in the production of final goods or intermediaries, differed from each other in their organisations. Two of them introduced a normal multidivisional structure after a series of trials and errors. The profit responsibility of each division was not clarified, the allocation of tasks between the management committee and divisions was vague, and moreover, the integration of production and sales into one division was not easy. This was also the case of the remaining one company, which was engaged in petrochemicals. This company, *Takeda Chemical* introduced sales divisions, while factories were placed under the direct control of the head office.

Thus in the case of Japanese chemical companies, the multidivisional structure became predominant, though primarily *not* in its classical form.

7.3 ELECTRICAL AND ELECTRONIC COMPANIES

There were 14 concerns in the electrical engineering industry. Nine of them which were engaged in comprehensive, heavy or communication electrical industries are examined here. The remaining five, which mostly supplied household electrical equipment will be discussed in the next chapter. The development of the Japanese electrical equipment industry belongs to the post-war era. In 1920 only four such concerns were listed among the largest 100 firms. In the interwar years, the electrical departments of mining or shipbuilding concerns, which had been engaged in repairing the electrical equipment of mines or supplying electric appliances for ships, were organised as separate companies. Some of them entered into special partnership with foreign companies, such as *General Electric* and *Siemens*. New management and accounting methods were introduced from these foreign companies. After the Second World War, these pre-war firms intensified their relationships with their oversea partners. Patterns in the import of technologies changed due to the emergence of new market opportunities and of new companies. Japanese companies became used to introducing excellent technologies from foreign companies, and this naturally led to competition among Japanese companies over the introduction of the same technologies. The time-lag between the introduction of new technologies and its application into production was short in post-war Japanese electrical engineering companies. In the 1960s investment in research and development rose sharply, up to a level equivalent to that of their European counterparts.

The pre-war firms had become diversified by 1940, and the post-war firms which began with one or two sorts of household electrical equipment or radio receivers, had become diversified by 1970. In the long run the production quantity of household electrical equipment exceeded that of heavy electrical engineering. The share of heavy electrical machinery in the total output of electrical engineering products decreased from 44 per cent in 1950, to 36 per cent in 1955 and to as low as 24 per cent in 1965.

Organisational change took place in the early phases of development. By 1960 five of nine concerns had adopted the multidivisional structure, and all of them had introduced it by 1970, although with some variations. Prior to this they had experienced management decentralisation or even divisional forms.

Hitachi[22] was a unique as an electrical equipment company in 1950, because electrical equipment represented less than one-third of its total products. The nature of their products, consisting of heavy machinery, rolling stock, steel products, and wire and cable, pushed the company to a fully diversified firm in 1950. Some of these products were the results of acquisitions, or of vertical integration. However, most were developed with the company's own technology. By 1950 the company had been equipped with three corporate research institutes with some works laboratories, each laboratory specialising in one or more industrial area. The organisation of the company began with the functional structure, and was reformed into a multidivisional one in 1952. The divisions were originally 'staff divisions', but during the 1960s divisions gradually took over the management of production units and operating departments. However, the nature of the staff divisions has remained until the present, and the operating units still maintain their autonomy.

Investment priority was given to heavy electricals during the first half of the 1950s, though this did not contribute to the heavy electricals' shares in the total output of the company.[23] During the first half of the 1950s, diversification into measuring instruments and chemical products was attempted, which meant an expansion of *Hitachi*'s product lines into unrelated areas. Structurally *Hitachi* experienced many changes; in 1950 the head office was reorganised into four functional headquarters and the sales headquarters was charged with the control of branch offices. The division headquarters, which was concerned with production, was divided into six sub-units, each in charge of the planning of factory management and sales. Senior and ordinary managing directors were appointed as headquarters managers, and important problems were discussed by the headquarters managers' committee. Following this reform a divisional structure was introduced in 1952. The end of a long strike and the boom of the Korean War were aided in reconstructing the firm's foundation. The top management was named the 'Important Business Committee'. However, each factory and branch office was placed under the direct control of the president, and factories were operated through a self-supporting system. Each of eight divisions was still a 'staff division', mainly in charge of planning and monitoring.

During the latter half of the 1950s, *Hitachi* chose electrical equipment for its major area of investment, and began to manufacture household electrical equipment by applying heavy electrical engineering technology and research on new areas such as electron tubes. The company had an established policy of developing independent technologies, and had no special links with foreign electrical companies. This policy was maintained throughout the expansion into new fields of electrical equipment. The steel and cable branches of the firm were separated into independent companies, and this was later followed by a similar separation of the chemical products division. In spite of the separation of these branches, the number of divisions increased towards the mid-1960s. Throughout the decade following 1955, the characteristics of the divisions remained unchanged. Divisions were accompanied by neither production nor sales units, although they were able to control factories and branch offices. Only the top management organisation changed slightly when managing directors were divorced from responsibilities as division managers.

During the severe recession of the early 1960s, they planned a series of organisational reforms, but these took some time. In order to make profit control more complete, it was planned that production and sales units were placed under divisions. However, each of *Hitachi*'s factories manufactured various kinds of products and could not be divided into divisions by product. After 1962 the divisions were gradually equipped with production units, and by 1964 all the divisions owned their own factories. Profit centres were moved from factories to divisions. By this reorganisation, redundant expenditure, staff and activities was removed. However, the sales function remained independent of divisions.

During the economic recovery following 1965, *Hitachi* invested heavily in household electrical equipment and electronics, the latter including computer and communication equipment. This choice did not directly reflect on the share of each product line. However, towards the beginning of the 1970s, household electrical equipment and electronics developed, each representing a quarter of the total sales of the company, another half being shared equally by heavy electrical and heavy engineering products. Together with this changing strategy a large-scale structural reform began to take place. This time, not only the production units but also the sales departments (except for local branch offices) were placed under the control of division managers. Local branch offices were divided into sections corresponding to their respective divisions. Another important change was to be found in the sub-division of operating units, and the grouping of these divisions into division headquarters. The technology of electrical engineering and electronics was changing rapidly and the traditional operating units were unable to adapt themselves to these changes. Existing divisions were divided and reorganised according to the nature of the technologies of the new products. Thus, though the divisions were equipped with sales function for promoting the self-supporting system, each factory was allocated with internal capital according to the amount of its assets. Interest was charged on internal capital and internal loans. Factories under divisions and not divisions themselves undertook financial responsibility. By this reform, the divisions remained and division headquarters were set up. However, the factories actually became divisions, and the 'divisional structure' which had appeared in 1952 was revived. Twenty-six factories became 'production divisions' under divisions, and the main task of the divisions in the classical sense was to coordinate the relationship between factories and factories, and between sales and production.

Along with such specification, *Hitachi* combined divisions into groups between 1967 and 1969. Like in the heavy engineering companies, demand for large-scale equipment increased towards the end of the 1960s. First attempts were made to combine chemical engineering and electrical machinery into one division headquarters. Thus the organisational problem of this giant company were found to be in adjusting the contrary tendencies between the systematisation of product-markets and the specification of production technology. The choice in the 1970s raised the more difficult question of coordination under such a structure. Instead of its traditional all-round strategy, the company decided to concentrate on developing electronics and heavy electrical engineering. Household electrical equipment contributed to a high turnover, but investment in this field was curbed. As a result, the share of the heavy electrical and electronic branches grew gradually. However, each division or factory of *Hitachi* retained strong decentralising tendencies and a central allocation of resources was not easy.

Until the company introduced the divisional structure in 1949, *Tokyo Shibaura Electric*[24] (*Toshiba*) had been administered by a self-supporting factory system, in which each factory controlled sales and planning. The multidivisional system was completed during the 1950s and 1960s, but in the 1970s it reorganised into a more loosely structured system.

Its early organisation was that of a holding-company structure derived from the merger of two large-scale companies. One of the predecessors was a weak electrical company, and the other a heavy electrical firm. Both companies had technological ties with *General Electric*, and their merger brought forth a fully diversified electrical company ranging from household electrical and communication equipment, and heavy electrical machinery. The self-supporting system of factories was, after a heavy loss and a large-scale labour dispute, a prerequisite to obtaining financial support from banks. The divisional structure of 1949 was not of a complete one, but was a mixture of divisional and functional principles, in which electrical machinery and communication equipment branches were organised into full divisions, while measuring instruments and electrical lighting bulbs were organised into production units, with their sales activities forming a separate sub-unit. The areas covered by the divisions accounted for less than half of the company's sales. The motive for adopting this structure was 'to simplify the company organisation according to the product-market areas, to coordinate various product lines more efficiently, and to reconstruct the company by paying attention to the initiatives of each division and production unit'. The top management organisation, consisting of directors was formed, in which the department managers were required to take part in meetings when the topic discussed concerned their own departments. An internal auditing system was established, though it did not last long. The top management organisation was divided into the managing committee consisting of the president and managing directors, and the operating committee in charge of planning each function. Meanwhile the production units consolidated sales function and became full divisions. Local branch offices were set under the direct control of the president, but were directed by the division managers. In spite of these reorganisations, recovery only came slowly and it was only in 1953 that the company began to grow smoothly.

As the company grew into mass-production goods, organisational reform again became necessary. The sales departments of the electrical light bulbs and measuring instruments divisions were separated and formed a sales company. In setting up this sales company, eight existing local sales companies were also consolidated. Local branch offices were engaged in the sales of products of the electrical machinery and communication equipment divisions, while mass-production goods were handled by this sales company.

Between 1955 and 1965 more than half of *Toshiba*'s financial resources were allocated to heavy electrical engineering,[25] with another fifth going to the household electrical branch and 18 per cent to electron tubes. More than a quarter of all investment was in research and development. As a result, these three areas became equal in their sales by 1965. During the decade following 1955 the number of product lines and affiliated companies increased, and these necessitated the development of the top management. Five senior managing directors were appointed to assume the responsibility of each function. These senior managing directors were, instead of the president, in charge of a number of departments and affiliated companies, and a sales control department was set up to support them and make plans for marketing. The company had been production oriented, but tried to change to marketing orientation. By 1962 due to technological innovation and the emergence of new kinds of products which resulted from it, imbalances of sales and human resources among divisions appeared, and the existing divisions were unable to cope with this new situation. To render a balance among divisions, large divisions were divided and to monitor them, a management committee was founded in 1962, and the general staff was also formed. This reorganisation also enabled the firm to meet the setback of the mid-1960s as well as the liberalisation of trade.

After 1965 large scale investment was made in colour televisions, air conditioners, atomics, elevators, and computers.[26] The importance of heavy electrical engineering rose during the decade after 1965. Having merged with *Ishikawajima Heavy Industries* to prepare for the growing demand for power source equipment, *Toshiba* eventually acquired *Ishikawajima Turbine*. With such a wide range of technologies, only *Toshiba* was able to maintain high shares in power plants and high profits among the stagnant heavy electrical engineering companies. Before that time, managing directors were members of top management and were in charge of particular divisions. By removing this dual nature from the managing directors, they were able to devote themselves to top management function and decision making in conjunction with the president. Another change was made by increasing the autonomy of each division. The authority for decision making at the operating levels was delegated to the division managers. A new system of monitoring the division's performance was adopted. Capital and assets were allocated to each division as internal capital. Together with the specification of divisions, divisions were grouped. By this reorganisation seven groups were formed to accept large-scale orders.

After the oil crisis, resources were allocated to electronics. The management structure was also improved. All the business concerns of the company were divided into three sectors, namely heavy electricals, household electricals, and communication equipments, each representing approximately equal shares in the total output of the company. The vice-president and senior managing directors were appointed heads of the sectors and made almost all decisions.

Mitsubishi Electric[27] was able to recover thanks to the Electric Development Plan of the government, which brought about an increase in demand in the heavy electrical industry. The organisational structure of the company changed from the self-supporting production-unit system to the multidivisional one in 1958, but changed again to decentralisation throughout the 1960s. The divisions were grouped as sub-units below the top management, and were replaced by the division headquarters by 1980. Throughout these processes, the relative autonomy of the factories remained.

The technological tie-up with *Westinghouse* was revived in the early post-war years, and its importance is indicated in the formation of the Department of Production Technology which took charge of the relationship with *Westinghouse*. However, it was necessary for *Mitsubishi Electric* to develop magnetic and insulating materials to make full use of *Westinghouse*'s technology. Soon the company re-examined its dependence on heavy electrical engineering and developed household electrical equipment. The technologies for the new growth areas were not only introduced from *Westinghouse* but from *Western Electric*, *RCA*, *IBM*, and *MAM* (France). To the corporate research institute of *Mitsubishi Electric*, which had been established during the war, were added new branches which were engaged in comprehensive electrical industry. It was planned that the share of household electrical equipment be increased to 60 per cent of total sales, and nearly 60 per cent of financial resources were allocated to the household and mass-produced electricals branches between 1955 and 1965, and as a result these products to represent 40 per cent of the total sales by 1965.[28] In 1958 the multidivisional structure was introduced replacing the self-supporting factory system. Under the new system the units immediately below the top management consisted of the heavy electricals, electronic, household electricals, and overseas divisions. At first managing directors were appointed as division managers, and were made responsible for production, sales, and profits in their own divisions. Profit responsibility was made thoroughly clear from the outset because the assets of the company were allocated to each division, and the rate of return of each division was monitored according to the long-range plans. The management committee was reinforced in order to be able to coordinate the divisions and make decisions more swiftly. For these purposes, the general staff was formed and the responsibilities of the management committee were clarified. The tasks of the managing directors were separated from those of the division managers.

After 1965 the development of new market through the supply of new products was made a strategic goal. For this purpose research and sales functions were emphasised. It was after the mid-1960s that the company established basic technology of its own. However, the ratio of research and sales expenditures to the total sales did not increase during the decade after 1965: the latter remaining at 17 per cent, the former gradually increasing from 1.2 to 2.2 per cent.[29] Towards the end of the 1960s a series of structural reorganisations again took place. The company intended to intensify the function of the divisions on the one hand, but subdivided them on the other. The 'Business programme system', under which the plan for the year was drafted by the division managers and not by the head office, was introduced in 1969. Another reform was the 'control of funds system', by which each factory was made a profit centre, which was formerly assumed by divisions. Factory managers were made responsible for the profit of their factories. Internal capital was assigned to each factory according to the amount of its fixed assets, and interest was charged by the head office on working capital. In actuality, factories became divisions.

In parallel with such specification of operating units, the relationship between these units was made clear by the introduction of 'system divisions'. These divisions were set up to cope with the tendency of divergence in activities caused by management decentralisation, and to cope with large-scale orders more easily. This 'system division' had no production function, but engaged in planning, developing and marketing. Due to the rapidly changing pattern of demands, such a structure proved to be inadequate and thus it had to be developed further and four division headquarters were set up in 1977 as a result. The existing 11 divisions were broken up, and 18 new ones formed. These new divisions were oriented to their own markets, and only sales and were only assigned with planning functions. These 18 divisions were grouped into four division headquarters, each of which was in charge of production functions. The 'sales' divisions were made profit centres, and factories cost centres. Local business offices were controlled by the sales headquarters which was responsible to the top management as were other division headquarters.

The organisational structure of *Fuji Electric*[30] changed from the self-supporting system of production-units to a functional structure in 1949, to the divisional one in the early 1960s. Having been formed with *Siemens* (*Schuckertwerke*) as the largest shareholder, this firm was, in 1950, even more committed to heavy electrical equipment than *Mitsubishi Electric*. The company restored its technological as well as financial relationship with *Siemens* after the war. In an attempt to diversify into household electrical equipment, heavy electrical engineering technology was applied, but the share of heavy electrical machinery increased during the first half of the 1950s. The organisational reform in 1949 reflected the strategy of diversification. The company divided its sales function into three departments by product-market criteria. In addition to heavy electrical engineering, household and weak electrical equipment, which each required their own marketing practices, were formed as departments. The management committee was reinforced, and the company's functions were assigned to each member of the management committee. This centralised functional structure was established by 1950.

Between 1962 and 1964 a divisional idea was introduced and developed. First, four management units, each responsible for a product-market area or a function, were set up in 1962, and this structure was reformed into a divisional system the next year. The two divisions, namely the heavy and the light electrical divisions, being controlled by senior managing directors, were made profit centres, and charged with planning and sales responsibility. The production function was, at first, separated from these divisions. As a background to this reform, a significant increase in household electrical equipment and mass-production goods required different marketing methods from that of heavy electrical engineering. During the slump of the mid-1960s, technical staff were assigned to the operating divisions to integrate marketing and technological research. Furthermore the company separated its household electrical equipment from the mass-production goods division in order to rebuild it. However, the share of household electrical equipment in the total turnover of the company decreased after its peak in the mid-1960s. The company began to emphasise its own technology, particularly in basic materials such as resins and semi-conductors, and efforts were made to establish a central research institute along these lines. In the meantime, factories were placed under the control of divisions and the main functions were finally integrated under the divisions. The factories' profits and the divisions' sales were clarified by the introduction of the 'settlement of the factory account system' in 1966. However, with the introduction of this system, factories were again separated from the divisions. The emergence of large-scale orders such as industrial plants assisted this trend. Divisions by product-technology criteria took place by a new principle which was much more oriented to markets. In 1968 a Controlling Headquarters was set up and charged with the coordination of divisions, while the Factory Headquarters were put in control of factories. Therefore although the name 'division' remained even after 1970, centralisation was pushed forward.

In spite of these organisational reforms towards the end of the 1960s, the profits of Household Electrics Division did not recover and finally the company withdrew from that field. The management structure of *Fuji Electric* moved from a centralised and functionally departmentalised one of the 1950s to the normal divisional one in the early 1960s. The delegation of authority to divisions was observed along with this process. By trial and error the production units under divisions were made more independent in the late 1960s, and as a result had to be counter-balanced by centralisation measures later.

Three companies were identified as suppliers of communication equipment, though they showed differences in their strategy during the three decades after 1950. *Nippon Electric*[31] had diversified within communication equipment, as well as having a share in electronic appliances by 1950. As a scheme for the reconstruction of the company, the management intended to reduce its scale, including reducing the number of employees and closing down of some production units. *Nippon Electric* revived its technological tie-up with *ISE* by offering it one third of its shares. *ISE* technologically supported *Nippon Electrics*, accepted engineers, and recognised the latter as the exclusive user of patents in Japan. Eventually shareholding by *ISE* decreased to 15 per cent of the issued capital of *Nippon Electric*. *Nippon Electric* also began to develop radio interests, this being caused by the start of commercial broadcasting, and communication equipment branches in response to the special procurement boom of the Korean War, and also as a response to the five year plan of the *Telegraph and Telephone Corporation*. At the same time the company reorganised its product lines as the first stage of factory rationalisation, then introduced production management techniques and quality control. One of the production units was made into a self-supporting radio division, which was charged with the sales and the production of radio receivers. Other factories were made to specialise in the production of either radio or wired communication equipment, while their sales activities were centralised. In order to restore Japan's communication network, *vis-à-vis* the strategic situation in the Far East, GHQ made inquiries into communication equipment companies, and found that the management organisations (particularly that of top management), of these companies were extremely weak.

Between 1955 and 1964, investment in radio communication and electronic appliances increased, and the sales of these branches also increased gradually.[32] The high proportion of wired communication equipment meant, however, that the company was still considerably dependent on the *Telegraph and Telephone Corporation*. The organisational reform of 1956 was made in response to retardation in the carrier supply branch and partially in the wired communication branch. Geographical groups were reorganised into product divisions through the integration of technology and manufacturing. Thus, instead of having two factory managers who had been charged with a wide scope of authority, five division managers were appointed and borne with responsibility for the research and production of each product line. This production division (divisions without sales function) system was regarded as a kind of decentralised management system, but sales function were still carried out centrally. Furthermore, the idea of profit responsibility was not clarified.

A multidivisional structure was introduced in 1961, by which time *Nippon Electric* had already adopted divisional ideas because some of their activities, such as the radio receivers and mass-production goods divisions, had already been divisionalised. In spite of the production division system of 1956, production costs could not be reduced. Thus five divisions were set up and delegated with the authority necessary to carry out the functions of technology, sales, and manufacturing in their own product lines. Managing directors were appointed as division managers. The general staff, such as the sales supervising department and the planning section, was formed. But this was not the end of organisational reform, as the management had noticed that the organisational system was falling behind the expansion and the strategy of the firm.

Towards the mid-1960s, K. Kobayashi proposed that the direction of future development should be towards both communication equipment and computers, which at that time were not yet closely related to each other. He appreciated that the electron tube branch would intermediate technologically between these two branches, and set these three branches as the company's domain. During the decade following 1965, electronic equipment and components took the place which had until then been occupied by communication equipment. Exports, especially those of electronic components increased rapidly. The structural reform of 1965 corresponded to these new necessities. The function of the top management was made clear; until that time managing directors had also held the posts of division managers, confining them to a particular division instead of allowing them to undertake the responsibilities of general executives. Firstly, the management committee was set up to discuss the general problems of management. Secondly the firm reinforced the divisional structure. Some divisions were considerably larger than others, and within such large divisions there were mixtures of the sub-units which dealt with various product-markets. Such divisions were sub-divided, and 23 divisions had appeared by 1969. Each was made a profit centre, in charge of the technology, sales, and production of its own product lines. Thirdly the firm consolidated sales organisation according to the market criteria and reorganised them into Public Sales Headquarters or Overseas Sales Headquarters, etc. This ambivalence between the divisional structure and the sales headquarters system was successfully integrated within a matrix organisation in 1970. Marketing activities which were well conformed to the characteristics of the products or sales techniques became more important. The sales departments which were included in divisions were separated. Under this matrix structure 30 divisions were made profit centres. These divisions constituted six groups which were in charge of production and technology, while the sales function was divided into four groups. By optional combination, the company was able to accommodate various kinds of market demands. This system was particularly suitable for the diversifying market, which extended from supplying mass-produced appliances to large-scale orders.

After 1974 *Nippon Electric* adopted a strategy of developing electronics and maintaining its communication equipment branches, and this strategy proved to be successful, because these two fields became much more closely related than they had before, in areas such as satellite, or data communication. The main direction of development was in these highly integrated areas, as well as in electronic appliances which represented a quarter of the company's output.

Fujitsu[33] was, in 1950, more specialised in the production of communication equipment than *Nippon Electric*. For its reconstruction, *Fujitsu* began with closing its unnecessary production units. Its technological tie-up with *Siemens* (*Halske*) was revived, which brought wireless communication, telephone, semiconductor, and electron tube technologies to the company. Demand from *Telegraph and Telephone Corporation* contributed much to the recovery and initial development of this company. The organisational structure in 1950 was quite simple. In 1952 the company separated the production units from the head office organisation, and the management structure of the company was composed of the head office with sales department and factories with production and purchasing departments. The firm also reinforced its sales activities, though they were dependent on the sales organisation of *Fuji Electric*.

In the second half of the 1950s, the firm decided to enter into the production of computers. The government was supporting domestic technology under the Five Year Plan for the Promotion of the Electronic Industry. Financial resources were accumulated as a 'computer reserve fund', though investment in this new area was slow until 1964, when the amount of investment reached a sum equal to that in communication equipment.[34] By 1959 the firm had enlarged its sales department further and sub-divided it into four units, each of which was in charge either of a particular market or of a particular product line. In 1961 the company adopted the divisional structure, consisting of communication and the electronics divisions. Through this measure, the company was divided into two parts, each in charge of its own sales, technology and production. They became aware of the differences in technology and marketing between electronics and communication equipment. Operating units were divided and allocated to each division without much difficulty. In the following year, the Computer Headquarters which was in charge of the production, sales, and technology of computers was set up within the Electronics Division (i.e., it became a division inside a division). On the other hand there were production or local sales units which did not belong to these divisions, but directly to the president. As a general background to such reorganisation, the company's rapid expansion as well as the technological innovation in the computer industry made *Fujitsu*'s traditional functional structure insufficient. In order to unify sales activities and rapidly changing technology, as well as to make profit management complete, a multidivisional structure was adopted. President Okada stated that, 'In the future the assets should be divided and allocated to each division, and profit should be made clear.'

After 1968 the runaway growth of computers caused the company to be classified as a less diversified firm. The ratio of research and development funds to the total sales increased from 2 per cent to 8 per cent during the decade after 1964. Between 1968 and 1973 the company is estimated to have spent more than 70 per cent of its total fixed investment in computers and electronics interests.[35] Through organisational reform which dealt with the growing demands for data communication, part of the communication division was reorganised into the electronics division. Taking into account of the importance of electronic appliances such as semi-conductor devices, *Fujitsu* set up a new division. In spite of these measures, the share of computers rose, and it quickly took the place of communication equipment.

After the oil crisis, the full-liberalisation of computers came on the agenda. In order to meet *IBM* in the Japanese market, machinery comparable to that of *IBM* had to be developed, and managerial efficiency had to be realised. Expenditure on research and development took up 6 to 7 per cent of total sales after 1974 and in addition to large investment in computers, electronic appliances also required considerable amounts of capital. Structural reorganisation into a decentralised divisional system followed these changes. A system in which the profit and loss of the enterprise was calculated on the divisional bases was created, and *Fujitsu*'s complicated organisation was simplified. The profit and loss of each division was to be controlled by dividing it into sales and production profits. For this purpose a Sales Headquarters and a Division Headquarters were set up in each division. Some of the tasks of the head office, such as financing, supplying materials and labour management, were moved to the divisions.

In *Fujitsu*'s divisional structure, the number of divisions was small and did not increase in the course of time. The transformation from the traditional multidivisional structure to the division headquarters system was thus not very distinctive.

Oki Electric[36] began its post-war development in a situation similar to that of *Fujitsu*. *Oki* was the oldest communication equipment company in Japan, with no particular foreign partners. To introduce developed technologies, the company had to find foreign companies which would support it, but the major foreign companies already had interests in Japanese electrical concerns. Finally, *CIT* (France) and *Raytheon* (US) supplied necessary technologies without holding shares in *Oki Electric*, which sought its market in the field of communication equipment. More than three-quarters of its sales were derived from telephone equipment, which continued to represent a dominant share until the mid-1960s. Diversification was limited within the scope of communication equipment. Early organisational reforms were mainly concerned with the shop floor level and involved the introduction of scientific management. Problems above this level were solved through the self-supporting system of local factories. Production units were made specialise in either wired or radio communication equipment.

After 1955, the company expanded its interests in telephone equipment, and then planned to make inroads into electronics. Investment was therefore made equally in these two areas.[37] This strategy brought *Oki Electric* technical skills in the field of peripheral equipment, which played an important role when the company moved into computers later. This strategy also brought about a series of new production units, each of which was made to specialise in a particular product line. Organisational problem developed regarding how these production units should be controlled and coordinated. In 1958 the 'production unit system' was introduced, and a planning department was founded as the general staff.

Owing to its heavy investment, the slump of 1965 hit severely *Oki Electric*. In the course of recovery after 1966, new markets were developed in electronic components and electronic switchboards. The divisional structure, consisting of two divisions was adopted in 1966. This was quite similar to the divisional structure adopted by *Fujitsu*. In *Oki*'s case, however, the number of divisions gradually increased. Each of the six divisions was in charge of both production and sales, but did not directly control the factories.

Oki Electric modified this divisional structure in 1972; the sales headquarters was set up, and existing sales departments were separated from divisions so they could be brought together under the sales headquarters. Most of the divisions became 'production divisions' and these divisions began to specialise in technology and production. Then differentiation within the sales headquarters took place, which brought about the creation of five sales headquarters according to the market or product. In spite of this structural reform the company's profits did not increase after 1972. Long-range plans were reconsidered, and new profit sources besides the *Telegraph and Telephone*

Corporation were looked for. Management systems suitable for a private market were studied. In addition to the rate of return of each division, the profitability of each product lines was investigated, and it became apparent that only a few products, among a total of 30, raised profits. To solve this problem, the company adopted a full-divisional structure in place of the production divisions. In addition, 'Strategic Business Units' for the important products in each division were founded, and each such unit had a manager, who was responsible for the unit and his staff. A kind of matrix structure appeared, which was able to quickly respond to the various sorts of market needs. The top management staff, covering technology, oversea activities, and production, was fortified. Electronic devices were chosen as the company's strategic products.

Nippon Denso,[38] which had once been *Toyota Motor*'s electrical appliance factory, was separated from *Toyota* in 1949. At that time the company manufactured household electrical equipment as well as radiators and car appliances. The firm started to introduce the divisional system in the early 1960s and completed it in 1963. 'Production divisions' were formed, while sales activities were carried out by the sales department of the head office.

After the special procurement boom of the early 1950s, the company diversified into electrical distribution and control equipment. However, unlike those electrical companies which had originated in the electrical departments of mines and shipyards, diversification into comprehensive electrical equipment was curbed. The market for automobile electrical appliances grew rapidly after 1955, and governmental support for the promotion of the mechanical engineering industry helped the company to fully enter automobile electrical equipment. *Nippon Denso* made a technological tie-up with *Bosch*. The product lines of the company increased within the field of automobile electrical equipment.

Organisation developed swiftly. In the beginning, the company was based on a functional structure with a central staff department. In 1961 the firm centralised research and development, and partially introduced the divisional system. The production planning and the sales planning staffs were formed. In the following year divisionalisation took further steps. Production functions were sub-divided into four units according to product lines (e.g., the Air-conditioning Product Division). In 1963, these product divisions had design, inspection and technology functions added to them. The divisions were made profit centres, and were assigned with not only day-to-day duties but with long-range planning duties as well. Division managers were separated from the members of the management committee. Thus, except for sales, all functions were moved to divisions. The reason for this was that demand came directly from a single auto-mobile manufacturer; *Toyota Motor*, and direct sales of all kinds of electrical appliances to this particular firm were the main sales activities of *Nippon Denso*. Thus the organisation of the sales func-tion was formed according to the market, by consolidating sales activity, rather than by letting the divisions sell separately. In reality, this company was a single function company until the mid-1960s.

Even after the mid-1960s, the Japan's electrical appliance manu-facturers were still underdeveloped and could not effectively cope with foreign companies. In order to prepare for the liberalisation of foreign capital, much attention was paid to the quality and cost of products. Product management methods were introduced, and tech-nological research was promoted. *Nippon Denso* and its affiliated companies set up a joint research centre. By 1970, production for *Toyota Motor* decreased to approximately half of total output. Tech-nologically, *Nippon Denso* had caught up with *Bosch* and *Lucas* by the early 1970s with the emergence of electronic appliances, whose basic patents were supplied by *Texas Instrument* and *Western Electric*. Nevertheless, *Nippon Denso* still remained a supplier of electrical appliances for automobiles throughout the 1970s. During the two decades starting from 1960, the technological development of these products was rapid and many new products replaced older ones, making reorganisation of the divisional structure necessary. The division headquarters structure was finally introduced in 1976. The sales function remained separate from these division head-quarters despite of the growing new market outside of *Toyota*. This was chiefly because the systematisation of products which were related to more than two division headquarters proceeded and made it more efficient to separate sales functions from the operating div-ision headquarters.

The last large-scale electrical concern to be dealt with is *Matsushita Denko*,[39] the sister company of *Matsushita Electric Industrial*, and a wartime aircraft company. It entered the production of wiring de-vices and conduit tubes after the war. In the first half of the 1950s *Matsushita Denko* increased the ouput of resins and entered lighting fixtures, the latter soon coming to represent nearly 30 per cent of total sales. Based on skills of their own, in development since the pre-war era, the company introduced new plastic and resin technologies from *St. Regis*. This helped *Matsushita Denko* to enter the housing materials market, and eventually made it into a comprehensive housing company. The organisational structure in the beginning of the 1950s is characterised as a self-supporting factory system, but in 1952 it was reorganised into a Business Promoting Unit system, a kind of the divisional structure. This developed into a normal multidivisional structure in the latter half of the 1950s.

In the early 1950s with 2000 workers the scale of the company was still small. The company was divided into twelve Business Promoting Units, each of which was in charge of sales and production. Actually it was a divisional structure, though each division was too small. Between 1955 and 1964 the company began to co-relate resins and plastics with electrical equipment, particularly with lighting fixtures or wiring devices, and to apply these skills to housing components. Investment was concentrated on the resins and housing material branches. The consolidation of these two departments proceeded, because the output of the share of resins went down while that of housing materials increased.

Meanwhile close coordination among the Business Units became necessary. A Division Headquarters was set up in 1956 as the Business Units Staff. Soon, a Sales Headquarters was also added, and it consisted of several sales departments by products. The division of labour between the sales departments in each Business Unit and those in the Sales Headquarters was as follows: Business Units were still responsible for the sales of the products in charge, particularly for planning and designing of products and sales, the controlling of the sales, while the Sales Headquarters was in charge of sales channels and distribution. Finally in 1959, instead of the 'three-headquarters system', the divisional structure was officially adopted. The sales and production under the Business Promoting Unit system was separated again, under the headquarters system, but it became necessary to unify these functions to cope with the rapidly growing market. The autonomy of each division was established, and the training of the division managers, who were capable of carrying out and coordinating all functions, was one of the primary purposes of the multidivisional structure at the time. Divisions were delegated with some of the tasks, which had formerly been carried out by the Sales Headquarters. The local branch offices however, did not come under these divisions. These offices were made into self-supporting units and each was responsible for a particular.

After 1965, *Matsushita Denko* rapidly discarded wiring devices and housing appliances, and became a comprehensive housing company. New products, such as pollution prevention equipment or systematised products required closer inter-divisional relationships. In order to avoid unnecessary competition among divisions, a 'consolidated divisional structure' was introduced in 1971. This grouped several small and related divisions together, and made them cooperate in areas from production to sales. The development of original 'combined' products was attempted. In the next year, managing directors were appointed to take charge of these Consolidated Divisions so as to clarify the responsibility.

Of the 14 electrical equipment concerns listed among the largest 100 firms of 1970, nine mainly supplied producer final goods. These nine firms had originally produced either heavy electrical or communication equipment. Most of them had been technologically and financially affiliated with foreign companies before the war, and such relationships were restored after the war. Until the mid-1960s foreign partners played important roles in the reconstruction of Japanese firms, in their rationalisation of production, and in diversification particularly through utilisation of electronic technology.

Several forms can be distinguished among the organisational structures of Japanese electrical equipment companies. Two of them are important here. The first group consists of those companies which were established in the pre-war era, and dealt with heavy electrical machinery. These companies rebuilt their foundation by adapting themselves to the opportunities created by the Electricity Development Plan, the fixed capital investment in minings and steel industries, the special procurement for the Korean War, and to the brisk investment in heavy industries after 1955. They entered the household electrical equipment field, which grew rapidly during the decade since 1955. Their production units were traditionally powerful, and led these concerns to take irregular forms of the divisional structure. Prior to the adoption of the divisional structure, the self-supporting factory system was popular, and even after its adoption divisions were sometimes composed of sales and staff functions. Instead of centralising operating functions, management decentralisation was further promoted through the adoption of the divisional structure. Factories were made profit centres and the divisions were, when they had factories, allocated with internal capital. These companies sometimes adopted the divisional structure in order to enter household electrical equipment. From the end of the 1960s, these companies began to group divisions together as demand for heavy electrical equipment became more systematised. The division headquarters system was adopted, in which a division headquarters had several sales divisions by products and factories.

The second group of electrical equipment companies were those which were concerned with communication equipment. They began their post-war history with the First Five Year Plan of the *Telegraph and Telephone Corporation*, and had diversified into household and industrial electronicals and computers by 1970, though there were differences both in the timing of and the degree to which this strategic choice was made. The 'production divisions', which were composed of the production and staff functions, were widely observed. In these cases the sales function was separated from the divisions and centralised. In the 1970s the sales function was reorganised according to market criteria. They became the first adopters of the matrix structure.

7.4 HEAVY ENGINEERING COMPANIES

As in Britain, heavy engineering industry has been one of the largest employing industries in Japan. Some shipbuilding firms were even the forerunners of the modern large-scale companies. These firms developed during the First World War due to the rapid increase in the transportation of goods made necessary by the war, and the decline of the supply of Western ships to Asian countries. The Japanese industrial structure which, until that time, had been dominated by textiles and mining, was transformed by the development of various industries, led by the shipbuilding industry. By 1920, shipbuilding concerns such as *Kawasaki Dockyard*, *Mitsubishi Shipyard*, and *Osaka Iron Works*, became large enough to be comparable with *Vickers*, *John Brown*, *Armstrong-Whitworth*, and *Cammell Laird* in terms of assets and employees. Diversification started just after this boom. During the boom of the First World War, shipbuilding firms invested surplus profits in related industries, and during the following recession work had to be found in other industrial areas. The introduction of shipbuilding without the prior development of its related industries forced shipbuilders to self-supply parts and appliances such as metals, electrical equipment and turbines. The technical skills which they accumulated through this self-supply of parts provided them with skills in important industrial fields which were useful for diversification. The proportion of non-shipbuilding branches increased in the inter-war years, although these various activities were gradually separated as subsidiaries. The rise of large-scale non-shipbuilding companies in engineering industry was observed towards the end of the 1930s, but there were differences in the ranks of the pre-war and the post-war large-scale firms.

Immediately after the Second World War, Japanese shipbuilding companies had lost their large domestic market consisting of the Navy and the shipping companies, whose demands had always super-ceded the shipbuilding industry's production capacity. The ship-building companies had to seek markets abroad, where they could compete with European shipbuilders only through lower production costs and short-time delivery. Technological innovations in the 1950s such as seal welding, block building, and advance fitting, were contrived under such market pressure.

Mitsubishi Heavy Industries[40] was formed in 1964 through the merger of three large companies, which had appeared as a result of the dissolution of the former *Mitsubishi Heavy Industries*. By the mid-1930s, this ancestor had accumulated necessary technical skills, not only for building mercantile or naval ships, but for constructing turbine and diesel engines, rolling stock, building materials, ord-nance, aircraft, automobiles, and other heavy engineering products. These technical skills were inherited by the three descendants of *Mitsubishi Heavy Industries*, and later became the motivating power behind their diversification. More than 25 production units of the pre-war *Mitsubishi Heavy Industries* were located throughout the various parts of the country. After the war, in order to reconstruct the company a system, in which each production unit was self-supporting, was established. Under this management system not only the receival of orders and production but also financing was del-egated to each factory on the assumption that inefficient units would naturally be closed down. The managers of these units had to put much effort into finding financial resources, and had no time to pay attention to the operation of their factories. The weakness of the head office caused unnecessary competitions among its production units.

Shin Mitsubishi Heavy Industries, which took over the original *Mitsubishi Heavy Industries*' factories in central and western Japan, was engaged in the production of automobiles and industrial machin-ery in addition to ships. The shipbuilding branch, despite its low share of sales, played an important role in the initial development of the company. Owing to the company's diversified activities, main product lines effectively supplemented each other since 1952; engines and automobiles grew between 1952 and 1955, machinery and ship-building between 1955 and 1957, engines and aircraft after 1957, and finally from 1958 onwards many new kind of industrial machinery. With these product lines, the company enjoyed the highest growth rate among the descendants of *Mitsubishi Heavy Industries*.

Structurally, the early self-supporting production unit system soon came to be replaced by the 'Profit Responsibility System' of each factory, under which each production unit was equipped with a full set of functions, except for financing. The product lines among the factories were not rearranged at all, and the central board of directors was held in rotation by the production units. Both systems, the production-unit structure and the 'profit responsibility system', contained centrifugal elements. The appearance of new kind of industrial machinery made it necessary to consolidate *Shin Mitsubishi Heavy Industries'* sales function. In contrast to shipbuilding, orders for which had been directly accepted by each production unit, industrial machinery orders were accepted through the *Mitsubishi Corporation* (*Mitsubishi Shoji*) and these orders were transferred to the sales department of the head office of *Shin Mitsubishi*. Moreover, automobiles, agricultural machinery, and engines, which were produced on an estimate basis, required well organised marketing, and this could only be attained with a company-wide effort. Purchasing also became centrally coordinated. By 1957, the company had reorganised its structure into a functional form, but immediately after this reform a divisional style of management was introduced. Managing directors, who had been responsible for one of the functions, were made responsible for each of a product-market area, and the management committee was transformed into a body whose members coordinated product lines.

Mitsubishi Shipbuilding became diversified on the principle that, 'the rise and fall of machine manufacturing determines the destiny of the company'. The emphasis on general engineering, however, was not attained until 1959, because heavy investment in shipbuilding had to be made after 1955. Both competition among *Mitsubishi Ship-building*'s factories, resulting from the self-supporting system, and the duplication of product lines gradually became centrally coordinated and each factory was in turn made to specialise into one or two product lines such as large-scale ships or mining machinery. *Mitsubishi Shipbuilding* established a top management and its staff by 1960, and management centralisation took place; a managing director had been assigned to each product line and by 1959, a senior managing director had been appointed to take charge of each function. A central purchasing department was formed in 1960.

Between 1961 and 1963, the company moved towards decentralisation again. Production units, each having manufacturing, sales, and technology functions, were reorganised into several divisions, though these divisions were not made profit centres. Divisions were formed inside the production units, and not vice versa.

The third descendant, *Mitsubishi Nippon Heavy Industries*, took charge of nine factories situated in the eastern part of Japan. Shipbuilding represented a dominant share in 1950, but by 1955 diversification into large vehicles and then into construction machinery, boilers, and industrial equipment had begun. The organisational problem for this company was, like the other descendants of *Mitsubishi Heavy Industries*, how its factories should be rationalised. Therefore, company-wide organisation remained a secondary issue. *Mitsubishi Nippon Heavy Industries* naturally went for the self-supporting production unit system, and it was to these units that factory rationalisation was entrusted. At the top, the holding-company structure was gradually reformed into a functional one, and a sales deparment was formed in the head office. The transition from the functional to the divisional structure was also gradually prepared for. The sales department of the head office was divided into the product-market areas, while each factory began to specialise in particular products. The adoption of the multidivisional structure had been discussed in the past, but it was not realised because the company had already accepted the divisional principle in practice, such as motor-vehicle department, etc. The senior managing directors, who were charged with a single function, were each made responsible for a single product by 1961.

The central and branch offices of these three descendent firms had been placed in the same buildings. However, these three companies had been competing in some product lines since the beginning and this competition became more intense as each company diversified. After the shipbuilding slump of the early 1960s, industrial and construction machinery as well as automobiles became the new areas of rivalry. *Mitsubishi Nippon Heavy Industries* specialised in large cars, while *Shin Mitsubishi Heavy Industries* did so in smaller cars. This balance began to collapse when it came to smaller trucks, medium-sized buses, and particularly tractors, which had been one of the main product fields of *Mitsubishi Nippon Heavy Industries* but was then entered jointly by *Shin Mitsubishi Heavy Industries* and *Caterpillar*. Further background to the merger of these three companies was the new competitive environment brought about by the liberalisation of foreign trade. In order to strengthen their positions, Japanese companies aimed at expanding their scale, and large-scale mergers took place after 1960.

In the post-merger organisational structure, the three *Mitsubishi* heavy engineering companies were reorganised into five divisions of the new *Mitsubishi Heavy Industries*, and by this was intended the centralisation of the diversified enterprise. However, the new divisional structure was nominal, partly because each production unit still remained as a profit-centre and partly because the coordination of the product lines among the production units was difficult, particularly in the redistribution of employees and assets to the five new divisions. Such centrifugal forces were checked by appointing a senior managing director to the head of each division, but the power of each production unit or of engineering-production function was too strong for the introduction a modern management structure with a market orientation. Under this divisional structure, each production unit took charge of manufacturing or shipbuilding, while each division had a technological department and one or more sales departments, although sales activities had to be supported by the centrally controlled branch offices and *Mitsubishi Corporation*. The necessity of managerial innovation to strengthen the divisions and the head office was pointed out and attempted from time to time, and finally in 1977, due to the increase in the large-scale orders which extended to several divisions and production units, the division headquarters system was introduced. In spite of these centrifugal trends among the factories, *Mitsubishi Heavy Industries* quickly adapted themselves to the new market opportunities and performed quite well.

Kawasaki Heavy Industries[41] has been a rapid diversifier into various lines of engineering products including aircraft and transportation equipment. Before the Second World War the company had manufactured steel construction goods, reciprocal and diesel engines, turbines, boilers, electrical motors, rolling stocks, automobiles, and factory plants. Further integration backward into the self-supply of steel was also carried out. All these activities were initially operated in their own factories, but eventually some of them were moved into separate companies such as *Kawasaki Sharyo* or *Kawasaki Aircraft*. The steel interest of the company was separated in the early post-war period, making shipbuilding *Kawasaki Heavy Industries*'s primary product. An incomplete functional structure, consisting of four manufacturing departments and a sales department, solved the organisational problems of early days. This was reformed into a multidivisional structure in 1961, turned back to a mixture of the divisional and functional structure in 1966, and finally reorganised into the division headquarters form in the late 1960s.

The main issue of its early post-war development was in technological and organisational modernisation and rationalisation at the shop floor level. Manufacturing departments were divided into three production units ('Factory System') in conformity with the product lines to delineate where final responsibility for the cost of each product would rest. In concert with the establishment of three specialised factories, the firm reinforced its sales department of the head office and divided it into four departments according to product types. Finally the top management organisation, consisting of managing directors and its general staff was formed in 1954, although its main task was to control production. *Kawasaki Heavy Industries'* relationships with *Kawasaki Sharyo* (transportation equipment) and *Kawasaki Aircraft* were tightened when diversification into machinery and construction materials was planned in the mid-1950s.

The introduction of the multidivisional structure took place in 1961. Below the top management four divisions were formed: shipbuilding, machinery, precise machinery, and construction materials, and each were made profit centres, and were each responsible for supplying their own materials, manufacturing, and sales. Until the mid-1960s approximately 60 per cent of total sales were made up by shipbuilding. The managing directors were appointed as division managers, but apart from this the structure adopted by *Kawasaki Heavy Industries* was a typically multidivisional one. Engineering concerns experienced difficulties in adopting the normal multidivisional structure because of the problems of dividing production units according to the product-market criteria. Construction materials were produced in the same workshops that made the ship parts. *Kawasaki* had already divided its production units into product lines under the 'Factory System'. Management decentralisation according to the divisional principle proceeded until 1965, when the top management was separated from the tasks of the division managers.

This classical multidivisional form, however, was modified in 1966, when the firm amalgamated an engineering company. The latter was made the Second Engineering Division, but the sales function of the two engineering divisions were separated from these Engineering Divisions and unified into one sales headquarters. Furthermore, the sales departments of two other divisions were also separated and consolidated into the sales headquarters, which stood in line with the divisions. Finally these divisions and sales headquarters were put together and reorganised into three product groups controlled by the members of the management committee. The next organisational change occurred in 1969, with the merger with *Kawasaki Shatai* and *Kawasaki Aircraft*. A mixture of the division headquarters system and the divisional structure was adopted. Five division headquarters, each consisting of one sales headquarters and several divisions, and four independent divisions with full functions were set up. Two amalgamated companies came to constitute the divisions of the new *Kawasaki Heavy Industries*, their product lines without being re-allocated. This merger was made in order to increase the company's international competitive power, but the lack of organisational difficulty at the time of merger meant, in a sense, that there was little effect of scale-economy as a result of this merger. The consolidation of research and development by these forebears was also attempted, but there was little co-relationship among ships, aircraft, and motorbicycles. Meanwhile diversification was promoted by these two periods of mergers, and by 1970 the share of shipbuilding was reduced to less than a quarter of the company's total sales. However, the amalgamated branches did not continue to grow satisfactorily, and towards the mid-1970s, industrial machinery, motors, and factory plants grew to be the main products of *Kawasaki Heavy Industries*. The head office was vested with greater power in 1976, particularly in research and sales functions. The company tried to integrate the sales headquarters of the division headquarters into one so as to meet large-scale orders which extended over several divisions, and thus to increase the company's market orientation. As a result, the General Sales Headquarters was placed in the head office to coordinate the sales activities of the division headquarters.

The organisation of *Mitsui Shipbuilding and Engineering*,[42] originated in a functional/line form in which the head office was composed of administrative and trading functions, while the production departments were placed in the factories. In 1962 the firm adopted a divisional system in its production unit, reorganised this system into a normal multidivisional structure in 1967, and moved into a division headquarters system in the 1970s.

Mitsui Shipbuilding and Engineering had traditionally depended heavily upon shipbuilding. In addition to old customers such as *Mitsui Lines*, demand from overseas had increased by the mid-1950s. The management structure was built with the objectives of rationalising the production process and promoting marketing abroad. The head office consisted of finance and sales departments, while the shipyard had shipbuilding, engineering, and industrial machinery departments. The reform in the management structure began in 1962. 'Semi-divisions' were set up in the shipyard, and these were responsible for accepting orders, production, and profit, and the special staff was assigned to these sub-units. The firm divided the sales function of the head office into two departments according to product lines. More complete divisions were introduced in 1967, the intention of which was to establish workshop management means of quality control, to clarify profit responsibility and to prepare for diversification. The directors, who were responsible for the profit of the 'semi-divisions' as well as for the coordination of 'semi-divisions' and sales departments, were appointed. 'Semi-divisions' were given control of sales departments. Senior managing directors were appointed as division managers, and thus had to deal with long-range policies and operating problems at the same time.

In the early 1960s, a long-range plan was drafted, and with it the firm intended to reduce the share of ships in its total sales to 47 per cent by 1967, and 38 per cent by 1972. However, the shipbuilding boom of 1963 prevented this reduction. The expansion of *Mitsui Shipbuilding*'s shipyard fell behind that of others, and heavy expenditure was made after the boom. Furthermore, this priority of investment in its shipyard continued throughout the slump of 1965. Nearly 85 per cent of all fixed capital investment went into shipbuilding.[43] Even when it amalgamated *Fujinagata Shipbuilding*, *Mitsui Shipbuilding* would not have utilised *Fujinagata*'s technical skills in chemical engineering.

In 1967, when the former 'semi-divisions' were renamed as 'divisions', the sales functions of the head office were moved to these operating divisions. The division managers were separated from top management tasks. This reorganisation did not end in the formation of a normal multidivisional structure. A 'project division headquarters', which was in charge of large-scale industrial plants extending to various divisions and subsidiaries, was set up. Interests were developed in engineering branches, and these were accompanied by enormous investment (amounting to 40 per cent of the total investment) after 1974, and this again necessitated organisational improvement.[44] Three divisions engaged in engineering products were consolidated into one division headquarters, and the Project Division Headquarters was also replaced by this new division headquarters.

Hitachi Shipbuilding and Engineering[45] was another firm whose strategy remained centred on shipbuilding. The share of shipbuilding amounted to nearly 70 per cent of its total sales in 1950, and rose further throughout the 1950s. The company's early management structure was one consisting of trading departments in the head office, and production units. In 1963 the company set up a product headquarters, which developed into a multidivisional structure in 1964. In spite of further measures to reorganise its management structure, however, the firm did not move into a full-divisional organisation until the present.

In 1949, a five year plan, aimed at the modernisation of the company's shipyard was drafted by the Staff Department. This plan was accompanied by the expansion of the sales department and the establishment of a functional structure. The firm's simple head office was subdivided into six sales departments according to product-market areas. This organisational reform enlarged the head office, though it was put into practice without increasing the number of salaried employees: the ratio of salaried employees to wage workers was 23.6 per cent in 1946, 28.3 per cent in 1950, and around 27 per cent in the 1950s.

As the export market of shipbuilding was unstable, the firm had to make up for it by adding industrial machinery to its product lines. From 1957 onward, full-scale diversification was begun, extending to new areas not directly related to shipbuilding and marine engineering. This diversification strategy was hindered both by the temporary cessation of investment in Japanese industries in the early 1960s and by the shipbuilding boom of 1963. Although *Hitachi Shipbuilding and Engineering*'s interests in shipbuilding were dominant, new fields, such as mass-production goods, required marketing techniques completely different from those of shipbuilding. This led to the adoption of a new organisational structure, and a provisional type of headquarters structure, based on a mixture of the functional and the divisional forms, was introduced. The company's activities were divided into shipbuilding and engineering by divisional criteria, and into service, sales, and factories by functional criteria. The Service Department took the initiative in accepting orders, and profit responsibility was jointly assumed by the service and the sales departments and by the factories as well. In 1964 a move toward the divisional structure started, though it was far from the typical one with a full set of functions. The firm set up four divisions, each consisting of a design and a sales department. Factories were placed under the direct control of the top management, and made profit centres. There were reasons why a full-divisional structure was not adopted; each of the company's production units were engaged in various product lines, and if the full-divisional structure were to be adopted, each production unit would have be divided into three or four parts. Some products, however, were the materials of others, and the transfer processes would have become very complicated under such conditions. Another reason, was that factory managers could gain a wider perspective by taking responsibility for the production and profit of several product lines. The top management was able to secure two information lines, one from division managers and the other from factory managers.

The divisional system of 1964 did not necessarily lead the company to diversification. Against the company's intentions, the engineering branch was allocated less than 20 per cent of financial resources between 1965 and 1973, and heavy commitment to shipbuilding had left *Hitachi Shipbuilding and Engineering* with huge shipyards.[46] The defect of this divisional structure was found in the incessant necessity for coordination between the divisions and the factories. For instance, the factories had to inquire to the division about plans for accepting orders in order to fix their own budgets. Such problems were solved in 1967, when the division headquarters structure was introduced. The Shipbuilding Division Headquarters was assigned four factories which were devoted primarily to shipbuilding. The division headquarters controlled production and sales, and were allocated with internal capital according to the amount of their assets. Under this structure, however, factories remained as accounting units, and were soon separated from the division headquarters again. The division headquarters took charge of sales and planning – planning for accepting orders, production, technological development, and capital investment – but as most orders were accepted individually, the division headquarters took a leading position over the factories. This organisational form required close coordination between the divisions and the factories as well as between divisions. Furthermore, the division headquarters were renamed as Sales Headquarters. Being based on the headquarters system, the company introduced a matrix structure into the Engineering Sales Headquarters, by which the headquarters became able to relate various markets with technology and products. This enabled them to accept large-scale orders, such as industrial plants, which required various sorts of engineering products.

Ishikawajima Heavy Industries[47] was not primarily concerned with shipbuilding at its inception. Transportation equipment, particularly cranes, together with motors and boilers, were its main products in early phases of its development. These products brought a great deal of profit to the company, although their dominant shares were gradually overtaken by industrial machinery. By 1950, the sales function consisted of three departments each in charge of a particular product line and area. The production function was divided into six departments according to product lines. The self-supporting system of production units, often observed among heavy industries, had been abolished by then, and the centralisation of main functions had already been attained. Following the sub-division of the production function, the firm eventually sub-divided its sales function.

In 1960, the company amalgamated with *Harima Shipbuilding* which brought with them large-scale dockyards. *Harima Shipbuilding* had been planning to enlarge its engineering branches, while *Ishikawajima Heavy Industries* was capable of raising capital. These two concerns had few duplicate product lines and this merger thus brought *Ishikawajima Heavy Industries* further diversification, as well as the position of the world second largest shipbuilder. The share of shipbuilding in its total sales became higher than those of both *Mitsubishi Heavy Industries* and *Kawasaki Heavy Industries*, though the share of industrial machinery did not decline after the merger. The multidivisional structure was introduced at the time of this merger. Five divisions were delegated with total authority in production and sales. Each had its own factories, and was made a profit centre. At first, division managers were appointed from among the managing directors. After the merger, the firm promoted factory specialisation. After 1960 some modification was made on this multidivisional structure. The top management had noticed that the authority of division managers was not being fully exercised. Managing directors were divorced from the responsibilities of division managers, and made to concentrate on their tasks as top management personnel.

The next organisational reform came with in the separation of the sales function from the divisions. Throughout the 1960s, as production technology advanced and new products appeared, specification of product lines proceeded, and the number of divisions increased accordingly. On the other hand, large-scale demand which covered the product lines of several divisions began to appear. In order to strengthen market orientation, the sales function was re-organised into three headquarters by product-market as well as by geographical areas. In effect each division was made to specialise in production, though remaining a profit centre.

This structural reform was made in 1968, and was a timely response to changing market needs, i.e. increasing demand for sets of com-pound products. The sub-division of product lines proceeded under this organisation, which was unable to meet such compound pro-ducts. Profit responsibility was not as clear as compared with that in the typical multidivisional structure. In order to solve these prob-lems, a division headquarters structure was introduced in 1974 and seven division headquarters were set up through the reorganisation of existing divisions and production units. Divisions were regrouped into division headquarters to correspond with the pattern of market demands. Each division headquarters was delegated with the func-tions of production, marketing, and further of financing, that is, some of the head office's functions were shifted to the division head-quarters. Under this structure, the profit centre was placed on the division headquarters and not on the division.

Since the late 1950s *Ishikawajima Harima* had been famous for its strategy of expansion, but was unable to maintain it after 1974. The drastic decline in orders, especially those of shipbuilding, led the company to rationalise its production units. The divisional structure was taken over by the functional one because the self-supporting system of product lines had become unattainable. The management structure was simplified; The new Sales Headquarters took charge of marketing and engineering to cope with various market demands, while the Production Headquarters controlled five production units, each of which had one or more factories and was grouped by a geographical area. *Ishikawajima Harima* intended to get rid of the inflexible nature of the divisional structure. This was, however, a temporary measure, and in 1980 the firm reintroduced the division headquarters system, in which each division headquarters was equipped with a full line of functions. In such a diversified firm, business activities should be grouped together according to the nature of technology, production and market with which they dealt.

Since the reorganisation of the production-unit form into a func-tional structure, the operating units of *Ishikawajima Heavy Industries* were controlled through the functional departments. Since the merger of 1960, the new firm was administered by the full-functional or full-divisional structures. Throughout the period of organisational reforms since the 1960s, its factories remained under the divisions or department, and were not directly controlled by the top management.

Among the product lines of *Sumitomo Machinery*[48] in 1950, were transportation equipment, metal processing machinery, turbines, iron frames, and speed gears, but more than 20 per cent of its sales consisted of other sorts of mass-production goods. Management decentralisation took place in 1954, when two product groups were divisionalised and other factories were made self-supporting operating units. However, it took another 13 years before the whole company had moved into the multidivisional structure.

Organisational reform began at the shop floor level, as in other engineering companies. Then the management attempted to establish process control and reorganise traditional hierarchical orders. During the slump which followed the special procurement boom of the Korean War, structural reform was discussed, and in 1954 a divisional system was adopted to mass-production goods. New divisions were made profit centres and given responsibility for sales and manufacturing functions. Following this reform, the self-supporting factory system was introduced, and this was extended to all the product lines of the company.

The balance between industrial machinery which was produced to order and mass-produced machinery changed frequently. Between 1955 and 1965 industrial machinery increased in response to the brisk investment in Japanese heavy industries. To deal with this sort of large-scale machinery, *Sumitomo Machinery* became associated with *Uraga Shipbuilding*, which had a large-scale marine engineering department. Meanwhile *Sumitomo* was planning to equip itself with mass-production lines.

The divisional system had extended to the whole company in 1967. Industrial machinery, transportation equipment, and chemical engineering divisions were set up in 1967 and 1968. These were full-divisions in charge of sales, technology, and manufacturing functions, although some managing directors were appointed as division managers. A merger with *Uraga Shipbuilding* followed divisionalisation. This merger had been under discussion since 1964, but mutually agreeable conditions were not easily arrived at. *Uraga Shipbuilding*'s financial situation had been bad, and this would have become a burden for *Sumitomo Machinery*. Furthermore for an engineering firm to have a shipbuilding branch was a doubtful necessity. The merger brought the new combine large workshops which had formerly belonged to *Uraga Shipbuilding*. The first step taken by this new company was to invest heavily in the shipyard, expecting to utilise the engineers and workers of the former *Uraga Shipbuilding*. Shipbuilding recovered quickly after the merger. The consolidation of both companies' product lines was also attempted in some products such as cranes and bridges. Thus the technical skills of *Uraga Shipbuilding* were revived in the new company. The organisational problem of the merger were solved by turning *Uraga Shipbuilding* into two divisions of *Sumitomo Shipbuilding and Machinery*. Such a measure, however, worked against the principles of multidivision by product, since the new firm set up a second engineering division whose products would partly overlap with those of the first Engineering Division. Before long a division headquarters system was introduced, which modified a provisional holding company style organisation into a multidivisional form.

Toyoda Automatic Loom Works[49] dated back to 1926 when it was incorporated and inherited weaving loom technology which had been developed by the original family enterprise. Eventually its product lines extended to automobiles, special steel, and cotton yarn although these unrelated activities had been separated during the war. By 1950 the company had been outgrown by one of its offsprings, *Toyota Motor*, and was now primarily engaged in the production of textile machinery. The company introduced the divisional structure in 1960, returned to the functional form between 1965 and 1970, and reintroduced the divisional structure in 1970.

Sales from automobile parts and engines, however, increased rapidly in the 1950s, peaking in the mid-1960s. Diversification into automobile parts was pushed forward by the anticipated decline of textile machinery. The company began with repairing US Army heavy vehicles, then advanced into producing special motor vehicles and buses, as well as automobile parts for *Toyota Motor*. This policy resulted in a stable performance for the company. Between 1955 and 1965 large investment was made in forging equipment for the manufacture of engines and parts.[50] At that time decision-making was carried out by the top management which represented each function of the company, but *Toyota Motor* shared its chairman, president, and some other executives with *Toyoda Automatic Loom Works*. The top management organisation was reformed in 1956. A management committee was set up, each function was strengthened, and staff services in sales and sub-contracting departments were introduced. By 1960 it became apparent that there were differences in production and marketing methods between textile machinery and motor vehicles. A multidivisional structure was adopted in 1960 for the first time. Among the divisions were those of forklifts, agricultural machinery, and motor vehicles, in addition to the spinning and weaving machinery divisions. However, some irregularity is observed in this organisation, in that the textile machinery divisions had neither factories nor sales departments, and were mere staff divisions, other functions being conducted by the production-control department or the textile machinery sales department, both of which were under the direct control of the top management. Spinning and weaving machineries were similar to each other in their manners of production, and were sold to the same textile companies or to the sub-contracting weaving mills of such textile companies, and need not have had different operating departments. The remaining divisions were, on the other hand, full-divisions with manufacturing and sales functions. The top management organisation was also modified. Instead of the management committee, a formal division headquarters meeting was founded, and was entrusted with decision making for the company together with interdivisional coordination. The division headquarters meeting was composed of managing directors, some of whom – the president and the vice-president – were the highest level managers of *Toyota Motor*.

This irregular multidivisional structure soon reverted to a functional structure, which continued until 1970. The main reason for this reversion was the poor results shown by some divisions. Agricultural machinery was not successful, and orders from the US Army ceased. Incredibly enough, there was no increase in the total sales of the company between 1960 and 1965. Advancement into wagon cars was planned, and structural reorganisation was necessitated.

In the long run dependence on the *Toyota Motor*'s strategy increased as sales of textile machinery were taken over by those of motor-vehicle equipment. The relationship between these two companies proceeded on various levels. At first, sales of motor-vehicle parts increased, later giving way to engines. Both of these were exclusively manufactured for *Toyota Motor*. Secondly from 1960 on, *Toyoda Automatic Loom Works* manufactured complete motor vehicles – industrial trucks, small trucks, and forklifts – forming a division of labour with *Toyota Motor* which specialised into ordinary passenger cars. Capital investment in these product lines increased towards the mid-1970s.[51] Thus *Toyoda Automatic Loom Works* took charge of manufacturing special motor-vehicles within the *Toyota* group, and this was, to a certain extent, the result of the company's independent decision. Thirdly from 1970 the share of automobile assembling in the total sales of this company rose rapidly, which illustrates its increasing dependence on *Toyota Motor*. Together with the production of compressors for air conditioners, the ratio of those of its products that were directly connected with *Toyota Motor*'s assembly lines rose to 60 per cent of total sales.

The multidivisional structure was adopted in 1970 for the second time. Four divisions were made full divisions, each consisting of sales and manufacturing functions. Due to the recovery of textile machinery and the rapid growth of motor vehicles, each field became firmly established, and the multidivisional structure became the most efficient organisational structure for the 1970s.

Kubota,[52] which was one of the first firms to adopt the multidivisional structure, was a family firm in 1950. The company was engaged primarily in various series of iron castings, and among them cast iron pipes for water service were its main products. Demands came from the agricultural sector, and the company began to get involved in the production of agricultural machinery and combustion engines through forward integration. Its organisation in 1950 was that of an incomplete functional form. A multidivisional structure consisting of five divisions was adopted in 1950 to clarify responsibilities. The managing directors were appointed as division managers, and were engaged in the coordination of production, sales and designing of each product lines. At the top level of management, each of these managing directors was assigned a function of his own, though it is not certain whether this measure was effective. At that time the concept of the multidivisional structure was quite new, and it was apprehended that it would have a decentralising nature. In order to check the centrifugal effect, the company strengthened the top management by setting up a management committee which was given powers of control and coordination. Subsequent organisational reform followed along these lines; in 1952 the sales planning department was founded to promote marketing, and in 1960 a division headquarters was organised to control the divisions.

In the 1960s the company diversified into industrial machinery which gradually took the primacy which had formerly belonged to iron casting. *Kubota* adapted themselves to this change by increasing the number of divisions. The separation of the top management from the operating divisions had been carried out by 1960. Managing directors took charge of control, financing, materials, and the division headquarters, while non-executive directors were appointed as division managers.

From the end of the 1960s traditional products fell into a slump. Measures were taken to strengthen these product lines' marketing organisation, and to diversify into new products. Housing equipment, environment control systems, and pumps for various purposes were among the newly-appearing products. New divisions were added, and existing divisions subdivided. In 1971, *Kubota*'s President Hiro, pointed out the difficulty inherent in increasing the number of divisions. The president could not simultaneously pay attention to all divisions, for the number of divisions had increased to 14. In order to respond to market demand however, divisions had to be further subdivided. The firm introduced the division headquarters system to solve these countervailing trends. Divisions were grouped into six units, which could be controlled without much difficulty by the top management which could also promote unified strategies.

From 1974 onward, *Kubota*'s diversification strategy was re-examined. However, judging from the direction of capital investment and from the share of each product line in the total sales, diversification still continued, and the company still remained in the unrelated industry category.[53] To establish powerful leadership, the firm reformed its organisation and founded a 'Top Management Committee' in place of the existing managing board. The new top management committee was composed of the president, the vice-presidents and some of the senior managing directors, while the functions of the head office were transferred to the division headquarters.

Komatsu[54] was not based on the ordinary multidivisional structure. The company was traditionally engaged in iron casting and forging, then integrated forward to industrial and mining machinery. During the Second World War it manufactured tractors, which were to become its main products at the start of its post-war reconstruction. The production of tractors, however, had to be altered with the changing economic policy of the government. In effect, its products consisted mainly of construction and mining machinery, cast and forged iron, and industrial machinery, as well as special procurement services for the US Army. However, the company's long term plans were set in expanding the production of bulldozers. Shell casting was large enough to cover the recession in civilian demands in the first half of the 1950s.

During the construction boom which came after 1955, *Komatsu* became fully dependent on the production of bulldozers. The seller's market continued until 1960. The company's biggest organisational problems were found in the establishment of a functional structure through reinforcement of the top management and in the organisation of production. Marketing organisation was also important for this industry because each product was considerably expensive and after-sales service (such as replacement components) was extensively required. These, in turn, required a vast amount of financial and human resources in this area. The sales activities of *Komatsu* depended to a larger extent on the branch offices of a general trading company. Production also had to be reorganised. The production management department was set up to control the capacity of each factory, to handle orders most efficiently, and to plan production. The management tried to re-allocate product lines, a serious necessity because the company was rapidly moving from a mixture of civilian and military industry to strictly civilian industry. Finally, the top level management was established by forming a managing board and a general staff department in 1959. Decision-making, which had formerly been carried out individually by the managing director in charge of each function, were centralised in the managing board.

However, this environment which was so favourable to *Komatsu*, did not last long. In 1960 *Komatsu* created a long-range management plan, which aimed at diversification into agricultural machinery, motor pumps, and industrial plants. At the same time, however, the company had to prepare for the liberalisation of trade in bulldozers. In order to compete with *Caterpillar*, which was planning to advance into the Japanese market through a joint venture with *Shin Mitsubishi Heavy Industries*, *Komatsu* spent almost all of its financial resources in construction machinery.[55] Towards the mid-1960s, its organisational structure was simplified. Sales departments were consolidated into a single headquarters, and technological and then foreign activities were similarly consolidated. Furthermore, the firm abolished the headquarters to simplify information channels. By these measures, all product lines except bulldozers, were reorganised into the agricultural machinery and the industrial plants divisions, both of which had sales and technology functions but were not charged with a production function. In effect, the strategy for competing with *Caterpillar* overcame the strategy of diversification. The share of construction machinery in the total sales increased year by year, reaching 68 per cent in 1970. Industrial vehicles also increased their share during the same period. Cast and forged iron, which had initially constituted one of the company's main products, were completely integrated into other product lines by becoming their materials.

In the mid-1960s there was discussion as to whether or not this sort of partial adoption of the divisional system was effective. Eventually, this partial divisional structure had reverted to the functional form by 1970. As domestic demand for bulldozers was filled, *Komatsu* planned to export its products, and to further diversify into industrial plants. As far as exports were concerned though, *Komatsu* could not compete directly with *Caterpillar*, but remaining the marginal supplier in Asia and South America, and made its way into socialist countries. The divisional structure was partially adopted for the second time for purposes of diversification. This time three divisions were set up, covering forklifts, industrial plants and engines, and industrial machinery. There were also the main product lines which were still administered by a functional structure. This structure has continued until the present, although the number of divisions has decreased. Again the strategy of diversification was undone by the expansion strategy of bulldozers.

The organisational structure of *Komatsu* frequently swayed between the functional and the partially divisional structure. Another characteristic was found in the centralisation of authority in the head office. Expansion due to the firm's rapid growth brought forth various organisational problems often seen in this kind of bureaucratic organisation. The firm tried to simplify its structure and centralise its operations. In order to supplement these measures, much use was made since the mid-1960s of informal organisational activities such as project teams, quality control circles, and various committees.

The nine companies examined here dealt with the production of transportation equipment, such as ships and various sorts of industrial use vehicles. By 1963, when the Japanese shipbuilding industry encountered its second boom, these companies developed in different directions. Some of the five of the companies intensified their interests in shipbuilding, while others expanded in engineering. A similarly divergent trend was observed in the cases of four engineering companies. Two tended to specialise in transportation equipment, while the other two diversified.

The multidivisional structure was introduced in the first half of the 1960s. Six companies adopted it between 1960 and 1964. However, the chief motive behind this organisational reform was not in mitigating centralised control, but in solving problems arising from mergers. Their strength derived from engineering excellence and the self-supporting system of factories.

Most of the nine concerns in heavy engineering introduced the multidivisional structure, but only a few maintained the full-divisions which were responsible for at least the sales and manufacturing functions. The reallocation of product lines in the initial period of the divisional structure was a difficult task, and made it impossible for each division to have its own production units. The reason for this was partly technological; production was carried out by order, and this meant that various products were completed in the same workshops. More importantly, however, powerful production units made it difficult to reorganise and absorb the production units into divisions. The transitional character of the multidivisional structure was also caused by conflicting trends in demand and technology. The market demand for engineering products became more and more systematic, while products became more and more specific. The division headquarters structure was introduced to solve these countervailing trends. In cases such as these, each division headquarters controlled several production divisions and a sales division, together with having further authority delegated by general office.

7.5 SUMMARY

Technological skills, either introduced from foreign countries or accumulated and developed independently, have been the mainsprings of development for firms in chemicals, electrical equipment and heavy engineering. The development of these firms depended on supplying new products. This is illustrated in the following tables which show the product diversification of the companies in these branches. The process of diversification was rapid, particularly in heavy engineering in the 1950s, electrical equipment in the 1950s and 1960s. The growth rate of these companies was also high during the same period; 200 to 400 per cent every five years.

As has been pointed out, almost all the companies examined in this chapter adopted multidivisional structures. However, there were many variations which did not follow in the typical form of the multidivisional structure. These variations were important because

Japanese Management Structures

TABLE 7.1 Diversification by three-digit industry classification

	1950				1960				1970				1980			
	S	D	R	U	S	D	R	U	S	D	R	U	S	D	R	U
Chemicals	2	4	2	2	2	4	2	3	2	2	4	3	2		6	2
Electrical engineering	3	5	5	1		6	8			3	10	1	1	2	10	1
Heavy engineering		4	7			1	8	2		1	6	2		1	7	1

Note: *S* = single product, *D* = dominant product, *R* = related product, *U* = unrelated product

TABLE 7.2 Diversification by four-digit industry classification

	1950				1960				1970				1980			
	S	D	R	U	S	D	R	U	S	D	R	U	S	D	R	U
Chemicals		2	6	2	1	2	5	3		3	5	3		2	7	2
Electrical engineering	3	2	8	1			14				13	1			13	1
Heavy engineering		3	8			1	8	2			7	2		1	7	1

Note: *S* = single product, *D* = dominant product, *R* = related product, *U* = unrelated product

they were influenced by the same traditionally strong production units or the changes in products and market. The transition among these sub-categories is shown in Tables 7.1 and 7.2.

NOTES

1. Channon, *op. cit.*, pp. 130–60; Dyas and Thanheiser, *op. cit.*, pp. 291–8.
2. Yoshitaka Suzuki, 'The Strategy and Structure of Top 100 Japanese Industrial Enterprises, 1950–70', *Strategic Management Journal*, vol. 1, 1980.
3. Shintaro Takahashi, 'Reorganisation of the Multidivisional Structure and the Headquarters System', in *Kozo henkakuka no soshiki tenkai* (Organisational Development under the Structural Change), ed. Kigyo kenkyu kai (Business Study Society), 1975, pp. 50–65; Giichi Hosono, 'The Multidivisional Structure and the Management Planning', *Kigyo kaikei (Accounting)*, Oct. 1963, pp. 61–7; 'Mitsui Toatsu', *Kik*, Mar. 1972, pp. 8–11; Hosono, 'The Coordination of Management Planning under the Multidivisional Structure', *Kj*, Feb. 1971, pp. 24–30; 'The Stipulation of the Amalgamation on Chemical Industry', *Kk*, Aug. 1968, pp. 10–19; see also ibid., Jan. 1968, pp. 18–23; 'The Aim of Mitsui Chemicals' Emergence', *Nu*, Jan. 1969, pp. 45–9; *Nks*, 14.9.1959, 7.5.1960, 13.6.1962, 31.8.1964; *Nss*, 12.10.1978, 6.10.1980.
4. *Reports to the Minister of Finance*, 1960–69.

5. *The Fifty Year History of Showa Denko*, 1977; Shuichi Saito, 'Showa Denko', in *Kindaiteki keiei soshiki no jitsurei* (Cases of Modern Management Organisation), ed. Susumu Takamiya, 1953, pp. 85–118; Japan Productivity Center (ed.), 'Showa Denko', *Choki keiei keikaku* (Long-Range Management Planning), 1961, pp. 158–63, pp. 528–9; 'Showa Denko', *Tk*, 22.11.1975, pp. 86–91; see also ibid., 19.6.1971, pp. 92–5; 28.12.1974, pp. 126–7; 31.3.1979, pp. 86–90; 'Showa Denko', *Tg*, Jan. 1977, p. 12; *Nks*, 9.9.1963, 6.1.1978; *Nss*, 31.7.1978.
6. *Reports to the Minister of Finance*, 1955–64.
7. Ibid., 1974–80.
8. *The History of Sumitomo Chemical*, 1981; Minoru Horimoto, 'The State of Chemical Industry and Management Organisation', in *Sk*, vol. 3, no. 4, 1969, pp. 58–64; Susumu Takamiya (ed.), 'Sumitomo Chemical', *Kindaiteki keiei soshiki no jitsurei, op. cit.*, pp. 313–18; Niihama City (ed.), 'Sumitomo Chemical's Advance to Petrochemical Industry and the Movement of the Sumitomo Group', Niihama sangyo hattatsushi (The Industrial History of Niihama), 1973, pp. 400–25; *Kagaku* (Company publication), Apr. 1969, p. 8; see also ibid., Sep. 1969, p. 8; June 1970, p. 13; Aug. 1970, p. 11; *Tokyo* (Company publication), Dec. 1971, p. 1; *Sumitomo Chemical Osaka seizosho shonaiho* (Company publication), 10.7.1961, pp. 2–3; 'Sumitomo Chemical', *Kj*, Nov. 1956, pp. 2–26; 'Sumitomo Chemical', *Kk*, Jan. 1980, pp. 36–7; 'Sumitomo Chemical', *Ec*, 11.5.1976, pp. 98–9; 'Sumitomo Chemical', *Tk*, 9.1.1965, pp. 159–61; see also ibid., 21.2.1970, pp. 52–6; 6.9.1975, pp. 90–95; *Nks*, 28.4.1955, 31.3.1959, 4.3.1963, 2.12.1977.
9. See Horimoto, *loc. cit.*
10. *The History of Mitsubishi Chemical Industries*, 1981; 'Mitsubishi Chemical Industries', *Kk*, Jan. 1980, pp. 34–5; 'Mitsubishi Chemical Industries', *Tk*, 12.7.1975, pp. 88–93; see also ibid., 30.10.1976, pp. 102–7; 12.4.1969, pp. 88–9; 17.11.1969, pp. 141–3; 29.5.1976, pp. 98–101; *Nks*, 24.6.1963, 26.12.1969, 6.3.1976.
11. *Reports to the Minister of Finance*, 1960–64.
12. Ibid., 1974–80.
13. Kan-ichi Nakayasu, *Munen muso* (Free from Contemplation and Scrutiny), 1965; do., *Watashi no rirekisho* (My Life History), 1980; *The Life of Kan-ichi Nakayasu*, 1984; Mainichi Shinbun Seibuhonsha Keizaibu (ed.), 'Ube Industries', in *Asu ni idomu 'Kigyo shinjidai'* (The Age of Challenging Business Enterprises), 1984, pp. 122–47; 'Witness to Postwar Industrial History XI', *Ec*, 16.3.1976, pp. 78–85; Seiichi Fujiyoshi, 'Transforming Limitable Mineral Resources into Illimitable Industrial Products', *Kik*, Nov. 1965, pp. 74–80; Kiyoshi Ozawa 'Ube Industries', *Tk*, 7.11.1980, pp. 48–51; see also ibid., 31.1.1976, pp. 88–92; 30.8.1980, pp. 108–11; 'Ube Industries', *Kk*, June 1972, pp. 18–21; *Nks*, 12.4.1963, 5.4.1965, 12.1.1966, 29.9.1971.
14. *Reports to the Minister of Finance*, 1965–73.
15. Ibid., 1974–80.
16. *The Sixty Year History of Dainippon Ink and Chemicals*, 1969; Kazuhiko Yoshida, 'The Multidivisional Structure of DIC and its Future Problem's *Kj*, Aug. 1978, pp. 24–7; 'Dainippon, Ink and Chemicals', *Kik*, Dec.

1962, pp. 62–4; 'Dainippon Ink and Chemicals', *Tk*, 11.1.1969, pp. 94–7; *Tg*, Jan. 1977, p. 15, *Nks*, 24.5.1960, 11.1.1980, 12.10.1980.

17. *Nihon Sekiyu Kagaku Kogyo Seiritsu Shiko* (A Treatise on the Rise of Japanese Petrochemical Industry), 1970; 'Mitsubishi Petrochemical', *Kk*, May 1966, pp. 40–45; see also ibid., July 1972, pp. 70–73; Nov. 1976, pp. 18–20; Aug. 1977, pp. 76–81; 'Mitsubishi Petrochemical', *Tk*, 23.9.1978, pp. 97–8; see also ibid., 24.3.1979, pp. 108–11; *Nks*, 15.9.1960, 25.12.1960, 25.3.1974, 6.7.1975; *Nss*, 2.8.1977, 9.6.1977, 20.8.1977, 2.4.1980.

18. *The History of Sekisui Chemical*, 1964; Yoshiro Hoshino *et al.*, 'Sekisui Chemical', *Ck*, vol. 2, no. 4, 1963, pp. 317–40; Kazuo Noda, 'Sekisui Chemical', *Ec*, 16.4.1963, pp. 72–6; 'Sekisui Chemical', *Tk*, 15.11.1975, pp. 126–31; see also ibid., 8.7.1978, pp. 98–9; 18.2.1961, p. 84; 'Sekisui Chemical', *Ma*, June 1968, pp. 17–24; *Nks*, 16.3.1964, 25.12.1964, 15.2.1965; *Nss*, 18.1.1975.

19. *The One hundred and Eighty Year History of Takeda Chemical Industries*, 1962; *The Two hundred Year History of Takeda Chemical Industries, with Supplement* (2 vols), 1983; Junji Hirata, 'The Process of the Middle-Range Planning', in *Senryaku keiei keikaku sakutei no jissai* (The Practice of Strategic Planning), ed. Kigyo kenkyu kai, 1982, pp. 153–65; 'Takeda Chemical Industries', *Tk*, 6.3.1971, pp. 86–9; see also ibid., 1.3.1958, pp. 59–61; 10.6.1972, pp. 84–8; 2.4.1977, pp. 90–94; 13.5.1978, pp. 88–92; *Nks*, 18.11.1963, 30.10.1973, 20.12.1976.

20. *Reports to the Minister of Finance*, 1955–64.

21. Ibid., 1965–73.

22. *The History of Hitachi* vols I (1960), II (1965), III (1971), IV (1985); Yasuo Okamoto, *Hitachi to Matsushita* vols I, II, 1979; Masao Fujie, 'Hitachi', in *Kindaiteki keiei soshiki no jitsurei, op. cit.*, pp. 330–54; Susumu Takamiya (ed.), 'Hitachi', *Kaisha soshiki* (Company Organisation), 1959, pp. 179–97; Iwao Futami, 'Hitachi', in *Saishin choki keiei keikaku no jitsurei* (Recent Cases of the Long-Range Management Planning), ed. Toyohiro Kono, 1978, pp. 62–87; Etsuzo Yamashita, 'Rationalising a Giant Enterprise', *Ks*, Apr. 1966, pp. 76–8; 'Hitachi', *Tk*, 20.1.1962, pp. 94–7; see also ibid., 22.7.1967, pp. 98–103; 14.12.1968, pp. 52–63; 22.8.1970, pp. 64–9; 29.7.1972, pp. 92–6; 18.3.1978, pp. 94–8; 19.4.1980, pp. 86–9; 11.10.1980, pp. 90–93; *Nks*, 14.1.1956, 26.3.1959, 2.2.1960, 8.8.1960, 16.8.1960, 30.9.1962, 22.10.1962, 4.2.1963, 19.2.1964, 24.5.1967, 21.8.1969, 10.11.1969, 25.5.1970.

23. *Reports to the Minister of Finance*, 1950–55.

24. *The Eighty-Five Year History of Tokyo Shibaura Electric*, 1963; *The One Hundred Year History of Toshiba*, 1977; Jo Yamaguchi, 'Tokyo Shibaura Electric', in *Kindaiteki keiei soshiki no jitsurei, op. cit.*, pp. 467–71; Keizai Doyukai (Japan Committee for Economic Development) (ed.), 'Portfolio Management System by Strategic Business Unit (SBU)', *1980 nendai no kigyo keiei* (Business Enterprise in the 1980s), 1980, pp. 147–59; Jo Kosaka, 'The Development of International Business and Its Promoting System', in *Sozo ni chosen suru soshiki kakushin* (Organisational Innovation Aiming at Creativeness), ed. Kigyo kenkyu kai, 1981, pp. 197–209; Shin-ichiro Sumino, 'The Operation and Problems of

Internal Capital System', *Sangyo keiri* (Industry Accounting), 1970, pp. 23–8; Shiro Shimaya, 'Rational Organisation: Toshiba's Emergent Target', *Ck*, vol. 4, no. 3, 1965, pp. 108–17; 'Tokyo Shibaura Electric', *Tk*, 14.2.1970, pp. 62–7; see also ibid., 5.9.1970, pp. 74–9; 9.10.1976, pp. 98–9; 14.1.1978, pp. 150–55; *Tg*, Jan. 1977, p. 9; *Ec*, 28.10.1975, pp. 94–5; *Nks*, 1.8.1954, 26.5.1953, 13.8.1958, 1.4.1959, 22.10.1962, 22.4.1963, 29.10.1966, 3.5.1970, 23.5.1973, 4.4.1977, 29.1.1979, 5.5.1980; *Nss*, 29.7.1975, 1.4.1976, 22.8.1978, 18.7.1979.

25. *Reports to the Minister of Finance*, 1955–65.

26. Ibid., 1965–73.

27. *The History of Mitsubishi Electric*, 1982; Japan Productivity Center (ed.), 'Mitsubishi Electric', *Choki keiei keikaku, op. cit.*, pp. 320–23; Kingo Imai, 'Mitsubishi Electric', in *Saishin choki keiei keikaku no jitsurei, op. cit.*, pp. 88–121; Keizai Doyukai, 'Planning Market-Oriented Strategy and Structure', *1980 nendai no kigyo keiei, op. cit.*, pp. 193–202; Masanori Tanaka, 'Monitoring of Research and Development: the Case of Mitsubishi Electric', in *Kenkyu kaihatsu hyoka jissen shiryoshu* (Practices for Monitoring Research and Development), ed. Kigyo kenkyu kai, 1982, pp. 293–5; Imai, 'The Present State of the Multidivisional Structure', *Kj*, June 1975, pp. 7–10; Akira Ishikawa, 'Monitoring Performance in the Multidivisional Structure', *Kj*, Feb. 1977, pp. 11–15; Imai, 'The Trend of New Multidivisional Structure', *Kj*, Aug. 1978, pp. 28–33; Yasuo Okamoto, 'Dynamism of Reorganisation in the Management Structure', *Kik*, Mar. 1965, pp. 56–62; 'Mitsubishi Electric', *Tk*, 15.10.1977, pp. 90–94; *Nks*, 2.12.1958, 14.12.1959, 26.8.1963, 9.7.1969, 10.11.1969, 20.6.1977.

28. *Reports to the Minister of Finance,* 1955–65.

29. Ibid., 1965–74.

30. *The History of Fuji Electric*, 1957; *The History of Fuji Electric*, vol. II, 1974; Masamoto Koga, 'Fuji Electric', in *Kindaiteki keiei soshiki no jitsurei, op. cit.*, pp. 355–68; Seishi Taka, 'The Multidivisional Structure of Fuji Electric', *Mg*, Feb. 1964, pp. 20–22; 'Fuji Electric', *Tk*, 29.1.1966, pp. 118–21; see also ibid., 28.9.1968, pp. 70–75; 19.3.1977, pp. 95–6; 24.12.1977, pp. 144–5; *Nks*, 4.10.1958, 9.12.1963, 12.12.1966, 7.3.1968, 27.8.1976, *Nss*, 9.7.1976, 10.2.1978, 27.2.1978.

31. *The Seventy Year History of Nippon Electric*, 1972; *The History of Nippon Electric: Ten Years Thereafter*, 1980; Tomomi Mitobe, 'Strategic Management Structure and Middle-Range Planning by Operation Group', in *Senryaku keiei keikaku sakutei no jissai, op. cit.*, pp. 145–52; Masao Miya, 'Practices Monitoring Research and Development', in *Kenkyu kaihatsu hyoka jissen shiryoshu, op. cit.*, pp. 133–49; Akira Koike, 'Problems of Internal Transfer Price in Multidivisional Structure', *Kj*, Feb. 1971, pp. 18–23; Yasuo Yoshioka, 'The Present State and Problems of Internal Transfer System', *Kj*, June 1975, pp. 11–15; Sheigo Matsumoto, 'Monitoring System of Divisional Performance', *Kj*, Feb. 1977; Masazo Shimizu, 'Nippon Electric', *Tg*, Jan. 1977, p. 8; 'Nippon Electric', *Tk*, 16.9.1972, pp. 92–3; see also ibid., 26.7.1975, pp. 86–91; 12.2.1977, pp. 82–87; *Nks*, 11.5.1964.

32. *Reports to the Minister of Finance*, 1955–64.

33. 'Fujitsu', *Tk*, 2.10.1971, pp. 88–9; see also ibid., 20.4.1974, pp. 84–7; 22.4.1978, pp. 86–91; *Nks*, 21.10.1971, 15.10.1972, 3.7.1974; *Nss*, 6.1.1981.
34. *Reports to the Minister of Finance*, 1955–64.
35. Ibid., 1968–73.
36. Heihachiro Murota, 'SBU System and Matrix Structure', in *Sozo ni chosensuru soshiki kakushin, op. cit.*, pp. 89–95; Haruo Mitsui, 'Long-Range Business Planning and its Committee's Regulations', *Kj*, May 1971, pp. 40–47; 'Oki Electric', *Ma*, Sep. 1979, p. 63; 'Oki Electric', *Tk*, 8.7.1972, pp. 92–3; *Nks*, 24.4.1958, 4.4.1979.
37. *Reports to the Minister of Finance*, 1955–64.
38. *The Fifteen Year History of Nippon Denso*, 1964; *The Twenty-five Year History of Nippon Denso*, 1974; 'Nippon Denso', *Tk*, 29.7.1967, pp. 122–3; see also ibid., 1.5.1971, pp. 74–7.
39. *The Fifty Year History of Matsushita Denko*, 1968; *The Sixty Year History of Matsushita Denko*, 1978; *Nks*, 8.1.1958, 1.9.1959.
40. *The History of Shin Mitsubishi Jukogyo*, 1967; *The History of Mitsubishi Zosen*, 1967; *The History of Mitsubishi Nihon Jukogyo*, 1967; Yoshinori Tsukahara, 'Mitsubishi Zosen', in *Kindaiteki keiei soshiki no jitsurei, op. cit.*, pp. 301–12; Japan Productivity Center (ed.), 'Shin Mitsubishi Jukogyo', *Choki keiei keikaku, op. cit.*, pp. 344–51; Jun Kawada, 'The Matrix System in the Engineering Business Promoting Division', in *Sozo ni chosen suru soshiki kakushin, op. cit.*, pp. 96–104; 'Mitsubishi Heavy Industries', *Tk*, 11.4.1964, pp. 68–72; see also ibid., 9.1.1965, pp. 171–3; 27.11.1965, pp. 66–72; 7.1.1967, pp. 154–6; 4.3.1967, pp. 68–75; 27.1.1973, pp. 88–97; 2.8.1975, pp. 82–87; *Nks*, 1.6.1956, 24.5.1957, 6.7.1959, 29.6.1960, 16.5.1961, 11.3.1963, 29.10.1963, 28.1.1964, 4.2.1964, 7.2.1964, 11.2.1964, 10.7.1965, 1.5.1967, 19.11.1977, 8.12.1977; *Nss*, 15.7.1975, 20.1.1977, 18.2.1977, 21.4.1977, 29.6.1977, 26.8.1977, 8.12.1977, 27.2.1978, 23.6.1980, 30.7.1980.
41. *The History of Kawasaki Heavy Industries*, 1959; Shoichi Kita, 'Kawasaki Heavy Industries', in *Kindaiteki keiei soshiki no jitsurei, op. cit.*, pp. 259–69; 'Kawasaki Heavy Industries', *Kj*, Nov. 1956, pp. 26–41; see also ibid., Nov. 1977, pp. 28–30; Aug. 1978, pp. 6–9; 'Kawasaki Heavy Industries', *Tk*, 6.12.1952, pp. 59–60; see also ibid., 17.8.1963, pp. 90–91; 30.3.1968, pp. 94–5; 13.2.1971, pp. 86–91; 28.12.1974, pp. 133–4; *Nks*, 23.1.1956, 3.9.1960, 10.6.1961, 14.3.1969, 16.3.1981; *Nss*, 14.5.1976, 29.3.1977, 21.4.1977, 1.7.1977, 2.10.1980.
42. *The Fifty Year History of Mitsui Shipbuilding and Engineering*, 1968; Shu Taki, 'Mitsui Shipbuilding and Engineering', in *Saishin choki keiei keikaku no jitsurei, op. cit.*, pp. 173–93; 'Mitsui Shipbuilding and Engineering', *Tk*, 9.8.1980, pp. 116–19; *Nks*, 29.5.1961, 6.8.1962, 8.6.1964, 1.3.1967, 26.7.1979.
43. *Reports to the Minister of Finance*, 1960–73.
44. Ibid., 1974–80,
45. *The Seventy-Five Year History of Hitachi Shipbuilding and Engineering*, 1956; *The Ninety Year of Hitachi Shipbuilding and Engineering*, 1971; Keizai Doyukai, 'Clarification of Authority by the Matrix System', *1980 nendai no kigyo keiei, op. cit.*, pp. 175–92; Akira Sasao, 'Co-existence of

New Industries in the Traditional Companies 241

Multidivisional Structure by Functions and that by Products', *Kj*, June 1975, pp. 20–23; 'Hitachi Shipbuilding and Engineering', *Ma*, Mar. 1980, pp. 107–9; *Tk*, 4.4.1970, pp. 76–80; see also ibid., 7.10.1972, pp. 86–90; *Za*, 20.9.1978, pp. 44–7; *Nks*, 14.11.1953, 19.2.1963, 21.10.1963, 8.4.1968, 27.4.1971, 15.3.1977, 2.12.1977.

46. *Reports to the Minister of Finance*, 1965–73.
47. *The One-Hundred and Eight Year History of Ishikawajima Heavy Industries*, 1961; *The Fifty Year Brief History of Harima Shipbuilding*, 1958; Gen-ichi Nagase, 'Spin-out Strategy for the Improvement of Business System', in *Senryaku taisei to katsuryoku soshiki no shintenkai* (New Development in the System for Strategy and the Structure for Excellence), ed. Kigyo kenkyu kai, 1979, pp. 273–81; Takao Tanaka, 'Overseas Expansion and Multinationalisation of Ishikawajima-Harima Heavy Industries', in *Nihon takokuseki kigyo no shiteki tenkai* (Historical Development of Japan Multinational Enterprise), ed. Mitsuo Fuji-i *et al.*, 1979, pp. 139–60; 'The Aims of Structural Reform', *Chosa jiho* (Company publication), Dec. 1974, pp. 2–7; 'The Aims of Structural Reform', *Aieichiai* (Company publication), July 1978, pp. 4–5; see also ibid., July 1980, pp. 4–5; Kuniyoshi Urabe, 'Top Management System in the age of Managerial Improvement', *Seisansei* (Productivity), Aug. 1962, pp. 32–8; 'Long-Range Management Planning for the Improvement of Business System', *Mg*, Nov. 1963, pp. 18–21; 'Ishikawajima-Harima Heavy Industries', *Kik*, Mar. 1972, p. 14; 'Ishikawajima Heavy Industries', *Tk*, 16.7.1960, pp. 68–9; see also ibid., 10.10.1964, pp. 60–63; 30.12.1967, pp. 132–3; 6.12.1969, pp. 72–9; 27.10.1973, pp. 94–5; 4.10.1975, pp. 86–91; 24.3.1979, pp. 102–6; 28.7.1979, pp. 92–5; *Tg*, Jan. 1977, p. 14; *Ec.* 26.11.1963, pp. 76–80; *Nks*, 2.7.1960, 8.8.1960, 17.9.1960, 4.10.1960, 15.4.1963, 10.6.1963, 14.1.1965, 9.12.1974, 4.7.1978, 25.4.1979; *Nss*, 1.7.1980, 9.7.1980.
48. *Annual Reports of Sumitomo Machinery for 1950–70*; 'Sumitomo Machinery', *Tk*, 13.1.1962, pp. 58–9; see also ibid., 30.1.1965, pp. 82–7; 1.4.1972, pp. 84–5; *Nks*, 10.8.1954, 22.4.1959, 23.2.1960, 5.7.1960, 23.5.1968, 9.4.1970, 29.10.1976, 14.2.1977.
49. *The Forty Year History of Toyoda Automatic Loom Works*, 1967; 'Toyoda Automatic Loom Works', *Tk*, 28.5.1960, pp. 62–4; see also ibid., 26.9.1970, p. 93; 10.4.1971, pp. 96–7; *Nks*, 2.2.1955, 21.7.1978.
50. *Reports to the Minister of Finance*, 1955–64.
51. Ibid., 1965–73.
52. *The Eighty Year History of Kubota*, 1970; *The Recent Ten Year History of Kubota*, 1980; Ryozo Tanaka, 'Intensification of Strategic Planning Function', in *Senryaku taisei to katsuryoku soshiki no shintenkai, op. cit.*, pp. 115–19; *do.*, 'Long-Range Management Planning for Low Growth Age', in *Senryaku keiei keikaku sakutei no jissai, op. cit.*, pp. 179–89; 'Kubota', *Mg*, Aug. 1963, pp. 15–18; *Ma*, Oct. 1978, pp. 63-70; *Tk*, 16.12.1972, pp. 88–92; see also ibid., 5.10.1974, pp. 91–4; 18.10.1975, pp. 106–11; *Nks*, 23.12.1963, 12.4.1970, 24.8.1976.
53. *Reports to the Minister of Finance*, 1974–80.
54. *The Fifty Year History of Komatsu*, 1971; Keizai Doyukai, 'Thorough Realisation of Management for Users', *1980 nendai no kigyo keiei, op.*

cit., pp. 95–104; Minoru Kuroda, 'On the Head Office/Branch Office Accounts: the Case of Komatsu', *Kj*, Mar. 1961, pp. 30–33; Shiro Sakuma, 'Pursuit of Optimum Organisation Form: the case of Komatsu', *Ks*, Sep. 1966, pp. 17–20; 'Komatsu', *Tk*, 24.7.1965, pp. 78–9; see also ibid., 2.10.1971, pp. 86–7; 9.9.1972, pp. 94–5; 19.10.1974, pp. 82–5; 23.8.1975, pp. 88–91; 4.2.1978, pp. 90–94; *Nks*, 17.8.1958, 14.10.1963, 20.9.1964, 30.11.1964, 1.11.1965.
55. *Reports to the Minister of Finance*, 1960–70.

8 New Companies in the Post-War Mass Market

8.1 INTRODUCTION

Companies in food, oil, automobiles, household electrical and other endurable consumer goods developed dramatically in the post-war period. There were only two concerns in oil, one in automobiles, and one in household electricals among the largest 121 firms in 1935, and only one of them remained in the ranks of the largest firms of the post-war era. By 1970 the number of the concerns had increased to eight in oil, 11 in automobiles, and five in household electrical equipment. In food, the large pre-war firms, which had mostly supplied semi-finished materials, were overtaken by new firms which produced finished consumer goods. These companies supplied new products to the Japanese market and developed rapidly along with their major product lines. A market for consumer goods appeared and developed rapidly after 1960, and the growth rate of these companies was generally high, probably the highest among all the industrial branches in the 1960–80 period.

Limited opportunities for the transfer of technological skill was a common characteristic of these industries, though this lack was made up for by the rapid growth of their major products. Their low level of diversification was remarkable when compared with companies in the other groups of industries which were examined in previous chapters, or even when compared with their European counterparts. This is shown not only by the three-digit industry classification but even by the four-digit category.

The number of sample companies in oil and automobiles was large throughout the three decades following 1950, though concentration ratios were high. Between 1955 and 1970, almost all oil products and automobiles were supplied by companies which were the members of the largest 100 firms. Food, brewing and dairy products showed high concentration ratios, and large-scale firms in food were mostly found

243

TABLE 8.1 Low diversifiers by four-digit classification

	1950		1960		1970		1980	
	S	D	S	D	S	D	S	D
Oil	6	1	3	5	4	4	4	4
Automobiles	1	8	0	4	0	5	0	2
Miscellaneous	0	1	0	0	0	0	0	1
Steel	0	3	1	2	0	4	0	2
Nonferrous metals	0	1	0	1	0	1	0	1
Materials	1	1	1	1	0	2	0	2

Note: S = single product, D = dominant product.

TABLE 8.2 Low diversifiers by three-digit classification

	1950		1960		1970		1980	
	S	D	S	D	S	D	S	D
Oil	6	1	5	3	5	3	5	3
Automobiles	9	1	10	0	10	1	10	1
Miscellaneous	0	2	0	2	0	2	0	1
Steel	2	4	2	5	0	6	0	5
Nonferrous metals	0	3	0	3	0	6	0	5
Materials	1	1	1	1	0	2	0	2

Note: S = single product, D = dominant product.

among these two sub-categories. In oil, there were entries by large-scale companies in the 1970s. They were 'combinato' refineries, set up by groups of companies and supplied oil products to other members of the same industrial complex. Besides exceptions such as these, new entrance was difficult. The reasons differed from each other. Oil refining required huge amounts of capital but had no guarantee of high profitability. In automobiles, established brand names and distribution channels were important barriers to new entries.

There is another product-market characteristic which the companies examined here had in common, and which might well have influenced the organisational form of these companies. Most of them supplied finished consumer products. They had relatively lengthy production processes, from raw materials to final distribution. As in food processing and household electrical equipment, close contacts with the market were highly necessary. However, such market characteristics created neither vertical integration, nor functionally departmentalised structure in these firms. They had organisational alternatives: some completely internalised marketing functions within a single firm and built up the functional structure, others set up or affiliated sales subsidiaries to gain control over outlets. The problem was in determining which type of organisational forms was more firmly integrated, or which type of coordination was more efficient throughout a long period of time. In some cases these large-scale companies became the manufacturing subsidiaries of other operating companies or often formed groups with other firms in the same industries. Whatever the case, all were new phenomena that were observed in the post-war era.

8.2 FOOD AND DRINK COMPANIES

By 1970, the pre-war food companies, represented by sugar refining firms, had been almost completely replaced by the new firms in final food processing. This change was caused not only by the emergence of a mass-market for food consumption, but also by new entries, the loss of Japan's overseas colonies, the appearance of new kinds of food, and finally by technical changes in food processing, transport and preservation. As for demand, the development of large city markets and change in eating habits were among the largest factors. In 1950 a quarter of the total population of Japan lived in cities with over 100 000 inhabitants, and this ratio had risen to 40 per cent in 1960 and to nearly 60 per cent by 1980. During the 25 years following 1955, the consumption of rice *per capita* decreased by 30 per cent, while that of meat and dairy products increased seven- and five-fold respectively.

Of the largest 100 firms in 1970, three began in dairy products, three in sea food or cold storage, and one each in flour-milling and condiments. In addition there were three brewing companies. Milk product and condiment companies were engaged in the processing of miscellaneous sorts of food, particularly of semi-perishable in 1950, but they tended to specialise in either their original products or in new products during the following two decades. Those companies beginning in sea foods and flour-milling started from the 'dominant product' category, and by the end of the 1950s, diversified into food processing or feed stuff through forward integration. Both specialisation and diversification, however, were implemented by adding downward processes, which were rooted in the same changes in the

Japanese pattern of living. Development in processing technology, transport, and in storage both in the distribution channels and in the final consumers, also influenced companies which diversified. Instead of the traditional items, fresh, frozen, freeze-dried, and semi-processed products became dominant in the market. More important still was the increasing dependence on overseas supply of raw materials. By 1970 more than 90 per cent of the wheat consumed in Japan was imported, and though the total quantity of fish harvested exceeded home consumption, difficulties increased in self-supplying some sorts of fish, particularly expensive ones. These companies intensified their purchasing and sales functions, and their original nature as mere processors of primary products became weak.

The growth rates of these companies were high throughout the three post-war decades. Their sales expanded at least 100 times (when calculated in yen), though the period of high growth differed among industrial branches. Throughout such rapid expansion, they extended their geographical coverage from local or urban areas to the whole country. This in turn resulted in the increase in the number of field-units, especially in the early phases of development, though recent times have seen the reduction in the numbers of these units. The number of operating units was nevertheless larger than the case of other industries. Compared with the development of the pre-war food companies, which depended on mergers or acquisitions to a considerable extent, the post-war production units of these companies were mainly set up and extended independently. The size of the production units, however, was not decisive in their development. Rather, the purchase of raw materials and marketing became barriers to new entries. Half of the firms showed a high level of family ownership or control in 1950, which was gradually replaced by other types of control.

These dramatic changes in market and product must have had influence on the organisational structure of these companies. Here, a word is necessary regarding the brewing companies; they have been administered through a centralised and functionally departmental-ised structure, though they were able to adopt a multidivisional structure by geography as their British counterparts or Japanese sea food companies did.

The foundations of *Nippon Suisan*[1] were laid between 1936 and 1938 by the merger of several fishing and fishing-related companies which had *Nippon Sangyo* as a common holding company. In 1950, due to war damages and post-war regulations, the company was primarily based on whale processing factories, then it acquired several fishing, refrigerating and food-sale firms, and had further acquired large trawlers by the mid-1950s. These led the company into trawling, northern sea fishing, and sea food processing. The company's organisational structure began as an autonomously decentralised one. Its local branches such as those in Tobata and Hakodate Offices formed the basic units of activities. Central coordination schemes, such as the formation of a sales department in the central office, and then of fishing and processing departments, proceeded throughout the 1950s and 1960s, and finally the processing factories were moved from under the control of the branches to that of the head office. In the 1970s, however, the relationship between the head office and the local offices was reformed by making the functions of both parts more distinct.

The early leading position of the local branches resulted from the heavy commitment of *Nippon Suisan* to fishing in which each local branch had its own fisheries, often inherited from its corporate predecessor. The local branches were also engaged in the processing and sales of sea food. Profit responsibility was placed on each of such branch offices. From the latter half of the 1950s the head office, with the support of its planning department, emphasised the necessity of changing its basic activity from fishing to processing by increasing the latter share to 50 per cent of the sales of the company. The company was traditionally weak in downward branches. Its products were distributed either through wholesale markets or the company's special agents, who in turn sold to local wholesale merchants. Five primary agents were nominated, and formed a group through which *Nippon Suisan's* canned products were efficiently distributed. For sausage outlets, ten local sales companies were set up, which are estimated to have dealt with seven to eight per cent of the total sales of *Nippon Suisan*, and also added secondary wholesalers to the members of the group. By such reorganisation, *Nippon Suisan* became able to form a relationship with its distribution channels which by then were limited to special agents. The foundations of the switch from activities on sea to those on land were completed by the mid-1960s. However, the company continued to invest heavily in the construction of trawlers. In effect the upstream branches became predominant again, not only in their capital investment but in the amount of their sales.

In the face of new circumstances in the fishing industry since the late 1960s, *Nippon Suisan* began to reexamine its strategy which laid primary importance on fishing. One of the new circumstances they had to take into account was the increasing demand for more sophisticated products instead of fresh fish obtained within the local market. Another new circumstance was the international fishing situation which had gradually become severe for a company with heavy dependence on fishing. Because of the nature of technical skills of the fishing industry, diversification into food industries had been limited. *Nippon Suisan* could not easily cross the barrier beyond the primary processing. Between 1965 and 1973, the company adapted itself to new circumstances both in strategy and in structure. Financial resources were shifted from ships to factories and purchasing, particularly of foreign products which had been developed through the joint venture between the company and its overseas partners.[2] Food processing, which by 1970 had come to be directly controlled by the head office, was showing a poor record of performance in spite of its increasing share in the total sales of the company. Finally, in 1973, the local offices acquired control of the local factories again, and were made responsible for production and sales in their own regions. This, however, was not a mere revival of the previous geographical divisions. The firm had to respond to a broader market. For this reason local divisions were grouped into two parts, which were in turn coordinated by the sales headquarters manager of the head offices.

Taiyo Fishery,[3] which started its post-war history with the expansion of its fishing interests, gradually moved into food processing and the merchandising of sea food products processed by its subsidiary companies. Under the powerful leadership of the founder's family, aggressive expansion and vertical and horizontal integration were promoted, all of which were continued until the end of the 1960s. A wide range arose in the flow of goods from fishing through processing to sales and the effective scheduling of these became more complicated. Various sub-units, regional, functional and divisional ones, were rearranged into a multidivisional structure by geography, in which each of the local offices was charged with fishing, processing, sales, financing, and planning functions. This organisation, being formed around the local production units as its nucleus, continued until the late 1960s, when the multidivisional structure by products was introduced.

Though *Taiyo Fishery* paid much attention to the elaboration of its managerial organisation, namely, the formation of the management committee with its general staff in the early 1960s, the influence of the founder's family was strong throughout the formation of its strategies. In 1960, the Nakabe family still possessed nearly 40 per cent of the company's shares, and also held the company presidency as well as of its three vice-presidencies. As the other members of the management committee were appointed as local managers, the amount of the central office's responsibilities increased as the merchandising of its subsidiaries' products became the company's major business. Capital expenditure was made in 70 subsidiaries in the course of this diversification. Between 1955 and 1968, the fixed assets of the main body increased by 200 billion yen, while those of the subsidiaries by 100 billion yen. These included dealings not only in sea food products, but of fertilisers, oils and fats, sugar, and agricultural and meat products. Furthermore, the operating units were separated from the local offices to form separate companies. The quantity of these subsidiaries' products increased enormously. Sea food, in particular, increased to represent one third of the sales of *Taiyo Fishery* in 1955, and to 50 per cent in the following two decades. The sales of the various products were undertaken by *Taiyo Fishery*, and distributed through its outlets. These measures, however, were not taken to maintain control by the founder's family. In a company so heavily committed to merchandising, purchasing and sales techniques were highly important, and it was not easy to control other activities such as fishing and food processing. The formation of subsidiaries and the separation of factories were promoted for this reason, but this process and the control were incomplete. In the late 1960s, the organisational structure became a mixture of the geographical divisions and of the holding company form with 13 subdivided functional departments. The aggressive expansion ended in a poor result in 1968. It was then planned that investment in subsidiaries would be rearranged and the company's organisational structure reformed.

Five division headquarters were formed and basic activities such as fishing, processing, and merchandising were allocated to each of them. At first, these headquarters were responsible for sales in addition to fishing or processing, and the local offices continued to have production and sales functions. However, this system was gradually modified into one consisting of five basic areas of functional activities. The local offices were gradually separated from the responsibility for production and sales of their own products. This organisational reform reflected the company's changing policy of intensifying its interests in sea food products and strengthening the top management. In 1960 *Taiyo*'s top management was staffed by the founder's family and the operating middle and lower management by salaried managers: by the end of the 1970s, the top management was supported by a strong central staff consisting of more than ten special business areas.

Nippon Reizo[4] took over the cold-storage interests of the original *Nippon Suisan*, and began operations in ice-manufacturing and frozen sea-food. The company had planned from the start to develop a food processing branch. The company's organisational structure evolved from one consisting of autonomous local production units, into a multidivisional structure by geography, and further, with the diversification into new products which were to be supplied to wider markets, into a multidivisional structure by products.

Organisational problems in *Nippon Reizo*'s early history are found in the difficulties it had in controlling its nearly 200 local factories, which had recovered from war damages without financial support from the head office. The necessity of integrating the freezing industry with sales functions and of establishing close relationships among local units was suggested by *GHQ*. It advised *Nippon Reizo* to strengthen its internal control through the formation of management regulations and a budgetary system. These measures were carried out by 1954. In 1952 the self-supporting system of branch offices was put into practice, and in 1954 the self-supporting product line system was introduced. The latter, however, could not take the place of the former, because the compilation of the budget and managerial control was performed by the branch offices. There were 13 such branch offices, each of which was in charge of 4–18 factories, and several sales offices. The above measures increased the tasks of the head office, in which the number of the highest level managers had increased to six – three vice-presidents and three managing directors. The planning committee evolved spontaneously from a breakfast meeting of the head office's departmental managers. It became necessary to shift the main business from the declining field of ice-manufacture to cold storage and food processing, and these new businesses could be neither planned for nor started given the existing geographical divisions. Food processing included not only sea food products but live-stock and various kinds of other food. The new fields of activities also included foreign trade, which also could not be carried out by the existing branch offices.

These new endeavours required new outlets and new types of sales activities. At first products like canned sea food were distributed by local special agents, but as competition became keen towards the early 1960s, the firm changed this method. It was planned that the amount of sales per agent would be increased. In place of the existing 50 agents, the firm set up its own branch offices, whose sales departments reorganised secondary wholesale merchants, and endeavoured to establish a mass-marketing organisation. These activities were supervised by the sales department of the head office.

Next came frozen food, which was started by supplying department stores, and then large customers such as schools or factories. The transportation of frozen food required special equipment and a direct sales method was chosen. The company set up several local sales companies, which directly supplied these products. Based on these experiences and distribution capacities, *Nippon Reizo* began to enter the home markets. Supermarkets or chain stores, which were at that time developing in large cities were chosen as new outlets. From the mid-1960s, *Nippon Reizo* increased its share in live-stock. Existing wholesalers were utilised, but gradually products were directed to large-scale customers and large retailers in urban areas. Here again sales companies were set up in order to supply directly to these customers and retailers. Adaptation to the developing urban markets, changing retailing methods, and large-scale customers, through setting up its own sales companies in place of the traditional wholesalers is, therefore, the characteristic of *Nippon Reizo*.

To coordinate these activities which were gradually becoming complicated, organisational reform into a multidivisional structure by product was started. Five operating units with profit responsibility were formed. However, the firm maintained the self-supporting system of the branch offices, and this system continued to play an important role in the budgetary and managerial control. Between 1963 and 1964 some central coordination schemes were attempted. The firm reformed the management committee, which had been an adviser to the president, into one which was in charge of deliberating important matters. Also the firm strengthened its divisions, making them into full-divisions which could coordinate production and sales activities. On the background, the business environment of the frozen food industry began to alter; the consumer demand, food processing technology, and methods of transport and refrigeration all changed. Too much decentralisation was not effective in the newly developing market. Between 1964 and 1970, 52 factories were closed down, and the branch offices, still in control of the production and sales units, were consolidated. The geographical divisions were, by the early 1970s, reorganised into product divisions.

Nisshin Flour Milling[5] developed a network of local factories throughout the country in the early post-war era, which the founder had acquired before the war. Unlike the other large-scale food companies of the post-war era, *Nisshin Flour Milling* had long contained the elements of a basic material supplier. Efforts were first made to increase production capacity by modernising the flour-milling process, and production did in fact double between 1950 and 1960 even though the number of operating units was increased only slightly. By then, the shares of the company had already been diluted among institutional shareholders, though the founder's family still held the post of president. The functional organisation, consisting of sales, production and finance departments, was established in 1950. This changed into a multidivisional structure in the late 1960s, and again into a partly functional structure by 1970.

Diversification was limited to the areas of flour milling by-products in the early post-war period, but a full-scale entry into feedstuff was started by utilising the core processing skills and sales techniques between flour milling and feedstuff. Forward integration into food processing and chemical products followed. Factories for the production of feedstuff were bought up and subsidiaries were set up in food processing and chemical branches. This brought about product diversification, which took *Nisshin Flour* into the areas of consumer final goods like processed food, though the ratio of the latter continued to remain at approximately 10 per cent of the total sales of the firm. To control such a diversified enterprise with an increasing number of factories, local offices and subsidiaries, a series of organisational reforms were begun in 1967. *Nisshin*'s major subsidiaries were gradually made to specialise in the sales function of particular products such as feedstuff and processed food, while production of these was transferred to *Nisshin Flour Milling*. Close control was maintained over these subsidiaries by assigning head office staff as their highest and middle level managers. Outlets for these new products were found among large-scale food dealers and wholesale flour merchants. Towards the end of the 1960s, the activities of the company, including those of its subsidiaries, were reorganised into three product groups: flour milling, feedstuffs, food and sales. This system had been elaborated by 1970, when the head office was equipped with a general staff, controlling, and sales functions, and the operating units were grouped into four product divisions. The subsidiaries which undertook sales activities came under the control of the divisions, and the sales and production of flour which was operated by *Nisshin Flour*

Milling, was also made to constitute a division. Furthermore, geographic groups were formed: 23 factories and 19 sales offices, including those of the subsidiaries, were combined into six regional groups, which were controlled by the members of the board. These reforms paved the way for the development of food branches in the 1970s, though the main product lines still consisted of flour and feedstuff.

The organisational structure of *Ajinomoto*[6] was simple throughout the early post-war period, consisting of trading departments in charge of purchasing and sales, and three factories. This system was reorganised into a functionally departmentalised form in the early 1950s when the Sales Department was set up and the Control Department assumed the management of the factories. Local trading offices were then set up to organise special agents. In the early 1960s divisionalisation took place.

Beginning as an entrepreneurial activity in condiments by S. Suzuki, the company diversified into vegetable oil, starch and other products, but increasing demand for seasonings at home and abroad pushed the company into specialisation in glutamic acid soda. The firm adopted new technologies such as zymosthenic and synthetic processes, and invested heavily in the condiment branch.[7] As the background to the introduction of mass production methods, markets for condiments were developing from large cities to local areas, as well as from home use to business use. The company endeavoured to sell to the Farmers' Purchasing Society, and to set up its own sales companies in addition to the existing wholesale merchants. Furthermore the company began to sell directly to urban supermarkets, while the sales force of the sales subsidiaries canvassed small-scale retailers. These rapidly expanding activities were coordinated by a new organisation. In 1952 operative departments with special staff were formed, as was a management advisory committee consisting of the departmental managers. In the late 1950s new management techniques such as controllership or long-range planning were introduced, and finally between 1958 and 1960, the authority of managing directors and of departmental managers over routine operations was clarified. Almost simultaneously, the chairman of the company, who was also its founder, took over the representative power of the company and became the member of the management committee. These suggest that managerial procedures were becoming more formal and that middle management was beginning to develop in an entrepreneurial firm.

A gradual move to a divisional structure started in 1962 with the introduction of a new accounting system to branch offices, local sales offices and factories. These operating units were made profit centres and charged internal interest. However, this reform was not accompanied by the delegation of authority until the Vegetable Oil Division, which equipped with planning, production and sales functions, was established. Then the Food Department and the Overseas Division were formed by the mid-1960s. Under the new divisional structure, international activities and diversification were pushed forward. For the latter, *Ajinomoto* planned several times to hold down the proportion ratio of condiments, and succeeded in this by the mid-1970s. Semi-perishable goods such as vegetable oil and mayonnaise were added to their product lines. These products required the reduction of a long distribution channel. In place of the middlemen, the firm developed its own trading offices, and set out to promote sales, advertising, market research, and the education of the sales force as parts of a campaign to stimulate marketing. In the course of diversification, joint projects with foreign food companies such as *Corn Product Refining* or *Kellogg* brought about not only the acquisition by *Ajinomoto* of production technology necessary for diversification, but also of marketing skills. For international activities, the company was one of the forerunners among Japanese firms in switching from export to oversea production. In this strategy, the condiment branch still maintained a dominant position. Though no large-scale organisational change took place after the mid-1960s, *Ajinomoto* discarded the influence of the founder's family after 1974, and the members of the management committee were separated from routine operations and made to specialise in strategic decision making.

For milk products companies, the market was not only small but also fluctuated for seasonal or climatic reasons in the early phases of their development. After 1960, a steadily growing market for fresh milk appeared and the share of fresh milk in the total sales of milk products companies rose rapidly. Three companies increased their market share of total fresh milk production, which amounted to 37 per cent in 1955 and 63 per cent in 1965. They also maintained more than 70 per cent of markets of other sorts of milk products. Their ratios of concentration in fresh milk, however, fell down after 1970 due to the rise of new distribution channels, such as supermarket stores, as well as to the growth of local milk producers who were able to make use of these new channels.

Meiji Milk Products[8] went a step ahead of other companies in preparing to develop fresh milk markets. By 1950 the number of its factories had increased to 44, most of which they had bought in and around large cities such as Tokyo, Osaka, and Nagoya. Acquisition continued in the early 1950s, owing to which the centrifugal tendencies of the production units and the different managerial practices remained in spite of the prior formation of the functional structure. To tighten up the top and the middle management an organisational reform, consisting of the formation of a management committee and of office regulations, was carried out. The company set up eight regional offices to combine its factories with wider market, and formed a functional structure with line and staff in 1960. However, these managers were not sufficient given the firm's rapid expansion. Further affiliation was made of local milk companies, and existing food wholesalers were converted into sales subsidiaries.

A product divisional system was partly introduced in the mid-1960s, and was replaced by a mixture of a functional and a geographical system in the early 1970s. Although this company continued to spend its financial resources mainly on its fresh milk interests until the mid-1970s, they were unable to maintain their market share.[9] *Meiji Milk* diversified into food processing, through subsidiaries at first, but eventually within the company itself. To deal with these growing activities, the food processing and ice-cream branches were divisionalised in 1965 and 1966 respectively. However, these measures did not last long. Towards the end of the 1960s, factories were separated from these product divisions and put under the direct control of the top management, while the sales and marketing functions based on geographical areas were reinforced. Existing local offices were grouped into several general sales offices, and were made units of profit responsibility. There are two conceivable reasons behind the change from a product to a geographical system. One was *Meiji*'s efficiency in consolidating its sales activities and distribution channels to meet the emerging large-scale general food retailers. Milk products were formerly distributed through specialised retailers such as pharmacies or milkmen, who dealt with one or two product lines. These were quickly overtaken by the new types of food stores which sold numerous kinds of milk products. The other reason was the changing weight given to sales over production. The number of the local offices amounted to 32, while some of the production units were closed down. Sales activities were actually operated through local sales subsidiaries, whose numbers had increased to 24 by 1965. Sales functions were separated from production function, and the former took the initiative in the company's growth. Product divisions were combined into one production department, through which the production of diversified lines was controlled.

In contrast to *Meiji Milk Products*, *Snow Brand Milk Products*[10] was slow to enter the fresh milk market, due to the remoteness of its main production units from large cities. However, they had maintained a strong network of fresh milk collection, and also had high market shares in milk products. In the course of embarking on activities in new regions and product diversification into semi-perishable milk products, the organisational structure of the company moved from a functional to a divisional form, then swayed between divisions by geography and by product.

The company had once decided to set up sales subsidiaries in order to capture markets, but changed its strategy later and instead came to depend on special agents. Among them were general food wholesalers and specialised wholesalers in milk products. However, as their product lines extended, particularly to various perishable and semi-perishable goods, their outlets also diverged. For traditional products such as canned milk or butter, a sales promotion department was set up to supervise and educate their agents and retail stores, who were also assisted in the introduction of up-to-date equipments like refrigerators. For fresh milk, sales companies were set up in conjunction with local farmers' societies, which sold directly to milk stores to be widely distributed among consumers. These activities were operated through *Snow Brand*'s branch and local trading offices, whose numbers amounted to 43 by the mid-1960s. The early organisational problems of *Snow Brand* were not only in the controlling of its many production units which numbered more than 400, but also in the coordination of the interests of its shareholders consisting of farmers. Having originated from the farmers' co-operative union, the company's policies were heavily influenced by this union. In 1952 top management was established by forming a functionally departmentalised structure with line and staff, and the controller system and long-range planning was also adopted. The multidivisional structure by geography was gradually introduced over 1959 and 1960 based on the strategy of geographical expansion. Originating in Hokkaido, *Snow Brand* started to build factories for fresh milk to supply local cities throughout Japan. This programme had succeeded by the mid-1960s, and this was accompanied by extraordinary growth in its sales after 1955. In addition to its original head office, a Tokyo Head Office was set up, and each of the two head offices had the production, sales, planning and controlling functions, as well as a management committee which were required to report to one another. Below these twin head offices were placed product sub-divisions, which were limited to the planning and controlling functions. However, in 1963 the company's structure moved into the multidivisional form by products. In the early 1960s, differences in production, sales and management methods between milk products and fresh milk gradually became apparent. Fresh milk interests expanded rapidly, and this in turn required special distribution channels as well as preservation and transportation skills. The number of distributing agents increased. For milk products the situation was different in that the liberalisation of trade was approaching.

The management structure was reorganised in 1969, largely due to changes in retailing methods. Formerly, *Snow Brand*'s products had been sold by various specialised retailers: powdered milk by pharmacies, fresh milk by milk distributors and milkmen, canned milk and butter by general food stores. The shares of these retailers came to be increasingly substituted by supermarkets. In addition, the growth of the fresh milk market began to slow down. Entries into supermarkets and other 'help-yourself stores' required the unification of distribution channels as well as an increase in general sales powers and different sorts of services. Geographical divisions took the place of product divisions and the former were made profit centres. The number of such profit centres increased from two to eight, and this system was expected to contribute to training the top management of the next generation. In the central office, 18 departments were set up to assume the staff function of each product or the operating function. The members of the top management were separated from posts of departmental responsibilities. The purpose behind this reorganisation was explained as follows. Planning ability became highly necessary to meet the entries of foreign companies or of new companies in the milk products market. In addition, the nature of production and marketing of each particular product became indistinct due to the emergence of new methods of processing and storage and of new distribution channels (such as the supermarkets). Furthermore the scale of new projects became larger and the existing small production units were reorganised into new factories with mass production equipment. However, all of these problems were not necessarily best solved by this new organisation. On the level of sub-units below divisions, a dual system of regional and product sub-divisions remained. Fresh milk and ice-cream were produced by the factories of all the regional divisions and sold through the trading offices of these divisions, but milk products were produced by one of the branch offices and sold by other branches. A solution was found in strengthening the regional divisions and consolidate the staff departments of the general office. It was also necessary to strengthen the general management functions to coordinate them all.

After the oil crisis, the firm endeavoured to diversify into food processing. Dairy farming began to lose its footing and the raw milk supplies decreased. For this policy, one of the subsidiaries was used. Existing milk distributing stores were also converted into 'convenience stores', which handled various sorts of foods. In contrast to this diversification policy, the divisional structure was abolished, and the functional structure introduced in 1980.

Another dairy products company, *Morinaga Milk Industry*[11] was separated from *Morinaga Food Industries* in 1949. The latter held more than one-third of *Morinaga Milk*'s shares, and though this decreased to 7 per cent in the early 1970s, interlocking directorships became still prominent in later years. This limited the diversification of *Morinaga Milk Industry* in its early phases of post-war development. Unlike other milk products companies, the functional structure was its basic organisation, though its priority changed from production to sales.

Until the early 1970s, this company continued to specialise in fresh and powdered milk. A strong sales organisation for powdered milk had been established, particularly among pharmacies in the pre-war era. Special agents were the middlemen between *Morinaga* and these retailers. However, the firm came to adopt a rebate system, called the MGL system, in order to directly control these retail stores, and this enabled the company to keep track of the flow of their products. Financial resources were concentrated on the fresh milk branch prior to the mid-1960s, and its market share overtook that of *Meiji* by 1965.[12] For geographical expansion, contracts were made with local firms for the supply of fresh milk instead of increasing the company's own factories. Local demand was filled by these affiliated companies. *Morinaga Milk Industry*'s own production capacities were gradually intensified. The number of local sales offices was also small because much of the company's sales activities were carried out by the trading company inside the *Morinaga* group.

In the mid-1960s, president Ono and his staff decided upon a policy of further extension of the fresh milk interests. They were convinced that this was the best way to meet the liberalisation of trade in milk products, since there would be no competition from foreign companies in the fresh milk market. Financial resources were again concentrated on the enlargement of milk plants,[13] and the company's market share in fresh milk caught up with that of *Meiji*. To capture control over the outlets of the fresh milk, the company took over the employees of its sales subsidiary and became a fully multifunctional firm. However, financial performance in the late 1970s was poor when compared with the other two companies described previously, partly because of the 'arsenic milk' case and partly because of the low profitability of the fresh milk branch. Diversification was belated and its sales was overtaken by that of *Meiji*. Towards the end of the 1970s, *Morinaga*'s organisational structure came to resemble those of other milk companies which had strengthened their sales functions. For diversified products, the company set up ice-cream and milk foods departments, and they in turn were controlled by the sales head-quarters.

Unlike British brewing companies, all of Japan's large-scale brewing concerns were administered by a centralised functional structure. Three companies accounted for 95 per cent of the total amount of beer brewed in Japan in 1970, a quantity equal to approximately half of that brewed by all the British breweries, or one-third of that brewed by German breweries. During the three decades after 1950, the amount of production increased 30 times, reaching 4.5 million kilolitres per year by 1980 and making beer the most popular alcoholic beverage in Japan.

There were no mergers during the three post-war decades. On the contrary, there was a dissolution of *Dai Nippon Brewery*, which in the pre-war years, had grown through mergers. In spite of the rapid development of the brewing industry, there were few new entries throughout the post-war period. Moreover, the minimum economic production unit scale was only some 30 to 40 thousand kilolitres in the early 1970s, and in this respect, barriers to new entries were low. However, new entrants either withdrew, or encountered difficulties before making progress. This was partly due to the distribution system which consisted of sole sales agents, and partly to the licencing requirements for dealing in beer. Under the pretext of ensuring the collection of alcoholic tax, the number of dealers was limited so as to avoid over-competition among them. In spite of the rapid expansion of the market, this system certainly put new companies in a disadvantageous position, as they could not develop new marketing channels of their own, while existing channels were affiliated to the established breweries. Thus tremendous efforts were required to break into the market. For instance, *Takara Brewery*, which was not one of the largest 100 firms, had to set up its own sales subsidiary when it entered the beer market. The oligopolistic structure of this industry was related to the nature of the product, beer having been newly transplanted in the Japanese market. Brewing companies did not have to pay attention to the divergent tastes of consumers, since beer was not rooted deeply in Japanese daily life. Rather, they supplied unified, high quality, and mass-produced goods, brewing only lager-type beers with little product differentiation. This was in contrast not only to the European brewing companies, which showed a high degree of product differentiation, being based on local differentiation in tastes, but also to other branches of the brewing industry in Japan, such as 'sake' or soy sauce where small companies still produced various lines of products. The management structure of Japanese brewing companies was influenced by such industrial organisation.

In 1950, *Kirin Brewery* held 29 per cent of the Japanese beer market, while *Nihon* (later *Sapporo*) *Breweries* and *Asahi Breweries* 37 and 34 per cent, respectively. By 1970, the share of *Kirin* amounted to nearly 60 per cent, while those of *Sapporo* to 21 per cent and of *Asahi* to 13 per cent. In 1950 *Kirin*'s production units were located throughout Japan. Those of the other two companies were concentrated in either the eastern or western half of the country. Such positioning was favourable to *Kirin* when urban markets began to expand rapidly.

Sapporo Breweries[14] developed a highly centralised organisational structure. *Dai Nippon Brewery* was divided into *Nihon* (later *Sapporo*) *Breweries* and *Asahi Breweries* in 1949, and *Nihon Breweries* inherited its production units located in the eastern part of the country. Their sales agents were also situated in the eastern half of Japan, and these factors became barriers to the distribution of their products to the other half of the country. *Nihon Breweries* put considerable effort into penetrating into the western part of Japan until the mid-1960s, where they set up branch offices and organised sole sales agents for them. As the two descendants of *Dai Nippon Breweries* began to develop beyond their own territories, they became aware of inefficiencies in their activities in the new areas and of their weak competitive power against *Kirin*. This led to the discussions of a merger between *Sapporo* and *Asahi*, though it was never carried out. The market share of *Nihon Breweries* declined in the 1950s, and this pushed the company to product differentiation. The decline of the market share seemed to have been caused by small investment, but the former was not the effect but was in fact, the cause of the latter. The largest problems for this company until the mid-1960s were how to sell their products, and how to closely coordinate the production and sales of perishable goods which required high transportation cost. Both production and sales were centrally carried out by the head office. At the outset the organisational structure immediately below the top management was composed of sales, raw materials and individual factories. A production department was eventually set up, and one of the managing directors became the departmental manager. In the late 1950s, managing directors were set free from operational responsibilities, and the hierarchy from the top management to departmental managers and to the operating executives was finally established. Branch offices had their own factories and 'stock points' (warehouses), while the final adjustment between production and sales, and between regions was made by the sales unit of the central office.

The strategy and structure of *Nihon Breweries* became highly market-oriented in the mid-1960s. A minor product differentiation within lager beers was attempted. A merger with *Asahi Breweries* was also discussed, but it was pointed out that the coordination of the sole sales agents of both companies would be a primary difficulty, in that regional allocation had now caused their duplication.

After 1965, financial resources were spent on sales activities.[15] The head office was reorganised into sales and production headquarters, and the president undertook the duties of sales headquarters manager. These measures were taken to recover their declining market share. In the latter half of the 1970s, this structure was modified into a normal one. Investment in production increased, and that in sales decreased.[16] The headquarters were abolished, and each function was assumed by a managing director. Prior to these changes, the general staff section was set up for drafting long-range plans.

Asahi Breweries[17] took over the factories and branch offices of the former *Dai Nippon Brewery* located in western Japan. Their wholesalers were also largely located in the western half of Japan. The first measure they took was to reorganise these wholesalers as their sole sales agents, and to block *Kirin*'s entry into the western market. This method was soon imitated by *Kirin* and *Nihon*. *Asahi* diversified into soft drinks early in its development, and the share of soft drinks was 20 per cent of the company's total sales by the mid-1950s. The amount of sales, capital investment, and the ratio of sales expenses were higher than those of *Nihon* (*Sapporo*) until the mid-1960s.[18] Though simple, *Asahi*'s management structure was formalised from the outset. The head office was separated from operating units, and the managing directors who constituted the top management were separated from operating activities. At the middle management level, heads of departments were engaged in planning, and delivered the decisions of the president to operating managers or made reports on operating units to the management committee. Such an early experiment in the functional structure had its basis on the simple nature of the products and the production units. This organisation controlled the activities of *Asahi*'s five factories and ten branch offices.

In the meantime, a decrease in *Asahi*'s share of the beer market continued, and the top management was shaken up several times. However, no effective policy was taken until 1980. Minor differentiations in lager and high expenditures in marketing were not necessarily successful. Diversification into soft drinks, however, improved the company's position and in the late 1960s nearly 40 per cent of the company's profit came from this branch. They also invested in distilling in the 1970s. In spite of such diversification, the management structure did not change basically. The separation and unification of the responsibilities of the managing director and those of the departmental manager were repeated over and over after the mid-1960s.

The miraculous development of *Kirin Brewery*[19] is often explained as resulting from the favoured location of its production units and branch offices. However, it may well be added that the company also paid serious attention to the quality of its products, particularly in the standardised quality of its beer and the careful selection of raw materials. Sales expenses were small, and the number of the company's sole sales agents did not increase. Though *Kirin*'s market share was the smallest amongst the three breweries, the sellers' market continued in the early post-war period. Instead of distributing its products throughout the country, *Kirin* laid much emphasis on the urban markets. Products were distributed through special agents, 20 per cent of whom were affiliated with this company. In building up a stronger organisation of wholesalers, *Kirin* gave priority to those who had been their agents in the pre-war era, but had to add others who had experience in dealing with alcohol. The number of their wholesalers had become 646 by 1950. Then reorganisation in distribution methods was started in the early 1960s. Wholesalers and retailers began to discount prices, the former paying the latter a rebate during the recession of 1960. This was partly a result of the excessive number of wholesalers, who were exclusively responsible not only for sales, but for transportation and the collection of bills. The company adopted a new method of distribution, in which orders were made by each retailer, though they were intermediated by the wholesalers, and the products were directly transported from factories to these retailers. This gave *Kirin* a direct hold on its final distributors. The company expanded its factories and equipment more vigorously than other brewing companies during the 1960s. This was, however, necessitated by the increasing demand for the *Kirin* brand. In the 1960s, the firm was setting up new factories every other year. Fixed assets increased by 17 to 68 per cent every year.[20] Though *Kirin* had long-range plans in the beginning of the 1960s, the sites of their new factories were not carefully chosen, and factories were built instead in places where supply was unable to fill demand. From their inception, the rate of these factories' operations reached 100 per cent, and, in turn, they also required a huge capital investment. However, the increase of Kirin's market share was not so rapid when compared with the amount invested. The marginal construction cost per unit of output was high, reaching three times the costs of the other two companies. *Kirin* had to increase the number of its factories regardless of high equipment costs. By the mid-1960s the number of its operating units had increased to 19 – eight factories and 11 branch offices. And these activities were administered by a mixture of the functional and the line structure, in which the operating units reported directly to the president.

Kirin's increasing market share boosted the operating expenses of the other two companies. Policies to hold down its own market share were taken by *Kirin* towards the late 1970s. The period of the sellers' market was over, and transportation costs went up, particularly in urban areas. Modern marketing and distribution methods were adopted: the sales headquarters began training the sales force, who had been accustomed to conservative alcohol retailers, and adopted the minimum unit of orders to reduce transportation time. Management resources were transferred to distilling and soft-drink production.[21] Some of *Kirin*'s new products were sold through their beer distribution channels, but new channels had to be developed for others. Each branch office set up new units in charge of juice or milk. The management structure of this company was a typically functional one since the mid-1960s.

In spite of the geographical separation of the market and production units, and despite their enormous size, Japanese brewing companies coordinated and controlled the flow of goods through a centralised functional structure. This differed from the case of British breweries, in which geographical divisions were popular forms of management structure. There were reasons for the Japanese breweries' choice. Firstly, despite its relatively small economic scale and inherent high transportation costs, the central coordination of the flow of goods, particularly among regional demands, was not so difficult in the brewing industry. It was even more efficient to coordinate regional fluctuations of demand, which were often under the influence of weather and other kinds of regional factors, than to establish geographical divisions. Secondly, there were no regional differentiations in taste. These companies developed by internal growth and had no elements which prevented the homogeneity of products.

Most of the concerns in food industries developed downward into distribution of their products either through their own branch offices, sales subsidiaries, or affiliated special agents. Such strategies for gaining control over outlets often ran against the anti-monopoly law. However, the above descriptions should be enough to understand the outline of the direction of their development as well as the differences observed between them. The activities of these companies were administered through various forms of organisational structures, particularly by geographical divisions or functional departments, and moved among the several types of basic forms. Except in one case in which the transition from the functional to the divisional structure was accompanied by management decentralisation, most of them intensified central control of local units and of the flow of goods, especially in their earlier reforms.

The major problems these firms had to solve by structural reforms were the parallel changes in the methods of supplying raw materials, product diversification, the appearance of perishable and semi-perishable goods which required speedy distribution, and the emergence of new outlets. First the appearance of perishable and semi-perishable goods prompted the introduction of the multidivisional structure by geography which was most suitable to maintaining the value of products through the efficient scheduling of flows in processing and distribution. Next came product diversification, which required not only different processing skills but also different distribution channels. At the same time, due to the increasing import of raw materials, regional divisions with their own local production units lost their advantages of access to raw materials. The multidivisional structure by product was introduced mostly in the mid-1960s. Then geographic divisions gradually developed with the emergence of the new market channels, though which they were able to deal with various sorts of food products. However, the choice between product and geographic divisions was not a clear-cut one, and these two systems still co-existed until the late 1970s. New geographic divisions differed from those of the early post-war period in that the latter were based on local production units, while the present ones oriented marketing in a particular area.

8.3 OIL COMPANIES

There were eight oil concerns listed in the largest 100 firms in 1970. Two of them were single function firms specialising in oil-refining, four had completely integrated refining and distribution, one had formed a complicated network of refining and distribution with a world major oil company and one of the major's subsidiaries, and in the case of one other, the amount of oil it sold exceeded that refined by its own refineries. This gap between the amount of oil refined and that sold, however, was more or less observed in all the oil companies, because there were 13 oil sales companies to more than 30 oil refining companies. Seven of these eight concerns integrated refining and sales. The institutional arrangements of Japanese oil companies, which coordinated the basic functions of business enterprise and allocated resources, were set forth by the world majors and the Japanese government. Their industrial organisation and, to a certain extent, managerial hierarchies were structured by these two external factors.

Foreign oil companies, including the world majors, played a unique role in the Japanese oil industry. Unlike in Germany, the world majors did not set up 100 per cent owned subsidiaries in Japanese oil industry: *Esso*, *Shell*, and *Mobil Oil* were oil sales companies in Japan. They supplied crude oil to Japanese oil refining companies, provided them with capital by becoming their majority or minority shareholders, and sometimes distributed products for Japanese oil companies. It was the Japanese side that took the initiative in introducing foreign capital. In 1950 Japanese oil companies were technologically far behind foreign oil companies. Domestic oil companies were short of capital for modernising their refineries, and were also without governmental support like other energy industries such as coal or electricity were receiving. In addition it was necessary for oil companies to secure constant supplies of crude oil, and these were controlled completely by the world major oil companies.

The government laid restrictions on the activities of foreign oil companies. After the liberalisation of crude oil import in the early 1960s, the government further intervened in the coordination of production by allocating refining capacity to each company. This measure, which was taken to avoid over-production and excess in equipment, resulted in severe competition among the oil companies for the allocation of new capacities. As the allocation was determined on the basis of each company's market share, investment was made as soon as the equipment plans were approved, and competition among companies was transformed into one for the market share.

The constitution of the sorts of oil which were refined by the Japanese oil companies showed similarities among all the firms, but the problems which arose from their distribution differed from product to product. Lubricants, heavy oil, and naphtha were for industrial use, and they are classified as 'fabricated basic materials'. Gasoline and most light oils are used by final consumers. In the early post-war era, the ratio of lubricant was generally high. In the late 1950s and 1970s, the ratio of heavy oil rose to 35 or 40 per cent of their total sales. Given that its price was relatively low in comparison with other countries, the volume represented by heavy oil was high. As the oil companies sold heavy oil and naphtha to large-scale companies in electricity, chemicals and steel in large lots, the organisation of distribution was relatively simple. Oil companies or their parent firms sold directly to the industrial companies. On the other hand, the ratio of gasoline in their total sales began to rise starting from the 1960s, finally rising to some 40 per cent in the late 1960s, but dropping back down to around 30 per cent by 1980. Light oil which was also for final consumer use gradually rose up from 15 to 18 per cent of total sales between 1960 and 1980. In terms of sales amount, more than half of oil products were distributed to the final consumers' market. The oil companies competed for the formation of distribution channels. The pattern of supply was more or less similar to all the oil firms. These companies made use of special agents, each having its own garages locally. Thus, there were relatively many wholesalers engaged in retailing in oil distribution. Most of these agents were affiliated with a particular oil company by sole-sales contracts involving rebates and other financial help. In some cases, local garage owners were supplied with oil by these sole-sales agents. In both cases, the oil companies controlled the flow of goods by affiliating the oil distributors. Many of these special agents appeared in the 1960s, when the demand for oil increased rapidly. Recently, mass-distributors such as the Agricultural Cooperative Association or trading companies began to form their own distribution channels, becoming independent of particular oil companies.

Japanese oil companies adapted themselves to the ever-increasing demand for oil, which had surpassed that for coal by the early 1960s, growing more than one hundred-fold during the two decades since 1950. In doing so, they relied much on the institutional arrangements described above, as well as on their own internal management structures. However, their internal organisations were relatively simple, partly because they were not diversified, for instance, into petrochemicals unlike their European counterparts.

The activities of *Nippon Oil*[22] have been administered by a mixture of a holding-company and functional structure. Though it had its own refineries, most of its products came from subsidiaries, while the company itself was mainly engaged in sales activities. Recently the company is often classified into trading industry.

Nippon Oil had six oil refineries in 1950. To secure its supplies of crude oil, the firm made a contract for commission refining with *Caltex*. This developed into a joint venture with *Caltex*, resulting in the formation of *Nippon Oil Refining*. *Caltex* supplied capital and crude oil, while *Nippon Oil* offered two of its refineries. All of the new company's products were distributed by *Nippon Oil*. Although the typical functional structure had been formed by 1950, *Nippon Oil* had to solve two, often contrary, problems. One was to maintain its initiative over *Caltex* in management. *Nippon Oil* avoided the introduction of *Caltex*'s financial resources into its own enterprise, but set up a separate company jointly with *Caltex*. A holding-company style was the result of such motives. However, the company had to efficiently coordinate the flow from the supply of crude oil through refining to distribution, which was becoming more and more important in order to meet a rapidly expanding demand for oil. A stronger top management was needed, and the management committee, the concept of which was imported from the United States, was formed. Managing directors were excluded from departmental management.

With the formation of *Nippon Oil Refining*, *Nippon Oil* became a holding company with the sales function of the former. *Nippon Oil*'s top management consisted of a senior managing director, three managing directors, and the head office staff. They became general managers being engaged in planning, budget control, research, and organisation. Although *Nippon Oil* continued to have its own refinery, its main development in production was observed among its subsidiaries. Thus the company developed as a holding and sales company, with only 18 per cent of its oil products being produced by its own refineries in 1960.

It was its strong distribution channel that supported *Nippon Oil* in maintaining its leading position among the Japanese oil companies. Eight of its business offices and three refineries were controlled through a functionally departmentalised structure. Long-range plans, which also applied to *Caltex* and were prepared by the general staff, were started in the late 1950s. In 1957 *Nippon Oil*, *Nippon Oil Refining*, *Koa Oil* and *Caltex* formed a joint committee to investigate supply and demand, and to make a plan for the group. *Caltex* supplied crude oil and financial resources. The declining market share of *Nippon Oil* was partly due to the Japanese government policy of giving priority to purely domestic oil companies. However, *Nippon Oil* did not attempt to self-supply crude oil, but continued to cooperate with *Caltex*.

Nippon Oil and *Caltex* took equal shares in setting up *Nippon Oil Refining*,[23] and each sent the same number of directors to that company. Below the board of *Nippon Oil Refining*, the executive committee in charge of drawing plans for equipment and capital was formed. Between 1951 and 1962, the company was administered through its own organisation consisting of general affairs, labour, operating, and accounting departments as well as two refineries. The four departments acted as the advisory staff to the executives who directly controlled the refineries. The company developed rapidly in the 1950s, accompanied by an increase in the number of operating units and employees. This brought about the necessity of examining the means of allocating managerial tasks and of operation. It became apparent that the scale of the head office was too large for a firm which specialised in refining. Thus *Nippon Oil Refining* intended to simplify its head office.

Meanwhile, the management also became aware of the necessity of promoting rationalisation of production and sales according to the consistent policies of *Nippon Oil Refining* and *Nippon Oil*. The similar management tasks of both companies were consolidated in

1962. The accounting department and four refineries were left in *Nippon Oil Refining*'s own organisation, while all of its other management tasks were moved to a joint organisation with *Nippon Oil*. In the following year, the general staff of both companies were consolidated into a single body.

Thus, the lines of authority were unified especially at the top and the middle management levels, although these two companies were legally separate for each other, each with its own assets and operating units. In this sense, the control of *Nippon Oil* over *Nippon Oil Refining* became tighter than in the case of the traditional holding company structure. This organisational reform was necessitated, on the part of *Nippon Oil Refining*, by the coming liberalisation of crude oil imports.

Showa Oil,[24] which was formed during the Second World War in line with the government industry control policy, went into a partnership with *Shell Oil* in the early post-war era. The pattern of co-operation with a world major oil company differed from that of *Nippon Oil*, though its chief motive was, as in the cases of other oil companies, in securing the supply of crude oil as well as obtaining financial resources. There was discussion of a merger with *Shell*, but *Shell* became the holder of a 50 per cent interest in *Showa Oil*. The company had eight production units in 1950, and products were distributed partly through its own sales organisation and partly by *Shell Oil*. Financial resources were spent in the expansion of refineries at the beginning, then towards the early 1960s, in that of sales organisation.[25] Emphasis was gradually switched from the supply of heavy oils to that of gasoline. These activities were coordinated by the functional structure, though refineries were directly responsible to the top management. Organisational problems in dealing with the flow from crude oil to oil products became more complicated when the firm separated one of its refineries as *Showa Yokkaichi Oil*. The latter became a refining subsidiary, which refined for *Showa Oil* and *Shell* by commission. Both *Showa Oil* and *Showa Yokkaichi Oil* were supplied with crude oil by *Royal Dutch*. *Shell* undertook approximately two-thirds of *Showa Yokkaichi Oil*'s oil products, and a quarter of those of *Showa Oil*. In order to avoid overlapping of their activities in production and sales, the merger of *Showa Oil* and *Shell* was again discussed, but this resulted in failure.

After 1965 *Showa Oil* further developed its sales activities. As the number of garages was being limited by the *Ministry of Trade and Industry* since 1965, the company relocated them to main roads where demand was rising remarkably, and standardised them to reduce construction costs. Furthermore, the meter-sales system was introduced to increase control over individual garages. The company's own refining capacity did not increase since 1965, and the major part of its new investments were made in sales, particularly in the formation of distribution channels.[26] An organisational reform was carried out in 1965, and the functionally departmentalised structure was formed. The operating units, which had previously been directly responsible to the top, now came under the control of the departmental managers. A line and staff organisation was also introduced, and the members of the board were made responsible for functional departments. Lines of authority were also unified by this measure. To deal with the products for *Shell*, *Showa Oil* formed the Direct Sales Department.

Toa Nenryo Kogyo[27] was set up as an oil refining firm in 1939. The managers of the former *Ogura Oil* undertook the management of the post-war *Toa Nenryo*. After the war, *Standard Vacuum* – a joint subsidiary of *Standard Oil of New Jersey* and *Socony Vacuum* – joined the management of *Toa Nenryo Kogyo*. Fifty-one per cent of its shares were transferred to *SVOC*, which in turn, secured supplies of crude oil, offered technological and managerial advice, and distributed products for *Toa Nenryo*. The modernisation of management was started by the initiatives of *SVOC* directors. The traditional accounting department was divided into a controller and a treasurer. Internal auditing was introduced and the traditional general affairs department was abolished. Production and technological departments were newly set up, and a budgetary system and the regulation of operational tasks were formed.

The latter half of the 1950s saw remarkable development in the oil industry. *Toa Nenryo* expanded its refining capacity, and integrated backward and forward, though it did not step into sales activities. The company equipped itself with its own tankers, and entered the petrochemical industry through a subsidiary, but the firm itself remained a single function firm which specialised in refining. Management practices which had been introduced from the United States were reconsidered after 1955. The main problem was that the excessive specification of the organisation, which prevented a flexible coordination among tasks, was unsuitable for the training of management. The secretarial, legal, inquiry and sales-staff departments were abolished, the general affairs department revived, and the planning department was set up. In short, the American way of job specification did not fit Japanese management practices.

The major holding company of *Toa Nenryo* was dissolved in the late 1960s as a direct result of the Anti-trust decrees, but also fundamentally due to the falling strategic importance of far-eastern crude oil. *Toa Nenryo* entered into a direct partnership with *Esso* and *Mobil*. The coordination of the stages from the crude oil supply to the distribution of the finished products did not change in spite of the reorganisation of parent companies. *Toa Nenryo* was able to concentrate its efforts on the thorough rationalisation of production. *Esso Standard*, the sales company, preferred automobile oil, which was the most profitable of petroleum products, and therefore *Esso* and *Mobil* supplied light crude oil. Such a combination brought *Toa Nenryo* the highest profitability of all the oil companies throughout the 1970s.

Mitsubishi Oil[28] was set up jointly by the pre-war *Mitsubishi* and *Associated Oil*, US. After the war, *Associated Oil* (later, *Tidewater Oil*) financed the reconstruction of *Mitsubishi Oil*, and later *Getty Oil* inherited this co-partnership. As soon as *Mitsubishi Oil* was registered as an oil sales company, it set up a trading department in the head office and trading offices in large cities. The firm delivered its products directly to large-scale consumers, and indirectly, through special agents, to small-lot markets. The number of *Mitsubishi*'s local agents reached 137 in 1955. *Mitsubishi Oil* had a wide market among the *Mitsubishi* group companies, particularly as an outlet of heavy oils, and it aimed for stable profitability rather than market shares. The expansion of the company's refining capacity was slow when compared with other oil companies. In 1950, the organisational structure of the company was composed of the functional departments and the operating units, each of which was directly responsible to the board. The modernisation of its organisation began in 1952. The internal control and the general staff were introduced in the mid-1950s. A gradual move to the functionally departmentalised structure was observed in the 1950s. Managing directors in charge of functions were appointed, who at the same time were responsible for the operating units.

However, in 1960 the production department was abolished, and factory managers were put under the direct control of a managing director. Meanwhile, the number of sales agents increased to 182, and that of garages to 1746, which equalled ten-fold growth during the decade following 1955. In contrast to its increasing number of branch offices, the number of *Mitsubishi Oil*'s refineries remained unchanged. In the late 1960s, it was planned to set up a joint oil company in the northern part of Japan, and it was expected that the sales channels of existing companies would be utilised. *Mitsubishi Oil* joined this project, and undertook the supplies of crude oil and distribution of the products for this joint subsidiary. By then the company had affiliated some influential agents who had a country-wide network of branch offices. Their offices were, together with those of the existing local wholesalers, grouped into nine geographical units, each of which was controlled by a branch office of *Mitsubishi Oil*. This again prompted the organisational reform at the higher level of management. Production and technology functions were separated from sales and transport functions, each of the former two being placed under the control of the members of the board. The production director was made responsible for production department and refineries. The managing directors left operating activities, when the departmental headquarters system was adopted in 1975. The new departmental headquarters were equipped with their own line and staff and were controlled by the managing directors. Such decentralisation, however, did not last long, and in 1977 departmental headquarters were replaced by ordinary functional departments.

Although classified as a native oil company, *Maruzen Oil*[29] was financially supported by *Union Oil* and several foreign banks throughout the period of its post-war reconstruction. In the pre-war era, the company had been engaged in the distribution of lubricant oil in the western part of the country. After the war, the company opened up full lines of oil products by building up its own refinery, though lubricant and heavy oil remained as its main products. Financial resources were concentrated on the expansion of production units and the introduction of new technologies. These measures were taken not merely to reconstruct the company but to meet the increasing demand for oil. The problem was in how to develop its sales organisation, because its dealers were concentrated in a few large cities in the western part of Japan and specialised in the lubricant oil trade. A branch office was set up in Tokyo, and this branch and the refineries were made directly responsible to the top management. An aggressive expansion policy followed. Markets in the central and eastern parts of Japan were embarked upon, aimed at increasing *Maruzen*'s market share and integrating upward and downward stages, such as crude oil transport or petrochemicals.

Furthermore, *Maruzen* branched out into the north-eastern and northern part of Japan in association with a local oil company. With these developments as a background, a functionally departmentalised structure was formed in 1958. However, the company had to strengthen its distribution channels because their control over local agents was weak. *Maruzen*'s local agents were in a financially weak position, and should have been supported by *Maruzen*. A series of organisational reforms took place in sales activities. Firstly, the firm increased the number of its local trading offices. Secondly in 1962, the Sales Department of the head office was separated to form a legally independent company that would bear the responsibility of sales activities. And finally, in the same year eight local sales subsidiaries were set up, and integrated the following year. This rapid expansion, which elevated the company to the position of the third largest company in the Japanese oil market, had bad results. Crude oil was expensive and its self-transportation, too. The weakness of *Maruzen*'s sales channels had not been improved. Production units were relatively small and separately located. These were all disadvantageous factors in an over-competitive market. In 1963, *Union Oil* again came to support *Maruzen* financially, and the top management of *Maruzen* was renewed. A reconstruction advisory committee was also sent from the Business Circle (*Zaikai*).

An organisational reform took place. To avoid one-man management, a 'council system' was adopted for decision making, and the function of auditors was strengthened. The planning section, in charge of long-range policies, was enlarged. Sales organisations had to be fortified and a merger with the company's sales subsidiary took place, making *Maruzen* full-functional. To integrate the flow of goods to the final distributors, *Maruzen Oil* adopted a 'meter-sales system', according to which the petroleum in each garage was owned by *Maruzen*. The next step was to introduce a system of profit responsibility into its local branches and petrochemical interest. This system was further extended to *Maruzen*'s refineries in 1966 for purposes of cost reduction. A fairly large amount of financial resources were spent in the sales branch. Between 1965 and 1973, two-fifths of fixed investment was appropriated towards sales activities, which strengthened the financial position of their sales agents as well as control over them.[30] The sales agents of *Maruzen Oil* were generally small in their scale, and *Maruzen* had to make the investment on their behalf.

Daikyo Oil[31] was a lubricant producer, and integrated backwards into oil refining in the post-war period. After the war, the firm was reconstructed as a Japanese owned company, and due to this, the company remained as a relatively small firm with poor distribution channels and few financial resources. The company's internal structure was quite simple. The head office had trading and technological departments, while its refinery and two branch offices reported directly to the top management. The authority of each position was not clear: plans were drafted by directors and the management advisory committee had not been formed yet. In 1959, a formal departmental structure was introduced, and the planning and the auditing systems were adopted. This structural change was necessitated by the rapid expansion of oil refining capacity in the late 1950s, which was caused by the continuous fall in the price of crude oil. The influence of the falling price of crude oil did not stop here, for it also brought about over-competition between the oil companies, and naturally led to the regulation of the output. For *Daikyo Oil*, consolidation of the sales departments of Japanese owned small companies was planned, but *Daikyo Oil* did not join the syndicate because *Daikyo*'s financial position was not so bad.

Unlike other oil companies, *Daikyo Oil* continued to depend on a single refinery, and the expansion of capacity was made without increasing the number of its refineries. On the other hand, the number of its branch offices and garages rapidly increased, and by the mid-1960s, the company had to build up a structure which enabled the promotion of sales activities. Coal wholesalers were used as *Daikyo*'s agents, the Trading Department was expanded, and the human resources of this department were supplied by the rationalisation of the refinery. Eventually, the amount of sales exceeded that of production, and this gap was filled by joining with some other refining companies. There were some problems in this inter-firm coordination. These refineries did not necessarily supply the light lines of oils which *Daikyo Oil* and its thousands of garages needed most, because their affiliated refineries were located in 'industrial complexes' and supplied heavier lines of oil. To fill this quality gap, *Daikyo*'s own refinery had to be made to specialise further into light oil. *Daikyo Oil* also tried to self-supply crude oil by investing in an oil mining company and by direct trade with Arab countries in the 1960s. The reason for this was that it was forced to supplement its insecure supply of crude oil because the company lacked a partner among the world majors. Vertical integration in such forms prompted the firm to build up a functionally departmentalised structure which was completed in 1970 in a form which comprised management, production, and sales departments and a general planning staff. The management department was in charge of the supply of crude oil. This structure also prepared for the construction of a new refinery, diversification, restraining pollution, and the expansion of high-grade lubricants. After the oil crisis, however, the number of levels in the hierarchy was reduced to make decisions and their execution swifter. The functional departments were abolished and the operating units were again made directly responsible to the top management.

Idemitsu Oil[32] originated as an oil retailer, integrated backwards into primary wholesales after the war, and further into refining and transport. Since the early 1950s the company had extensive oil retailing channels, through which American or Iranian oil was distributed. In the face of the Japanese government policy of promoting domestic refining, this company entered self-refining of oil. The activities of this company were quite peculiar in comparison with those of other oil companies. It has been a personally owned company even after it became the second largest oil company in Japan. Financially, *Idemitsu* depended on loan capital. In 1955 *Idemitsu* bought oil refining equipment as a first step toward advancing into refining. Almost all the financial resources necessary for this plan were supplied by banks. For sales the company avoided agents or wholesalers and preferred direct retailing. The thinking of *Idemitsu*'s founder was that crude oil be bought directly by *Idemitsu* at a low price, transported at low cost by *Idemitsu* tankers, stocked in *Idemitsu* storage tanks, delivered by *Idemitsu* lorries and sold directly to the consumer through *Idemitsu* branch offices. In short, he aimed at reducing transaction costs by integrating vertically. *Idemitsu* set up 23 branch offices and more than 50 sales units, all of which were engaged in direct sales. Of course the company also had to use other local retailers who had their own garages. It was not, however, the role of the branch offices to control these retailers, though their branch offices were occasionally asked for advice by local retailers. Owing to this unique strategy, *Idemitsu*'s sales had, by the mid-1960s, risen to a level close to that of *Nippon Oil*, the largest Japanese oil company. These growing activities were, however, coordinated and controlled by an informal structure. Managing directors were in charge of one function each, but any formal organisation was avoided. At the top management level, a management committee was not formed. In the 1970s, the company advanced into the purchase of crude oil, and integrated the whole process from the supply of raw materials to the sales of oils. Diversification into gas and other new fuels brought about the creation of additional sales departments. Management decentralisation was promoted: branch offices were made self-supporting units. Each was allocated internal capital, and was authorised to take charge of financing. To plan and monitor these activities, the general planning office was set up in the latter half of the 1970s.

As has been examined briefly, the internal structures of Japanese oil companies have been simple. Most of them began their post-war development with a line or incomplete functional structure. Some still remained as single function companies, and some, like *Idemitsu* or *Maruzen*, promoted management decentralisation, while others formed functionally departmentalised structures as their sales to the final consumers developed. Product diversification was strictly restrained. Those companies that once went beyond the single product category (according to the three-digit classification) did so either by increasing by-products such as paving materials or by entering petrochemicals. In both cases, the share of these new products remained slightly above five per cent of the total sales of each company. However, it was not so much their low diversity as the industrial organisation of the Japanese oil industry that kept the internal structure of oil companies relatively simple. First of all, the supply of crude oil was beyond the control of the Japanese oil companies. Secondly, the power of the world major oil companies were strong in the rapidly expanding markets. The main field of activities of Japanese oil companies has long been in refining process, in which they pursued the economy of scale. Later, particularly in the 1960s, they began to pay much attention to marketing, partly because success in marketing determined governmental grants of additional refining capacity, but mainly because new demand from the final consumers expanded rapidly by the growing number of cars taking the places of heavy lines of oils. Thirdly, in addition to these, refining by commission or joint refining put the coordination of activities beyond the control of individual firms.

The formation of a strong top management organisation was observed in the early post-war period, particularly in the case of those which had American partners. In *Nippon Oil*, *Toa Nenryo*, and *Mitsubishi*, the modern management apparatus such as controllers, budgetary systems, and the management committee were adopted, though these measures were too drastic to maintain their archetypical forms. Furthermore, functionally departmentalised structures had to be reformed into simpler ones, partly because of the special character of Japanese industrial organisation and partly because of divergence from Japanese practices. In Japanese-owned companies, by contrast, the development of formal organisations was observed towards the end of the 1960s in face of the bad performance of these companies.

8.4 AUTOMOBILE COMPANIES

There were 11 automobile companies among the largest 100 firms in 1970. Almost all of them were administered either through a functional or a simple line structure. By contrast, various forms of inter-firm coordination, including groupings, sub-contracting, and particularly sales subsidiaries developed around large-scale automobile firms. Naturally the range of product lines of individual companies was limited. More than half of these firms diversified into the production of trucks, motorcycles, and parts. Except for one, however, these companies were classified in a single business category by the three-digit industry classification. The total sales of these 11 companies were twice those of four British firms, or three-quarters those of eight German firms in 1970.

These companies manufactured trucks, buses, motor-tricycles, and motorcycles in 1950. *Toyota*, *Nissan*, *Isuzu*, and *Hino* started in trucks, *Nissan Shatai* (then *Shin-Nikkoku Kogyo*) in buses, *Toyo* and *Daihatsu* in motor-tricycles, *Nissan Diesel* (then *Minsei Industry*) in engines, and *Fuji*, *Suzuki* and *Honda* in motorcycles. The motor-tricycle companies embarked on the production of small trucks in anticipation of a decline in demand for motor-tricycles due to the emergence of small trucks. By 1960, however, 'light' trucks or 'light' automobiles had become their main lines, and after 1961 they had begun to produce passenger-cars. The motorcycle companies also became involved in automobile production after 1960. The truck manufacturers had been trying to enter passenger-car production from the beginning, though they had to remain in truck production due to technological limitations. There were two ways of solving the technological limitations. One was to enter a partnership with a foreign company, beginning with importing parts and knocking them down, and then gradually advancing into independent production of the necessary parts. *Hino* (*Renault*), *Isuzu* (*Rootes*), and partly *Nissan* (*Austin*) developed along these lines from 1952. The other way was to supply all the parts independently through the reorganisation and rationalisation of subsidiaries and subcontracting firms; this was the path chosen by *Toyota*.

During the 1960s reorganisation and grouping among these companies proceeded. This was partly because of governmental policy regarding the automobile companies which were to meet the competition of foreign automobile companies. They had to acquire international competitive power by growing large. The *Toyota Group* consisted of *Toyota*, *Toyoda Automatic Loom Works* which specialised in cars for industrial use, and *Nippon Denso* which supplied parts. *Daihatsu* and *Hino* joined the group, though their relationships with *Toyota* differed both from each other and from other members of the group. At that time *Daihatsu* was strong in light cars, while *Hino* was strong in buses. The *Nissan Group* consisted of *Nissan*, *Nissan Diesel Motor* which specialised in trucks and buses, and *Nissan Shatai* specialising in the construction of specialty cars. *Fuji Heavy Industries* took part in the production of light cars, and *Isuzu* also joined the *Nissan Group* but soon left it again. The companies whose names are given above were all among the largest 100 firms in 1970. There were, of course, other members included in these two groups, but they were outside the largest 100 firms. There were attempts for the formation of other groups, but nothing came of them. Thus, except for the three independents, most automobile companies became affiliated with either *Toyota* or *Nissan* by 1970.

In addition to coordination of product lines among group members, the coordination of production and sales is also observed at the inter-firm levels of organisation. Some companies set up their own sales companies, specialising themselves in manufacturing. Others integrated production and sales functions within single firms. For such durable consumer goods as automobiles, not only mere distribution but aftercare and sales finance were necessary, and these were implemented by hundreds of dealers. The distribution channels of the domestic market can roughly be divided into three types; the first, in which the automobile companies set up 'general sales' companies through which their products were distributed to the local dealers; the second, in which the automobile companies directly supplied their products to their local dealers; the third, in which the automobile companies sold directly to the final consumers through their local trading offices. The first two have widely been observed throughout the three decades under examination. In both cases, local dealers were affiliated with the automobile companies – or their sales companies – through shareholding, interlocking directorships, and exclusive transactions. Each dealer, in turn, had its outlets throughout the prefecture allocated to it, where it sold one or several lines of products of a particular automobile company. Whether or not these functions were controlled through the direct lines of the manufacturing companies, constituted an important organisational problem for the Japanese automobile companies.

Until 1950, when its sales department and spinning and electrical appliance branches were separated, *Toyota Motor*[33] was a multi-function and multi-product firm. Its sales organisation was built up by S. Kamiya after the examples of *G. M.* Japan. The separation of the sales from production function as a legally independent firm has often been referred to in terms of the condition of financial support from banks. In the early post-war period its production increase rapidly. Towards the end of the 1940s the increased production under the slump required aggressive sales activities, resulting in an inability to collect bills, and further leading to a company-wide financial crisis. They recognised the necessity of separating production finance from sales finance as a measure for securing both supplies of raw materials and the payment for workers. Through this measure *Toyota Motor* was not only freed from the burden of sales finance, but from all sales activities. *Toyota Motor Sales* made sales plans, according to which orders were placed with *Toyota Motor*. The sales company bought all the products of its manufacturing partner. *Toyota Motor*'s bills were accepted by *Toyota Motor Sales*, and were guaranteed for rediscount by the Central Bank. The promissory notes accompanied by monthly payments were also guaranteed for loans from city banks. *Toyota Motor Sales* was not only a distributor, but a sales and marketing company engaging in market research, product planning, and services for *Toyota Motor*. Thus *Toyota Motor* was able to concentrate all its financial resources on production, including the purchasing of foreign machinery, the modernisation of assets, and the development of new equipment. When other automobile companies were introducing foreign technologies, *Toyota* chose to develop its own. It also introduced various sorts of management techniques such as quality control, modern production methods, the rationalisation of transportation, etc. These were further developed by the company into unique production management methods. Towards the end of the 1950s, a mass production system was established. A large-scale factory was newly built. The company had to re-examine the quality control system of its parts suppliers, which *Toyota* had adopted in 1953, in order to secure the supply of good quality parts. Various production techniques first introduced into *Toyota Motor* spread to its suppliers, which came to be integrated to *Toyota*'s production system by the mid-1960s. The suppliers were concentrated on the same locality as *Toyota*'s factories, which contributed to the economy of production scale and the reduction of transportation costs.

This mass production system was accompanied by mass marketing carried out by the sales company. *Toyota Motor Sales* inherited *Toyota Motor*'s dealers. When government control of automobile distribution was removed after the war, *Toyota* affiliated the best of these dealers and placed them in each locality. Instead of intervening in the management of dealers, *Toyota* made use of local capital and merchants. Between 1953 and 1961, *Toyota Motor Sales* began to form a fourth distribution channel, according to classes of car. In some regions, more than two of *Toyota Motor Sales*' dealers appeared. The functional structure was reformed into a simple line form, in which large production units were removed from under the control of the production department and made directly responsible to the top management. Along with this reform, top management organisation was gradually built up. A planning committee was formed to accommodate proposals from all levels of the hierarchy, and a management committee was formed for important decision making. A Supreme Council was formed jointly with *Toyota Motor Sales*.

In coordinating the flow of supplies and products, *Toyota* depended heavily on organisations formed outside the firm. About 250 subcontracting firms supplied parts accounting for more than 70 per cent of the total production costs of *Toyota*. *Toyota* also made use of 250 sole-sales dealers in its sales activities. This system might be classified as a vertically semi-integrated structure, though the nature of control differed between the upstream and downstream stages. In the upstream, the adoption of the 'super-market production system' by *Toyota Motor* abolished its own warehouses, and forced suppliers to turn their production processes from lot-production to assembly lines. This, however, did not necessarily mean that the suppliers' production processes were completely integrated to *Toyota*'s, nor that the suppliers were completely controlled by *Toyota Motor*. The reduction of production costs or the introduction of assembly lines on the part of suppliers made them specialise in some particular parts on a mass production basis, and their production capacity eventually exceeded *Toyota*'s demands. The higher group of suppliers began to provide other automobile companies or other industries, while those which could not meet *Toyota*'s requirements had to become secondary subcontracting firms. Thus there was always a mobility in which some became independent of, while others became more dependent on, *Toyota Motor*. In the downward stages, on the contrary, the local dealers were tightly organised by the sales departments of *Toyota Motor Sales*, leaving them little mobility. There was a large information gap between the dealers and the sales company, and the former had to depend heavily upon information supplied by the latter.

By the mid-1960s the labour productivity of *Toyota Motor* had caught up with that of European companies. However, to meet the giant US companies, at that time 20 times larger than *Toyota*, in the Japanese market, the scale of production had to be further expanded. For this purpose, *Toyota Motor* went into a partnership with *Daihatsu Kogyo* and *Hino Motors*, which were commissioned to produce *Toyota* cars. These partnerships intended co-operation in planning of new product lines and of technology, in export and in the rationalisation of supply. In the meantime, a mass market for automobiles had developed, and *Toyota* made inroads into this market by adding another distribution channel consisting of 70 local dealers situated in each prefecture and large city. A full-line policy was developed by adding products aimed at a wider class of consumers. *Toyota* used the same parts for various classes of cars as much as possible and thus attained low production costs.

The ratio of exports in the total sales increased in the second half of the 1960s: it was 15 per cent in 1965, 26 per cent in 1970, 35 per cent in 1975, and 43 per cent in 1980. Not only the shares of exports, but also their qualities shifted from trucks for Asian markets to passenger cars for the US market. Export activities were operated through the Export Headquarters of *Toyota Motor Sales*, and dealers in the US and European countries, where the number of dealers was much larger than in Japan's market, since the sole-sales agency system was not in use in those countries. *Toyota*'s high profits in the 1970s came from exports rather than from the domestic market.

Though quite irregular as a functional structure *Toyota Motor*, lacking both production and sales departments, its managerial functions such as accounting, production techniques, equipment control, export, and labour and personnel were highly centralised. The members of the Toyoda family held important positions in the highest levels of management in *Toyota Motor* as well as in its group companies.

Hino Motors[34] began its post-war history in the manufacture of trucks and buses, then embarked upon car production in a partnership with *Renault*. *Hino* put much effort into the reconstruction of its parts and component suppliers and the fortification of the group as a whole. In 1948, its sales department was separated as *Hino Diesel Sales*, and C. Amano was appointed its manager. In 1953 when *Renault* was put on the market, *Hino Motors* set up another sales company, *Hino Renault Sales*. This was the first attempt among the automobile companies that separated sales department, being supported by the concept that manufacturers should not produce according to their own conveniences but to the demands of the market. Such demands of the market could best be answered to by companies specialising in sales. In spite of early attempts to build up sales organisations, the number of *Hino*'s dealers was still limited and the development of distribution was thus belated. The company's main product lines gradually shifted from large diesel-engine cars to smaller ones towards the mid-1960s, and to adjust to this change, its two sales companies were merged in 1958. However, there were few changes in the organisation of the local dealers. The organisational structure remained a production-centred one. The size of the head office was small, and it had only an accounting and a general affairs department. Major functions such as production, technology, materials, and research belonged to factories. The position of the head office rose as the planning function became more important and as exports increased.

Just as *Hino* was about to develop small passenger cars, it encountered the 1965 slump and the liberalisation of imports. Although its larger car branches, which represented about 80 per cent of the total sales of the company, were not so badly damaged, a mass production system had to be established in the smaller car branch. *Hino Motors* went into a partnership with *Toyota Motor* in order to acquire technological support. The company sent trainees to *Toyota* and was able to learn a lot about production management. The influence of *Toyota* did not stop with the reorganisation of the factory line or the acceleration of its workings. *Hino* also had to fortify its control over the parts suppliers through its purchasing department. Alterations were also necessary in the company's sales organisations. *Toyota* dealers amalgamated 26 of the 59 *Hino*'s local dealers, mainly those engaged in the sales of smaller cars formerly belonging to *Hino Renault Sales*, while *Hino Motor Sales* reorganised its own dealers with the gravity on the sales of larger cars. After the mid-1960s, the ratio of trucks sales increased as a result of a tie-up with *Toyota*

Motor. New kinds of managerial tasks beyond the level of the shop floor, such as research and overseas activities also appeared. Unlike *Toyota* where a separate sales company handled exports, in *Hino*'s case the manufacturing company directly handled all overseas activities, including the export of its products. The centralisation of *Hino*'s management began in the late 1960s. Each director was given control over one function, and the planning section was enlarged to become general staff. The production function was also departmentalised, and placed below the board.

As a member of the *Toyota* group, *Hino Motors* was assigned to the construction of small trucks. *Toyota* supplied engines, and *Hino* manufactured the rest of the necessary accessories. *Hino* was also engaged in the production of ordinary trucks, whose export played an important role in the early 1970s. The expansion of the domestic market due to public investment also contributed the development of its truck interests. The increase in exports to developing countries, as well as the successful assimilation of *Toyota*'s technical skills, enabled *Hino Motor* to maintain a position relatively independent of *Toyota Motor*.

Throughout the thirty years under examination, the basic pattern of *Hino*'s organisation on the operating level remained unchanged. *Hino Motors* was in charge of production and export, while *Hino Motor Sales* was in charge of the distribution of products to the domestic market. Under this pattern, centralisation proceeded as the export increased and as research and development became more important.

Daihatsu Kogyo[35] started as an engineering company, and had made inroads into motor-tricycle production in the pre-war era. In the early post-war years, the firm was engaged in forging and the production of diesel engines, as well as motor-tricycles. To meet the rapid expansion of the motor-tricycle market, *Daihatsu* encouraged each of its factories to specialise in a particular product or material. The management structure was formed as a functionally departmentalised one, in which *Daihatsu*'s two factories were controlled by a production department while the other functions were executed through an 'Operating Department'.

Daihatsu developed in two directions. One was the expansion of its sales organisation for motor-tricycles; traditionally the firm had an extensive network of local dealers, numbering 62 in 1951 and 68 in 1956, in addition to about 500 sub-dealers. *Daihatsu*'s early products required substantial repairs and services because they often had mechanical problems. Thus, the traditional workshop type dealers constituted the company's main sales units. The other direction was in the development of engine and forging interest. Engines and forging products differed from motor-tricycles in both management method and market, and a separate division was set up for these products. The new division had two factories and a sales department, and dealt with diesel engines and forgings.

In the late 1950s, the demand for small trucks was taking the place of that for motor-tricycles. *Daihatsu Kogyo* adapted itself to this change and entered passenger car production. It thus became necessary to reorganise its factories according to modern production principles. Not only cost accounting and process management techniques were introduced into their own factories, but the factories of parts suppliers were modernised. *Daihatsu* sent their foremen and technicians to these suppliers whom they advised regarding the work process, the lay-out of the factories, and the improvement of their machine tools. The flow of materials and parts, however, were coordinated separately by the Purchasing Department and by the factories respectively. *Daihatsu*'s control over its dealers was also fortified. Unlike the dealers of other automobile companies, those of *Daihatsu* were not sole-sales agents. When *Daihatsu* embarked on the production of 'Lilliput' motor-tricycles, the company began to form its own dealers in addition to the local sales companies. *Daihatsu* began to give advice regarding the sales activities and accounting methods of the dealers, and also sent its staff to them. Such measures, however, came to be substituted by increasing the number of production units situated in the various parts of the country. *Daihatsu* also made use of sub-contracting companies for the fitting of finished Lilliput motor-tricycles. A strong top management was set up to control these diverse activities, and then a management committee was formalised in 1958. Main product lines were reorganised into a functional headquarters structure, consisting of technology, trading, and production headquarters, while diesel and foreign divisions were gradually built up as profit centres. All these measures were completed by the early 1960s.

Meanwhile the preferences of customers were changing from small trucks to passenger cars just at the time when the company started to produce passenger cars. In comparison to their earlier products, the production of passenger cars required a higher level of technical skills and precision in processing and fitting the components. *Daihatsu* converted their truck factories into passenger car factories. Supplies and sales were both important. The supply organisation of the company was reformed and control of materials and accesories was centralised into the Ikeda Works, as opposed to their partial control by the central Purchasing Department. Furthermore, the firm reorganised their parts suppliers. About 30 of these were consolidated, and others were made to specialise in particular parts, and some were developed as specialist component producers and were able to sell their products to outside markets. About 230 suppliers were thus reorganised around *Daihatsu*. In sales, existing dealers with local origins, and not necessarily *Daihatsu*'s sole-sales agents were gradually consolidated and allocated particular areas. In some areas *Daihatsu* set up new dealers. The sales headquarters was moved to Tokyo to coordinate and control the local sales activities more efficiently. However, it was not easy for *Daihatsu* to adapt itself to the passenger car market. *Toyota Motor* advised them both in technology and sales. *Daihatsu*'s diesel division was separated, and then its sales function was separated into a new company in 1968. The sales function was moved to *Daihatsu Motor Sales*, in which *Daihatsu Kogyo* held 60 per cent of the shares while *Toyota Motor* and *Toyota Motor Sales* had 20 per cent respectively. *Daihatsu Motor Sales* was modelled after *Toyota Motor Sales* which sent its directors to the new company. Their cooperation also extended the co-development of new model cars and the subcontracting the *Toyota* cars. Investment policy since the organisational reform, however, was not very brisk in comparison to *Daihatsu*'s rivals, such as *Toyo Kogyo*. Its fixed capital investment during the decade before the oil-crisis amounted approximately to 60 000 million yen, which is equivalent to a quarter of that of *Toyo Kogyo*.[36] This modest investment policy resulted in crisis for the company, especially in export and 'light' car production. *Toyota Motor* sent management to *Daihatsu* and changed its policy to a more aggressive one. Financial resources were concentrated on small cars for popular use. Thus the mass-production system specialising in particular product lines was completed in the late 1970s. The organisational structure remained production-centred.

Nissan Motor[37] went the other way round to the three companies described above in organising and coordinating its production and sales functions. Until 1949 its production and sales had been carried out through separate companies. There is a brief but decisive history behind this. In 1937, the original *Nissan Motor Sales* was set up, but eventually it was integrated with a governmentally controlled distributor under the war structure. Just after the war, the second-generation *Nissan Motor Sales* was set up as the general agent for *Nissan Motor*, and 47 dealers, one from each prefecture came under the control of this sales company. *Nissan Motor* did not hold the shares in *Nissan Motor Sales* until 1951, when the company took over a major part of the activities of *Nissan Motor Sales* and made the latter specialise in distribution among large-scale customers. Direct sales by the manufacturing company was chosen, and the reasons for this consolidation were more or less similar to the separation between the two functions in the case of *Toyota*. A legally consolidated firm would have ensured a closer relationship between the manufacturer and its dealers, enabled the former to react quickly to the changing market demands, and would eventually reduce sales costs. In *Toyota* the relationship between the manufacturing and sales companies was much closer, being based on shareholding, interlocking directorships, and above all, equal positions between the two parties. In *Nissan*'s case, the relationship was similar to the traditional general agent system. By this consolidation the management structure of *Nissan Motor* became a functional/line one, comprised of sales and purchasing departments and of factories. In the early 1950s, the main factory of *Nissan Motor* was still being requisitioned by the US Army, and production had to be carried out by its nine separately located factories. A complicated means of supplying parts to each of these factories developed. The long-range plans for the early period dealt mainly with the reallocation of product lines among factories, very necessary for the establishment of mass-production methods. The reform in the sales organisation followed. A sales staff department was set up, and the operating sales department was divided up into six sub-units by geographical areas. Under such a system this company mainly supplied various types of trucks and buses.

In the latter half of the 1950s, *Nissan Motor* embarked on the production of a medium-size car in a partnership with *Austin*, but at the same time, emphasis was put on a research and development system in the field of smaller cars. Such a divergent policy resulted in the production of two lines of cars. Centrifugal trends in production became apparent and forced *Nissan* to adopt a self-supporting system in the production units, whose managerial practices differed from each other. Such trends had to be balanced by forming a strong top management. The management committee was formed for the promotion of long-range planning. The coordination of production and sales was performed by the planning committee. However, the standardisation of the shop floor level practices into a unified speed, work practice, and organisation was a difficult task. Control over the parts suppliers had been fortified since the mid-1950s. At first *Nissan* introduced mass production and modern management techniques into its factories, and later in the late 1950s quality control. In the early 1960s *Nissan* gave advice on the lay-out of the production processes of their parts suppliers, and also made it possible to coordinate the flow of materials from 108 suppliers to the fitting lines of *Nissan Motor*. The raw materials for these suppliers were purchased centrally by *Nissan Motor* in order to reduce costs.

Nissan Motor encountered managerial problems in the mid-1960s in preparing for both the liberalisation of trade and passenger car production. Not only had a huge amount of capital been invested in fixed equipment since the early 1960s, but cooperation with other automobile companies, and the rationalisation of affiliated and sub-contracting companies was also pursued. First, a minimum scale had to be attained in order to be able to cope with American companies in the Japanese market. In addition to *Nissan Diesel Motor* and *Nissan Shatai*, both of which had already been affiliated with *Nissan Motor*, *Fuji Heavy Industries*, *Aichi Machine Industry*, and for a short period of time *Isuzu Motor*, went into partnerships with *Nissan Motor*, and manufactured special lines of cars for the latter. Secondly in 1966, a large-scale merger with *Prince Motors*, another large automobile company, took place, and *Prince Motors* was organised into a division of *Nissan Motor*. In sales the merger took an irregular form. *Prince Motors* had made use of a sales company as the outlet of its products to local dealers, while *Nissan* in turn directly distributed its products. Both systems survived in the new company and the products of the Prince Division were distributed through a sales company as before. Finally, they had to secure a supply of various parts with good quality. Traditionally these suppliers produced single items or parts of components according to a blue-print sent from *Nissan Motor*. *Nissan Motor*, however, intended to develop them into specialised component producers which had their own technical skills and enable them to supply complex and finished components. Cooperation among the suppliers was also necessary to promote their specialisation, and the conservative attitude of the parts suppliers had to be changed. *Nissan* tried to introduce production management techniques such as quality control and value analysis. Meanwhile, cooperation among parts suppliers based on mutual division of labour saw little progress. The merger with *Prince Motors* was thus a chance to reorganise the suppliers into a hierarchical structure. *Nissan Motor* dealt only with the primary suppliers, who in turn organised second-ary and tertiary suppliers under them. Financial and human resources were allocated to these suppliers throughout the 1960s in an attempt to transform them into specialised parts suppliers, as well as to strengthen the unity of the group. The number of subsidiaries was also increased during the same period. The amount of capital invested in them increased by 20 times during the 1960s.[38] All these contributed to the establishment of a mass-production system for various lines of auto-mobiles. The increasing amount and kinds of tasks brought about the development of a big head office where departmental headquarters and the general office were situated.

Nissan's development after 1974 is characterised as a process of expansion. The company was controlled by a functionally depart-mentalised structure throughout the 1970s, though it had a division in subordinate lines. Its major production units still maintained relative independence in their management practices, and were directly re-sponsible to the top management. *Nissan*'s export ratio amounted to 40 per cent by the mid-1970s, and overseas activities were carefully controlled by the Overseas Division Headquarters. The domestic sales organisation was more centralised. In order to catch up with *Toyota*, the president himself undertook the position of sales depart-ment manager. It had 255 local dealers which were classified into five product lines. In addition it had nearly 50 dealers supplying parts and diversified products, although the product lines of the former *Prince Motors* were still distributed through a general sales company.

The forerunner of *Fuji Heavy Industries*[39] was a giant aircraft company which grew enormously after 1938, with 102 factories and 250 000 employees in 1945. Most of these factories were closed down and the company was divided into 12 offshoots after the War, five of which got together to set up *Fuji Heavy Industries* in 1953. Each of these five companies had originally been a single function and single unit firm, engaged in product lines such as railway vehicles, buses and motor-scooters. The resumption of aircraft production made them join up with each other to form a new company. Automobile pro-duction was chosen as a new field of activity, though there was a strong tendency among them to cling to aircraft production. Initially, it was a fully diversified firm, though the range of its diversification was limited within transportation equipment. Its organisational struc-ture for the first six years was a decentralised one, consisting of production units which had a fairly wide scope of authority over production, of the sales departments, each dealing with one of the product lines, and of the head office. Members of the central board were sent from these production units.

The development of the company was rooted in the production of motor-scooters, the firm then advancing into the production of light four-wheel vehicles by the end of the 1950s. During the decade before 1964, financial resources were equally allocated to each of the production units, namely, to the diversified activities of the company. In 1955, the sales of *Fuji Heavy Industries* amounted to as much as that of *Honda Motor* but went down to a half of the latter in 1964. The weakest aspect of its activities immediately after the consolidation were in sales. It had a wide range of products from scooters to rolling stocks, each requiring a different organisation, different distribution channels, and different marketing techniques. Moreover, the company was planning to make inroads into automobile production, which added another requirement for the formation of a sales organisation. In 1954, the firm started to form an organisation of local dealers, which were eventually located in every prefecture, and sold their scooters and light automobiles through these. In the upward processes, suppliers were organised by each of the production unit of *Fuji Heavy Industries*, each one specialising in engines or body production. Apart from the financial burdens necessary for the formation of its own distribution channel, new activities created a complex flow of goods, and in 1959 the multidivisional structure consisting of three self-supporting divisions with a full line of functions, was adopted. The functions of the head office were strengthened by the setting up of a planning department. In the following year, the largest of the divisions was dissolved into three functional headquarters which were directly controlled by the top management. However, in 1961, these functional headquarters were reorganised into a division so as to clarify the authority and responsibility of the division managers.

After the mid-1960s the company began to concentrate its limited financial resources on the 'light' automobile branch. Other divisions such as buses, aircrafts, and railway vehicles did not show satisfactory results, and *Fuji* was unable to enjoy the advantages of diversification. Though nominally divisions, these were actually based on production units which *Fuji Heavy Industries* had inherited from their forerunners. The management tried to reorganise them according to product-market areas, and establish a self-supporting system. Furthermore, *Fuji Heavy Industries*' sales channels were weak compared with those of other automobile companies. At first use was made of existing distributors when *Fuji* entered passenger car production, because financial resources could no longer be spent on building up new channels. However, since *Honda* had had success in using unaffiliated dealers, *Fuji* followed its example. In 1968 the company moved into a partnership with *Nissan Motor*. Unlike other automobile companies, though, *Fuji* aimed at maintaining diversification. However, *Fuji* also tried to develop itself as a producer of passenger cars. Strategic plans aimed at setting up a specialised factory for ordinary passenger car production by making use of the high profits of the 'light' automobile branch which would naturally result in high dividends and the increase in its own capital. The leading position of 'light' automobiles did not change easily, though its market was approaching its peak. These factors necessitated a modification in the divisional structure in 1968. The Light Automobiles Division was reorganised into functional headquarters such as production, planning, and technology, all of which were, like other divisions, directly responsible to the top management.

The forerunner of *Nissan Shatai*[40] was also an aircraft company, having moved into the production of bus and truck bodies in the late 1940s. However, the production equipment was poor in quality, and modernisation did not proceed. When this company was reorganised by the Industrial Reconstruction and Reorganisation Act, it was confronted with a financial crisis and was unable to raise capital on the stock exchange. *Nissan Motor*, which had constantly ordered bus bodies from *Nissan Shatai* (at that time named *Shin Nikkoku Kogyo*), acquired 87 per cent of the shares in the latter and sent a president to oversee its reconstruction. The sales directed to *Nissan Motor* rose from 26 per cent to 37 per cent of its total output during the first half of the 1950s.

The management structure of *Nissan Shatai* remained a decentralised one. The head office had accounting and general affairs departments. Its two local offices were equipped with financing, trading, and purchasing functions, and the production function was completely delegated to the factories. Meanwhile, the relationship with *Nissan Motor* became much closer: instead of constructing bus bodies, *Nissan Shatai* entered the production of components and the construction of the non-standardised lines of *Nissan Motor*. Therefore, the local operating units of this company seemed to belong to *Nissan Motor* rather than to the head office of *Nissan Shatai*. All these were observed in the latter half of the 1950s. The next step was to concentrate *Nissan Shatai*'s financial resources on its Hiratsuka

Factory in order to develop it as a passenger car factory on the mass production basis, though the main task assigned to the company was to manufacture small trucks, caravans and the other special cars of *Nissan Motor*, as well as their own micro-buses.[41] The trading function was centralised by 1960, though *Nissan Shatai*'s production for the consumer market continued to decrease as that for *Nissan Motor* increased. By the mid-1960s the head office had been separated from the operating unit, and formed a planning – mainly production planning – department.

After the mid-1960s the company further intensified its nature as a single function firm. The only products handled by their own Trading Department were micro-buses, and the remaining part of the company was exclusively devoted to manufacturing for *Nissan Motor*. *Nissan Shatai*'s Kyoto Factory was modernised into one based on the mass production of wagon cars, and added also to its lines were caravan type variations of *Nissan* products. By 1960, the company had reorganised its purchasing system. *Nissan Shatai* had its own suppliers, but they were reorganised according to the *Nissan* method: first, leading members were chosen from among *Nissan Motor* suppliers, and these in turn were charged with the control of *Nissan Shatai*'s secondary suppliers; secondly, *Nissan Shatai* acquired shares in seven leading suppliers; and finally in 1971, *Nissan Shatai* established its own group consisting of 82 affiliated suppliers. The factories of *Nissan Shatai* were made directly responsible to the top management. The head office became specialised in the purchasing and technology functions, while the production management and the production departments were set up in each factory. Research and development gradually became independent of *Nissan Motor*. The majority of its sales activities were still carried out through the distribution channels of *Nissan Motor*, though direct relationships with customers, such as after sales service and supplying parts and components became necessary, as did the development of *Nissan Shatai*'s own channels in order to keep up with the changing market.

The forerunner of *Nissan Diesel Motor*[42] began as a supplier of diesel engines for *Nissan Motor*. In addition it also used to produce its own buses and trucks. The sales activities of this company were also operated through the sales organisation of *Nissan Motor*, but in 1960 the firm set up a separate sales company jointly with *Nissan Motor*. Eventually, this sales company, *Nissan Diesel Sales* came to organise 66 local dealers as outlets of *Nissan Diesel*'s products. Just after the formation of this sales company, however, *Nissan Diesel* intensified its nature as the diesel department of *Nissan Motor*. The production of large trucks and buses with diesel engines for *Nissan Motor* increased, while engine production for outside markets decreased. Its sales department was abolished in the late 1950s.

In the beginning *Nissan Motor* held no shares in *Nissan Diesel Motor*, but in 1953 it acquired a 35.1 per cent interests in *Nissan Diesel Motor* (which later increased to 52.5 per cent), and sent directors to the latter.[43] After 1965 the production of trucks, which were to be distributed through *Nissan Diesel Sales* increased while those commissioned by *Nissan Motor* decreased. Trucks were also produced for the export market, and this required the company to organise a structure able to deal with overseas activities. By the end of the 1970s, the company had established an export department in the head office, and it was this department, not the sales company, that was charged with oversea activities. The planning department was also set up in the head office. In contrast to the case of *Nissan Shatai*, the management tasks of *Nissan Diesel* were centralised in the head office. Thirty-one departments in the head office reported to the top management, and engaged in operative activities or staff services. Both *Nissan Shatai* and *Nissan Diesel* were reconstructed by *Nissan Motor* in the early post-war era, by becoming its suppliers of parts such as bodies or engines, but both eventually developed into the finished car manufacturers by equipping themselves with mass production fitting lines. In the course of their development these two firms gradually accumulated technical skills of their own or established their own markets in specially product lines.

Izuzu Motors[44] was the largest Japanese automobile company in 1950, manufacturing trucks and buses, and moving into the production of diesel engines in the early post-war period. The company was outgrown by *Toyota* and *Nissan* in the 1960s, when the latter two companies increased their shares of passenger cars production by organising the systems of mass production and mass distribution. *Isuzu* had long been a truck manufacturer, and trucks traditionally held the major part of the automobile market. In order to acquire the technical skills necessary for the production of passenger cars, *Isuzu* had to go into a partnership with *Rootes Motors*, and this continued until the mid-1960s, and the number of cars produced amounted to the largest among such co-partnerships. Managerial problems in the company's early days were primarily found in production. Firstly, each of *Isuzu*'s three factories was made to specialise in the production of one of the main parts of automobiles, and the activities of these factories were coordinated by the functional department of the head office. By 1955, the head office had been equipped with a full line of functional departments from purchasing to sales and export, and departmental managers were separated from the responsibilities of both top management and the operating units.

From the mid-1950s a long-range plan was put into action. It aimed at the increase in the production of both trucks and passenger cars. *Isuzu*'s factories were traditionally organised in a system in which each produced particular parts. This was reorganised into a new system in which every factory was made to produce particular lines of finished automobiles. Parts were supplied by its 400 sub-contracting companies. In doing this, financial resources were first allocated to truck interests, then from the early 1960s, to passenger car production.[45] Factories were separated from the control of the production department and became directly responsible to the highest level management. Production was in fact decentrally carried out by each of the product lines under the new system. The expansion of the automobile branches, however, was not accompanied by the expected results, for trucks and engines still amounted to 90 per cent of *Isuzu*'s total sales in 1965. In every car model from the *Hileman* to that of the mid-1960s, the company was unable to attain the minimum economic scale of passenger car production in this period. One of the main reasons for this was in *Isuzu*'s weak passenger car sales organisation, which was different from that of trucks. Passenger car markets were gradually shifting to the final consumers, and these were products that had to be sold in quantity. It was in the mid-1960s that the Sales Headquarters was formed and was charged with the control of sales branches. *Isuzu*'s sales organisation was, like its production, reorganised according to product types, though operations were controlled and coordinated centrally by this sales headquarters.

Since the mid-1960s, *Isuzu Motors* entered into a series of partnerships with other automobile companies in order to attain a scale of production. In 1966 *Isuzu* formed a partnership with *Fuji Heavy Industries*, though this was dissolved in 1968 when *Isuzu* tried to form it into a tripartite group by joining *Mitsubishi Heavy Industries*, which also had an automobile branch then. However, *Mitsubishi* came to link up with *Chrysler*, and *Isuzu* thus had to find a new partner. In 1970 *Isuzu* formed a partnership with *Nissan Motor*, through which *Isuzu* was to undertake the construction of *Nissan* cars, but this too dissolved the following year, when *General Motors* decided to acquire 34.2 per cent of the shares in *Isuzu*. *Isuzu* thus came to be engaged in the knocking down of *G. M.* cars, which were distributed through *G. M.*'s sales organisation overseas. This changed the position of the company from one of heavy dependence on trucks and buses to heavy dependence on passenger cars. However, *G. M.*'s support could not immediately put an end to *Isuzu*'s decline, and its recovery was postponed until the late 1970s, when exports of small trucks and cars through *G. M.*'s sales organisation brought a profit to the company.

Throughout the 1960s decentralising trends in managerial functions continued. Each factory was delegated with the necessary managerial authority. At the level immediately below the top management came headquarters by products and functions. For instance, the Small Car Sales Headquarters was in charge of the sales activities, while the Large Car Production Headquarters was charged with research, technology, and the production of larger lines of cars including the control of factories. Towards the late 1970s, the organisational structure was reformed into a market-oriented one. The production function was consolidated under one sub-unit which controlled all the factories, and the sales functions were reorganised into sales, export, and component headquarters.

Toyo Kogyo[46] was a family-owned company that had been engaged in mechanical engineering and motor-tricycle production in the pre-war years. After the war, its production of motor-tricycle grew rapidly, representing 90 per cent of the sales of this firm. Towards the end of the 1940s, more than ten engineering firms, which had originally been engaged in aircraft production, were entering the motor-tricycle industry. *Toyo Kogyo*, which started to manufacture motor-tricycles before the war, had organised local sales agents, and by 1948 had established distribution channels by placing an agent in every prefecture. Sub-dealers were chosen as new local agents, but they were not necessarily the sole-sales agents of *Toyo Kogyo*. This system was maintained until the mid-1960s. These agents were supervised by the local branches of *Toyo Kogyo*. In the head office, a relatively simple line structure by products was developed into a functionally departmentalised structure in the early 1950s.

The latter half of the 1950s saw a dramatic change in the motor-tricycle market. Small trucks appeared and their prices gradually fell. Motor-tricycles were superior to small trucks in their capacity of transport, and had a wide market established among small-scale firms. At first, *Toyo Kogyo* advanced into the production of motor-tricycles of higher quality, though gradually came to notice difficulties in competing with small trucks, whose ownership at this time was a status symbol. Between these two products, 'light' motor-tricycles, or super-mini motor-tricycles appeared, but were gradually taken over by 'light' trucks. *Toyo Kogyo*, though not quick to adapt itself to these new markets, advanced into the production of trucks in 1958 and soon into 'light' motor-tricycles, then in the early 1960s into passenger car production. An extraordinary growth in sales necessitated a reform of its family management. A management committee and general staff were introduced. In 1956, traditional product lines such as mining and industrial machinery were grouped into divisions. In the automobile branch, sales activities were emphasised: the company had strong distribution channels, which were to come under the three Regional Sales Controlling Departments.

In the first half of the 1960s *Toyo Kogyo*'s management recognised that the private passenger car market was expanding more rapidly than that of commercial-use automobiles, and moved from truck to small passenger car production. For this purpose, it became necessary to establish a mass production system, and this was promptly implemented. High profit and the position of the third largest automobile company in Japan were the results of these changes. The management also appreciated the necessity of forming new distribution channels besides existing ones, because trucks and passenger cars involved different markets and sales techniques. *Toyo Kogyo* formed a new organisation consisting of one dealer each in every prefecture, and held 49 per cent of each dealer's shares. Furthermore, *Toyo Kogyo* attempted to increase the number of the operating units of the local dealers to 1000, and this was attained by the end of the 1960s. After 1965, this franchise distributing system was changed, and plural dealers were set up particularly in large cities. For overseas markets, *Toyo Kogyo* had depended on local distributors through special agent contract. However, after 1965 *Toyo Kogyo* began to set up their own distributing companies in large markets.

Rapid expansion in the 1960s increased the number of sub-units below top management. It was necessary to reorganise nearly 30 departments into a more unified organisation. In 1970 five functional headquarters together with a general planning section and a separate division were formed. Towards the early 1970s, major efforts were made in the production and technological functions while the sales function was left as it was. Such changes as well as rapid expansion required a huge amount of investment with loans from banks. As a late-comer to the automobile market, the company concentrated its efforts on the development of the rotary engine in order to pass the exhaust gas regulation and to survive in the competitive automobile market. When the company entered the mass production of rotary engines, it was severely hit by the oil crisis. This engine was not necessarily efficient in fuel consumption, and the interest charged on loans became a burden. Although no major organisational reforms were made, the *Sumitomo Bank* intervened, resulting in a shake-up in the top management and the end of the owner-management structure. Domestic sales activities were strengthened. *Toyo Kogyo*'s relationship with *Ford*, which had begun in the early 1970s, was transformed from a mere technological tie-up into a much closer relationship. In 1978 *Toyo Kogyo* began to supply components to *Ford* and to construct cars under contract for *Ford*. In 1979 *Ford* took a 25 per cent interests in *Toyo Kogyo*.

Honda Motor[47] was set up after the war, and started its development with motorcycle production. In the early 1950s the company attempted to embark on the mass production of motorcycles, and new outlets were found among bicycle retailers. Their products were initially distributed by sales agents, and often by sub-dealers. T. Fujisawa, the senior managing director of this small firm, formed a distribution system extending from the manufacturer to its local branch offices and thousands of retailers. The new forms of distribution were quite different from that of other automobile companies, which more or less depended on a limited number of affiliated dealers and their retail outlets. *Honda*'s distribution system was rather similar to the typical downward integration observed in large-scale American firms. However, the difference between *Honda* and other automobile firms was, at this point, due mainly to the different nature of their products; *Honda* sold motorcycles, while other firms supplied trucks and motor-tricycles. In 1958, at the time of introducing a new model to the market, *Honda* again invited local merchants to be retailers of its motorcycles. However, the products were distributed not through *Honda*'s own branch offices but through local agents to 600 retailers. More interestingly, such characteristics particular to *Honda*'s distribution channel reappeared when the firm made inroads into four-wheel vehicles. The company, like more than 40 other neighbouring motorcycle manufacturers, encountered difficulties twice in the 1950s, but the fame and esteem of *Honda*'s products had been established by the end of the 1950s. Without delay the company advanced into the American and then the European markets. The ratio of exports to their total sales increased from five per cent in 1960 to 31 per cent in 1964. Such exports were accompanied by *Honda*'s after-sale service with a supply of parts. Marketing and sales were thus closely integrated with production. Unlike other automobile companies, *Honda* did not affiliate part suppliers permanently, but utilised a more flexible supply from any good-quality manufacturers. Having experienced success in motorcycle production, *Honda* entered the production of four-wheel vehicles. By that time, other motorcycle and motor-tricycle companies had already begun the production of four-wheel vehicles. *Honda* again invited motorcycle dealers that had originated as bicycle retailers to be dealers for their four-wheel vehicles. The number of these dealers amounted to 23 000 in 1967. To coordinate the flow of their products, *Honda* increased the number of their local trading offices from a dozen to 90, and these carried out wholesale functions. Also 283 service factories were set up to reinforce the activities of the retailers who could not easily provide various automobile services by themselves. As well as their own trading offices, *Honda* continued to make use of local agents not only in the distribution of motorcycles but in that of four-wheel vehicles. Such local agents lacked links among them-selves, and this was one of their defects, compared with the activities of *Honda*'s branch offices. However, local agents were expected to play roles of a kind different from what could be attained by well organised and centrally controlled trading offices. Organisational problems in the mid-1960 were, in addition to the build-up of the sales organisation and their integration with the mass production system, how top management should be separated from daily oper-ational activities. The management structure by then was composed of a sales and an accounting department and of production units, whose leadership was assumed by members of the top management. Operational authority was delegated to their subordinates in 1964, while the top management were made to devote themselves to general management tasks.

Honda's international activities took off rapidly after 1965. First, export of finished products, followed by the formation of assembly factories overseas, whose numbers increased to 30 by the early 1970s, and finally, oversea production proceeded after the mid-1970s. In the domestic market, sales of four-wheel vehicles increased, reaching more than half of total sales in the early 1970s. The top management organisation was elaborated upon and the highest level managers were separated from operative functions. In the early 1970s, manag-ing directors were grouped into one of three committees in charge of managerial resources. They reported to the senior managing directors' meeting. At the same time, the strategic groupings by geography, such as the North American group, were formed, whose memberships were again constituted by managing directors. Head office functions such as finance, purchase and sales, and the production units came below these two kinds of groups consisting of managing directors. Operative managerial functions were, in turn, distributed among the production units.

Suzuki Motor[48] had originated as a weaving machinery manufacturer, then embarked on motorcycle production by combining mechanical processing skills, which they had acquired through armament production during the war, with the forging technology of the textile machinist. The sales organisation was divided into three areas, and a distribution channel, consisting of general agents, local agents, and retailers was formed. At first, the trading department of the company which had used to deal with textile machinery, sold 'bicycle engines' (engines fitted to bicycles). However, the market and the sales methods of 'bicycle engines' were completely different from those of weaving machinery. Moreover, the market was expanding so rapidly that the company could not catch up with demand. To sell systematically, *Suzuki* had to depend on general agents, who had established relationships with local agents in the automobile or bicycle trade, to intermediate between *Suzuki* and the retailers. At that time, *Suzuki* was a single unit company, and was engaged in the production of bicycle engines and textile machinery. A simple functionally departmentalised structure evolved in the first half of the 1950s.

The company extended its product lines to four-wheel vehicles in the mid-1950s, particularly to 'light' trucks. Until the mid-1960s, the modernisation of management procedures was pursued on a company-wide basis. On the shop floor level, scientific management was introduced from the US, and in keeping with this concept, a new factory was built to manufacture four-wheel vehicles on a mass-production basis. In sales, *Suzuki* began to acquire shares in their dealers who were placed under its direct control. *Suzuki* made direct contact with local agents, who, in the western part of Japan had origins that traced back to automobile dealers, and in the east to bicycle wholesalers. In the following year, *Suzuki* decided to increase the number of its local agents, which numbered 150 by 1960. *Suzuki*'s products were handled by these agents and sold by 6000 retailers. On the other hand, the company had been strengthening its control over these agents since 1959, by acquiring their shares, sending them managers and making them exclusive dealers of *Suzuki*'s products. In the head office the management committee and a planning section were formed, and these engaged in long-range company planning and general policy making. The textile machinery branch was separated as a division in 1958, then as an independent company in 1961. Finally three headquarters, consisting of administration, production, and trading were set up, and authority was delegated to these headquarters. From this classical and formal organisational structure, the company moved into a different one in the latter half of the 1960s. Rapid expansion in production, including an increase in the number of production units, occurred after 1965, and this, in turn, resulted in the expansion of sales channels. Four-wheel vehicles led this process by taking the place of motorcycles, though in exports the latter still played a dominant role. The sales functions of these two products were separated from each other, and were further divided into regional groups. *Suzuki* advised its agents to divide their organisation into two parts, and thus separated the distribution channel of motorbicycles from four-wheel vehicles. By 1970, they had 190 local agents, 53 of which were their affiliated companies. The production units, each with several factories, came under the direct control of the top management. Thus sub-divided units engaging in production, sales and service, were placed below the top management.

Though *Suzuki* was already a big firm with the most modern production units, their organisational structure resembled that of small-to-medium-sized enterprises. A similar trait is also observable in *Suzuki*'s strategy from the early 1970s. As an automobile concern, the company specialised in 'light' trucks and special 'light' passenger cars. This allowed them to enjoy tax and administrative privileges, which enabled them to lower the prices of these lines of vehicles. However, competition in the market for higher class cars among 'light' automobile producers raised the prices of these cars, which came to resemble ordinary small cars. Market demand was changing, and the customers preferred the latter. Moreover, *Suzuki* attempted to develop a technology to prepare for the exhaust gas regulation, but could not easily succeed in it, although the company expressed an optimistic expectation on its 'Epic engine'. It was in the latter half of the 1970s, during the second oil crisis, that the company successfully manufactured cheap lines of light automobiles with good cost performance. The organisation of the company changed little. The

TABLE 8.3 Management structures of Japanese automobile companies

	1950	1960	1970	1980
Toyota	F	Mfg	Mfg	Mfg
Hino	Mfg	Mfg	Mfg[a]	Mfg[a]
Daihatsu	F	F+D	Mfg+D	Mfg+D
Nissan	F	F	F+D	F+D
Fuji	—	MD	F+D	F+D
Nissan Shatai	MDG	F	Mfg[b]	Mfg
Nissan Diesel	F	Mfg	Mfg[a]	Mfg[a]
Isuzu	F	F	F	F
Toyo	F	F+D	F+D	F+D
Honda	F	F	F	F
Suzuki	F	F+D	F	F

[a] with export or overseas departments
[b] with a weak sales department

F = financial structure
MD = Multidivisional structure
F + D = partly divisionalises structure
Mfg = single function

middle management at the departmental level was lean, and the number of the managing directors was lean, and the number of the managing directors was also small.

The organisational structure of the Japanese automobile companies just below the top management was either a functional structure – sometimes with an additional one or more separate divisions – or a single function form with a sales company. Such organisational forms were primarily intended to coordinate the flow of goods from the manufacturers to their local dealers, while upward branches such as these supplying parts and components were controlled by production units. As is shown in Table 8.3, these organisational forms seldom changed once they were established. Nearly half of the firms listed specialised in manufacturing functions, while their sales activities were operated through separate wholesale companies, which in turn organised local dealers. The chief advantages of such a system derived from the nature of the automobile industry as a supplier of finished consumer goods. From processing raw materials and various parts to distribution to the final customers, goods flow through a lengthy number of subdivided and specified stages, with money flowing in the opposite direction. Such flows could not easily be controlled from a single central office. Sales companies undertook the coordination of downward stages to the customers. The wholesale activities of the Japanese automobile companies were operated either through their sales headquarters or separate sales companies, and most of the Japanese automobile companies excluded wholesale merchants. More importantly, the automobile companies (or their sales companies) affiliated local retailers as outlets for given product lines in particular localities. The number of these dealers was small, but they had their own operating units allocated to them. A few automobile companies, particularly those which originated in motor-cycles, developed a different distribution system, making use of local agents (wholesalers) and thousands of retailers. Gradually these local agents were either replaced by the trading offices of the automobile companies or affiliated to the latter, but continued use was made of thousands of retailers even after the entry into passenger car production.

Similarly, most activities in upward processes, such as supplying parts and materials, were carried out through subsidiaries and subcontracting companies. The relationship between the automobile companies and these parts suppliers can be termed as federations, which are neither a complete integration nor a market relation. However, the automobile industrials were able to utilise such relationships to enjoy advantages both of market and hierarchies. The companies did not have to pay fixed costs in supplying parts and components, for they were able to secure them on time and in a condition as if they had been processed in their own factories. However, these part suppliers were able to become specialised manufacturers on a mass-production basis, accumulate their own technical skills, and find outlets outside the group.

The number of companies which integrated production and sales within a single firm decreased during the three decades after 1950. The number of their departments increased as they grew large, but it eventually became necessary to reorganise these departments into larger functional headquarters. Some of them added one or more separate divisions. This does not indicate product diversification on their part, but shows the elements of their origin as engineering or aircraft companies, occupations that came to be replaced by automobile production. Even *Fuji Heavy Industries* which had been fairly diversified and had adopted the multidivisional structure in the past, concentrated its activities on automobiles production.

Centralisation and decentralisation were somewhat different problems in the above management structures. In the companies with an established tradition, production units had much initiative in administration, and as a result decentralisation proceeded. *Nissan Motor*, *Fuji Heavy Industries*, *Isuzu*, and *Hino* had such tendencies for a long time. These firms tried to centralise their activities through the consolidation of research and development, the introduction of the multidivisional structure, or transferring their emphasis from production to sales. On the other hand, companies of post-war origin, like *Honda* or *Suzuki* took the delegation of authority seriously. Both pursued decentralisation while building up their general management organisations.

8.5 MISCELLANEOUS COMPANIES IN CONSUMER DURABLE GOODS

Nine concerns among the largest 100 manufacturing firms in 1970 are still to be examined. All of them supplied finished consumer goods and developed by establishing distribution outlets for final consumers. Two of them were in chemical products, five in household electrical equipment, and the remaining two in miscellaneous industries. All grew dramatically after the war, still retaining the influence of founders' family. Though they diversified either by applying core technical skills or by extending marketing channels to new areas, the relative importance of the additional products in their total sales remained low.

Fuji Photo Film[49] developed rapidly in the post-war period, beginning with the production of X-rays and movie films, then increasing its photo film interests in the first half of the 1950s. By 1955, *Fuji Photo Film* outgrew its rival, *Konishiroku Photo Industry* in terms of both total sales and shares in the film market. Efforts were made in the rationalisation of production and in the foundation of a black-and-white photo-film factory. Diversification was limited to photo-chemistry and optical apparatus by utilising the market which was common to these products. Following improvements on the shop floor level, which brought unsatisfactory results, management reorganisation became inevitable. *Fuji Film* attempted to build up a centralised management structure, with written regulations, a clear division of labour between the line and the staff, defined responsibilities of each position, and a clear-cut lines of authority. The firm then formed a management committee in 1956. The reinforcement of sales organisation was carried out, by dividing the sales function into four sub-units by products. The number of trading offices was increased, directly controlled laboratories for processing were set up, and then in the early 1960s, a country-wide network of laboratories for colour film was established in cooperation with local photo shops.

A large-scale investment was made in the second half of the 1960s, when colour film was replacing black-and-white. Sales expanded by three times during the five years between 1965 and 1970. This expansion required new market, which were acquired through the affiliation of processing laboratories and their local agents. A progressive rebate system was used in organising the agents. Of five major film wholesalers, *Fuji Photo Film* had succeeded in affiliating four by the early 1970.

The functional structure, which continued until 1970, was partly divisionalised. Two branches, namely, optical machinery and magnetic materials, became divisions, though these divisions only undertook sales activities. The overseas divisions which controlled sales and service activities were also added. The background to these changes began in around 1960. The first factor was the appearance of duplicating machinery and magnetic materials. A subsidiary was set up in 1962 in conjunction with *Rank Xerox*, while *Fuji Film* remained lowly diversified until 1970. The second was the liberalisation of foreign capital in the early 1970s. *Fuji Film*'s strategy to compete with *Kodak*, which was ten times its size, was double-sided. *Fuji Film* tried to maintain and increase its share in photo-film both at home and abroad. By 1975, when domestic demand for colour film had reached its peak, the company increased export to 21 per cent of its total sales. At the same time, the company attempted to increase its shares in optical machinery, magnetic materials and printing materials, which had increased to 35 per cent of *Fuji Film*'s total sales by the late 1970s. Photo-copying machinery manufactured by the joint-subsidiary did well. Capital investment was built up in these interests.[50] However, these divisions were abolished by the mid-1970s. Between 1974 and 1980, nearly 60 per cent of its total investment was spent in the film branch, the sales of which amounted to 60 per cent of the company's total sales. This ratio, in fact however, indicates a poor showing in the film branch in comparison with the previous decade when half of *Fuji Film*'s capital was allocated to film interests and their share was 70 per cent.

Shiseido[51] has long been engaged in cosmetics, even when it was still a family enterprise. Its post-war reconstruction started with supplying daily necessaries and reorganising distribution channels. By 1950 the basic form of its present organisational structure had appeared. In the 1950s it was still a single unit firm, and it had 46 sales companies throughout the country. This was the first firm which utilised such sales companies for distribution. Beyond these sales companies, chain stores were built up and cosmetics were sold through these outlet. Toiletries, on the other hand, were taken up by a general sales company and distributed through thousands of local wholesalers to retailers. Toiletries were bulky products, and had to be dealt with through a larger number of stores, and could not be easily controlled by *Shiseido*'s well-organised distribution network. Gradually the share of cosmetics in the company's total sales increased. Above such operating levels, a planning department was set up to integrate and coordinate the production, sales, and finance functions, which had autonomously generated. Financial relationships with the company founder's family ceased quickly. The company's first five-year plan was proposed in the beginning of the 1950s, and aimed at increasing sales and reorganising sales channels in addition to improving the quality of products and the financial position of the firm. *Shiseido* sent finance staff to its local sales companies. The importance of top management function was also realised. The managing directors who had been appointed as heads of functional departments were separated from lines and made general managers. In contrast with the other newly-founded companies examined in this chapter, *Shiseido* had no strong leaders throughout the period of post-war rapid development. Rather, the company was operated by salaried managers, whose educational backgrounds were not necessarily high.

Shiseido's main efforts have been directed to organising its sales network. As well as the local sales companies, retailing shops, which had been organised into a series of chain stores in the early 1950s, were controlled by the local sales companies so as to maintain resale price levels. These retailing shops were classified into four groups according to the share of *Shiseido*'s products in their sales, and 5000 service staff who belonged to the local sales companies visited them. Such a strategy was a reflection of the firm's investment policies; *Shiseido* has invested more in local sales companies and show rooms than in factory equipment. The ratio of sales and administrative expenses has been constantly high, reaching 50 per cent of the total sales throughout the two decades since 1960. Among *Shiseido*'s product lines, cosmetics necessitated such sales expenditures and organisation, and the result was a further increase in the share of cosmetics in the company's total sales. The functional structure developed gradually, and the number of departments increased from six in 1955, to eight in 1960, 14 in 1970, 15 in 1980.

There were five electrical equipment companies among the largest

100 firms in 1970 which specialised in consumer final products. *Matsushita Electric Industrial,*[52] the largest of them, had always attached much importance to the elaboration of its own management structure. Since its adoption of the multidivisional structure for the first time in the pre-war era, the company experienced many periods of organisational reforms. The initiative came from K. Matsushita, the founder of the firm, who well appreciated the significance of the management organisation and its decentralisation.

The personal leadership of K. Matsushita was strong in 1950 and still was in the 1960s, though the size of the firm had already grown to more than half that of *Toshiba. Matsushita*'s main product lines consisted of radio receivers and batteries, followed by electrical lighting lamps and cockers. In the process of the post-war reconstruction the firm faced a company-wide crisis. K. Matsushita attempted a full reorganisation of factories, product lines, sales agents and the head office. Head office staff was appointed to each of the functional departments, and factories were made self-supporting units. In 1950 the divisional structure was reintroduced as the final measure of its reconstruction. The president, the vice president, and a senior managing director were appointed division managers, and the head office was simplified. After this the company promoted product differentiation and specification policy within each product line. As a result, the number of divisions increased to seven in 1953, 19 in 1959, and 29 in 1962. As each of these divisions was made responsible for one product line of household electrical equipment, and as the kinds of household electrical equipment increased rapidly after 1955, new divisions subsequently appeared. At first, each of these divisions was fully responsible for the sales of its products, which were distributed to the retailers through local agents. In the early 1950s, *Matsushita* set up a central sales department which controlled the sales activities of divisions and carried out advertising. Then followed the formation of local branch offices, and of a loose association of retailers handling the products of *Matsushita*. The distribution channels consisting of branch offices, local agents, and loosely affiliated retailers became more extensive when the firm set up local sales companies in conjunction with local agents. These local sales companies were extended throughout the country by 1960, and carried out the wholesale function more efficiently than local sales agents. Thus the company integrated the wholesale stage by means of 100 such sole sales companies.

Some modification was seen in this divisional structure. To

coordinate the sales activity of the divisions, the top management staff was reinforced. The growth of sales in the first half of the 1950s did not improve the financial position of the company, and a second structural reform took place in 1954. Four headquarters were set up, and the Division Headquarters was charged with the control of divisions, while the Sales Headquarters was put in control of the branch offices. Managing directors were appointed as headquarters managers. In addition divisions and branch offices were allocated with internal capital, on which interest was charged by the head office. Thus the structure of the company was transformed from the ordinary multidivisional structure to a mixture of the divisional and functional structure. An extremely specified division, engaged in a single product line, could not efficiently carry out nation-wide marketing.

The five-year plan of 1955 called for 30 per cent annual growth and the 'full line' policy in household electrical equipment. The second half of the 1950s saw new entries, particularly of heavy electrical companies, into the household electrical equipment market, which finally led to competition accompanied by price reduction. *Matsushita* attempted to avoid price reduction by strengthening its control over its distributors. The number of sales companies was increased, and retailers were organised into sole sales and semi-sole sales chains. Thus the basic pattern of present distribution from manufacturer through *Matsushita*'s sales companies to affiliated retailers appeared, though local branch offices, agents and semi-sole-sales retailers were not completely excluded. The company lacked the applied technology in the heavy electrical branches, which was necessary in the manufacture of refrigerators and washing machines. This was to be acquired by affiliating a company. Once these plans were realised, activities overseas became *Matsushita*'s main goal after 1960. Its main products changed from electrical lamps to radio receivers in the first half of the 1950s, to television sets in the second half of the 1950s, and to household electrical equipment in the 1960s. After 1960 structural reorganisation was mainly concerned with the top levels of management. The firm formally set up a joint decision-making system for the top management. Although management decentralisation was promoted and division managers had been delegated with a considerable degree of responsibility until that time, in practice the founder of the company was always consulted. The firm enlarged its head office and added a planning headquarters for these purposes. The number of division headquarters in charge of divisions was also increased to five in 1959.

These measures, however, were not able effectively to meet the recession of the mid-1960s. Local sales companies were the first to run into a dead end. Only 25 or so of 170 local sales companies made profits. After the recovery, *Matsushita* had to face consumer movements and a long slump towards the beginning of the 1970s. They also had to overcome the import restriction of the developing countries. These circumstances pushed the company towards overseas investment, the balance of which began to increase rapidly after 1967. At home, fixed capital was mainly invested in consumer electronic equipment.[53] The ratio between household electrical equipment and consumer electronics had alternated from the 1960s.

Through the experience of the harsh years, the management recognised the defects in the separation of sales function from divisions. During the brisk period divisions assigned their products to these local branch offices, and the latter in turn to the sales agents. The sales agents did not sell what they got in stock by their own judgement, but sold what was assigned by *Matsushita*. Marketing was directly connected with production, and thus research directly related to marketing was required. K. Matsushita realised the importance of the autonomy of local sales companies. A full divisional structure was adopted for the third time, under which each division was to sell its own products to the sales companies without passing through local branches. These divisions were also charged with total responsibility for their products, including exports and overseas activities. Local sales companies were made to purchase on their own accounts, though they were obliged to handle *Matsushita*'s products. In addition to internal capital, an internal interest system was adopted. The sales headquarters set up local sales companies, so that the sales organisation would become complete. Along with such decentralisation, the financial staff of the head office was sent to each division to report its performance to the top management. Following this reform, the division headquarters, which had increased to 17, were abolished in 1972, and 63 divisions were reorganised into 12 groups. The formation of division headquarters between the top management and operating divisions prevented a swift flow of information, and gave division headquarters a considerable degree of authority in practice, though they were expected to coordinate divisions. Authority was delegated further down to these 63 divisions. Such management decentralisation was believed to be highly necessary for fostering the next generation of leaders.

After 1974 the investment priorities were placed on expansion to overseas countries, and on the development of communication equipment. *Matsushita*'s overseas investment rose above £200 million in 1978, though investment in communication equipment did not increase as had been planned.[54] The multidivisional structure which was established in 1972 was to be re-examined in 1975. In face of the depression following 1974, the central staff sought a management system which could control divisions more efficiently, and therefore reorganised the divisions into several groups, which were supervised by senior managing directors. By these means *Matsushita* aimed at a production and marketing strategy, as well as fluent communication and regulation between divisions, swift decision-making, and the avoidance of duplicate investment among divisions. Three General Division Headquarters were set up in 1975. The Radio Communication General Division Headquarters was charged with 29 divisions. However this structure did not last long. When the president changed and the vice presidents resigned, the General Division Headquarters were abolished. Divisional autonomy was stressed for the fourth time, and *Matsushita* separated its production units as independent companies. As a result, 20 divisions were made full divisions with production and sales, while 20 others had only sales, and these distributed the products of the manufacturing subsidiaries.

Sharp[55] was the brand name given to the products of *Hayakawa Electric*, and also the name of its general sales company which was separated in 1956. After narrowly surviving the disorder of the post-war period, which greatly retarded the recovery of radio receiver producers, *Hayakawa Electric* developed into the production of television sets. After 1955 extensive investment was made in the household electrical equipment branch, particularly in refrigerator and washing machine factories.[56] *Hayakawa Electric* introduced the multidivisional structure in 1963, and then amalgamated *Sharp* in 1967. Soon after this consolidation, however, the company returned to the functional structure again. As for distribution and marketing, *Hayakawa Electric* separated its sales department, and made use of a sales company from 1956. This measure was taken in order to make relations with local wholesalers more efficient. The shares of radio, television set, audio equipment, and household electrical equipment in the total sales of *Hayakawa* had become roughly equal to each other by 1960. The multidivisional structure which was introduced in 1963 was composed of communication equipment, household electrical equipment, and industrial electrical machinery. The company itself was a single function firm, and built production divisions, while all the products of these divisions were handled by the sales company. In spite of these measures the performance of the company did not improve until the mid-1960s. In this divisional system, managing directors were separated from division managers.

After 1965 electronics branches grew rapidly and calculators, medical electronic equipment, and industrial electronics became the main products of the new division. A vast amount of capital was invested in the Electronic Division in the latter half of the 1960s. Against the recession of the mid-1960s, the company reinforced its sales function. In place of local wholesalers and agents, 54 local sales companies were set up, and 14 service and credit companies in 1965, and aimed at reorganising its distribution channels. In effect, *Hayakawa Electric* formed two levels of wholesale activities. One was *Sharp*, the general sales company, and the other consisted of local sales companies formed since 1965. The general sales company was consolidated into *Hayakawa Electric* in 1967, and the new company with full functions was named *Sharp*. At the same time the production division system gave way to the sales headquarters system. Divisions remained as production divisions, while their products were handled by a single Sales Headquarters. Furthermore in 1970, the Sales Headquarters was sub-divided into three headquarters by product. These sales headquarters undertook marketing for particular product lines. Until the mid-1960s the main product lines of the company were for consumer use, such as household electrical equipment, television sets and audio equipment. By 1970, however, electronics for industry use had increased in quantity, representing one third of its products, and these required different distribution channels from those of consumer products. Local sales companies were made to specialise in particular product lines, such as household electrical equipment or business machinery. Finally, these local sales companies were reorganised into nation-wide wholesale companies by products towards the end of the 1970s. As a background to this supermarkets and other mass-sales retailers unaffiliated with any electrical equipment manufacturers appeared, and their sales expanded rapidly. The local sales companies which were formed for local wholesalers could not effectively deal with the rising nation-wide mass retailers.

Sanyo (Sanyo) *Electric*[57] started in the production of generating apparatus for bicycle lamps, and quickly went into the production of radios and washing machines. The number of its product lines increased year by year, pushing the company into becoming a general weak-electrical company by 1960. Organisational change took place quite frequently. *Sanyo* was incorporated in 1950, although it retained the characteristics of a family concern. A formal organisation of a functional type was introduced in 1951 in which managing directors were appointed as heads of departments, and the multidivisional structure with a full line of functions and profit responsibility was adopted in 1961. However, this system moved towards the functional form in 1970, was fully divisionalised again in 1972, and was reorganised into the functional form in 1975.

Markets for *Sanyo*'s ever increasing product lines had to be developed and organised. At first *Matsushita Electric Industrial* undertook *Sanyo*'s sales functions, and the products were sold by electrical equipment shops. Iue, *Sanyo*'s founder, took over the sales function, visited bicycle retailers, from whom he acquired information regarding reliable wholesalers, then made contact with these wholesalers by inviting them to his factory and even to his home. As soon as distribution channels were formed in the western part of the country, he set up branch offices in Tokyo and Kyushu. When the company made inroads into radio production, and particularly after embarking on television set production, other distribution channels had to be added. Repair was the main work of traditional radio shops. *Sanyo* turned these into electrical equipment retailers. Towards the end of the 1950s competition in the household electrical market became intense, due to the entries of the heavy electrical companies. After setting up local branch offices, *Sanyo* had to ensure the effective control of the flow of their products from local agents to retailers. *Sanyo* began to organise retailers, and the number of its affiliated retailers became 4400 by the mid-1960s. Prior to this, the company completed the affiliation of local wholesalers, who became the sole sales agents for *Sanyo*'s products. Where they could not secure such agents, local sales companies were set up. There was also a labour dispute in *Sanyo*. These influenced the structural form of the company. *Tokyo Sanyo Electric* was set up as a separate company producing refrigerating equipment. To fill the financial needs of this new production unit, and to avoid the spread to it of labour disputes, and in order to adopt a different wage standard, setting up a separate company was an appropriate measure.

The divisionalisation of *Sanyo Electric* started in 1961. As the firm grew rapidly, its management became aware of the necessity of drawing on new ideas which originated from the bottom level of the hierarchies of the firm. The main problem in *Sanyo*'s transition to the multidivisional structure was in the lack of personnel capable of assuming positions as division managers. For a company like *Sanyo*, which in a decade had grown from a small workshop to an enterprise with ten thousand employees, it was impossible to cultivate division managers who could deal with research, manufacturing, sales and financing at the same time. To hire them from outside was not feasible either. The solution was to make the transition process gradual. The first division was set up in 1961, and other divisions were organised in the following year one by one. These were divisions with a full set of functions. Divisions were made profit centres, but the profit responsibility of each division was not rigorously required. The sales headquarters was reorganised into the marketing staff. Although a network of affiliated retailers had been formed, these retailers also handled the products of other electrical equipment companies, and as competition for affiliation became keen, some left *Sanyo*. *Sanyo* raised the standard of its affiliated retailers, and aimed at setting up 1000 retailers 80 per cent or more of whose sales consisted of *Sanyo* products. The number of such shops had become 7000 towards the late 1970s.

After the economic recession of 1965, which hit the household electrical equipment market most severely, *Sanyo* began to set up overseas subsidiaries, which were not only in charge of export and sales, but also of overseas production. Boom continued for five years, and the sales of the company increased by more than three times during the same period. Towards the late 1970s, however, the company was again confronted with difficulties, such as the dumping problem in the American market. The multidivisional structure was re-examined, and the sales and production functions in the division were separated from each other. The Production Division Headquarters was put in charge of technology and supplies of materials, and under this the Production Divisions were placed and made to specialise into particular product lines. In general this reorganisation was aimed at centralising leadership by maintaining the advantages of the divisional structure. This did not last long, for the company was not easily able to recover from the slump, and the multidivisional structure was again adopted. However, after its oil-crisis, the company simplified the organisation and separated manufacturing and sales for the third time. Three division headquarters were made to specialise in the production function, while the sales function was divided into two sales headquarters. The latters were not only expected to organise the local retailers, but to educate the employees of the local agents, to group them, and to organise joint advertisement.

Sony,[58] whose forerunner had been set up in 1946, engaged in the production of communication equipment and electro-magnetic appliances since its inception, and also came to enter the production of tape recorders and radio receivers. From its creation, *Sony* aimed at competition in the world market, which it participated in from the mid-1950s. By 1965, more than half of its sales were due to exports, especially to North American and other developed countries. For this purpose financial resources were allocated to research and development, reaching 4 per cent of its total sales by 1965.[59] Overseas investment was also commenced early in *Sony*'s development. *Sony* had developed high quality household electrical equipment even prior to the maturing of the domestic market. Contrary to traditional practice which utilised general trading companies for export, the company chose direct export through its own sales organisation abroad. In the US, for instance, a sales company was set up, and its trading offices wholesaled *Sony*'s products. Where *Sony* had no such trading offices, sales agents were appointed.

The company did not set up a formal organisational structure for a long time, even though it was, by 1965 a large company with more than 6000 employees. *Sony*'s vice-president pronounced that a formal hierarchical structure with limited areas of command and responsibility was not appropriate to the Japanese labour market and business, based on his experiences during an overseas assignment. The main problem was in middle-level management. *Sony* had to keep this level mobile to promote innovation. If a new task appeared, several persons should take charge in rotation. In practice, however, differentiation of managerial tasks arose, and functional departments such as sales, overseas sales, and production appeared during the 1960s. Just after such an explanation by its vice-president was repeated, the company adopted the divisional structure in 1970, which was further expanded into the division headquarters structure in the 1970s.

Victor Company of Japan[60] was founded in 1922 as a subsidiary of *U.S. Victor* to supply audio equipment for the Japanese market. When the latter was acquired by *R C A*, *Mitsubishi* and *Sumitomo* took part in the management of the Japanese *Victor*. In 1950 half of *Victor*'s total sales consisted of records, and the other half of radio receivers and record players. Divisionalisation started during the 1960s and proceeded gradually; the main product lines were first divisionalised and then in the late 1960s the whole company.

Unlike the other electrical equipment companies, *Victor* was slow to recover after the war, and finally *Matsushita Electric Industrial* was invited to reconstruct its management. The programme of reconstruction by *Matsushita* was a unique one. Instead of excessive dependence on records, radio receivers and record players were set as new areas of development, and these were to compete with *Matsushita*'s product lines. *Victor* was not acquired by *Matsushita*, nor did the former become a mere subcontracting company for the latter. In fact *Matsushita* got a rival company among its group members. The main product lines in *Victor*'s five-year plans were television receivers in the second half of the 1950s and stereo sets in the first half of the 1960s. These plans were successfully carried out. For outlets for their products, *Victor* adopted a set of distribution channels different from other electrical equipment companies. Instead of using local agents or setting up local sales companies, the firm completely integrated the wholesale function internally, and built up an organisation of their own local trading offices. These trading offices sold their products to retailers. When service and credit requirements grew large, these were moved to separate companies.

The introduction of the divisional structure had been discussed since 1963, and was gradually implemented. Record interests had actually been divisionalised. The Stereo Production Department integrated the sales function, and in 1964 the television set branch, also fast-growing, was divisionalised. Thus the production system by product lines was clarified, and these product divisions acquired sales function in order to develop marketing most effectively. By 1966 all the other product lines were divisionalised. The number of divisions continued to increase, and these were made profit centres in 1967. *Victor*'s divisionalisation began in the main product lines and then spread to the whole company. Managing directors were separated from the responsibilities of division managers. After the adoption of the divisional structure, the coordination of the flow of products was still a classical form. Divisions had their own local trading offices, whose number increased rapidly in the 1960s, and came to be enough to cover the whole country, and their products were distributed through divisions through their local trading offices to the retailers. But when the division headquarters structure was adopted in 1969, managing directors assumed the posts of the division headquarters managers.

A series of organisational reforms into the divisional structure, however, lost their bases in the early 1970s. Profits and sales declined for three years successively. Under such conditions the company was forced to separate its record branch. Though this branch had been the most profitable business of the company, the planning, manufacturing, and marketing technique of records differed completely from those of electrical equipment, and owing to the development of small-scale records printers, a more flexible system had become necessary. The record industry was also changing into a leisure industry. Except for the production function, *Victor*'s record interests were separated. The reconstruction of the firm was carried out by the company's new president who had been sent from *Matsushita Electric Industrial*. Although no special organisational reform was taken place this time, measures were taken in its practical operation. The autonomy of divisions was expanded. The sales and marketing functions were reinforced: division staff and factory engineers were sent to sales offices in order to experience practical marketing, and the sales headquarters was made a general staff department. Finally, the trading offices were separated into local sales companies the same as in other electrical equipment companies. By 1976, 23 of *Victor*'s 114 sales offices were reorganised into separate companies. The company tried to increase the number of its affiliated shops, which were relatively few compared with those of other electrical equipment companies. The number of these affiliated retailers, at least 50 per cent of whose sales consisted of *Victor* products, was only 400 in 1974, but it was planned to increase this number to 1500 by 1980. On the other hand, *Victor* had a relatively high ratio of mass-sales retailers. More than 40 per cent of their products were sold by these types of retailers. The reorganisation of distribution channels after the mid-1970s, therefore, seemed to go against the general trends in the outlets. These measures improved the financial position of the firm, though the growth rates of all its product lines were still slow.

Nippon Gakki[61] is engaged in the production of furniture, woodwork, and motorcycles in addition to various kinds of musical instruments. Musical instruments had long been manufactured for school use in Japan. *Nippon Gakki*, under the brand name of *Yamaha*, developed a new market for home use musical instruments. For the development of new outlets, the firm set up music classes, in which a substantial amount of financial resources were allocated from the second half of the 1950s, and these classes contributed to creating new demand for musical instruments, particularly for pianos and electric organs. After 1955, the company developed rapidly, with a 30 per cent annual growth rate. The products of the company were distributed through an organisation of special agents, which had been created by the mid-1960s. Six hundred such agents accounted for three quarters of Yamaha piano and organ sales, while the remaining quarter were made directly through its own branch shops. This is in contrast with the case of its rival *Kawai Musical Inst.*, in which 70 per cent of piano sales came from directly managed shops. In both cases, though manufacturing companies more or less operated their own retail shops, *Nippon Gakki* utilised fewer directly managed shops for retailing. This was simply because leading musical instrument shops had already become special agents of *Nippon Gakki*, when *Kawai* started. *Nippon Gakki* coordinated the flow of products to retailers through its eight local offices. The motorcycle interest of the firm was soon moved to a separate manufacturing company, but their products, together with imported musical instruments and records, were sold by the branch offices and showrooms of *Nippon Gakki*. These activities including those of subsidiaries were controlled by a typical functional structure.

By the mid-1960s, the firm had thoroughly mechanised piano production process replacing traditional hand-manufacture. The principle of mass-production was introduced to all manufacturing processes, and processes from woodworking to piano tuning were integrated. New factories based on these methods were set up in the first half of the 1960s. These changes were to make *Nippon Gakki* the world's largest piano manufacturer. Use was not made of trading companies in exporting, instead *Nippon Gakki* chose to export directly to overseas dealers. For this purpose *Nippon Gakki* set up overseas sales companies and developed its own distribution channels among the dealers abroad. An analysis of annual reports, however, does not reveal a resulting drastic increase of capital investment during the period.[62]

In the latter half of the 1960s, when its share of the piano market had reached 70 per cent, the company developed new demand in electronic organs in the domestic market, and in pianos overseas. Diversification into various leisure industries brought about the multidivisional structure in 1973.

To curb its monopolistic position as a piano producer *Nippon Gakki* promoted diversification and overseas expansion in the latter half of the 1970s. Overseas investment, especially in motorcycle production amounted to a substantial sum. In order to control these diversifying branches, the multidivisional structure was abolished in 1978. In its place, a functional headquarters system was founded, bringing the advantages of management decentralisation. The company president concurrently took the position of the sales manager, and the company's organisational structure was simplified.

K. Hattori,[63] the world-famous watch-maker for its brand name *Seiko*, was utterly unknown until the mid-1960s. It had acquired excellent technical skills from foreign products by the end of the war. The rationalisation of production processes, namely, the full integration of all the processes of watchmaking into one factory, was undertaken after the war. A strong sales organisation was also formed during the same period, and it consisted of 100 wholesalers and 4600 retailers in the domestic market in the early 1960s. These increased by sales 20 times during the fifteen years from 1950, but the company's fame was still limited to within the domestic market. This family-owned enterprise was structured as a hierarchy of holding companies. In production, two subsidiaries were engaged in watch making, while *Hattori*'s own factory-made clocks. As sales from the clock branch accounted for only 15 per cent of all sales between 1950 and 1965, *Hattori* was dependent on its two subsidiaries for a major part of its production. *Hattori*, on the other hand, was engaged mainly in planning and sales, and controlled the *Seiko* group, and therefore the task of *Hattori* resembled that of the head office of a holding company. However, all of the shares in the two subsidiaries and 40 per cent of those in *Hattori* were held by two holding companies, whose shares in turn, were held by the members of the founder's family.

Hattori's export ratio, around 10 per cent of its total sales in the early 1960s, began to rise rapidly after 1965. This development was initiated by the Tokyo Olympic Games, but a large amount of research and development expenditure was necessary to gain international competitive power. The two production companies began to accumulate their own technical skills and initiative in planning and research began to shift to the production subsidiaries, which had no direct relationships with the markets. In some areas, competition and overlapping investment between the production units began. Although there was little of a technological relationship between the principles of the various watch mechanisms, such as quartz or mechanical, and digital or analogue, the *Seiko* group could boast of their excellence in all of these areas. *Hattori* moved to tighten the control of sales activities. From among the wholesalers, 50 leading firms were chosen as special agents, who were requested by *Hattori* to buy their products, and who in turn requested *their* retailers to buy these goods. The number of these retailers had become 23 000 by 1970.

Hattori set up or made contracts with one sole-sales agents for each overseas country. Throughout the three post-war decades, the top management of *Hattori* was elected from the founder's family, while the executives of the production companies were promoted from employees within these companies. When *Seikosha*, the clock-making department of *Hattori*, was separated into a legally independent unit, *Hattori* became a sales company of the *Seiko* group.

Technological innovations in watch making resulted in a new situation in the company's management. Control over the manufacturing subsidiaries of the *Seiko* group became weaker as these subsidiaries accumulated their own technical skills. To restore more efficient coordination, *Hattori* sent executives to its subsidiaries and tried to curb decentralising elements found among subsidiaries engineers. Outside the company, technological innovations also brought about new competition in price and in the production process. The market share of *Seiko* brand products declined throughout the 1970s, partly due to the appearance of extra-cheap digital watches made by a calculating machinery companies and partly due to the rise of foreign companies. *Hattori* made inroads into the low-priced goods under a different brand name.

8.6 SUMMARY

Companies in food, oil, automobiles, and other durable consumer goods appeared in the post-war period, and grew rapidly after 1960. All supplied finished consumer goods which were completely new to the Japanese market. As various types of demand grew all at once in a limited period, it became both necessary and possible to produce on a mass production basis, and to supply standardised products to relatively standardised markets. At the same time, these industries required a relatively high level of technical skills, and in some of them the supply of raw materials or parts and components were difficult problems. To coordinate and control the flow of goods and money through the long course from raw materials to final consumers was a major cause of complicated administrative problems. It was also necessary to build up distribution channel for their products. The solution of these companies was not the downward integration to wholesales and the formation of the typical functionally departmentalised structures. Although some of these companies followed this orthodox lines, as in the cases of *Honda* and *Victor*, most others either set up or reorganised local wholesalers as their sales companies, and further affiliated retailers.

There were two ways of coordinating the flow of products to the consumers. One was through the functional structure. In practice, however, the managerial hierarchies of these companies tended to develop into the direct line structure particularly on the production side. A huge amount of assets and a large number of employees were concentrated on a relatively few number of their factories, while wholesale operating activities were carried out by local sales companies. Senior members of the board were appointed to factories, and were made directly responsible to the president.

In another form, the companies were more or less specialised in one of the major functions of production or sales, while another function was carried out by subsidiaries or their parents. *Nippon Oil* and *K. Hattori* are the examples of such companies, which tended to specialise into sales activities. *Toyota Motor* and *Toa Nenryo* went other way. They were basically single function companies in form, in that their sales function was carried out by their general sales companies. The general sales company coordinated the flow of goods from its manufacturing partner to the retailers. But such an organisational form seems to have been related to the nature of their products rather than to the low diversity of these firms.

NOTES

1. *The Fifty Year History of Nippon Suisan*, 1961; *The Seventy Year History of Nippon Suisan*, 1981; Japan Productivity Center (ed.), 'Nippon Suisan', *Choki keieikeikaku* (Long-Range Management Planning), 1961, pp. 66–72; 'Nippon Suisan', *Tk*, 6.2.1965, pp. 98–100; see also ibid., 22.9.1973, pp. 118–19; 11.12.1976, pp. 90–93; 'Nippon Suisan', *Ec*, 24.12.1974, pp. 90–91; *Nks*, 14.9.1960, 2.12.1963, 3.8.1964.
2. *Reports to the Minister of Finance*, 1965–73.
3. *The Eighty Year History of Taiyo Fishery*, 1960; Shigeru Yamamoto, 'Taiyo Fishery', in *Kigyoho Kenkyu* (Studies in Business Law), June 1963, pp. 29–35; Kazuo Noda, 'Taiyo Fishery', *Ec*, 30.4.1963, pp. 76–80; 'Taiyo Fishery', *Tk*, 14.4.1973, pp. 106–7; see also ibid., 23.3.1974, pp. 78–82; 15.10.1977, pp. 98–9; *Nks*, 18.3.1963, 25.3.1967, 12.10.1969, 16.7.1971.
4. *The Twenty-Five Year History of Nippon Reizo*, 1973; 'Nippon Reizo versus Ajinomoto', *Ck*, vol. 12, no. 3, 1973, pp. 210–15.
5. *The History of Nisshin Flour Milling*, 1955; *The Seventy Year History of Nisshin Flour Milling*, 1970; *The Progress of these Ten Years*, 1980;

'Nisshin Flour Milling', *Ec*, 21.3.1978, p. 98; 'Nisshin Flour Milling', *Ck*, vol. 18, no. 2, pp. 221–25; *Nks*, 30.3.1964.

6. *The History of Ajinomoto*, vols I(1971), II(1972); Tetsuo Kono, 'Matrix System of Central Research Institute', in *Sozo ni chosen suru soshikika-kushin* (Organisational Innovation Aiming at Creativeness), ed. Kigyo kenkyu kai, 1981, pp. 105–11; Naomasa Mizoguchi, 'Monitoring of Activity in Research and Development Department', in *Kenkyu kaihatsu hyoka jissen shiryoshu* (Practical Materials for Monitoring Research and Development), ed. Kigyo kenkyu kai (Business Study Society), 1982, pp. 221–46; Nihon keieiseisaku gakkai (Japan Society of Business Policy) (ed.), *Keiei shiryoshu taisei* (Collected Materials of Business Adminis-tration), vol. II 1967, pp. 180–218; Kazuo Noda, 'Ajinomoto', *Ec*, 7.5.1963, pp. 72–6; 'Ajinomoto', *Tk*, 10.11.1956, pp. 72–3; see also ibid., 28.1.1961, p. 83; 17.10.1964, pp. 78–81; 9.1.1971, pp. 125–6; 28.12.1974, pp. 122–3; 25.10.1975, pp. 96–101; 2.11.1978, pp. 69–71; 26.1.1980, pp. 102–6; 'Nihon Reizo Versus Ajinomoto', *Ck*, vol. 12, no. 3, 1973, pp. 210–15; 'Seventy Years in Search of Tastes', *Ck*, vol. 17, no. 3, 1978, pp. 77–81; 'Ajinomoto', *Tg*, Jan. 1977, p. 22; see also ibid., Apr. 1980, p. 13; *Nks*, 24.2.1964.

7. *Reports to the Minister of Finance*, 1955–64.

8. *The Fifty Year History of Meiji Milk Products*, 1969; *The Sixty Year History of Meiji Milk Products*, 1977; 'Meiji Milk Products', *Tk*, 21.7.1962, pp. 46–8; see also ibid., 22.7.1972, pp. 100–1; *Nks*, 24.3.1975.

9. *Reports to the Minister of Finance*, 1965–73. Its share in the total fresh milk production was approximately 23 per cent between 1960 and 1965.

10. *The History of Snow Brand Milk Products* vols I and II(1961), III(1966), IV(1975); Kyotaro Tsujioka, 'Snow Brand Milk Products', in *Kindaiteki keieisoshiki no jitsurei* (Cases of Modern Management Organisation), ed. Susumu Takamiya, 1953, pp. 147–205; Y. Daikichi, 'Open Distri-bution Channel Policy of Snow Brand Milk Products' in *Ryutsu Mondai* (Problems of Distribution) ed. by G. Fukami, 1967; 'Snow Brand Milk Products', *Tk*, 21.1.1978, pp. 95–9; see also ibid., 18.10.1980, pp. 88–90; *Nks*, 30.12.1963, 19.3.1980.

11. *The Fifty Year History of Morinaga Milk Industry*, 1967; 'Morinaga Milk Industry', *Tk*, 12.10.1974, pp. 88–9; see also ibid., 3.7.1976, pp. 98–100; *Nks*, 14.6.1965, 26.10.1967.

12. *Reports to the Minister of Finance*, 1955–64.

13. See also ibid., 1960–64.

14. 'Sapporo Breweries', *Ma*, Sep. 1965, pp. 47–50; *Nks*, 26.3.1963, 27.3.1963, 28.7.1966, 14.8.1966, 26.8.1971.

15. *Reports to the Minister of Finance*, 1965–73.

16. Ibid., 1974–80.

17. Kikuo Yonekura, 'Asahi Breweries', in *Kindaiteki keieisoshiki no jitsurei* (Cases of Modern Management Organisation), ed. Susumu Takamiya, 1953, pp. 225–30; 'Asahi Breweries', *Tk*, 20.2.1971, pp. 76–9; *Nks*, 11.7.1972.

18. *Reports to the Minister of Finance*, 1955–65.

19. *The History of Kirin Brewery*, 1969; *The History of Kirin Brewery: A Sequel*, 1985; Tadao Konishi and Kaizo Hashimoto, 'Beer: Japanese

Industrial Organisation (16)', *Ck*, vol. 12, no. 46, 1973, pp. 390–436; 'Kirin Brewery', *Tk*, 25.3.1967, pp. 70–77; see also ibid., 20.7.1974, pp. 86–9; 21.5.1977, pp. 84–9; 'Kirin Brewery', *Ec*, 15.6.1976, pp. 94–5; Yoshio Hatakeyama, *Ma*, Mar. 1978, pp. 57–64; *Nks*, 29.4.1963, 23.4.1975, 12.1.1979.

20. *Reports to the Minister of Finance*, 1960–71.
21. Ibid., 1965–73.
22. *The Eighty Year History of Nippon Oil*, 1967; Japan Productivity Center (ed.), 'Nippon Oil', *Choki keieikeikaku* (Long-Range Management Planning), 1961, pp. 242–53; *do.*, 'The Case of Nippon Oil', *Sengo keieishi* (Postwar Business History), 1965, pp. 771–4; Kimi Ishikawa, 'Organisation and Management Planning', *Kj* Jan. 1960, pp. 27–32; 'Nippon Oil', *Tk*, 8.5.1971, pp. 82–5; see also ibid., 13.10.1973, pp. 96–7; 'Nippon Oil', *Ec*, 9.4.1963, pp. 68–72; 'Nippon Oil', *Kik*, Jan. 1965, pp. 144–8; *Nks*, 31.7.1957, 25.2.1963, 1.8.1963.
23. *The Thirty Year History of Nippon Oil Refining*, 1982.
24. *The Thirty Year History of Showa Oil*, 1974; 'Merger with Shell?', *Nu*, Jan. 1967, pp. 29–38; 'Showa Oil', *Tk*, 26.12.1964, pp. 158–9; *Nks*, 6.1.1966.
25. *Reports to the Minister of Finance*, 1950–64.
26. Ibid., 1974–80.
27. *The Thirty Year History of Toa Nenryo Kogyo*, vols I, II, 1971; *The History of Toa Nenryo Kogyo 1969–74*, 1974; *The History of Toa Nenryo Kogyo 1974–79*, 1979; 'Toa Nenryo Kogyo', *Tk*, 26.3.1977, pp. 97–100; *Nks*, 16.11.1964.
28. *The Fifty Year History of Mitsubishi Oil*, 1981; Susumu Takamiya (ed.), 'Mitsubishi Oil', *Kaisha soshiki* (Company Organisation), 1959, pp. 69–91; 'Mitsubishi Oil', *Tk*, 18.1.1975, pp. 86–7; *Nks*, 14.8.1958, 11.11.1963.
29. *The Thirty-Five Year History*, 1968; 'Maruzen Oil', *Kh*, Mar. 1963, pp. 76–84; 'Idemitsu Oil and Maruzen Oil', *Ec*, 22.1.1963, pp. 28–32; *Nks*, 1.6.1963.
30. *Reports to the Minister of Finance*, 1965–73.
31. *The Thirty Year History*, 1969; *The Forty Year History of Daikyo Oil*, 1980; 'Daikyo Oil', *Tk*, 6.9.1980, pp. 102–5.
32. *The Fifty Year History*, 1970; *The Fifty Year History*, Part II, 1981; T. Kato, 'Direct Sales Policy of Idemitsu' in ed. Fukami, *op. cit.*; 'Idemitsu Oil', *Tk*, 17.3.1962, pp. 42–3; see also ibid., 14.8.1976, pp. 112–16; 'Idemitsu Oil', *Ec*, 2.4.1963, pp. 78–83; *Nks*, 9.3.1962, 20.5.1963.
33. *The Twenty Year History*, 1958; *The Thirty Year History of Toyota Motor*, 1967; *The History of Toyota Motor*, 1978; *Motorizeishon to tomoni* (A History of Toyota Motor Sales, 1950–70), 2 vols, 1970; *Sekai heno ayumi*, (The Thirty Year History of Toyota Motor Sales), 2 Vols, 1980; Koichi Shimokawa, 'Outsiders of the Japan Company Limited' in *Nihon keieishi koza* (Japanese Business History) v, 1976; Kazuo Wada, 'The Formation of "Vertically Semi-integrated Structure"', *Academia*, no. 83, 1984, pp. 61–98; Fukashi Ichikawa, 'Toyota Motor', *Kh*, Oct. 1968, pp. 132–43; 'Toyota Motor', *Tk*, 9.1.1965, pp. 174–6; see also ibid., 6.8.1966, pp. 56–63; 1.8.1970, pp. 66–71; 14.4.1973, pp. 94–8;

21.6.1975, pp. 84–7; 11.9.1976, pp. 76–87; 24.12.1977, pp. 134–8; 7.10.1978, pp. 82–7; 7.4.1979, pp. 116–19; 22.12.1979, pp. 124–8; 19.7.1980, pp. 14–17; 27.1.1980, pp. 138–43; Masatoshi Tsuruta, 'Toyota Motor: Studies in the Modern Japanese Capitalism (67–9)', *Ec*, 17.6.1980, 24.6.1980, 1.7.1980; *Nks*, 29.3.1959, 15.2.1960, 25.3.1963, 24.2.1964.

34. *The Forty Year History of Hino Motors*, 1982; *The Thirty Year History of Hino Motor Sales*, 1978; Yoshiaki Miwa, 'Hino Motors', *Ma*, Jun. 1966, pp. 65–9; 'Hino Motors', *Tk*, 11.11.1978, pp. 98–101; *Nks*, 1.7.1964.

35. *The Sixty Year History*, 1967; 'Daihatsu Kogyo', *Tk*, 14.12.1974, pp. 86–7; see also ibid., 11.12.1976, pp. 100–01; 4.8.1979, pp. 114–16; 'Daihatsu Kogyo', *Ma*, Oct. 1980, pp. 69–73.

36. *Reports to the Minister of Finance*, 1964–73.

37. *The Thirty Year History of Nissan Motor*, 1965; *The History of Nissan Motor, 1964–73*, 1975; *The History of Nissan Motor, 1974–83*, 1985; *The Road to the Twenty-First Century: The Fifty Year History of Nissan Motor*, 1983; Kigyo kenkyu kai (Business Study Society) (ed.), 'Strategy for Internationalisation and its Promotion Structure', in *Sozo ni chosensuru soshikikakushin* (Organisational Innovation Aiming at Creativeness), 1981, pp. 230–39; Masao Hachiya, 'Nissan's Offense by Merger', *Ck*, vol. 4, no. 12, 1965, pp. 128–36; *Ck*, vol. 4, no. 12, 1965, pp. 128–36; 'Nissan Motor', *Kh*, Oct. 1964, pp. 109–17; 'Nissan Motor', *Tk*, 12.9.1970, pp. 52–6; see also ibid., 18.11.1972, pp. 86–90; 19.5.1973, pp. 90–91; 2.11.1978, pp. 96–103; 2.12.1978, pp. 80–84; 1.3.1980, pp. 76–9; 13.12.1980, pp. 14–16; 'Witness to the Postwar Industrial History XLII – XLIII', *Ec*, 19.10.1976, 26.10.1976; 'Tie-up between Nissan and VW', *Ec*, 23.12.1980, pp. 10–18; 'Nissan Motor', *Tg*, Jan. 1977, p. 13; *Nks*, 29.5.1955, 4.12.1959, 28.3.1960, 25.3.1963, 13.5.1963, 8.1.1965; *Nss*, 14.1.1981.

38. *Reports to the Minister of Finance*, 1960, 1970.

39. *The Thirty Year History of Fuji Heavy Industries*, 1984; 'Fuji Heavy Industries', *Tk*, 7.11.1964, pp. 72–3; see also ibid., 24.7.1965, pp. 82–3; 2.11.1968, pp. 54–5; 28.10.1978, pp. 102–03, 'Fuji Heavy Industries', *Ma*, Nov. 1980, pp. 74–80; *Nks*, 1.2.1953, 8.7.1954, 1.4.1955, 4.5.1959.

40. *The Thirty Year History of Nissan Shatai*, 1982.

41. *Reports to the Minister of Finance*, 1955–64.

42. 'Nissan Diesel Motor', *Tk*, 19.10.1968, pp. 102–03; *Nks*, 29.11.1960.

43. *Reports to the Minister of Finance*, 1955–64.

44. *The History of Isuzu Motors*, 1957; *Kuruma to tomoni hanseiki* (A half Century with Automobile), 1979; *Zoku kuruma to tomoni hanseiki* (A half Century with Automobile: A sequel), vol. I, vol. II, 1981; 'Isuzu Motors', *Tk*, 28.11.1970, pp. 22–3; see also ibid., 26.7.1975, pp. 92–4; 13.3.1976, pp. 80–84; 31.7.1976, pp. 90–92; 4.3.1978, pp. 110–14; 19.5.1979, pp. 82–5; 21.6.1980, pp. 126–8; 'Isuzu Motors', *Ck*, vol. 19, no. 77, pp. 116–18; *Nks*, 30.9.1963, 4.7.1971, 12.7.1971, 16.7.1971, 26.8.1971, 1.1.1978.

45. *Reports to the Minister of Finance*, 1955–64.

46. *The Fifty Year History of Toyo Kogyo*, 1972; 'Toyo Kogyo', *Tk*, 3.4.1965, pp. 97–101; see also ibid., 10.9.1966, pp. 102–05; 28.11.1970,

pp. 16–20; 25.3.1972, pp. 38–40; 8.7.1972, pp. 94–5; 3.2.1973, pp. 90–94; 26.1.1974, pp. 68–72; 9.11.1974, pp. 76–80; 14.2.1976, pp. 20–29; 12.11.1977, pp. 36–42; 14.1.1978, pp. 160–63; 2.6.1979, pp. 16–19; 'Toyo Kogyo', *Za*, 1.8.1978, pp. 32–39; see also ibid., 19.6.1979, pp. 18–24; 'Toyo Kogyo', *Ec*, 12.6.1979, pp. 50–53; Kazuhiko Hayashibara, 'Toyo Kogyo', *Ma*, Aug. 1976, Dec. 1977; 'Toyo Kogyo', *Ck*, vol. 19, no. 77, pp. 118–19; *Nks*, 9.2.1964, 11.1.1970, 4.7.1971, 8.10.1978, 14.3.1979, 12.7.1979, 25.10.1979, 3.11.1979, 31.10.1980, 12.11.1980.

47. *The History of Honda Motor*, 1975; Shimokawa, *loc. cit.*; Keizai Doyu-kai (Japan Committee for Economic Development) (ed.), 'Reorganis-ation of the Top Management into Functional Groups', *1980 nendaino Kigyokeiei* (Business Enterprise in the 1980s), 1980, pp. 203–13; 'Honda Motor', *Tk*, 21.11.1968, pp. 130–32; see also ibid., 1.4.1972, pp. 68–72; 28.12.1974, pp. 118–19; 15.8.1976, pp. 129–30; 30.4.1977, pp. 82–5; 5.8.1978, pp. 92–3; 2.11.1978, pp. 53–5; 26.5.1979, pp. 126–30; 'Honda Motor', *Kh*, Feb. 1963, pp. 76–85; *Nks*, 23.9.1960, 29.7.1963, 11.4.1964, 31.10.1977.

48. *Fifty Year History*, 1970; 'Suzuki Motor', *Tk*, 5.5.1973, pp. 106–07; see also ibid., 14.12.1974, pp. 83–5; 18.10.1975, pp. 102–05; 9.6.1979, pp. 88–9; 'Suzuki Motor', *Za*, 2.10.1979, pp. 113–16; Yoshiro Ikari, 'Suzuki Motor', *Ma*, July 1980, pp. 91–96.

49. *The Twenty-Five Year History of Fuji Photo Film*, 1960; Japan Pro-ductivity Center (ed.), 'Fuji Photo Film', *Choki keieikeikaku, op. cit.*, pp. 228–33, pp. 540–41; 'Fuji Photo Film', *Tk*, 4.6.1977, pp. 82–6; see also ibid., 21.8.1971, pp. 76–9; 3.7.1976, pp. 97–8; 'Fuji Photo Film', *Ec*, 24.6.1975; *Nks*, 15.6.1956.

50. *Reports to the Minister of Finance*, 1965–73.

51. *The Hundred Year History of Shiseido*, 1972; Kazuo Noda, 'Shiseido', *Ec*, 12.11.1963, pp. 72–6; Teruo Hanaoka, 'Shiseido', *Ks*, July 1966, pp. 66–7; Yoshihiro Tajima, 'Shiseido', *Ck*, vol. 3, no. 4, 1964, pp. 284–9; 'Shiseido', *Tk*, 5.8.1967, pp. 52–9; *Nks*, 1.2.1965, 30.9.1974; *Nss*, 14.1.1981.

52. *The Fifty Year Brief History of Matsushita Electric Industrial*, 1968; Yasuo Okamoto, *Hitachi to Matsushita* vols I, II, 1979; Hiroshi Omori, 'Historical Inquiry into Multidivisional Structure: the Case of Mat-sushita', in *Kigyosha katsudo no kokusaihikaku* (International Compari-son of Entrepreneurship), 1973, pp. 189–217; Japan Productivity Center (ed.), 'Matsushita Electric Industrial', *Choki keieikeikaku, op. cit.*, pp. 334–7; Junichi Yamamoto, 'Business Ideology and Policy of Matsushita; the Expert in Sales', *Kik*, July 1964, pp. 114–22; Shozo Amibuchi, 'The Aims of "New Organisational Structure" of Matsushita and Nippon Gakki', *Ma*, Apr. 1978, pp. 65–68; 'Matsushita Electric Industrial', *Kj*, Jan. 1956, pp. 115–18; 'Matsushita Electric Industrial', *Mg*, Aug. 1963, pp. 10–14; 'Matsushita Electric Industrial', *Tk*, 9.1.1965, pp. 168–70; see also ibid., 25.7.1970, pp. 60–65; 12.5.1973, pp. 86–94; *Nks*, 8.7.1963, 22.2.1964, 24.2.1964, 30.11.1964, 8.4.1968, 8.1.1970, 15.12.1972, 19.1.1975, 18.1.1978, 11.1.1979.

53. *Reports to the Minister of Finance*, 1965–73.

54. Ibid., 1974–80.

55. *The Fifty Years of Hayakawa Electric*, 1962; 'Hayakawa Electric', *Tk*, 9.5.1959, pp. 51–53; see also ibid., 20.2.1964, p. 62; 'Sharp', *Tk*, 26.2.1972, pp. 87–8; see also ibid., 4.9.1766, pp. 97–8; 26.8.1978, pp. 84–7, *Nks*, 4.4.1967, 6.1.1970, 2.12.1980, 8.1.1981.

56. *Reports to the Minister of Finance*, 1955–64.

57. *The Thirty Year History of Sanyo Electric*, 1980; 'Sanyo Electric'. *Kik*, Nov. 1969, pp. 53–8; 'Sanyo Electric', *Tk*, 20.3.1971, pp. 84–7; see also ibid., 23.6.1973, pp. 90–94; 28.5.1977, pp. 104–08; *Nks*, 23.9.1963, 10.1.1970, 31.1.1975.

58. Yasuo Okamoto, 'Dynamism of Management Structure', *Ck*, vol. 7, no. 3, 1968, pp. 192–203; Kazuo Noda, 'Sony', *Ec*, 11.6.1963, pp. 72–6; Yasunobu Otori, 'The Original Management Method of Sony', *Ec*, 30.7.1968, pp. 64–8; 'Sony', *Tk*, 20.6.1970, pp. 73–6; see also ibid., 25.12.1971, pp. 103–04; 26.8.1972, pp. 92–5; 26.8.1972, pp. 90–93; *Nks*, 15.6.1964, 13.1.1965, 27.2.1973, 28.2.1973; *Nss*, 14.9.1979.

59. *Reports to the Minister of Finance*, 1960–65.

60. *The Fifty Year History of Victor Company of Japan*, 1977; 'Victor Company of Japan', 20.5.1972, pp. 78–9; *Nks*, 28.2.1953, 8.2.1964.

61. *The History of Nippon Gakki*, 1977; 'Nippon Gakki', *Tk*, 17.2.1962, pp. 54–5; see also ibid., 27.2.1971, pp. 90–93; 13.11.1975, pp. 53–5; 25.6.1977, pp. 116–20; 15.3.1980, pp. 92–5; 14.6.1980, pp. 70–73; Shozo Amibuchi, 'The Aims of "New Organisational Structure" of Matsushita and Nippon Gakki', *Ma*, Apr. 1978, pp. 65–72; 'Nippon Gakki', *Ec*, 8.4.1975, pp. 98–9; *Nks*, 17.2.1964.

62. *Reports to the Minister of Finance*, 1955–64.

63. *A Chronology of Watches and Clocks*, 1973; 'K. Hattori', *Tk*, 6.10.1973, pp. 78–9; see also ibid., 28.5.1977, pp. 94–8; 2.11.1978, pp. 56–8; 30.8.1980, pp. 112–15; 'K. Hattori', *Will*, Dec. 1982, pp. 64–7; *Nks*, 4.5.1964, 9.1.1965, 13.11.1970.

9 Management Resources and their Development

9.1 THE DEVELOPMENT OF MANAGEMENT STRUCTURES IN JAPANESE INDUSTRIAL COMPANIES

This book has examined the development of managerial hierarchies of large-scale Japanese firms. We started with a hypothesis that a firm is formed when the market or other forms of outside transactions is substituted by an internal allocation of resources. A firm can develop through the internalisation of one kind of resource such as labour, capital, and the flow of goods.

The organisational structure of a firm is determined by the kind of resources which the firm has initially internalised. Two basic organisational forms, known as the functionally departmentalised structure and the multidivisional structure, for instance, can be regarded as organisations built upon the internalised flow of goods. This book has examined the management structures of major Japanese firms in their relation to kinds of management resources.

The emergence of multiunit firms in Japan was accompanied by the internalisation of the transactions of human resources. In the classical discussion by Coase, a firm appears by internalising the transactions of labour, and this is explained by the peculiar nature of human resources.[1] However, our argument is not necessarily based on the peculiar nature of human resources. There was no labour market in Japan which supplied various necessary skills to newly introduced industrial branches. Although the transactions of labour naturally lead to a long term employment, the internalisation of the transactions of labour in Japanese firms proceeded not because of such nature of human resources. Unless the employment system was formed in a manner which stimulated long term transactions of labour and the internalisation of skilled workers, a firm could not maintain its existence. Furthermore, not merely the length of services but the increasing initiative of firms in employment became predominant in the pre-war Japanese large-scale firms. In Japan, the internal labour market, characterised by inside promotion, life-time employment, and a wage system based on the length of services, emerged in the formation period of modern large-scale firms. This internalisation of labour was different from the introduction of the scientific management which also related to the managerial control of workers. Although such rationalisation of the shop floor was attempted in the 1920s, its full introduction had to wait until the 1950s. And unlike scientific management the internalisation of labour in Japanese firms found in the early twentieth century could not be solved on the shop floor level.

The internal hierarchies of firms developed for the purpose of controlling such human resources, particularly on the shop floor level. Those companies which internalised the transactions of labour adopted the line structure, and their managerial hierarchies appeared to be simple. Each operating unit was directly controlled by the highest level managers of the firm. In practice however, the number of ranks in the hierarchies increased, and the hierarchies became more complicated. Incentive systems such as promotion according to the length of service, were adopted, making the hierarchical ladder at the shop floor level more complicated. Ranks did not correspond with the line of authority, or each job.

There is no sufficient ground to suppose that Japanese firms were mainly built on internalised labour because their American counterparts were built on the internalised flow of goods and the European firms, on internalised financial resources. There may be many other industrialising countries besides these three areas. Moreover, Japanese firms do not have to confine themselves to the internalisation of labour. The coordination of the flow of goods or internal allocation of financial resources may become necessary in Japan.

In coordinating the flow of goods, early large-scale firms in Japan faced problems in securing a stable and low cost supply of raw materials. Most Japanese companies in the pre-war era were suppliers of semi-finished products. Raw materials amounted to a dominant part of the production cost, and their prices were liable to change. Except cotton spinning and wool textile firms, most of the pre-war companies in fabricated basic materials integrated backward to raw material branches, and became multifunction firms. Companies manufacturing producer final goods also integrated backward to the supply of parts and components. Such an upward integration brought about internalisation of the flow of goods, but the flow of goods was not always coordinated centrally, and was often left to individual operating units. Large-scale textile companies preferred market transactions in purchasing and sales, and in order to make full use of the market channel, they developed their own purchasing department or offices. Downward integration to weaving process was also observed, and even when they used outside weavers or finishers, the relative position of spinning firms became stronger.

The creation of the flow of goods inside the firms necessitated their coordination by managerial hierarchies. These managerial hierarchies of firms had to be reformed from a simple line structure to more complex ones. If the coordination of the flow of goods was centralised, the company was structured by functional departments. If such coordination was delegated to operating units, the organisational form became a production unit structure. However, in both of these structures the internal control of labour remained important, and influenced on the forms of organisations.

After the Second World War, such backward integration came to an end. Companies in fabricated basic materials declined, too. Like the textile companies of the pre-war era, companies in other fabricated materials could no longer expect cheap raw materials near their operating units or inside the firm. As they introduced a mass-production system, they had to look for supplies of raw materials abroad. Some made use of the market transactions of raw materials, and others secured them through long term contracts or by developing overseas mines or forests. These companies made inroads into processing branches, and employed processing factories or wholesale merchants. Companies in producer final goods also reduced self-supply of parts and components, and began to nurture outside suppliers by technological and financial aid or long term transactions, pushing them to develop as specialist part suppliers for the general markets. Companies in producer final goods diversified by applying the technical skills which they had obtained through self-supply of parts and components.

Companies in consumer final goods grew large in the post-war era by integrating downward to wholesales, and affiliating retail outlets. Companies in the automobile, gasoline, and household electrical equipment industries were typical examples. In some branches of industry, notably in automobiles, the suppliers of parts and components were affiliated with particular automobile manufacturers.

But, here again, mobility inside and outside the groups took place and those affiliated suppliers which acccumulated their own technical skills tended to develop into specialist part producers for the general markets. The functional structure was widely established in consumer final goods companies, while the multidivisional structure took the place of the 'production-units' form in producer final goods companies.

The internalisation of the transactions of financial resources, or the allocation of cash flow is only a very recent phenomenon in Japanese manufacturing firms. The accumulation of internal capital could not catch up with the increasing demand for new investment. The external capital market did not develop enough for the requirement of the expanding large-scale companies. Throughout most of the pre-war era, the capital of large-scale firms was raised by equity, and the ratio of their equity to their total capital was considerably high. The shares of these companies, however, were not necessarily distributed widely in the market. A portion of these were held by the founders of the companies, particularly in the cases of medium-sized textile firms, or were held by various types of holding companies – including the *Zaibatsu* – in industries other than textiles. The additional capital was not supplied by the shareholders' own money, but was more or less dependent on bank loans to the shareholders secured on their shares. Transaction of financial resources within segmented circles were observed. Such a segmented supply of financial resources, however, did not necessarily mean that the investment decisions of individual companies were made by these institutions outside the firms. The function and the forms of the pre-war Japanese holding companies differed individually. Holding companies shared a common characteristic in that they supplied initial financial resources within segmented circles. They emerged in a certain stage in the separation of ownership and control, as if to restrain this natural trend.

Since the last phase of the War, the equity ratio of Japanese large-scale firms quickly declined, and its position was replaced by loaned capital. This trend continued until the end of the period covered by this work. Throughout the most part of these three decades, fixed capital investment was financed by loaned capital, particularly from banks, and as a result financial groupings were formed around the banks. Each large-scale firm derived a large part of its financial resources from a particular bank, and the segmented circular flows of financial resources with banks at their centres were formed. This was the characteristic of the 'business group' in post-war Japan. Here again though, the banks did not take the place of the individual companies in investment decisions.

9.2 THE DIRECTION OF THE DEVELOPMENT OF MODERN FIRMS: TYPES AND STAGES

In comparison with their western counterparts, the Japanese large-scale firms were distinguished by internalisation of the transaction of labour. This characteristic was maintained until the post-war era, though the internal transactions of the flow of goods eventually became important too. The large-scale post-war companies, particularly those dealing in final goods, made use of affiliated companies to coordinate the flow of goods from purchasing to sales. In financial resources, whereas the shares of some pre-war large-scale firms were held by the *Zaibatsu*, most of the post-war firms were financed by particular banks inside the same business groups. Such characteristics in the allocation of resources have determined the basic forms of the managerial hierarchies of Japanese firms. Different forms of managerial hierarchies would result from other combinations of internalised resources. The experiences of American or European firms suggest such different possibilities. Are these national divergencies invariable, or, if not, is there any process of convergent evolution?

Whether a firm internalises the transactions of a particular kind of resource or not is determined by the comparative transaction cost between hierarchies and the markets (or the third type of institutional arrangements). The transaction cost in the market depends on the scarcity of a particular kind of resources or the uncertainties of its supply. Such comparative costs differ from market to market. Divergencies among nations result from the differences of such comparative transaction costs if the extent of a market overlaps that of a nation. However, the transaction cost of a particular kind of resources changes as the market develops. A firm may replace internal allocation with market transactions, and the border between the firm and the market will move in proportion to the reduction of the internalised resources.

Even if the extent of a market coincides with a country, a business enterprise of a particular country has to shift its main management resources in face of international competition. Comparative advantage in production costs, if it is derived from labour cost, would easily be lost in the face of upcoming firms in less developed countries where the cost of labour is lower. The more advanced countries would take advantage of the low transaction cost of goods, either by integration or by market transactions. Finally, they have to shift their main resources to financial resources when their followers attain low cost purchasing or sales. Thus there is a gradual change in the main management resources from labour to the flow of goods, and finally to financial resources. The Japanese firms examined in this book stayed in the first two phases. Firms in every country seem to take more or less the same course, though there are differences in the length of the period during which firms of a country were mainly based on a particular management resources.

A company can diverge from this pre-determined course without shifting its dominant resources. It can supply new kinds of products to the new markets by using the same management resources differently from the manner they were previously used in. Such diversification was realised by applying different strategies to the utilisation of the management resources developed inside the firm. Therefore, diversification should not be regarded as a strategy such as vertical integration, mergers, and mere expansion. If a company internalises the transactions of resources, it cannot make full use of these resources in the existing way and accumulate surpluses inside the firm. However, the company can use these resources in a different way.[2] If they internalise the transaction of labour, the company can accumulate a wide range of technical skills, knowledge, and technologies from their employees, and diversify by applying these assets. If the internalised resources are the flow of goods, the company can diversify by making use of the core distribution channel or the technical skills of parts production. The relatively low diversification of the companies in fabricated basic materials indicates that the flow of goods realised through backward integration brought them few such technical skills. If they are financial resources, a company can take over other companies in different industries even if they have no technological or market relations. These factors indicate that companies do not necessarily shift to other resources in the face of competition, but diverge from a simple evolution process through diversification, and maintain their competitive power by being based on the same management resources. If it is possible, national divergence is not easily replaced by a single direction of development in the management resources and managerial hierarchies.

NOTES

1. R. H. Coase, The Nature of the Firm, *Economica*, vol. IV, 1937.
2. Yoshihara, Sakuma, Itami & Kagono, *Nihon kigyo no takakuka sen-ryaku*, Tokyo, 1981.

Appendix

The Largest 100 Industrials of 1935 (by sales and assets)

	Sales (1000 yen)	Assets (1000 yen)	Employees
Food and drink			
Nichiro Gyogyo			
(Nichiro Fishery)	37 952	82 692	17 952[d]
Kyodo Gyogyo (Kyodo Fishery)	19 885	(17 910)	2 218[d]
Nippon Shokuryo Kogyo			
(Japan Food Products)	18 400	35 405	?
Taiwan Seito			
(Taiwan Sugar Mfg)	64 424	118 768	?
Dai-Nippon Sugar Mfg			
[*Dainippon Seito*]	77 081	116 160	?
Meiji Sugar Mfg [*Meiji Seito*]	71 938	92 717	2 643
Ensuiko Sugar Mfg			
[*Ensuiko Seito*]	34 358	99 056	1 802
Nanyo Kohatsu			
(Nanyo Company)	16 182	31 727	?
Teikoku Seito			
(Teikoku Sugar Mfg)	(13 432)	34 622	?
Meiji Seika			
(Meiji Confectionery)	16 183	(8 122)	1 862
Dai Nippon Brewery	64 916	136 677	3 390
Kirin Brewery	23 938	30 320	1 192
Noda Shoyu (Noda Soy-Sauce)	18 260	37 821	2 492
Nippon Flour Mills			
[*Nippon Seifun*]	61 192	40 810	c.800
Nisshin Flour Mills			
[*Nisshin Seifun*]	?	50 632	1 300
Textiles			
Toyo Cotton Mill [*Toyo Boseki*]	57 012	176 042	42 240
Kanegafuchi Spinning			
[*Kanegafuchi Boseki*]	243 825	212 636	30 156
Fujigas Spinning			
[*Fujigasu Boseki*]	53 279	82 579	15 673

(*continued on page 332*)

332   *Appendix*

Appendix   *continued*
The Largest 100 Industrials of 1935 (by sales and assets)

	Sales (1000 yen)	Assets (1000 yen)	Employees
Dai Nippon Spinning & Weaving [*Dainippon Boseki*]	40 815	129 915	25 745
Nisshin Spinning [*Nisshin Boseki*]	38 775	43 118	10 460
Naigaiwata (Naigai Cotton Spinning)	119 112	65 614	23 411
Kurashiki Cotton Spinning [*Kurashiki Boseki*]	c.16 000	41 533	8 656
Kishiwada Spinning & Weaving [*Kishiwada Boseki*]	31 558	25 235	8 422
Kureha Spinning [*Kureha Boseki*]	?	36 793	?
Fukushima Cotton Spinning [*Fukushima Boseki*]	?	28 431	?
Kinka Boseki (Kinka Spinning)	30 870	36 211	4 523
Nagasaki Boshoku (Nagasaki Spinning & Weaving)	17 790	(17 470)	3 738
Wakayama Spinning & Weaving [*Wakayama Boshoku*]	14 922	(10 715)	3 318
Izumo Seishoku (Izumo Weaving)	c.15 000	(17 249)	4 181
Hinode Spinning & Weaving [*Hinode Boshoku*]	19 822	(17 490)	3 790
Meisei Boshoku (Meisei Spinning & Weaving)	19 000	(10 946)	2 485
Shanghai Seizo Kenshi (Shanghai Spinning)	70 604	37 067	13 887
Omi Hampu (Omi Sail Cloth)	16 513	(15 382)	3 407
Tenman Orimono (Tenman Weaving)	21 817	21 457	3 380
Doko Boseki (Doko Spinning)	(?4 645)	22 268	?
Nikka Boshoku (Nikka Spinning & Weaving)	(?4 945)	31 586	?
Toyoda Boshoku (Toyoda Spinning & Weaving)	(?7 466)	28 082	?
The Nippon Weaving [*Nippon Keori*]	75 987	115 288	13 211
Showa Keito Boseki (Showa Wool Spinning)	15 219	27 225	2 579
Kyoritsu Muslin	21 632	(12 834)	2 762
Tokyo Muslin Boshoku (Tokyo Muslin Spinning &			

Appendix *continued*
The Largest 100 Industrials of 1935 (by sales and assets)

	Sales *(1000 yen)*	Assets *(1000 yen)*	Employees
Weaving)	*23 684*	*(38 117)*	*6 410*
Chuo Keito Boseki (Chuo Wool			
Spinning)	15 644	19 155	2 420
Toyo Muslin	25 460	26 189	8 448
Shinko Keori (Shinko Wool			
Textile)	21 705	(13 686)	7 584
Gunze Silk Mfg [*Gunze Seishi*]	51 500	35 678	21 450
Katakura Industry [*Katakura*			
Seishi]	54 552	79 531	21 597
Toyo Rayon	23 243	41 315	6 545
Kurashiki Kenshoku			
(Kurashiki Rayon)	*c.*20 000	45 180	5 600
Teikoku Jinzo Kenshi (Teikoku			
Artificial Fibre)	15 327	57 972	8 500
Asahi Bemberg Kenshi			
(Asahi Bemberg)	35 204	92 686	14 500
Nippon Rayon	(?8 988)	27 262	6 000
Teikoku Seima (Teikoku			
Cambric Mfg)	(10 934)	33 936	3 780
Paper			
Oji Paper Mfg [*Oji Seishi*]	169 311	347 976	9 534
The Japan Paper Industry			
[*Nippon Shigyo*]	18 161	40 365	?
Mitsubishi Paper Mills			
[*Mitsubishi Seishi*]	(12 380)	21 321	1 501
Chemicals and pharmaceuticals			
Dainippon Jinzo Hiryo			
(Dainippon Artificial			
Fertilisers)	19 155	78 239	3 452
Sumitomo Chemical [*Sumitomo*			
Kagaku]	16 572	31 586	1 934
Denki Kagaku (Electro			
Chemicals)	15 548	47 079	2 964
Nippon Chisso (Nippon			
Nitrogen)	18 696	190 265	1 569
Chosen Chisso (Chosen			
Nitrogen)	50 426	111 424	7 698[c]
Showa Hiryo (Showa Fertilisers)	22 177	39 082	?
Nippon Denki Kogyo (Nippon			

(*continued on page 334*)

Appendix   *continued*
The Largest 100 Industrials of 1935 (by sales and assets)

	Sales (1000 yen)	Assets (1000 yen)	Employees
Electro Chemicals)	14 961	57 314	?
Toyo Koatsu Industries	(1 926)	26 375	524
Manshu Kagaku Kogyo (Manshu Chemicals)	(4 356)	39 748	?
Nippon Soda Kogyo	25 142	23 916	?
Nippon Soda	(13 096)	23 231	3 200
Nippon Stuff Mfg [*Nippon Senryo*]	37 488	23 255	1 471
Dainippon Celluloid	16 495	30 331	2 134
Godo Yushi (Godo Oils & Fats)	16 581	18 792	940
Shionogi	15 070	(11 610)	?
Sankyo	*c.*20 000	24 435	1 500
Takeda Chobei Shoten	26 657	20 051	2 100[c]
Hoshi Seiyaku (Hoshi Pharmaceutical)	(*c*.3 700)	23 520	?
Oil and ceramic			
Nippon Oil [*Nippon Sekiyu*]	70 805	140 823	5 654
Ogura Sekiyu (Ogura Oil)	?	?	?
Asahi Glass	39 944	42 387	2 650
Asano Cement	34 701	137 371	5 107
Onoda Cement	14 802	48 195	3 906
Iwaki Cement	(8 298)	20 027	651
Osaka Yogyo Cement	(9 769)	19 838	600
Iron and steel			
Nippon Steel [*Nippon Seitetsu*]	300 737	487 119	45 847[a]
Showa Seikojo (Showa Steel Works)	24 657	109 940	*c.*20 000
Kobe Steel Works [*Kobe Seikojo*]	53 191	43 969	4 641[d]
Nippon Kokan (Nippon Steel Tube)	57 468	97 415	5 300[b]
Asano Kokura Seikojo (Asano Kokura Steel Works)	21 008	(11 092)	?
The Japan Steel Works [*Nippon Seikojo*]	19 398	41 911	?
Kokusan Kogyo (Kokusan Industries)	25 561	35 906	3 506
Sumitomo Metal Industries [*Sumitomo Kinzoku Kogyo*]	63 139	75 737	?

Appendix *continued*
The Largest 100 Industrials of 1935 (by sales and assets)

	Sales *(1000 yen)*	*Assets* *(1000 yen)*	*Employees*
Non-ferrous metals			
Mitsui Mining [*Mitsui Kozan*]	101 303	179 389	48 517
Mitsubishi Mining [*Mitsubishi Kogyo*]	75 686	154 195	24 191
Furukawa Kogyo Gomei (Furukawa Mining & Co)	*c.*15 000	49 472	?
Sumitomo Besshi Kozan (Sumitomo Besshi Mining)	17 484	27 592	4 186
Nippon Mining [*Nippon Kogyo*]	74 289	207 711	19 280
Fujita Kogyo (Fujita Mining)	16 695	69 188	6 316
Sumitomo Densen (Sumitomo Cable Mfg)	33 917	26 492	2 241
The Furukawa Electric [*Furukawa Denko*]	64 419	54 516	?
Toyo Seikan (Toyo Can Mfg)	17 513	(16 133)	569
Tokyo Rope Mfg [*Tokyo Seiko*]	14 328	(18 085)	2 006
Electricals			
Hitachi [*Hitachi Seisakujo*]	49 638	59 470	13 404
Mitsubishi Electric [*Mitsubishi Denki*]	22 202	29 205	2 900
Fuji Denki (Fuji Electrics)	16 645	16 783	1 461[d]
Shibaura Engineering Works [*Shibaura Seisakujo*]	28 349	31 792	*c.*5 280
Tokyo Electric [*Tokyo Denki*]	41 308	59 165	4 790
Nippon Electric [*Nippon Denki*]	16 712	20 466	2 680
Engineering and shipbuilding			
Mitsubishi Heavy Industries [*Mitsubishi Jukogyo*]	105 334	116 775	28 118
Kawasaki Dockyard [*Kawasaki Zosenjo*]	?	151 938	23 120[b]
Tokyo Ishikawajima Zosenjo (Ishikawajima Shipbuilding)	15 613	19 430	?
Harima Zosenjo (Harima Shipbuilding)	14 307	22 602	*c.*3 300
Asano Zosenjo (Asano Shipbuilding)	36 742	42 727	2 370
Uraga Dock [*Uraga Senkyo*]	(1 560)	21 785	3 350
Osaka Iron Works [*Osaka Tekkojo*]	(3 291)	23 785	4 600

(*continued on page 336*)

Appendix *continued*
The Largest 100 Industrials of 1935 (by sales and assets)

	Sales (1000 yen)	Assets (1000 yen)	Employees
Nippon Sharyo (Nippon Rolling Stock)	15 021	(16 342)	2 330[d]
Kisha Seizo (Railway Carriage Mfg)	(6 794)	19 364	3 790
Toyodashiki Shokki (Toyoda Loom Works)	(5 236)	19 242	3 450
Nippon Jidosha (Nippon Motor)	15 416	(7 958)	?
Aichi Clock and Electric Implement [*Aichi Tokei Denki*]	18 219	18 369	3 857
K. Hattori (Hattori Watch & Clock)	?	27 504	3 521[d]
Others			
Godo Keori (Godo Wool Textile)	0	32 277	0

Note: [a] 1934, [b] 1936, [c] 1937, [d] production employees, ? = data not known.

Index

acquisitions *see* mergers
affiliates 104
  automobile companies 97, 278
  and distribution 96
  origins 84–5
Agricultural Cooperative
  Association 267
Aichi Machine Industry 287
aircraft production 288
Ajinomoto 253–4
Akita Mokuzai 57
Alcoa 186
aluminium 181, 183, 184, 185
  technology 186
Amagasaki Seitetsu 144–5
Amano, C. 282
Arab oil 274, 275
Arrow, K. J. 6
artificial fertilisers 24, 29
  see also chemical industry
Asahi Benberg 53, 57
Asahi Breweries 261
Asahi Chemical Industry 122, 192
Asahi Glass 35, 69, 135–6
Asano Cement 42–3, 56
Asano group 46–7, 56, 60
  employees 62
Asia
  restricted imports 118
  and textiles 106
assets 89
Associated Oil (U.S.) 271
audio equipment 309
Australia, mines in 141, 145
authority
  and written rule 181, 194
  see also control; head offices
automobile companies 218, 219,
  229–31, 243, 277–302, 317,
  326–7

affiliates 97, 278
  and business groups 77
  distribution 278–9, 280, 289,
    290; companies 295;
    integration 296
  diversification 288, 289, 290
  entries 91, 244
  exits 91
  expansion 288, 295
  exports 281, 282, 283, 288;
    Honda 296, 297; trucks 292
  finance 279, 290, 295
  foreign competition 278, 287
  and government policy 278,
    280, 287
  head office 282, 288, 289, 290,
    291, 293, 298
  integration 280–1
  investment policy 285
  management committee 280,
    286, 287, 288
  mass production 279–80, 285,
    287, 288, 291, 295; rotary
    engines 296
  mergers 287
  and oil crises 296, 299
  partnerships 281, 286, 287, 293;
    foreign 277
  raw materials 287, 288, 297, 300
  research and development 282,
    283, 291, 294, 302
  sales activities 277, 278, 279,
    289, 293; companies 282, 286,
    291; dealers 283–4, 295, 296,
    298–9, 300, 301
  sales and assets 89, 93
  scientific management 298
  shop floor 286–7
  structure 102, 279–80, 288–9,
    298–302; changes 282–3,

284–5, 294–5
technology 279, 282, 291, 294;
  and exhaust gas 299;
  limitations 277; and
  partnerships 282, 292
top management 280, 281, 288,
  289, 297
wholesale activities 300–1
Ayukawa, G. 57
Azariadis, C. 5

banks 11, 68–9, 81
  and business groups 77, 79–80,
    82, 328
  Central 69, 80
  foreign and oil 272
  loans 295
  role of 45
  in Zaibatsu 61, 65, 70, 71
Belgium 7
Besshi Mines 159
Bosch 212, 213
Brazil, mines in 141, 145
breweries 243, 245, 246, 259–64
  entries 259
Bridgestone Tire 133, 134
Britain *see* United Kingdom
budgetary system 270, 276
building products 93
bulldozers 233, 234
bureacracies, defined 2–3
business groups 75–83, 328
  and automobile industry 77
  and banks 77, 79–80, 82
  and corporate control 77, 82
  and external debts 79–80, 82
  financial transactions 79–80,
    81–2
  and finished consumer goods 77
  and household electrical
    industry 77
  and information 77
  presidents 76, 81
  purchasing 81
  resource allocation 76, 86
  and shareholding 77–8, 81, 82
  and trading companies 80

Caltex 267, 268

cameras 90
Canada, mines in 141
canned products 247, 250
capital, raising 69
  see also shareholding
cartels 75, 107
  and copper 31
  development 37
  and market mechanism 2
  and multifunction firm 45
  in sugar 26
Caterpillar 220, 233, 234
cement industry 97, 103, 105
  decision-making 132
  distribution 132
  exits 91
  integration 24
  mergers 95
  organisation 23
  vertical integration 106
centralised management 28, 33
ceramics 103
  sales and assets 23, 89
  workforce 15, 16
Chandler, Alfred D.,
  hypothesis 3–6, 30
chemical industry 97, 176, 177–97
  budget control 122
  decision-making 182
  development 29, 33
  distribution 24
  diversification 99, 122, 178, 179,
    181, 182–3, 194–5, 236
  exits 90
  foreign technology 181, 182,
    183, 187, 194, 196
  head offices 184, 188, 190, 191
  integration 96
  mergers 178, 180
  ownership 48
  production units 178
  profit responsibility 184, 185
  raw materials 62, 185, 186,
    188–9, 192
  sales and assets 23, 89, 93
  structural reorganisation 179,
    180–1, 182–5, 188–9, 191,
    196–7
  workforce 15, 16, 19

see also pharmaceutical
Chosen Bank 65
Chosen Chisso Hiryo 48, 57
Chrysler,
  and Mitsubishi Motors 293
Chuo Keito Boseki 62, 64
CIT (France) 211
coal mining 187
Coase, R. H. 5, 324
cold storage 250
combinations,
  horizontal 94–5
Commercial Statistics 96
communications equipment 199,
  206, 207, 208–9, 210, 216, 308,
  312
companies, new, post-war
  243–318
  automobile 277–302,
  consumer durables 302–17
  food and drink 245–65
  oil 265–77
  see also individual industries
competition
  automobile companies 278, 287
  international 328–9
  oil industry 266
computers 199, 202, 209, 210
condiments 253, 254
consumer durable companies 132,
  302–17
decision-making 308
demand 303, 314
distribution 302, 304, 317; in
  electrical equipment 305, 306,
  309, 310, 314
diversification 302, 315
exports 307, 311, 312, 315, 316
head offices 305, 306, 307
innovation 312, 317
investment 303, 307–8
management committee 302
market for 243
mass production 315, 317
overseas subsidiaries 311
profit responsibility 311
research and development 312
sales activities 305, 311;
  companies 309; overseas

303, 307; retailing shops
  304; trading offices 302
structure 302–4, 315, 317–18;
  reorganisation 302, 305, 306,
  307–11, 313
top management 304, 306
wholesale functions 305, 316,
  318
consumer final goods 6, 88,
  89–90, 326–7
forward integration 97
mergers 94–5
structure 33
vertical integration 95
control
  and business groups 82
  corporate 44–72
  and sales 36, 378
  shareholding 78
  and subsidiaries 86
Cooperative Union of Farmers 30
copper 157, 158, 159, 160, 166
core technology 102, 103, 177
Corn Product Refining 254
corporate control 1920–40, and
  holding companies 44–72
cosmetics 89, 303–4
  integration 96, 97
cotton spinning firms 108, 124,
  325
  mergers 109
  organisation of 20, 23, 27–8
  raw materials 23
  workforce 15, 17
credit see banks; loan
crude oil 265, 266, 267, 269, 275

Dai Nippon Brewery 259, 260
Dai Nippon Printing 131
Dai-Nippon Sugar
  Manufacturing 25–6
Daido Steel 152, 155
Daihatsu 277, 281, 283–5, 300
Daiichi-Kangin group 76, 83
  directors 79
  internal transactions 82
  members of 76
Daikyo Oil 273–5
Dainippon Celluloid 30

Dainippon Ink and Chemicals 84,
  188–9
Dainippon Jinzo Hiryo 29, 64
Dainippon Spinning and
  Weaving 27, 28
Daishowa Paper
  Manufacturing 129–30
Daiwa Spinning 27
debentures, ratios of 61
decentralisation 36, 58, 101
  and decision making 58
  heavy engineering
    companies 218–19, 221, 228,
    231
  management 58
  resources 36
  and mergers 31–2, 33–6
decision making 71
  cement industry 132
  chemical companies 182
  consumer durable
    companies 308
  and decentralisation 58
  electrical and electronic
    companies 203
  executives 51–3
  heavy engineering
    companies 229
  and holding companies 54–6
  oil industry 273
  and shareholding 78
  steel industry 142
  and top management 51–3
  and Zaibatsu 44, 45
Deconcentration Act 109, 115
developing countries, exports
  to 307
directors, interlocking 258
  and business groups 78–9, 81,
  82
  and giant firms 83
  and manufacturing firms 97
  and shareholding 83
distribution 11, 62–5, 329
  see also individual industries
diversification 98–9, 329
  by product groups 100, 244
  see also individual industries
divisionalisation *see individual*

industries, structure
Doeringer 5
dominant product firms,
  diversification 98–9, 100
Dowa Mining, The 162–3
downward integration 106
drink *see* food industry

Electric Development Plan 203
electrical and electronic
  companies 89, 163–6, 197–216
  affiliation 97
  decision-making 203
  diversification 197, 198, 205,
    206, 211, 212, 215, 216
  exports 208
  operating units 200, 204, 209
  organisational reform 198,
    199–200, 201, 203–7, 210
  ownership 48
  production units 199, 200, 201
  profit centres 199, 204, 208,
    212, 215
  research and development 202,
    204, 205, 210
  sales 199, 201–2, 208, 209, 213
  and assets 23, 89, 93
  scientific management 211
  technology 198, 200, 202, 215
  top management 201, 207, 208
  workforce 15, 16
electrical engineering
  distribution 62
  diversification 236
electrical equipment
  companies 176, 304–14
  decision-making 308
  distribution 305, 306, 309, 310,
    314
  exports 307, 311, 312
  head office 306
  innovation 312
  investment 307–8
  profit responsibilities 311
  sales activities 305–6, 309, 311,
    313, 314
  structure 305–6, 308–9, 313;
    changes 307–11, 312–13
  wholesale functions 305, 313

electronics industry 308–9
see also under electrical and
electronic companies
employment/employees 61, 62
by industry 16
expansion of 15, 22
and government enterprises 15
long-term 19
minerals 15
in multiunit enterprises 14
recruitment 17, 62, 72
skills 14, 15, 17
textile industry 15–16, 17
traditional industries 15, 16
and training 18
turnover 17, 19
welfare 17, 18
engineering industry 89, 98
cost management 20
diversification 99, 103
mergers 95
organisation of 33–5
production units 33
sales and assets 23, 89, 93
skilled workforce in 17
see also electrical; heavy
engineering
Ensuiko Sugar Refining 26
entries 22, 71, 91
breweries 259
in new industries 14
environmental control systems 187
equity capital 65, 68
Esso 265, 271
Europe 6, 33
allocation of resources and
development 328
big business 7
breweries 259, 260, 264
diversification 99
divisionalisation 100, 177
holding company structure 9
mergers 94
executives 72
decision making 51–3
transitions 54
see also directors
exits 22, 71, 90–1
exports

automobile companies 281, 282,
283, 288, 296, 297
consumer durable companies
307, 311, 312, 315, 316
electrical and electronic
companies 208
shipbuilding 224
and steel industry 141, 153
textiles 27, 29
external debts 65, 67
and business groups 79–80, 82
ratio of 60–1
and Zaibatsu 60–1

fabricated basic materials 77,
105–69, 326
acquisitions 24
management structure 102
and mergers 24, 107
overseas activities 106
traditional companies 105–69;
nonferrous metals 156–67;
paper, printing and materials
124–37; steel 137–56;
textile 108–24
Fair Trade Commission 77, 78–9,
80–1
federations
and allocation of resources 11
and market mechanism 2
for purchasing and sales 72
with wholesalers 63
see also hierarchies
fertilisers 178–9, 181, 183, 195
and government policy 178
markets 184
financial institutions,
Zaibatsu 65, 68, 69
financial resources 10, 11, 58, 60
allocation 5, 6, 7, 65, 70; and
holding companies 7–8;
segmented 61, 67, 68, 72
and information 77
internalisation of 325, 327, 329
and organisational forms 10
financing, indirect 68
fine chemicals 184–5
finished producers goods 77
firms *see individual industries*

fisheries 246–50
    diversification 248
food industry 243, 245–65, 317
    and business groups 77
    development of organisation 29,
        41
    distribution 62, 246, 247, 251,
        254, 255, 257, 264; breweries
        262–3
    diversification 245, 246, 258,
        259, 264; breweries 261, 262,
        263; milk 259
    entries and exits 90
    growth rates 246
    head offices 247, 248, 252,
        256–7
    integration 245, 252
    market 244, 245, 259
    mergers 246, 260, 261
    middle management 253, 255,
        262
    operating units 246, 254, 263
    perishable goods 264
    preservation 245
    processing 248, 250, 252;
        technology 245, 246, 253
    profit centres 254, 255
    raw materials 246
    refrigeration 246, 247, 251
    sales: activities 246, 255, 261;
        and assets 23, 89, 93
    structure 246, 247, 248–9, 252,
        254, 255, 256–7, 258;
        breweries 262–3, 264;
        reform 251
    subsidiaries 249, 252, 256, 258
    top management 249–50, 253,
        255
    transport 245, 246, 261, 264
    workforce 15, 16
Ford, and Toyo Kogyo 296
forward integration 97, 101
frozen food industry 250, 251
Fuji Electric 56, 83, 205–6
Fuji Heavy Industries 277, 278,
    288–90, 300, 301
    and Isuzu Motors 293
Fuji Iron and Steel 141, 143, 148
Fuji Photo Film 302

Fujigas Spinning 27, 28
Fujinagata Shipbuilding 223
Fujisawa, T. 296
Fujita Kogyo 31
Fujita Mining 160
Fujitsu 209–10, 211
    functional structures 101
    /line structure: organisation of 9
        10, 11, 20; production
        units 107
    departamentalised structures 9,
        10, 20; textile companies 27
    development of 28
    transition to multidivisional 102
    furniture 314
Furukawa Coal Mining 64
Furukawa Electric 31, 41, 56, 64,
    163–4
Furukawa group 46–7, 56–7, 60,
    61, 65
    employees 62
    Related Companies of 59
Furukawa Mining 163
Fuyo group
    internal transactions 82
    members 76
    shareholding 78

garages 266, 274
    control over 269, 270, 271, 273,
        275
    and Ministry of Trade 269
gasoline 269
GDP, share of manufacturing
    in 66
General Electric 197
General Motors Japan 279, 293–4
Germany 2, 7
    automobile sales 277
    breweries 259
    output comparison 92–3
Getty Oil 271
glass industry
    integration 106
    markets 135, 136
    sales/assets 23, 93
    structure 136–7
    technology 135
    workforce 16, 19

Godo Yushi 35–6
goods transactions 72
  and business groups 80–1
  and growth of firms 7
  and information 77
  internalisation of 4, 6, 8, 22,
    328, 329
Goodyear 133
government
  employment in enterprises 15,
    17–18
  plan for electronic industry 209,
    215, 216
  policy 285; and automobile
    companies 278, 280, 287; and
    fertilisers 178; and oil 275; on
    production 113
groups *see* business groups

Hadley, E. M. 77
Harima shipbuilding 60, 226
Hattori, (K.) 316–17, 318
Hayakawa Electric 308–9
head offices
  automobile companies 282, 288,
    289, 290, 291, 293, 298
  chemical companies 184, 188,
    190, 191
  consumer durables 305, 306,
    307
  cotton spinning 21
  food industry 247, 248, 252,
    256–7
  and functional/line structure 9,
    11
  heavy engineering companies
    222, 223, 224
  Hitachi 198
  importance of 31
  and line structure 8
  nonferrous metals 157, 160, 161
  paper industry 125
  pharmaceutical industry 30
  and production units 11, 37
  trading departments 96
  Zaibatsu 15, 75
heavy electrical engineering 197–8,
  199, 200, 202
heavy engineering companies 176,

216–35
  decentralisation 218–19, 221,
    228, 231
  decision making 229
  diversification 216, 218, 220–2,
    223–5, 232, 234, 236; into
    automobile parts 229
  employment 15, 16
  head offices 222, 223, 224
  mergers 220, 221–2, 226, 228–9
  origin 216
  ownership 48
  product lines 220, 235
  production units 220, 224, 236
  profit responsibility 218, 220,
    223, 227, 228
  purchasing 218, 219
  sales 220, 226, 231
  structure 218–19, 220–36
  subsidiaries 217
  technology 216, 217, 235
  top management 219, 221, 223,
    225, 226
hierarchies
  and federations post-war 75–87;
    affiliated industrials 83–6;
    business groups 76–81;
    formation of 1920–40 13–38
  resources and structures 1–3;
    types of 7–9
Hino 281, 300, 301
  and Renault 277, 282
Hitachi 57, 76, 193–200
  as affiliate 83, 84
  head office 198
  products 198
Hitachi Cable 166
Hitachi Metals 154, 155
Hitachi Shipbuilding and
  Engineering 57, 224–5
Hokkaido Colliery and
  Steamship 152
holding companies 89, 327
  and corporate control 1920–40
    44–72; allocation of
    management resources
    58–66; development of 46–51;
    external institutions 44–6;
    strategic decision-making

51–8; wartime change and
continuity 66–71
and financial resources 7–8
Liquidation Committee 67
management 7
shareholding 49–51, 53
structure 9, 10; line 8;
multidivisional 7–8
and subsidiaries 49–51
and Zaibatsu 58
Honda 277, 290, 300, 302, 317
Honshu Paper 125, 127–8
horizontal combinations 24, 94–5
see also combinations; mergers
household electrical industry 89,
197, 199, 200, 205, 308, 309,
310–12, 326
and business groups 77
management structure 102
housing components 214
human resources 324
internalisation 1, 4, 15–22, 19,
36; and control 20; and
development of firm 8, 10;
and firm formation 6, 7
and lower management 8

IBM 203, 210
ice manufacturing 250
Idemitsu Oil 275–6
imports
cotton 62
liberalisation of 135
oil 266, 269
ore 140–1
raw materials, food 31, 264–5
see also individual industries
industrial complexes 91
Industrial Reconstruction and
Reorganisation Act 290
industrialisation 14
industrials, affiliated, and post-war
federations 83–6
industries, new, in traditional
companies 176–236
chemical and pharmaceutical
177–97
electrical and electronic 197–216
heavy engineering 216–35

information and business
groups 77
innovation *see individual industries*;
technology
integration 101, 106
automobile companies 280–1
chemical industry 96
cosmetics 96, 97
food industry 245, 252
glass 106
machinery 96
oil industry 274
resources, management 325–6
steel industry 138, 140, 141, 155
and textile industry 97
see also horizontal combinations;
mergers; vertical integration
Interchemical 130
investment 327
consumer durables 303, 307–8
overseas 97
and raw materials 106
shipbuilding 224
iron and steel industry 98, 105
exits 91
integration 24, 106
mergers 95
ownership 48
sales/assets 23, 93
workforce 16, 19
Ishige, Y. 180
Ishikawajima Heavy
Industries 202, 226, 227
Isibashi 133, 134
Isuzu Motors 278, 292–4, 300, 301
and Fuji Heavy Industries 293
and Rootes 277, 292
Itoh (C.) and Co. 49
Iwai Trading 62, 63
Izumo Seishoku 21

Japan Chemical Industries 119
Japan Paper Manufacturing 56
Japan Steel Works 152, 153
Jensen, M. C. 6
joint enterprises 84, 85
Jujo Paper 125, 128–9

Kamiya, S. 279

Kanebo 111–12
Kanegafuchi Spinning 35, 49, 68
Katakura Industry 27
Kawai Musical Instruments 315
Kawamura, K. 189
Kawasaki Aircraft 221, 222
Kawasaki Dockyard 33, 54, 216
Kawasaki Heavy Industries 139,
220–1, 226
Kawasaki Sharyo 221
Kawasaki Shatai 221
Kawasaki Shipbuilding 139
Kawasaki Steel 139, 143
Kellogg 254
Kigyo Shudan *see* business groups
Kinka Boseki 26, 27
Kirin Brewery 260, 261, 262–3
Kishiwada Spinning and
Weaving 26–7, 49
Koa Oil 268
Kobe Shipyard 34
Kobe Steel 60, 64, 76, 143–5, 155
Kokura Seikojo 31
Kokusan Kogyo 31, 33, 41, 42,
57, 64
Komatsu 232–4
Konishiroku Photo Industry 302
Korean War, effects of 111, 132
and electrical industry 198, 206,
215, 228
Kubota 231
Kuhara Mining 53, 57
Kuraray 120–1
Kurashiki Kenshoku 48, 53
Kurashiki Spinning 49, 120, 121
Kureha Shipping 26, 49
Kurehabo 111
Kyodo Gyogyo 57
Kyoritsu Muslin 49

labour
division of 2
internalisation of 4, 6, 88, 328,
329
shortages 131
technical skills 88
and top management 5
see also employment/employees;
human resources

large scale firms
1920–40, strategies 22–33
and allocation of resources
76–87
mergers 92
line structure 10, 20
decline in 22
and managerial control 8–9
live-stock 250, 251
loans 61, 65, 66, 68, 80, 328
and Mitsui group 79
and Sumitomo group 79–80
see also banks
lower management 2–3
function of 8
and holding companies 7
and human resources 8
and Zaibatsu 14

machinery, integration 96
management
committee: consumer durable
companies 302; oil industry
267, 276
structures *see individual
industries*
techniques *see* United States
see also lower management;
middle management; top
management
manager system 39
abolition of 32
managers, salaried 45, 51, 52, 54
manufacturing firms, development
of large-scale 1950–80 88–104
development direction 94–100
diversification 98–100
entries and exits 90–2
mergers and horizontal
combinations 94–5
positions and sizes 92–3
products 88–90
strategy and structure 100–3
vertical integration 95–8
market
breweries 259
glass industry 135, 136
internalisation of 245
mechanism 13; and cartels 2;

and resource allocation 2, 4, 6
research 254
urban 251, 253, 262
marketing *see individual industries*;
sales
Maruzen Oil 272, 276
Matsushita Electric Industrial
305–8, 310, 314
mass market 91, 104
for food 245
new companies in 243–318
see also companies, new
mass production 6, 91, 103, 105,
207, 326
automobile companies 279–80,
285, 287, 288, 291, 295
consumer durable companies
315, 317
and heavy engineering 228
paper industry 128
steel industry 140
and Toshiba 201
tyre industry 134
matrix structure 208, 212, 216
heavy engineering 225
Matsu Shokai 54
Matsukata, K. 54
Matsushita 83, 84
Matsushita Electric Industrial
213–15
Meckling, 6
Meiji Milk Products 254–6
Meiji Shoten 26
Meiji Sugar Manufacturing 26, 60,
63
Meisei Boshoku 53
mergers 94–5, 103, 168
automobile companies 287
cement industry 95
chemical companies 178, 180
consumer final goods 94–5
cotton spinning firms 109
and decentralisation 31–2, 33–6
engineering industry 95
Europe 94
fabricated basic materials 24,
107
food industry 246, 260, 261
heavy engineering companies

220, 221–2, 226, 228–9
and holding companies 7
iron and steel industry 95
large-scale manufacturing
firms 92
and multiunit firms 14
and organisational changes 31,
33–5
producer final goods 94–5
and product lines 34–6
semi-finished goods 94–5
shipbuilding 95
and steel 32–3
textile industry 71, 95
metal industry 31–3, 105, 157
integration 96
size of firms 93
middle management 37
defined 2–3
food industry 253, 255, 262
formation of 4
function of 8
and holding companies 7
role of 44
and Zaibatsu 14
middlemen 13, 64
see also wholesale function
milk
fresh 254, 255, 256, 257–8, 259
products 254–9
minerals
and distribution 62
employment 15
size of firms 93
structure 33
mines, foreign 156
mining 156–8, 159–61, 162–3, 167
Mitsubishi Bank 68, 69
Mitsubishi Chemical Industries
35, 69, 119, 135, 185, 186, 190
Mitsubishi Electric 64, 69, 203,
204
Mitsubishi group 41, 46–8, 55, 58,
60, 218, 312
affiliated companies 72
directors 79
employees 61
financial institutions 65
internal transactions 82

and loans 79–80
members 76
Mitsubishi Heavy Industries 33–4,
  69, 217, 219, 220, 226
Mitsubishi Kokuki 34
Mitsubishi Metal 158–9, 160
Mitsubishi Mining 69, 185
Mitsubishi Motors and
  Chrysler 293
Mitsubishi Oil 271, 272, 276
Mitsubishi Petrochemical 120,
  185–7, 190
Mitsubishi Rayon 119, 120
Mitsubishi Shipyard 18, 216
Mitsubishi Trading 62, 63, 64
Mitsubishi Zosen 34
Mitsui Bank 68
Mitsui Bussan 117
Mitsui Chemicals 179
Mitsui group 46–8, 58, 60, 61, 132
  affiliated companies 55, 72
  directors 79
  financial institutions 65
  internal transactions 82
  and loans 79
  members 76
Mitsui Mining 55, 68, 69, 178
  and Smelting 157–8, 159, 160–1
Mitsui Shipbuilding and
  Engineering 222–4
Mitsui Toatsu Chemicals 178, 183
Mizue Steel Works 146
Mobil Oil 265, 271
Mori Kogyo 58, 61, 65
Mori, T. 58
Morinaga Milk Industry 258–9
motor scooters 289
motor tricycles 283–4, 294
motorcycles 296–9, 314, 315
Moxley 84
multidivisional structure 9, 10,
  101–3
  and cartels 45
  changes from 108
  defined 4, 7–8
  Europe 100
  formation in U.S. 4, 5
  and holding companies 7–8
  increase in 22

and trading companies 44
  see also holding companies;
  structures; subsidiaries *and*
  individual industries
multiunit firms
  defined 7–8
  emergence of 13
  employees 14
munitions 70
musical instruments 90, 314–15

Nagasaki Boshoku 21
Nagasaki Shipyard 34
Nakabe family 249–50
Nakagawa, S. 56
Nakajima, K. 56
Nanyo Kohatsu 53
new industries in traditional
  companies 176–236
  diversification 176–7
New Zealand Aluminium Smelters
  Ltd 182
Nichia Seiko 149
Nichibo 113, 114
Nihon Breweries 260–1, 262
Nippon Chisso 49, 59, 61, 190
  employees 62
  financial resources 65
Nippon Chisso Hiryo 57
Nippon Denki Kogyo 58
Nippon Denso 212–13, 278
Nippon Electric 59–60, 70, 206–8
Nippon Gakki 314–16
Nippon Jidosha 57
Nippon Kogyo Bank 65
Nippon Kokan 33, 42, 145–7
Nippon Kyodo Shoken *see*
  securities; shareholding
Nippon Mining 57, 161
Nippon Oil 267–9, 275, 276, 318
Nippon Rayon 113–14
Nippon Reizo 250–1
Nippon Sangyo 57, 61, 246
  employees 62
  finance 65
Nippon Sharyo 33, 35
Nippon Shoken Hoyu Kumiai *see*
  securities
Nippon Shokuryo Kogyo 57

Nippon Soda Kogyo 49, 64
Nippon Steel 138, 147, 148, 149,
    152
  as affiliate 83
Nippon Suisan 57, 246–8, 250
Nippon Weaving, The
    development of 27, 28, 40
  shareholding 49
Nishiyama, Y. 139–40
Nissan Diesel 277, 291–2, 300
Nissan group 46–7, 83
  acquisitions 57
Nissan Motor 278, 285–8, 290–1,
    300, 301
  and Austin 277, 286
  partnerships 287, 293
Nissan Shatai 84, 277, 278, 287,
    290–1, 292, 300
Nissei Real Estate 84
Nisshin Flour Milling 252–3
Nisshin Spinning 27, 28
Nisshin Steel 84, 149, 155
Noguchi, S. 122
nonferrous metals 89, 105,
    156–67, 244
  divisionalisation 157–9, 160, 167
  foreign technology 156
  head office 157, 160, 161
  integration 24
  ownership 48
  profit responsibility 161
  raw materials 156, 157, 159,
    160, 166
  sales 156–7; and assets 23, 89
  structure 156–7, 158–62
  workforce 16

Ogura Oil 270
oil crises 135, 166, 311
  and automobile industries 296,
    299
  and paper industry 127
  and textiles 119
oil industry 83, 243, 265–77, 317
  affiliation 97
  budgetary system 270, 276
  competition 266
  decision-making 273

distribution 267, 268, 270, 271,
    272
  diversification 276
  entries 91, 244
  expansion policy 272
  foreign 83, 85, 265; capital
    265–6
  and foreign banks 272
  and government policy 275
  integration 24, 274
  management committee 267, 276
  production units 269
  products 266
  profitability 271
  refining 265, 273–4
  sales 271, 272
  and assets 23, 89, 93
  structure 268–9, 272
  reform of 270, 271, 273–4
  technology 265
  top management 275
  wholesalers 266
  workforce 15, 16
  see also crude oil
Oji Paper 68, 125–7, 128, 129
Oki Electric 210–11
Okura 57, 61
Onoda Cement 42–3, 53, 64,
    132–3
  employees 19
operating units 325, 326
  and factory managers 20
  and line structure 8
  see also individual industries
ores, nonferrous metals 156, 157,
    166
Osaka 21, 26, 62
  market 29
Osaka Denki Bundo 56
Osaka Godo Boseki 28
Osaka Iron Works 216
owner managers 53
ownership
  characteristics 50, 53
  and control 45
  dispersed 48, 50
  shareholders 47–8
Oya, S. 115, 116

paper industry   97, 103, 105,
     124–37
  diversification   127, 128
  exits   90
  head office   125
  innovations   125, 129, 130
  mass production   128
  and oil crisis   127
  raw materials   125–6, 127, 128,
     129, 130
  sales and assets   23, 89, 93
  structure   126–8, 129–31, 136;
     reform   126
  technology   125
  workforce   15, 16
partnerships
  automobile companies   277, 281,
     286, 287, 293
  Nissan Motor   287, 293
  and technology   282, 292
  Toyota Motor   281, 282–3, 285
perishable goods   264
personnel management   20
petrochemicals   83, 85, 179, 181,
     184, 189, 195
pharmaceutical companies   29, 30,
     176, 177–97, 194, 195
  distribution   62
Phillips Petroleum   182
photo film industry   302–3
pianos   314–15
Piore, M.   5
plastic processing   191
pollution   180
  and oil companies   275
  prevention equipment   215
post-war companies *see under*
     companies
Prince Motors   287
printing industry   124, 130–2, 137
  paper industry and materials
     companies   124–37
process industries   20
producer final goods   88, 90, 98,
     176, 326, 327
  diversification   101, 103
  divisionalisation   102
  mergers   94–5

product lines, and mergers   34–6
production units   327
  and decentralisation   33, 37
  functional/line structure   107
  and head offices   11, 37
  independence of   26, 31
  oil industry   269
  and purchasing   11
  responsibility of   37
  and sales   31
  steel industry   148, 152–3, 154–5
  structure   9, 33, 102; and
     management methods   10–11
  see also individual industries
profit responsibility *see individual
     industries*
purchasing
  in business groups   81
  control of   36
  development of   38
  federations for   72
  internalisation   13
  and operating units   11, 22
  *see also under individual
     industries*

radio receivers   206–7, 309, 312,
     313
raw materials   106–7
  cost   23–4
  and management resources   325,
     326
  supply of   58, 59, 62
  and trading companies   38
  *see also under individual
     industries*
Raytheon (U.S.)   211
record players   312, 313
records   312, 313, 314, 315
research and development
  automobile companies   282, 283,
     291, 294, 302
  consumer durable
     companies   312
  electrical and electronic
     companies   202, 204, 205, 210
  see also technology
resins   179, 180, 182, 189, 195,

213, 214
new types   191
Resource Nationalism   160
resources, allocation of
    management   1, 46, 58–67, 88
    and affiliates   83
    and business groups   76, 86
    capital investment   327, 328
    and decentralisation   36
    defined   1, 3
    development of   324–9; direction
        of 328–9; European   328;
        structures   1, 10, 324–8
    and federations   11
    financial   60
    and firm formation   5
    and holding companies   53, 327
    integration   325–6
    internalisation   324–6;
        financial   325, 327;
        human   324
    and international
        competition   328–9
    and large-scale firms   76–87
    and market mechanism   2, 4, 6
    mass production   326
    operating units   325, 326, 327
    raw materials   325, 326
    responsibility for   44, 45, 75
    and structures   1–11; aspects
        of   9–11; Chandler's
        hypothesis   3–6
    and subsidiaries   84, 85, 85–6
    technology   326
    and United States
        development   328
    and Zaibatsu   59, 61, 67
    see also human resources
rotary engines   296
Royal Dutch   269
rubber industry
    sales and assets   89, 93
    workforce   16

safety of chemical plants   180
salaried managers   45, 51, 52, 304
    transition to   54
sales   63, 89
    and control   36, 378

development of   37, 38
federations for   72
internalisation   13
nonferrous metals   156–7
and production units   11, 31
*see also under individual
    companies*
Sankyo   30, 49
Sanwa group
    internal transactions   82
    members   76
    shareholding   78
Sanyo Electric   309–11
Sapporo Breweries   260–1, 262
scientific management   4, 211, 325
    automobile companies   298
sea food companies *see* fisheries;
    food industry
    securities   78
    see also shareholding
Seiko   316–17
Seikosha   317
Sekisui Chemical   190–3
self-supporting factory
    system   211, 214
semi-finished goods   88, 90, 103
    diversification   100, 107, 108
    international activities   105
    mergers   94–5
    structure   168–9
semi-skilled workers   16
Shanghai Seizo Kenshi   48
shareholding   46, 47–8, 65–6
    and business groups   77–8, 81,
        82
    and control   78
    and decision making   78
    holding companies   49–51, 53
    and interlocking
        directorships   83
    and subsidiaries   85
    Zaibatsu   47–8, 71
Sharp *see* Hayakawa Electric
Shell   185, 190, 265, 270
Shibaura Engineering Works   34–5
Shin Mitsubishi Heavy
    Industries   217–18, 219, 220,
        233
Shinko Wool Textile   119

Shiobara Gomei 49
Shionogi pharmaceuticals 30
shipbuilding 103, 146–7, 216–29, 234
  affiliation 97
  development of 216–17
  exports 224
  investment 224
  mergers 95
  organisation of 34
  workforce 18
Shisheido 303–4
shop floor 20, 325
  automobile companies 286–7
Showa Denko 181–3
Showa Hiryo 30, 57–8
Showa Oil 269, 270
Siemens 197, 205, 209
silk industry 29, 97
single product firms,
  diversification 98–9, 100
size of firms 92–3, 331–6
skilled workers 14, 17
slumps 133, 307, 308, 311
smelting 156–7, 158, 162
Snow Brand Milk Products 256–8
Socony Vacuum 270
sole sales agents 63, 64
  cars 280, 285, 294
  Hattori 317
Sony 84, 312
Standard Oil 270
steel industry 137–56, 244
  decision-making 142
  diversification 142, 143, 146, 152, 155, 156
  and exports 141, 153
  foreign technology 137
  integration 138, 140, 141, 155
  mass production 140
  and mergers 32–3
  nationalisation 93
  production units 148, 152–3, 154–5
  profit responsibility 148
  purchasing 141
  raw materials 138, 140, 142, 145, 149, 155, 168
  sales 139, 143; and assets 89

structure 145, 146, 152, 154–5
technology 142
strategies
  decision-making 51–8
  and flow of goods 22–33
structures
  composition of 2
  and large-scale
    companies 1920–40 13–15;
    decentralised structures 33–6;
    internalisation of human
    resources 15–22;
    strategies 22–33
  see also individual industries
subsidiaries 84
  and control 56, 86
  food industry 249, 252, 256, 258
  heavy engineering
    companies 217
  and holding companies 49–51
  manufacturing 63
  overseas 109, 311
  and resource allocation 84, 85, 85–6
  and shareholding 85
  and top management 54–5, 56–7
  and Zaibatsu 54–5, 58
sugar manufacturing
  raw materials 24–5
  vertical integration 106
Sumitomo Bank 68, 70, 296
Sumitomo Besshi Kozan 31, 41, 59
Sumitomo Chemical 55, 59, 63, 70, 183–5
Sumitomo Densen Seizosho 59, 63
Sumitomo Electrical
  Industries 70, 165
Sumitomo group 32, 46–8, 58, 60, 69, 312
  banks in 70
  Connecting Companies 55, 59, 63, 72
  directors 79
  employees 62
  financial institutions 65
  internal transactions 82

and loans 79–80
members 76
shareholding 78
trading department 63
Sumitomo Hiryo 55
Sumitomo Machinery 228–9
Sumitomo Metal 32, 70, 141–3,
 159–61, 183
Sumitomo Shindo Kokan 32, 59
Sumitomo Steel Works 33
supermarkets 257
Suzuki 277, 300, 302
Suzuki, S. 253
Suzuki Shoten 64
syndicates 72
synthetic fibres 97, 109–11, 114,
 115–18, 119–23, 195
raw materials 124
synthetic rubber 134
systematic management 4

Taiwan 25, 26
Taiwan Seito 64, 66
Taiyo Fishery 83, 248–50
Takara Brewery 260
Takeda Chemical Industries 30,
 193–5, 197
diversification 194–5
sales 193
Taniguchi, T. 110
technology
aluminium 186
core 102, 103, 177
electrical and electronic
 companies 198, 200, 202, 215
food industry 245, 246, 253
foreign 105, 156, 197; chemical
 companies 181, 182, 183, 187,
 194, 196; steel industry 137
glass industry 135
heavy engineering
 companies 216, 217, 235
and management resources 326
oil companies 265
skills and trading companies 38
steel industry 142
transfer 243
United States 187
see also automobile companies

Teijin chemicals 115
Teikoku Seima 56
Teikoku Seito 53
Telegraph and Telephone
 Corporation 163, 206, 207,
 209, 211–12, 216
television sets 202, 308, 309, 313
Temman Orimono 21
Terada Gomei 49
Texas Instruments 213
textile industry 61, 98, 103, 105,
 106, 108–24, 325
distribution 64–5
employment 15–16, 17
exits 90–1
and integration 97
mergers 71, 95
organisation 27–9, 33, 38;
 changes 123–4
overseas subsidiaries 109
production 20
raw materials 62, 168
sales 108; and assets 23, 89,
 93
vertical integration 28
Tidewater Oil 271
Toa Nenryo 270, 271, 276, 318
Tobata Imono 42, 64
toiletries 304
Tokai Seitetsu 148
Tokyo Electric 34–5, 63
Tokyo Muslin Boshoku 26
Tokyo Rope 31
Tokyo Shibaura Electric *see*
 Toshiba
top management 2–3
automobile companies 280, 281,
 288, 289, 297
consumer durable
 companies 304, 306
and decision-making 51–3
electrical and electronic
 companies 201, 207, 208
food industry 249–50, 253, 255
functions 44, 45, 46, 71; and
 subsidiaries 56–7
heavy engineering
 companies 219, 221, 223, 225,
 226

and labour resources 5
oil industry 275
responsibilities of 5, 8
separation of 4
of subsidiaries 54–5
and Zaibatsu 15
Toppan Printing 130
Toray Industries 83, 117, 118, 123
Toshiba 33, 68, 200–3
research and development 202
Toyama Boseki 26
Toyo Cotton Mill 27, 28
Toyo Kogyo 294–6
and Ford 296
Toyo Muslin 26, 53, 57
Toyo Rayon 64, 68
Toyo Seikan 53
Toyo Seito 53
Toyobo 109–11
Toyoda Automatic Loom
Works 229, 230
and cars 278
Toyoda family 281
Toyota Motor 84, 212, 213, 228,
229–31, 277, 278, 279–81, 300,
318
as affiliate 83
partnerships 281, 282–3, 285
Trade and Industry, Ministry
of 138
and garages 269
trade, liberalisation of 126, 135,
189, 233, 258, 282, 287
oil imports 266, 269
trading companies 11, 63, 72
and business groups 80
and raw materials 38
role of 39; and multifunction
firms 44
and technical skills 38
and Zaibatsu 39, 61
traditional companies in new
industries 89, 103, 176–236
traditional companies in traditional
industries 89, 105–69
and mass production 103
workforce 15, 16
training and employment 4, 18
transportation costs 36

ore 139, 141
transportation equipment 228, 234
tyre industry
innovations 133–4
mass production 134
structure 133–5, 136

Ube Industries 187–8
unemployment 18
Union Oil 272
unit housing 192, 193
United Kingdom
automobile sales 277
breweries 264
companies 7
internalisation of flow of
goods 1–2
managerial hierarchies 13
output comparison 92–3
shipbuilding 216
United States 4–7
allocation of resources and
development 328
car production 281
management practices 10, 102,
267, 270–1, 276, 298; in paper
industry 126
managerial hierarchies 13
multidivisional structure 4, 101
oil 275
orders for Army 229, 230, 232,
286
technology 187
Unitika 113, 114–15
unskilled workers 17
Uraga Shipbuilding 228–9
urban markets 251, 253, 262
growth of 6
urea production 178, 179
USSR, mines in 141

vertical integration 24, 95–8
cement industry 106
consumer final goods 95
and line structure 9
and multifunction firm 4
sugar manufacturing 106
and survival 6
in textiles 28

see also combinations; mergers
Victor Company   84, 312–14, 317
vinyl   121
visible hand   5
   and labour transactions   4

wage system   19, 325
watches   90, 316–17
weaving   27
welfare of employees   17, 18
Western Electric   203, 213
whale processing   247
wholesale functions
   automobile companies   300–1
   breweries   263
   consumer durable
      companies   305, 316, 318
   and federations   63
   merchants   11, 37–8
   oil industry   266
   operating units   22
   ratio of   96
Williamson, O. E.   6
woodwork   314
workforce *see*
   employment/employees;
   human resources; labour
worsted companies   27

Yamaha   314–15
Yasuda   46–7, 60, 70
   affiliated companies   72
   employees   62
   financial institutions   65
   Holding Company   55–6
   subsidiaries   56, 60
Yawata Steel   141, 147–8, 149
Yoshino, Y.   77

Zaibatsu   14, 37, 46–8, 327
   allocation of resources   59, 61
   and control   44–5, 48, 51, 66–7;
      of subsidiaries   54–5
   and decision-making   44, 45
   and external debts   60–1
   financial institutions   65, 68, 69;
      banks   61, 65, 70, 71
   head offices   15, 75
   and holding companies   58
   managerial functions   14, 15, 45
   New   48
   resource allocation   59, 67
   shareholding   47–8, 71
   subsidiaries   58
   trading companies   39, 61
   see also individual groups
zinc   157, 158